First World War

and Army of Occupation

War Diary

France, Belgium and Germany

58 DIVISION
174 Infantry Brigade
London Regiment
8th (City of London) Battalion (Post Office Rifles)
11 November 1916 - 31 March 1918

WO95/3006/1

The Naval & Military Press Ltd
www.nmarchive.com
Published in association with The National Archives

Published by

The Naval & Military Press Ltd

Unit 10 Ridgewood Industrial Park,
Uckfield, East Sussex,
TN22 5QE England
Tel: +44 (0) 1825 749494

www.naval-military-press.com
www.nmarchive.com

This diary has been reprinted in facsimile from the original. Any imperfections are inevitably reproduced and the quality may fall short of modern type and cartographic standards.

Contents

War Diary	Copse U29c Near Warloy	09/05/1919	15/05/1919
War Diary	Millencourt Sector	15/05/1919	15/05/1919
War Diary	Reserve Millencourt Sector	16/05/1919	19/05/1919
War Diary	Lepz Sobsector Millencourt Sector	20/05/1919	25/05/1919
War Diary	Left Sub Sector Millencourt Sector	26/05/1919	27/05/1919
War Diary	Warloy	27/05/1919	31/05/1919
War Diary	Baizieux System	31/05/1919	31/05/1919
Miscellaneous	174th Infantry Brigade. Defensive Arrangements Millencourt Sector.	20/05/1918	20/05/1918
Miscellaneous	174th. Infantry Brigade Defensive Arrangements.	15/05/1918	15/05/1918
Miscellaneous	Appendix "A" Signal Communications.		
Miscellaneous	Appendix "B" to B,M/7/75/45 dated 20/5/1918.		
War Diary	Baizieux System Near Baizieux	01/06/1918	05/06/1918
War Diary	Daily Mail Woods Near Mirvaux	05/06/1918	10/06/1918
War Diary	Picquigny NW of Amiens	10/06/1918	12/06/1918
War Diary	Picquigny	12/06/1918	17/06/1918
War Diary	Villa Sector Rear. Franvillers	17/06/1918	18/06/1918
War Diary	Right Brigade Support Se Bresle	18/06/1918	24/06/1918
War Diary	Villa Sector Rear Near Franvillers	25/06/1918	25/06/1918
War Diary	Villa Sector Rear	26/06/1918	26/06/1918
War Diary	Barizie U.X. Syetem Near Baizieux	27/06/1918	28/06/1918
War Diary	Bazieux System Near Bazieux	29/06/1918	30/06/1918
Miscellaneous	174th. Infantry Brigade. Provisional Defence Instructions. Right Subsector-Right Sector-III Corps.	23/06/1918	23/06/1918
Miscellaneous	Appendix I. Summary Of Communications.		
Miscellaneous	Appendix II Work Policy		
Miscellaneous	Appendix III Administrative Arrangements.		
Miscellaneous	Ammunition		
Diagram etc	Circuit Diagram in Red		
Miscellaneous	Map to Accomdan		
Map			
Miscellaneous	8th Battalion London Regiment. Order No. 61	18/06/1918	18/06/1918
Operation(al) Order(s)	Operation Order 6th Bn London Regt	23/06/1918	23/06/1918
Miscellaneous	8th battalion The London Regiment. Order No. 60	16/06/1918	16/06/1918
Miscellaneous	8th Battalion London Regt. Provisional Order No. 46	23/06/1918	23/06/1918
Miscellaneous	8th Bn. London Regiment. Order No 62	26/06/1918	26/06/1918
Miscellaneous	174th. Infantry Brigade Reserve Brigade-Right Sector-III Corps Defence Scheme	27/06/1918	27/06/1918
Miscellaneous			
Miscellaneous	173rd Inf. Bde.	30/06/1918	30/06/1918
Miscellaneous	All Recipients	27/06/1918	27/06/1918
Miscellaneous	Amendment to 174th. Inf. Bde. Defence Scheme Appendix. 1	16/07/1918	16/07/1918
Map			
Miscellaneous	Appendix I. Tanks.		
Miscellaneous	Appendix II. Summary of Communications.		
Miscellaneous	Appendix III Administrative Arrangements.		
Map	Mapa		
Map	Diagrams of Communications		
War Diary	8th Bn London Reqiment War Diary Period July 1st to 31st 1918		
War Diary	Baizieux System Near Baizieux	01/07/1918	01/07/1918
War Diary	Support Bn. Left Brigade	02/07/1918	03/07/1918
War Diary	Support Bn. Left Brigade East of Lavieville	04/07/1918	05/07/1918
War Diary	Left Front Battn Left Brigade Sector	05/07/1918	05/07/1918
War Diary	Left Bn. Front Left Brigade Sector	06/07/1918	09/07/1918

War Diary	Left Front Bn. Left Brigade Sector	10/07/1918	12/07/1918
War Diary	Baizieux System Nr Baizieux	12/07/1918	17/07/1918
War Diary	Support Battalion Right Brigade E. of Bresle.	18/07/1918	22/07/1918
War Diary	Round Wood Behencourt Franvillers Road)	23/07/1918	28/07/1918
War Diary	Baizieux System Nr Baizieux	28/07/1918	28/07/1918
War Diary	St Laurence Farm Camp Near Baizieux	28/07/1918	30/07/1918
War Diary	Baizieux and Lavieville	31/07/1918	31/07/1918
Miscellaneous	Appendix Special		
Miscellaneous	Report On Special Operation By 8th Battalion London Regiment On 25/7/18		
Miscellaneous	Special Order by Brigadien Gencral C.G Higgins D.S.O. Commanding 174th Infantry Brigade. Appendix I	01/07/1918	01/07/1918
Miscellaneous	8th Battalion London Regiment. Operation Order No. 63 Appendix 2	30/06/1918	30/06/1918
Miscellaneous	8th Battalion London Regiment. Operation Order No. 64 Appendix 3	05/07/1918	05/07/1918
Miscellaneous	Appendix 4 Warning Order.	07/07/1918	07/07/1918
Miscellaneous	8th Battalion London Regiment Appendix	09/07/1918	09/07/1918
Miscellaneous	8th Battalion London Regiment. Operation Orders for Inter-Company Relief	09/07/1918	09/07/1918
Miscellaneous	6th London Regiment Appendix 5	11/07/1918	11/07/1918
Miscellaneous	8th Bn. The London Regiment. Order No. 67 Appendix 6	18/07/1918	18/07/1918
Miscellaneous	8th Battalion London Regiment Order No. 67 Appendix 7	28/07/1918	28/07/1918
Miscellaneous	8th Battalion London Regiment Appendix 8	30/07/1918	30/07/1918
Miscellaneous	8th Battalion London Regiment. Operation Order No. 65	12/07/1918	12/07/1918
Operation(al) Order(s)	8th Battalon London Regiment Operation Order No. 56		
Miscellaneous			
Miscellaneous	Administrative Instructions in Connaction with Operation Order No. 66		
Miscellaneous	8th Bn. The London Regiment	24/07/1918	24/07/1918
Miscellaneous	Administrative Arrangements	23/09/1918	23/09/1918
Miscellaneous	Provisional Defence Scheme Support Brigade Left Division III Corps.	13/09/1918	13/09/1918
Miscellaneous	Amendment No. 1 to 174th. Infantry Brigade Provisional Defence Schome for Green Line 18th Divisional Front.	23/09/1918	23/09/1918
Miscellaneous	Appendix II Signal Communications. Reserve Brigade-Centre Sector-III Corps.	31/07/1918	31/07/1918
Miscellaneous	Appendix III Administrative Arrangements		
Miscellaneous	Reference Reserve Brigade Defence Scheme	31/07/1918	31/07/1918
Miscellaneous	Provisional Amendments And Addenda to Defence Scheme	01/07/1918	01/07/1918
Map			
Map	Mapa		
Map			
Map	Appendix II Signal Communications. Reserve Brigade-Centre Sector-III Corps.	31/07/1918	31/07/1918
Diagram etc	Diagrams Of Communications. Reserve Bde Centre Dr III Corps		
Miscellaneous	Appendix III Administrative Arrangements.		
Miscellaneous	174th Infantry Brigade Defence Scheme	06/07/1918	06/07/1918
Miscellaneous	Appendix I Signal Communications		

Diagram etc			
Miscellaneous	Appendix 2. Work Policy		
Miscellaneous	Appendix 3 Administrative Arrangements.	07/07/1918	07/07/1918
Miscellaneous	Table Showing Approxinate Amounts Of Ammunition O.O In Brigade Sector.	07/07/1918	07/07/1918
Map			
Map	Map "B"		
Miscellaneous			
Heading	8th Battalion London Regiment August 1918		
War Diary	Lavieville Line And Baizieux	01/08/1918	02/08/1918
Miscellaneous	Baizieux	02/08/1918	02/08/1918
War Diary	Wargnies	03/08/1918	11/08/1918
War Diary	Copse J24 b.8.0	12/08/1918	12/08/1918
War Diary	Copse J24 b 80 and Round Wood	13/08/1918	13/08/1918
War Diary	Round Wood	14/08/1918	31/08/1918
Miscellaneous	17th Infantry Brigade Marrative Of Operations For The Period 22nd Augt. to 1st Sept	03/09/1918	03/09/1918
Miscellaneous	8th London Order No. B.	28/08/1918	28/08/1918
Miscellaneous	To Capt. Faber. 8th London Regiment.	02/09/1918	02/09/1918
Miscellaneous	Operation Order No 67 App No 1	01/08/1918	01/08/1918
Miscellaneous	8th Bn. Lodon Regiment. Warning Order App. No. 2	01/08/1918	01/08/1918
Miscellaneous	8th Bn. Londonregiment Operation Order No. 70	02/08/1918	02/08/1918
Miscellaneous	8th Battalion London Regiment Operation Order No. 71 App No. 3	04/08/1918	04/08/1918
Operation(al) Order(s)	8th Battalion London Regiment. Operation Order No. 79	05/08/1918	05/08/1918
Miscellaneous	Administrative Arrangements In Accordance With Operation Order No. 72 App No 4	05/08/1918	05/08/1918
Operation(al) Order(s)	8th Battalion London Regiment. Operation Order No. 79	05/08/1918	05/08/1918
Operation(al) Order(s)	Operation Order No 8th Bn. London Regt App No 5		
Map			
Miscellaneous	8th Lodon Order No. B	28/08/1918	28/08/1918
Miscellaneous	8th Bn. London Regt. Warning Order		
War Diary	Hindleg Wood Near Hem	02/09/1918	06/09/1918
War Diary	Ville Wood Moislains	07/09/1918	07/09/1918
War Diary	Sunken Rd Before Epehy	08/09/1918	10/09/1918
War Diary	Leramont	11/09/1918	15/09/1918
War Diary	Befure Ebeby	16/09/1918	18/09/1918
War Diary	Lieramont	19/09/1918	20/09/1918
War Diary	Templeux	21/09/1918	21/09/1918
War Diary	Templeux Quarry	21/09/1918	21/09/1918
War Diary	Templeux Harrylane	22/09/1918	24/09/1918
War Diary	Heilly	25/09/1918	26/09/1918
War Diary	Sany Berlette	27/09/1918	27/09/1918
War Diary	Chateau De La Haie	28/09/1918	30/09/1918
Operation(al) Order(s)	175th Infantry Brigade Order No. 145	11/09/1918	11/09/1918
Miscellaneous	175th Infantry Brigade Order No. 145	11/09/1918	11/09/1918
Miscellaneous	Appendix To Provisional Defence Scheme Support Brigade Left Division III Corps.	14/09/1918	14/09/1918
Miscellaneous	Provisgnal Defence Scheme Support Brigade Left Division. III Corps.	13/09/1918	13/09/1918
Map	Map A		
Map			
Miscellaneous	174th Infantry Brigade Provisional Defence Scheme	22/09/1918	22/09/1918
Map			

Miscellaneous	Diagram B		
Miscellaneous	8th Battalion London Regiment. Appendix I	14/09/1918	14/09/1918
Operation(al) Order(s)	8th London Regiment Operation Order No 76	15/09/1918	15/09/1918
Operation(al) Order(s)	8th London Regiment Operation Order No. 81	14/10/1918	14/10/1918
Miscellaneous	8th London Reg Order No. 77 Appendix III	17/09/1918	17/09/1918
Miscellaneous	Appendix IV OC Coy		
Miscellaneous	Appendix V OC Coy		
Miscellaneous	Appendix VI		
Miscellaneous	Narrative Of Operation 12th to 18th. October 1918 Appendix 4	15/10/1918	15/10/1918
Map			
Miscellaneous	Narrative Of Operations At Bersee 18/19 October 1918 Appendix 5		
Operation(al) Order(s)	8th Battalion London Regiment Operation Order No. 77 Appendix VII	26/09/1918	26/09/1918
Miscellaneous	58th Division.		
Miscellaneous	D.R.L.8		
Miscellaneous	58th Division	26/09/1918	26/09/1918
War Diary	8th London Regiment Post Office Rifles Oct 1st to 31 10 1918		
War Diary	Loos	01/10/1918	02/10/1918
War Diary	Panguste	03/10/1918	03/10/1918
War Diary	Loos	05/10/1918	09/10/1918
War Diary	Marqueffls Farm	10/10/1918	12/10/1918
War Diary	Sallaumines	13/10/1918	13/10/1918
War Diary	Courriere	14/10/1918	17/10/1918
War Diary	Mons Bersee	19/10/1918	19/10/1918
War Diary	Wattines	20/10/1918	20/10/1918
War Diary	Nomaines	21/10/1918	21/10/1918
War Diary	Nomain	22/10/1918	27/10/1918
War Diary	Rue Domprie	28/10/1918	31/10/1918
Miscellaneous	Narrative of Operation At Cite St Augustr. 4/5 10 18 Appendix I		
Map			
Miscellaneous	National War Museum Appendix 2		
Miscellaneous	Machine Gun		
Miscellaneous	Warning Order. 8th Battalion London Regiment. Appendix 3		
Operation(al) Order(s)	8th Battalion London Regiment. Operation Order No. 60	12/10/1918	12/10/1918
Miscellaneous	To O/C Coys		
Miscellaneous	174th L.T.M. Bty.		
Miscellaneous	Recipients of O.O. 132		
War Diary	8th Battalion The London Regiment Post Office Rible November 1918		
War Diary	Quesnoy Maulde	01/11/1918	08/11/1918
War Diary	F Lines	09/11/1918	09/11/1918
War Diary	Callenelle	10/11/1918	10/11/1918
War Diary	Beloeil	11/11/1916	11/11/1916
War Diary	Waudignies	12/11/1918	18/11/1918
War Diary	Beloeil	19/11/1918	19/11/1918
War Diary	Peruwelz	20/11/1918	28/11/1918
Miscellaneous	8th Bn, London Regt. Order No 89 Appendix I	01/11/1918	01/11/1918
Map			
Miscellaneous	8th Bn. London Regt. Order No. 90 Appendix II	05/11/1918	05/11/1918

Miscellaneous	To Headquarters 174th Inf. Brigade. Report of attempted raid of night 5/6 November 18.	06/11/1918	06/11/1918
Miscellaneous	To Headquarters, 174th. Infantry Brigade Further Report To Be Attached To Raid Report Of 3/11/1918.	06/11/1918	06/11/1918
Map	Appendix III Ref Sheets 38 and 45 1/40000		
Miscellaneous	8th Battalion London Regiment. Order No. 95 Appendix V	18/11/1918	18/11/1918
Miscellaneous	58th London Division	17/11/1918	17/11/1918
Miscellaneous	To Officers and men of the 8th Battalion London Regiment (Post Office Rifles)		
Map			
Diagram etc			
Miscellaneous			
Miscellaneous	Epehy		
War Diary	8th London Regiment Post Office Rible January 1919		
War Diary	Peruwelz	01/01/1919	29/01/1919
War Diary	Pernes En Artois	01/02/1919	28/02/1919
War Diary	Peruwelz	01/03/1919	01/03/1919
War Diary	Leule	08/03/1918	31/03/1918
Heading	Army Book No. 152 Lieut-Colonel Derviche Jones August 6-12-1918		
Operation(al) Order(s)	8th London Rt Operation Order No.	06/08/1918	06/08/1918
Miscellaneous	54th Brigade Is Corraing Out on	07/08/1918	07/08/1918
Miscellaneous	174 Inf Bde		
Miscellaneous			
Miscellaneous	7th Infantry Bde		
Miscellaneous	74th Inf Bde	08/08/1918	08/08/1918
Miscellaneous			
Miscellaneous	174 Bde Operation Report 9th Aug 1918.	09/08/1918	09/08/1918
Miscellaneous	Messages And Signals.	09/08/1918	09/08/1918
Miscellaneous	Conservation 007		

POST OFFICE RIFLES

8TH BATTALION

CITY OF LONDON
REGIMENT

1914-1918

HISTORY

OF THE

POST OFFICE RIFLES

8TH BATTALION

CITY OF LONDON REGIMENT

Compiled by.
Lt. Col. A. D. Derviche-Jones
D.S.O. M.C Commanding
the Post Office Rifles 1917 to 1919.

1914 TO 1918

ALDERSHOT:
PRINTED BY GALE & POLDEN, LTD.,
WELLINGTON WORKS.

1919.

311-Z4

On His Majesty's Service.

SECRET.

D. A. G.

G. H. Q.

3rd Echelon

745

SITUATION MAP UNBOLT

1:10,000

SPRIET

EDITION 2.

Scale 1:10,000.

TRENCHES CORRECTED FROM INFORMATION RECEIVED UP TO 23.10.17.

SITUATION
MAP

WO95/3006

56 DIVISION

174 BDE

1/8 LONDON REGT (POST OFFICE RIFLES)

1918 FEB — 1919 MAR

(ABSORBED 2/8 BN FEB 18)

EX 140 BDE 47 DIVN

SECRET

APPx "A"

OPERATION ORDER No. 11.

8th BATTALION. LONDON REGIMENT. Feb. 7th 1918.

---

1. The battalion will move to the forward Area tomorrow by march route, tactical trains and busses, details of which have been issued in ADMINISTRATIVE INSTRUCTIONS.

2. The Battalion will parade in Column of Route facing East on the HANGARD-AUBERCOURT Road at 6.am tomorrow, Feb. 8th, ready to move off. Head of the column to be at extreme EAST end of HANGARD village.
Order of march:- Band, B.C.A. H.Q., D. Sapping Platoon.
The battalion has orders to pass the cross roads ½ mile N of DEMUIN at 6.35.am.

3. Dress. Full Marching Order wearing Steel helmets.

4. The Battalion will relieve the 2nd Bn. BEDFORD Regt. in PIERREMANDE and AUTREVILLE, becoming C Bn. 90th Infy Bde., 30th Division.

5. All trench stores, aeroplane photographs, special maps, defence schemes and standing orders will be taken over, and receipts forwarded to Bn.H.Q. within 20 hours of relief.

6. Code word for Relief Complete will be "SEFILLED"

7. Brigade H.Q. will open at QUIERZY on Feb. 8th at an hour to be notified and will close at QUIERZY and re-open at SINCENY at 10.am, Feb.10th.

8. The Battalion will relieve the 2nd Bn Royal Scots Fus. on the night of the 9th/10th.
C & D Companies in the front line - A. Company in support and "B" Company as Counter Attack company.
Companies will take order as arranged at todays conference pending receipt of further instructions.

9. Each Company will leave 2 Signallers at the Details Camp.

10. Entraining States will be rendered to the Bn.O.R. by 7.pm tonight.

HUGH W PRIESTLEY.
Captain & Adjutant.

SECRET

 O.s. C. Companies.

H.Q.

WARNING ORDER

Battalion will move about 5.30.am on 8th and march to VILLERS BRETONNEAUX.

Thence it will entrain for forward area. Journey about 7 hours.

On arrival in forward area it will go in busses part of the way to Support Bn. billets and will march the remainder of the way.

It will be in Support billets for night of 8th - 9th and will move up into the line on night of 9th -10th.

Orders later.

W.B. VINCE
Lieut-Colonel.

8.9.18.

III

BATTLE HONOURS OF THE POST OFFICE RIFLES, AUGUST, 1914, TO NOVEMBER, 1918

Festubert	... May, 1915.
Loos	September, 1915.
Vimy	... May, 1916.
Somme—High Wood	September, 1916.
,, Butte de Warlencourt ...	October, 1916.
Bullecourt—Village	... May, 1917.
,, Hindenburg Line ...	June, 1917.
Ypres—Messines	June, 1917.
,, Wurst Farm	September, 1917.
,, Passchendaele	October, 1917.
Cambrai—Bourlon Wood	November, 1917.
St. Quentin—Crozat Canal	March, 1918.
,, Tergnier	March, 1918.
,, Noreuil	March, 1918.
,, Chauny	March, 1918.
Defence of Amiens—Villers Bretonneux	April, 1918.
Somme—Malard Wood	August, 1918.
,, Chipilly	August, 1918.
,, Bilfon Wood	August, 1918.
,, Marrieres Wood	August, 1918.
,, Epehy and Peizieres ...	September, 1918.
,, Ronnsoy	September, 1918.
Loos to Bauffe—Lens	October to November, 1918.
,, Annay	
,, Courrieres	
,, Wattines	
,, The Scheldt ...	

APPX 'B'

S E C R E T. Copy No: 8

8th Bn., London Regiment.

ORDER No: 12.

Map ref:
Sheet 70 D. N.W.
1,20,000

Feb. 9th
1918.

---

1. The 8th Bn., London Regiment will relieve the 2nd Bn., Royal Scots Fus. in the right sub-sector tonight the 9/10th as follows:-

C. Co. 8th Londons taking over from right front Company C. Co 2nd Bn., Royal Scots Fus.
D. Co. 8th Londons taking over from left front Company D. Co 2nd Bn., Royal Scots Fus.
B. Co. 8th Londons taking over from counter-attack Company B. Co. 2nd Bn., Royal Scots Fus.
A. Co. 8th Londons taking over from passive resistance Co. A. Co., 2nd Bn., Royal Scots Fus.

2. GUIDES. The Royal Scots are providing 1 guide per Co. and 1 guide for Bn. H.Q. to be at ROND D'ORLEANS at 3.15. p.m. Feb. 9th to take companies and Bn. H.Q. to R.E. Dump H.27.a.7.8. where 1 guide per company H.Q. and 1 guide per platoon and 1 guide for Bn. H.Q. will be waiting.

3. ORDER OF RELIEF and times for passing the starting point will be as follows:

Coy.	Starting Point.	Time of passing Starting point.
	Junction of Roads	
C.	(C.28.a.7.3.)	4.30. p.m.
D.	-do-	4.45. p.m.
A.	-do-	4.55. p.m.
B.	-do-	5. 5. p.m.
Bn.H.Q.	-do-	5.15. p.m.

4. INTERVALS. 250 yards between companies up to ROND D'ORLEANS forward of this 50 yards between platoons.

5. Lewis Guns will be carried.
A limber containing 42 magazines per company will leave Bn. H.Q. at 2. p.m. today under Sergt Parker. These magazines will be dumped at R.E. Dump H.27.a.7.8. to be picked up by L.G. teams as they pass.

6. C. & D. Company Officers trench kits and mess baskets will be dumped at Q.M. Stores by 3. p.m.
Bn. H.Q. A. & B. Companies Officers trench kits and mess baskets will be dumped at Bn. H.Q. by 3. p.m.

7. All trench Stores will be carried.

8. Orders for cookers and rations for Feb. 10th will be issued later.

9. Relief complete will be communicated to Bn. H.Q. by the quickest means by code word "FORT".

10. A map shewing dispositions to be at Bn. H.Q. by 4. p.m. Feb. 10th.

11. ACKNOWLEDGE.

HUGH.W.PRIESTLEY.
Captain & Adjutant.

Copy No:
1. Unit to be relieved.
2. O.C. 8th Bn.
3. O.C. "A"
4. O.C. B.
5. O.C. C.
6. O.C. D.
7. Bn. H.Q.
8. War diary.

July 11th, 1918 (officer in charge, Captain T. P. Croysdale), and to His Royal Highness the Duke of Connaught, at Blackdown, October, 1918 (officer in charge, Captain E. B. Davies, M.C.).

The first Commanding Officer of the Reserve Battalion was Lieutenant-Colonel F. Owen, T.D., who was also responsible for the start of the 2/8th, and who for over two and a half years rendered untiring and most valuable service to the Regiment. In April, 1917, he was succeeded by Lieutenant-Colonel B. Davie. In January, 1918, Lieutenant-Colonel P. E. Langworthy Parry took over the command, and infused much energy into the tactical training of officers and men.

COMMITTEES. Before proceeding to the fighting story of the Regiment, mention must be made of the ungrudging support, both financial and otherwise, given by the Postal Authorities, and the really excellent work of the various committees formed to look after the comfort of the men. The thousands of pairs of socks, the scarves, mittens, candles, footballs, books, magazines, boxing-gloves, games, and, above all, cigarettes, provided by these committees have administered largely to the well-being and recreation of all ranks, and entailed no little labour and self-sacrifice on the part of the friends of the Regiment. These committees have now been centralized into "The Post Office Rifles Benevolent Institution," with an influential committee under the Presidency of Colonel Sir Andrew Ogilvie, K.B.E., C.B. Communications for help and advice should be addressed to the Secretary, Mrs. Percy Ash, 130, Bunhill Row, E.C. 1.

2. THE 1/8TH BATTALION.

EARLY DAYS. The Post Office Rifles, like many other Territorial units, were on the way to their annual Training Camp when the news of the impending great struggle was received. The Battalion returned to London, and on the declaration of war was embodied and billeted in the various Post Offices of the Metropolis. Three of the eight companies acquired comfortable quarters in King Edward's Building, of the General Post Office, empty mail-bags, precursors of the generally useful sand-bags, being found to make fair substitutes for beds. After rapid moves, much marching, and frequent changes of billets, which provided a useful experience of what was to come in France, the Battalion eventually pulled up at Crowborough, where training commenced in earnest. Here many changes took place: a large number of the Battalion were transferred to the R.E., Army Post Office

CROWBOROUGH.

ADMINISTRATIVE INSTRUCTIONS in
connection with 8th Bn. London Regt ORDER No:11.

6.2.18.

1\. TRAINS. With reference to para 2 WARNING ORDER 6/31.1.18. the Tactical Trains provided on Feb 8th will consist of:-

2 Personnel Trains.
1 Omnibus Train.

Entraining Station: VILLERS BRETONNEUX.
Detraining Station: APPILLY.
Duration of journey about 7 hours.

The first personnel train leaves at 9. a.m. Feb 8th and will contain the 6th and 8th London Regiments.
The second personnel Train leaves at 10. a.m. with the remainder of the Brigade.
The Omnibus Train will leave at 1. p.m. with the following vehicles and personnel etc.

Vehicles.	Personnel.	Animals.
4 Cookers.	8.	8.
2 Water Carts.	4.	4.
1 Officers Mess Cart	1.	1.
1 L.G. Limber.	2.	2.
1 Medical Cart.	2.	1.
Chargers.	6.	6.
	23.	22.

The four cookers will carry rations in bulk for Feb 9th.
The two Water Carts will be filled before starting.
The L.G. Limber will carry 330 magazines in boxes
1 Cook per company will go with each cooker and act as brakesman, one water duty man per watercart for the same purpose. The M.O. Orderly will go with the M.O's. Cart. Sergt Flick will act as brakesman to the L.G. Limber.

There will be two covered wagons for stores etc on the Omnibus Train which must be loaded by 10. a.m. on the 8th.
All Transport for the Omnibus Train is to arrive at the station by 10. a.m. on the 8th. and will be under the orders of Lieut. D.W. Lamb

2\. TRANSPORT. All Transport not accommodated on the Omnibus Train will proceed by march route under the orders of Captain T.A.B. PURKIS.

3\. SUPPLIES. Rations for Feb 8th will be carried on the man and rations for the 9th on the cookers.
The Q.M. will arrange for one dixie per platoon and 4 for H.Q. Section to be taken to VILLERS BRETONNEUX by lorries to be loaded on Personnel Train, in order to provide tea on arrival in the new area

P.T.O.

which lasted from May 9th until near the end of the month, were designed to support the French attack some miles south at Souchez. On May 16th, while the attack was being continued in the neighbourhood, Richebourg, by the 2nd Division, the Battalion moved into the line at Festubert, and sustained many casualties. La Quinque, the Yellow Road, Willow Road, Welsh Chapel, and Dead Cow Farm, will bring back reminiscences of a not altogether pleasant nature to many who were there. On the 22nd "B" and "C" Companies took over portions of the old Hun line, which had been captured, and on the following day attacked and cleared some hundreds of yards of enemy territory, losing Lieutenants Hatfield and Moon (killed), and heavy casualties in other ranks. "C" Company having been heavily shelled, it was left to "D" Company to continue the attack, relying on bombs, with which, however, the enemy were better and more plentifully supplied. After obtaining the assistance of bombers of King Edward's Horse, the attack was successfully renewed on the 25th, and more enemy trenches taken, a strong point, known as J.3, holding out and defying capture. A further attack on this strong point was ordered for the morning of the 26th, but, fortunately, postponed to allow the position to be bombarded by heavy artillery. Some enemy who were seen to be retiring provided interesting and useful target practice.

When the Battalion eventually advanced to attack this post, an unforeseen incident occurred which materially assisted the attack. Some neighbouring British troops on the right moved in the direction of J.3, which they thought to be in British hands, at the very moment that the Post Office Rifles were commencing to attack it. This was too much for the Boche garrison, who hoisted the white flag and allowed the Post Office Rifles to capture one officer, forty other ranks, and some machine guns. So ended the first experience of the Battalion in actual battle, and gave them a reputation as a fighting unit which was well sustained in future contests. If the casualties were severe (in addition to those named, 2nd-Lieutenants Oliver Lawrence and Maclebone were killed, and 50 per cent. of other ranks killed and wounded), at any rate the enemy, whose artillery was many times stronger than the British, suffered quite as heavily, judging from the number of their dead lying around the captured territory, and also lost some tactical positions.

MAROC. After periods of rest at Philosophe and in the line by the Hulluch Road and Vermelles, the Battalion found themselves at Maroc, the Garden City, then a very

4. LORRIES. i. Two lorries will be available for transporting stores to VILLERS BRETONNEUX Station. The Q.M. will detail a guide to be at Brigade H.Q. [illegible] at 6. p.m. Feb. 7th to guide these lorries to Q.M. Store. These lorries will make two journeys i.e. 8. p.m. Feb 7 and 6. a.m. Feb 8th.

Two blankets per man will be taken on the two last lorries and blankets will be rolled in bundles of 10 securely tied and labelled and taken to the Q.M. Store by 6. 30. a.m. Feb 8th. A lorry will call at [illegible] at 4.30. a.m. Feb 8th to pick up D. Company's blankets and Mess boxes.

The Mess Cart will be loaded at H.Q. Mess at 5. a.m Feb 8th.

Surplus Mess Boxes to be at Q.M. Stores by 6.30. a.m

With the above exceptions all other stores are to be dumped at Q.M. Stores by 5. p.m. Feb 7th.

The Q.M. will arrange the necessary loading and unloading parties.

ii. On arrival at [illegible] Station on the 8th.

(a) Lorries will convey personnel to road junction G.[illegible]. From there, H.Q. and [illegible] Companies will march to billets in [illegible].

The remaining [illegible] companies to [illegible].

(b) Lieut. G.A. MONTGOMERY will act as embussing and debussing Officer.

(c) O. C. C. Company will detail an unloading party of 1 Officer and [illegible] Other Ranks to report to the detraining Officer Captain [illegible] for unloading Omnibus Train.

iii. After taking up the personnel as stated in para 4. ii. Lieut. G.A. MONTGOMERY will detail 6 lorries to return to [illegible] Station to take stores etc from the omnibus train to its destination.

Lieut. G.A.MONTGOMERY will be responsible for guiding the lorries to road junction G. [illegible] (Sheet [illegible]) and the Q.M. will be responsible for sending a guide to that road junction, as soon as he knows where he requires the stores to act as guide.

5. LEWIS GUNS. The 16 Lewis Guns will be taken to VILLERS-BRETONNEUX by the lorries. Sergt Parker will accompany them and hand them over to their respective sections as they arrive who will then be responsible for them.

HUGH.W.[illegible].
Captain & Adjutant.

Copies to all recipients. of ORDER No: 11.

APPENDIX "B"

MEDICAL ARRANGEMENTS.

A. REGIMENTAL AID POSTS.

Battalion in the line at H.27.d.8.7.

Battle Zone Battalion at H.27.a.1.2. (when new Battle Zone Battalion H.Q. there have been completed and taken over by the Battle Zone Battlion.)

B. RELAY POSTS.

(i) R.A.P. at H.27.a.1.2 . will be used as the Ist. Relay post.

(ii) 2nd. Relay post at G.25.a.2.3 .

C. ADVANCED DRESSING STATION.

SINCENY, at G.10.c.7.7.

A motor ambulance will be sent as forward as possible in advance of the A.D.S. as circumstances permit in order to assist the work of the Relay Posts.

D. 46th C.C.S.

NOYON, where wounded will be evacuated to.

E. Gas and slightly wounded. These casualties will be evacuat from A.D.S. to 2/2nd. Field Amb. CHAUNY.

E. SICK. Will be evacuated from A.D.S. to 2/1st. Field Amb. QUIERZY.

G. WALKING CASES. These will be evacuated through the above channel

APPENDIX "C"

ADMINISTRATIVE INSTRCUTIONS
in connection with
DEFENCE SCHEME.

1. AMMUNITION & RESERVE RATIONS.

The following is the Brigade establishment of ammunition:-

(a & b)	(a) Main Dump, SINCENY. G.$.d.9.2.	(b) Forward Dump, ROND D'ORLEANS.
S. A. A.	180000	100000
Grenades No. 5.	4780	960
" No. 23.	1200	600
" No. 24.	1650	1000
V?P.A. D.I. 1".	2680	1680
S. O. S.	100	100
Stokes shells complete with rings and green cartridges. ..	2300	1000
Pistol Webley.	1700	Nil.
	This dump is used for replenishing requirements of battle and forward zones.	This dump is kept intact and will be drawn on in case of emergency only.

(c). Forward Zone.

Keep.	Garrison.	S.A.A.	Water.	Rations.
Hill 89.	2 platoons.	30000.	80 gallons.	288.
Hill 98.	2 "	30000.	80 "	288.

(d) Battle Zone.

Keep.	Garrison.	S.A.A.	Water.	Rations.
BERNAGOUSSE Strong Point.	1 platoon.	30000	50 gallons.	288.
CLOS des VIGNES	1 "	30000	50 "	288.
ROND de L'EPINOIS	2 "	30000	50 "	288.
ROND D'ORLEANS	2 "	30000	50 "	288.

(e). RESERVE ESTABLISHMENT for Units in Battle and Forward Zones, other than in Keeps.

Each Section	-	2000 rounds S?A.A.
" Platoon	-	5000 " "
" Company	-	10000 " "
" Battalion	-	50000 " "

(f) BRIGADE RESERVE RATION STORE.

	Water.	Rations.
BERNAGOUSSE QUARRIES ..	200 gallons,	624.

(g). MACHINE GUNS. In both Battle and Forward Zones the following minimum establishment is laid down :-

(1) 10000 rounds (3000 of which are in belts ready filled) to be used only for repelling an attack by direct fire.

(2) 4 belts ready filled in addition retained for A.A. work on supposition that enemy attack will be preceded by low flying aeroplanes.

(3) 4 belts ready filled in addition to (1) and (2) to guns which are allotted S.O.S. lines.

(h). At billets etc. of all Units (other than those Units in Battle and Forward Zones), to include Field Coys. R.E., and Pioneer Battalion, 10000 rounds per Company.

This reserve is retained to allow of an extra 50 rounds per man being issued on receipt of messages "Prepare for attack" or "Man Battle Stations".

This ammunition is issued to Platoon H.Q., lids of boxes removed to facilitate distribution, but tin casing left intact to avoid deterioration.

(i). At each Lewis Gun post 2000 rounds in Magazines, and/5 boxes.

2. METHOD of REPLENISHING AMMUNITION.

Units submit indents by 9 a.m. daily. Requirements are sent up by Horse Transport under Brigade arrangements the same evening from Brigade Dump, SINCENY, G29,d,9,2.

3. WATER.

Forward Zone. There is a plentiful supply of drinking water at water point on road at H.27.a.5.9. Washing water plentiful from well at Battalion H.Q.

Battle Zone. Water is drawn from H.27.a.5.9. water point and from PIERREMANDE, and taken up in water carts.

Billetting areas. All villages have a number of good wells.

4. RATIONS.

Delivered by transport and pack animals by night to Battalion H.Q. and further. Route - PIERREMANDE or SINCENY - ROND D'ORLEANS - BARISIS road. Each Unit has one day's rations in hand at their Q.M. Stores.

5. COOKING.

This is done in villages and cookhouses close up to the line.

6. R.E. Stores.

The Divisional R.E. dump is situated at PIERREMANDE, G.28.b.4.0.

There are forward dumps at H.27.a.2.9. and H.16.a.7.2.

7. BATHS.

(a) The baths at H.21.c.3.2. are staffed and administered by the Battle Zone Battalion.

They are at the disposal of the Battalion in the front line, and the Battle Zone Battalion, und or mutual arrangements made by Commanding Officers concerned.

(b) SINCENY. Application for use of these baths should be made to Area Commandant, SINCENY.

(c) PIERREMANDE. Application for use of these baths should be made to a representative of the Area Commandant, SINCENY.

APPENDIX "D".

Units in Brigade Area and Headquarters.

174th Infantry Brigade H.Q	SINCENY.	G.10.b.4.3.
Forward Zone Battalion.		H.27.b.8.2.
Battle Zone Battalion.	PIERREMANDE.	G.28.b.8.0. (moving to H.27.a.1.0).
Divl. Reserve Battalion.	PIERREMANDE.	G.28.b.8.4.
198th M.G.Coy.	MARIZELLE.	G.13.b.7.3.
174th L.T.M.Bty.	SINCENY.	G.10.d.2.0.
511th Field Coy. R.E. (1 Section)	PIERREMANDE. BERNAGOUSSE QUARRIES.	G.28.d.2.9.
"D" Coy. 1/4th Suffolk Regt. (Pioneers).	AUTREVILLE.	G.22.a.3.4.
291st Brigade R.F.A.	SINCENY.	G.10.b.50.25.
Section, 182nd Tunn.Coy.R.E.	SINCENY.	G.10.d.05.85.
174th Inf.Bde. Tunn.Section.	BERNAGOUSSE QUARRIES.	
Brigade Transport Officer.	SINCENY.	
Brigade Gas Officer.	Left Coy. H.Q., FORWARD ZONE.	H.16.d.3.4.

---------------oOo---------------

Divisional H.Q.	QUIERZY.
175th Infantry Brigade.	G.10.a.9.5.
215th Infantry Regt.	FOLEMBRAY.
161st I.D.	FOLEMBRAY.
Battalion on Left. Forward Zone.	LA FORTELLE.
Battalion on Right. Forward Zone.	H.33.b.
Battalion on Right. Battle Zone.	BERNAGOUSSE QUARRIES.
Battalion on Left. Battle Zone.	H.1.c.8.2.

---------------oOo---------------

APPENDIX E.

GAS PRECAUTIONS.

1. The BASSE FORET DE COUCY Sector is one that offers opportunity to the enemy to employ gas projectors or gas shells on a large scale owing to the fact that most of the area is thickly wooded.

All commanders will aim at the highest possible standard of gas discipline in accordance with Gas Defence Instructions (SS.193).

2. The cover which his woods afford the enemy would enable him to instal projectors with little chance of their being observed by us.

All ranks will be constantly warned, in accordance with instructions already issued from time to time, of the possibility of these attacks and their characteristic features (simultaneous flash and reports of mortars, etc.)

3. There will be a sentry at or near every dugout in the Forward Zone near enough to give timely warning to the occupants, of a cloud, projector or gas shell attack. There will be no such thing in the Brigade as a "Gas Guard" or "Gas Sentry".

It is the duty of every sentry to watch for and report gas.

4. All ranks in the Brigade Area will carry box respirators. These will be worn in the ALERT position forward of the line G.30.central. - G.6.central.

SECRET. APPENDIX F.

COMMUNICATION OF HOUR FOR COUNTER-ATTACK,
"UNITS DIVISIONAL RESERVE".

The following method will be adopted in communicating the hour of the counter-attack to all concerned.-

1. The hour of the counter-attack will be settled by Brigade H.Q. as far as that may be possible.
Zero hour for the counter-attack will be communicated to all concerned. The hour will always be the clock hour or half-hour.

2. The Battalion Commander or Commanders carrying out the attack will establish their Headquarters together and as near to the zone of deployment of their troops as feasible, and mark their Headquarters with the Senior Battn. Commander's aeroplane strips.

3. Should the Battalion Commanders realise that they cannot get their troops into position in time for the assault at the hour fixed (i.e. 2 p.m.) they will fire two clusters of Red Very Lights (at a short interval, the first cluster at a quarter of an hour before Zero, i.e. at 1.45 p.m.), as a signal to the Artillery that Zero has been postponed half an hour. They will also, if possible, communicate the postponement in B.A.B. Code by 'phone to Brigade H.Q. and the Artillery, and to the Division for communication to the R.F.C., (via Corps H.Q.).

4. The Artillery (both Field and Heavy) will then reduce their fire, as much as possible, for 10 minutes before and after the zero hour fixed (i.e. from 1.50 p.m. to 2.10 p.m.), so as not to mislead the infantry into thinking that the barrage has commenced.

5. Should on the other hand the Battalion Commanders consider that the attack can proceed at the zero hour fixed, they will display, at their combined Headquarters, a white cross + (made of white strips 10' x 2') five minutes before zero hour (i.e. 1.55 p.m.).

6. Two contact aeroplanes will leave the ground together half an hour before zero (i.e. 1.30 p.m.) and on seeing the strips, the leading 'plane (to be nominated by the 82nd Sqdn. R.F.C.) will fire a succession of White Very Lights. These Lights will be the signal to the infantry for the assault to commence.

7. Each postponement will always be for 30 minutes.

8. A second postponement (i.e. to 3 p.m., instead of 2.30 p.m.) can if necessary, be made by the same means, i.e. by firing Red Very Lights again at 2.15 p.m. A third postponement (i.e. to 3.30 p.m.) can also be made, but a fourth postponement will indicate that the operation is cancelled for the time being.

9. The Artillery will always reduce their fire for 10 minutes before zero, so as to emphasize the moment for the attack, when the barrage falls.

-------o0o-------

174th INFANTRY BRIGADE.

DEFENCE SCHEME.

BARISIS SECTION

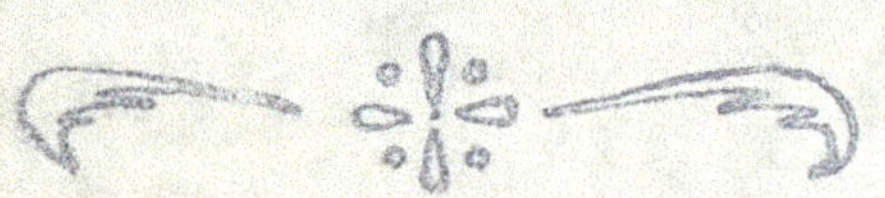

MARCH 1918.

DEFENCE SCHEMES

1918 MAR — 1918 JUN

S E C R E T. B.M./7/67/236.

Amendments and Addenda to
174th. Infantry Brigade Defence Scheme.

The following amendments and addenda to 174th. Infantry Brigade Defence Scheme are made :-

1. Para. 3.
Add new para. (c)

"All troops in any keep or defended locality will be under the command of the senior officer present."

2. Para. 7 b (ii). For "quarter of an hour's notice" read "one hour's notice."

3. Para. 7 b.

Add new para. (viii)

"Watches will be synchronized with Brigade H.Q. when the order PREPARE FOR ATTACK is sent out and thereafter at 12.15 p.m. daily during the precautionary period."

4. Para. 7 c.

Add new para. (ix)

"Any officer will carry out any of the instructions contained in para. 7 without waiting for the orders PREPARE FOR ATTACK or MAN BATTLE STATIONS, if in his opinion the situation demands it. When taking such action he will inform the corresponding units or formations on his flanks and report to his immediate superior."

5. Add new para. 10.

ALARM SIGNALS.

The following are the only alarm signals which will be used :-

(i) S.O.S. Signal by which troops in occupation of Forward Zone call for Artillery Barrage in case of definite enemy attack. Rifle Grenade, supplemented by Mortar Signals, giving the same lights :-

Signal : RED over RED over RED.

The responsibility of passing back S.O.S. Rifle Grenade Signals rests with the Infantry as far back as Battalion Head-quarters, Battalions in occupation of the Forward Zone. Further back it devolves on the Artillery to ensure that in the foggiest weather these signals can be seen by all batteries.

(ii) Test S.O.S. "GOLDEN RAIN ROCKET."

To test S.O S. arrangements, test to be acknowledged by R.A. by firing one round only per battery or detached section on the front from which the signal emanated. This does not include Silent Batteries.

In tests carried out by telephone or visual, the message will be worded - "TEST ONE ROUND."

(iii) The Patrol Signal. "GREEN VERY LIGHT." To be carried by Tally Patrols and to be fired to give the alarm to Infantry Garrisons. Action of Artillery will be governed by further action, i.e., communication from Battalion H.Q. Forward Zone, through Artillery Liaison Officer on duty at his H.Q., from Brigade H.Q., or S.O.S. Signal should such be discharged.

Commanders of Infantry Posts on seeing a GREEN Very Light discharged in their vicinity must consequently take immediate action to clear up the situation by sending forward a Patrol.

/ (iv) Aeroplane Flares.

(iv) Aeroplane Flares. Colour throughout Corps Front - RED.

To be kept in every KEEP and defended locality in the Forward and Battle Zones. They will be kept for emergency and only used when Contact Aeroplanes are sent over during or after an attack to locate our front. At least 30 flares are to be kept at each post. When called for they will be lit by Infantry in front line in most Forward Posts in groups of three.

(v) The Light Signal in use by the VIth French Army on our Right is as follows :-

S.O.S. Signal ... Rocket bursting into 6 stars.

6. Please acknowledge.

R. Davenport-Ward (signature)

Captain,
Brigade Major,
174th. Infantry Brigade.

20th March, 1918.

Copies to all recipients of
174th Infantry Brigade Defence Scheme.

the Aisne to Dommier, thence to Longpoint, where the Battalion entrained, arriving the same night at Abbé Wood. Here reserve positions were taken up, until on April 13th the Battalion was moved up to the front line at Villers Bretonneux, where a draft of two companies of the 8th Norfolk Regiment, seven officers and 250 men, reinforced the Battalion, and Major Browne became Second-in-Command.

VILLERS BRETONNEUX, April, 1918.

Villers Bretonneux will long live in the memory of those who had the misfortune to be there as one of the most unpleasant and hotly-contested positions in the defence of Amiens. Under continuous bombardment by day and night, by shells of all calibres—mostly gas—no place, not even the deepest cellar, afforded security. One gas shell knocked out ninety men of Headquarter's details, of whom fifty died from gas-poisoning. From April 17th to 19th there were more than 150 gas casualties, including Lieutenant-Colonel Soutten, Major Browne, 2nd-Lieutenants Howes, Bruggemeyer, Ward, and Hawley; while Captain Massey-Miles, M.C., one of the whitest and most gallant Battalion Medical Officers in France, died of gas-poisoning after a heroic attempt to succour others similarly poisoned, removing his gas-mask in order to do so, and thus courting an inevitable and agonizing death. Three Medical Officers were sent in quick succession in one day, two of whom became casualties, one killed and one wounded. The last to arrive, Lieutenant Macbean, of the American Army, survived the ordeal, and remained with the Battalion until the end of the war.

DOMART.

Lieutenant-Colonel Johnston took over the command on the 20th, with Major Edwards as Second-in-Command. Matters were still critical, and after a few days at Boutillerie the Battalion took up positions at Domart, until relieved by the French on the 27th, when they entrained to Neuf Moulin. In the last three days (25th-27th) one officer (2nd-Lieutenant Carter) was killed and two wounded (Captain Faber and Lieutenant Brown); while of other ranks 13 were killed, 83 wounded, and 43 gassed. The defence of Amiens was now secured, but at what cost! This story, bare of detail, of one Battalion during the terrible days of March and April, 1918, may read grimly enough, but this Battalion was one of many, and by no means exceptionally situated.

WARLOY, ALBERT.

After a week at Neuf Moulin, the Battalion moved to Warloy, and was employed in digging defence lines. The Division subsequently relieved the 47th Division, the Battalion moving first into the Henencourt and then the

Albert Sectors, immediately in front of that town. About this time Lieutenant Jacob became Adjutant, *vice* Major Priestley, Second-in-Command.

On June 28th Brigadier-General A. Maxwell, D.S.O., a former Commanding Officer of the 1/8th Battalion, was appointed to the 174th Brigade.

July 25th, 1918.

On July 25th a daylight raid on a large scale was carried out, about 300 men going over the top. The raid met with little opposition on the front attacked, except in the neighbourhood of the Quarry, where some platoons of "A" Company had a very hard time. A few prisoners were brought back, and many more in attempting to escape had to be shot; but during the return journey the raiders received heavy machine-gun fire from the flanks of the attack, and suffered heavily. 2nd-Lieutenants Roft and Alexander were killed, and four officers wounded (2nd-Lieutenants Tafner, Scarth, Johnson, and Hatchett). Casualties to other ranks were 113. On the whole, it seems probable that the casualties on both sides were about equal. One remarkable feature was that the enemy allowed the wounded to be got in without interference.

After a short rest at Round Wood, Franvillers (a place full of interest to those who had fought on the Somme in 1916), the Battalion moved to Baiseux, where they were joined by Lieutenant-Colonel Derviche-Jones, who had returned to take over the command of the Battalion from Lieutenant-Colonel Johnston, transferred to command the 7th Battalion.

BATTLE OF SOMME, August, 1918.

Plans for the great counter-offensive which [illegible] to make history were kept very secret. On August [illegible] the Battalion was marched and entrained to a back area at Wargnies, near Canaples, and preparations made for a long period of rest and training there. Actually, with the exception of a few days at Neuf Moulin, no opportunity had been given to train the Battalion, a large number of whom consisted of youngsters hurriedly sent out as reinforcements to make good the gaps caused by the enemy offensive. These lads were soon to show their mettle, even without the advantage of training. On the night of August 4th the Battalion was moved by night from Wargnies, and after entraining and marching, spent the day in a small copse on the Bray-Corbie road. A thick and continuous drizzle made things very uncomfortable, especially as the Battalion had to move up that night to relieve the 2nd Bedfords in the Sailly-Laurette Sector.

SAILLY-LAURETTE, August 6th, 1918.

A long march in the rain was followed by a long and

SECRET.

All recipients of 174th
Infantry Brigade Defence Scheme.

---

1. 174th. Inf. Brigade Defence Scheme (Copy No..19..) is forwarded herewith. This supersedes 90th Inf. Brigade Defence Scheme and amendments issued from time to time from this office, which will be destroyed. It will not be taken beyond Battalion H.Q.

2. Unit Commanders will at the first opportunity go through the Brigade Defence Scheme with their Company (M.G. Section) Commanders.

3. Units will furnish this office with their Defence Schemes based on the Brigade Defence Scheme by March 17th.

4. Please acknowledge receipt on form below.

R.M. Barrington-Ward
Captain,
Brigade Major,
174th. Infantry Brigade.

7th March, 1918.

---Cut Here---

174th Inf. Brigade.

Copy No..19. 174th Inf. Brigade Defence Scheme received.

/3/18. (sd)......................

difficult relief. The condition of communication and front trenches was deplorable, and relief had not been completed by dawn, when an assaulting Division of the enemy, specially trained for the occasion, attacked the 18th Division front on the left and the two left companies of this Battalion. These two companies ("A" and "D," under Captain Poulton and Lieutenant Wilkinson) put up a most praiseworthy defence, and, in spite of the fact that the Battalion on their left had been pushed back more than 400 yards, maintained their front line intact throughout, and, further, formed a defensive flank which the enemy was unable to penetrate. Much assistance was afforded by Lewis-gun fire from "B" Company (Captain Thomas), which swept across the line of the enemy attack and caused them numerous casualties. Some prisoners and machine guns were also taken in a bombing counter-attack initiated by 2nd-Lieutenant Pattinson. The enemy, though foiled in their attempt to pierce our lines, kept up an incessant bombardment of the front-line system with 5·9's, gas shells, and trench mortars. By the morning of the 8th, the date fixed for the great counter-offensive, the men of this Battalion were caked in mud from head to foot, had had practically no rest (this was only possible by leaning against the parados), and had repelled a determined attack by the enemy.

MALARD WOOD, August 8th.

In order to keep the impending attack secret and jump a surprise on the enemy, instructions for the attack were not issued until the morning of the 7th. The rôle of the Battalion was to clear certain copses, and clear and hold the west edge of Malard Wood. Actually this Battalion was in reserve, but circumstances, in the form of a thick mist limiting visibility to ten yards, thrust the Battalion in the forefront of the fight a few minutes after the battle commenced. The three days in the line, exciting and tiring as they were, had given them a better idea of direction than other troops could possibly have. The luck of the weather was with them from the start, and they were able to get right on top of the enemy before the direction of the attack was perceived. Two enemy Battalion Commanders and over 500 prisoners were taken by the Battalion, as well as numerous trench mortars and machine guns. The next day (9th) the Battalion was attached to the 175th Brigade, and ordered to co-operate in an attack by the 174th Brigade on Chipilly (which had given much trouble on the 8th), advancing on the left flank of the Division astride the Bray-Corbie road. An American Regiment participated on our right. The attack, which was entirely open warfare, was successful. The casualties to this Battalion were far lighter

CHIPILLY, August 9th.

S E C R E T. Copy No........19

174th Infantry Brigade

DEFENCE SCHEME

BARISIS SECTION.

Distribution over.

174th. Infantry Brigade.

DEFENCE SCHEME.

-------o0o-------

Re[punch hole] maps. Shoot ST QUENTIN 1/100,000.
Shoot 70 D N.W. 1/20,000.
Trench Map, ST GOBAIN 1/10,000.

BOUNDARIES. 1. The front held by the Brigade extends from the N.W. slope of LE CROTOIR Plateau in H.24.c. to the ROUTE CHALETTE (inclusive). Brigade and Battalion Boundaries are shown in detail on attached Map A.

215th Inf. Regt. (161st French Division) holds the sector on our right; 175th Inf. Brigade holds the sector on our left.

TACTICAL FEATURES. 2. The Brigade Front is sited along the Western slopes of a valley running South from the main valley of the River OISE. The enemy's front system follows the Eastern slopes of the valley. Our lines cross to the Eastern slopes of the valley at one point only viz. H.25.a. and b. where we have a footing on the spur running out Westwards from the enemy's lines.

On our right the French confront the enemy astride LE CROTOIR plateau. On the Northern edge of the plateau where our lines join the French the ground slopes steeply down to BARISIS village which is itself a smaller hill at the foot of LE CROTOIR plateau, flanked East and West by low ground.

West of BARISIS village the ground rises again to form a flat-topped hill on which PETIT BARISIS stands (Hill 89).

S.W. of Hill 89 the ground continues to rise to the CLOS DES VIGNES Spur (H.27); West of it the ground is open and very slightly undulating to the edge of the forest in H.21; North of it the ground falls towards the railway and rises again to the marked feature Hill 98 and Northwards again along the main ridge in the forest (H.9,10,16) on which we join the lines of the 175th Inf. Brigade.

In rear of the front system, from the steep slopes of the PATTE D'EPAULE (H.28,29) and CLOS DES VIGNES (H.28,27) Spurs the deep and broad valley S.W. of LE CROTOIR plateau and the open low-lying ground S. and W. of PETIT BARISIS is dominated.

Observation of the enemy's positions is strictly limited by the protection which the wooded country, through which his lines run, affords him. He has good observation of all our BARISIS positions from the spur in H.23.b. Equally the BASSE FORET de COUCY gives us covered approaches as far as the Eastern and Northern slopes of the CLOS DES VIGNES Spur, the edge of the forest in H.21., and Hill 98 with the outpost positions East of it.

ORGANIZATION OF DEFENCE. 3. The Defences of the Sector are organized into

(a) A Forward Zone.

(b) A Battle Zone.

These Zones are shown on Map A.

(a) One Battalion holds the Forward Zone. It is distributed in depth and will not be reinforced in the event of attack. Its role is to hold on to the last and delay and break up the attack.

Three coys. hold the outpost line, each distributed in depth and one coy. is detailed as a permanent garrison of the important keeps in rear of the Forward Zone on Hills 89 and 98.

All posts and keeps are to be capable of all-round defence.

(b) One Battalion (less one coy.) is a permanent garrison of the Battle Zone, with one coy. in Brigade Reserve. The Battle Zone is the Zone in which the main Battle will be accepted and fought and where reserve troops will be employed for reinforcement and counter-attack.

WORK and MAINTENANCE.

4. (a) Forward Zone.

The Battalion in the Forward Zone is responsible for the maintenance and development of all defences in its area. A R.E. Officer living near Battalion H.Q. is Works Officer, Forward Zone and assists the Battalion Commander in the organization and supervision of all work in the Forward Zone, distributing available sappers to the work in consultation with the Battalion Commander.

As an emergency measure, where concentration is required on urgent work in the Forward Zone, one coy. is available from the Battle Zone Battalion. This coy. is to be the coy. billetted at PIERREMANDE.

(b) Battle Zone.

The Battalion in the Battle Zone is responsible for the maintenance and development of the Battle Zone defences upon the lines laid down by Brigade H.Q.

A R.E. Officer is Works Officer, Battle Zone and assists the Battalion Commander in the organization and supervision of work done. Each of the three coys. garrisoning the coy. localities in the Battle Zone will work on its own defences.

The Divisional Reserve Battalion and one coy. Pioneers are concentrated on urgent tasks under the direction of Brigade H.Q. in consultation with the C.C. Battle Zone Battalion.

(c) Duties of R.E. and Infantry at Work.

Closest touch is essential at all times. Infantry and R.E. officers will reconnoitre tasks together beforehand and will make direct any arrangements of detail to assist the work or the comfort of the men.

The principles for work are

(i) Brigade H.Q. lay down what is to be attained.

(ii) R.E. point out how it is to be attained.

(iii) Infantry Commanders are responsible that it is attained.

(d) All working parties will proceed to their work armed and equipped (Rifle, Bayonet, Belt, Pouches, Braces, Steel Helmet and at least 100 rounds S.A.A. per man)

Whilst actually at work equipment may be taken off provided it is readily available.

All working parties are responsible for their own protection and will post a lookout sentry over arms. O.C. working parties are responsible for knowing where to find the Senior officer in the locality in which they are working (See para.7c v).

(e) Camouflage has a special importance in the Forward Zone where our positions are all under close enemy observation. All officers will pay special attention to camouflage and screens in their sectors to ensure that new screens are erected where desirable and that existing screens are kept from day to day in good repair. The enemy must be denied observation of our movement everywhere. All new work will be carefully camouflaged and kept concealed after its completion. Sods will be first cut from ground where trenches are to be dug and replaced carefully at the conclusion of the work. The element of surprise is not less valuable in defence than in attack.

PRINCIPLES OF DEFENCE.

5. (a) All defences will be organized in depth, that is to say that every unit down to platoons will be responsible as far as possible for finding its own supports and reserves, and for disposing of them in such a manner that the enemy, should he penetrate our outposts, will be met with continuous resistance throughout the Zone from supporting posts sited to cover and assist each other.

(b) All troops will hold their ground to the last, whether their flanks are turned or not.

(c) Surprise will be guarded against by good wire and control of No Man's Land, which will be patrolled every night on a plan organised from Battalion H.Q.

(d) The Forward Zone Battalion will not be reinforced. To deal with the temporary loss of a part of our positions local reserves of the three front coys. may be used for counter-attack.

The Coy. holding the keeps will not be involved in fighting forward of the line Hill 89 - Hill 98.

(e) Personnel of all Coy. and Battalion H.Q. are organised each as a unit under a definite commander. They are allotted defences in which they stand to at least once daily. Personnel of Brigade H.Q. is similarly organised.

NORMAL DISTRIBUTION OF TROOPS.

6. (a) Forward Zone.

One Battalion. Three coys. holding the outposts and one coy. in the line of keeps. 5 machine guns. 5 Light Trench Mortars.

(b) Battle Zone.

One Battalion (less 1 coy.) 11 machine guns.

(c) Brigade Reserve. (for Battle Zone).

One Coy. Battle Zone Battalion. 1 Coy. Pioneers. One section m.g's (4 guns). 3 Light Trench Mortars.

One Battalion of the Brigade is in Divisional reserve. Distribution of troops in detail is shown on attached map A.

ACTION IN CASE OF ATTACK.

7. (a) It is necessary to be prepared for an enemy offensive on a large scale under the following headings.

(i) An attack by the enemy along the whole Brigade front in conjunction with an attack on the front of the neighbouring Brigade and Regiment.

(ii) An attack on the French positions on our right (LE CROTOIR) involving the possibilities of the loss of LE CROTOIR and the rendering untenable of BARISIS VILLAGE in consequence.

To guard against this eventuality two main "keeps" are being constructed on Hill 89 and Hill 98 and posts to link those keeps to each other, to the present support line in the Left Coy. area (CARENCY Trench), and to the CLOS DES VIGNES Spur have been made. This line of keeps and posts is being wired throughout. See attached map B.

The CLOS DES VIGNES Locality, linking as it does with the 161st French Division Locality at BERNAGOUSSE, is of vital importance as this latter locality is the pivot on which the French systems of defence and switches in their Battle Zone hinge in the event of a serious and sustained attack from the S.E.

Close personal liaison with the French will be maintained by Officers Commanding Forward and Battle Zone Battalions and by their officers.

(b) If any warning is received that the enemy is likely to attack the following order will be sent out from Brigade H.Q.

PREPARE FOR ATTACK.

On receipt of this message which will be acknowledged by wire at once:

(i) Unit Commanders Forward Zone will take such action as they consider necessary to ensure increased vigilance and preparedness for attack. Patrols and listening posts will be ordered along every company front continuously throughout the night and early morning to watch for and report at once signs of hostile assembly.

O.C. Brigade Tunnelling Section reports himself to H.Q. Forward Zone Battalion and places his section at the disposal of the Battalion Commander.

(ii) All units in the Battle Zone and in Brigade and Divisional Reserve will hold themselves in readiness to move at a quarter of an hour's notice.

(iii) The following will report by wire to Brigade H.Q. the numbers present with their units in the reserve area:

O.C. Battalion in Divisional Reserve.
O.C. D. Coy. 1/4th Suffolk Regt. (Pioneers)
O.C. 511th Field Coy. R.E.
O.C. 174th. Light Trench Mortar Battery.

(iv) Liaison Officers will report as follows :-

From Forward Zone Battalions to flanking Battalions.

From Battle Zone Battalion to Forward Zone Battalion and French Battle Zone Battalion.

From units mentioned in para. (iii) to Brigade H.Q.

NOTE All liaison will be from North to South, i.e., every commander will be responsible for visiting his opposite number on his right flank.

(v) Working parties rejoin their units forthwith.

(vi) Battle police are told off to stragglers' posts by Forward and Battle Zone Battalions.

(vii) All units report completion of their arrangements as soon as possible by PRIORITY wire to Brigade H.Q.

(c) When an enemy attack is imminent or has begun the following order will be sent out from Brigade H.Q.

MAN BATTLE STATIONS.

This order may be sent without the previous warning in para. (b) above.

On receipt of this message, which will be acknowledged by wire at once :

(i) Battle Zone Battalion mans its positions with three companies on the front BERNAGOUSSE QUARRIES (exclusive) to ROND DE L'EPINOIS (inclusive) with Battalion H.Q. at H.27.a.1.0. One company (Brigade Reserve) moves to positions of readiness along line of PIERREMANDE - BARISIS Road in H.20.d. and H.27.a.

(ii) "D" Coy. 1/4th Suffolk Regt. mans its allotted positions with two platoons holding ROND D'ORLEANS. Defences, one platoon in posts North of these to the Left Brigade Boundary, one platoon in Company Reserve. along railway in H.19.c.

(iii) Machine Gun and Trench Mortar gun-teams stand to in their Battle positions. A G.S. Limbered wagon will report to O.C. 174th Light Trench Mortar Battery under arrangements made by the Staff Captain.

(iv) Other units fall in on their alarm posts.

(v) After the above order has been issued there will be no retrograde movement on the part of working parties. Working parties (including R.E.) will man the defences which they are working on or proceeding to or from, or the nearest defences. O.C. party will report to the Senior Officer of the locality, state strength of party and place himself at disposal.

(vi) Battle Police mount at stragglers posts in Forward and Battle Zones selected beforehand by respective Battalion Commanders. These to include SUNKEN Road H.27.b.80.15., R.E. Dump, H.27.a.8.8., ROND D'ORLEANS. Stragglers to be handed over to the nearest Infantry Commander.

(vii) Liaison arrangements as in para. b (iv) above.

(viii) All units will report completion of arrangements as soon as possible by PRIORITY wire to Brigade H.Q.

NOTE: System on which all the above telegraphic messages, acknowledgements and reports will be sent is dealt with in Appendix A.

For disposal of Battle Surplus Personnel see Appendix C.

ARTILLERY. 8. (a) Part of one Brigade R.F.A. covers the front and a proportion of the III Corps Heavy Artillery.

The artillery is distributed in depth to cover the Forward and Battle Zones. Certain guns in the Forward Zone are placed as silent guns and fire only in case of emergency to deal with hostile parties who may have penetrated our Forward Zone.

(b) In the event of a hostile attack or raid upon our front which does not involve the French on our right, certain French batteries are available to assist. This assistance is given on the demand, sent to the French from Brigade H.Q.,

DEFEND BARISIS.

(c) The substance of the foregoing paragraphs is shown in detail on the attached map C.

(d) When the order "MAN BATTLE STATIONS" is issued the

artillery open a bombardment of the enemy's positions by way of counter-preparation. This counter-preparation is divided into three periods as follows :-

(i) First Period. 8.45 p.m. - 3.45 a.m. (Counter-preparation A). Bombardment of enemy approaches etc. Enemy probably moving up to jumping-off positions.

(ii) Second Period. 3.45 a.m. - 7.45 a.m. (Counter-preparation B) Bombardment of probably jumping-off positions.

(iii) Third Period. 7.45 a.m. - 8.45 a.m. (Counter-preparation C.) Bombardment of Bridges.

(e) Forward guns are to be fought as long as possible. In this connection battalions are reminded that it is a paramount duty of the infantry to protect the guns to the last and that under no circumstances will infantry fail to accede to a request from the artillery to protect battery positions or to assist in getting guns away.

(f) Artillery liaison Officers from supporting batteries are attached to Battalion H.Q., Forward Zone for 48 hours at a time.

(g) Any heavy surprise bombardment by guns or trench mortars will be reported to Brigade H.Q. by PRIORITY wire.

MACHINE GUNS & TRENCH MORTARS. 9. (a) Machine Guns and Trench Mortars are disposed in depth throughout the Brigade area. Positions are shown on attached map A.

(b) One section machine guns and three Light Trench Mortars are held in Brigade Reserve.

(c) The principles of defence set forth in paras. 5 and 7 apply in their entirety to the Machine Gun Coy. and Trench Mortar Battery. The only reason for abandoning a battle position will be that, in existing circumstances, another position offers stronger and more favourable defence of the same ground.

(d) All machine gun and trench mortar personnel will

maintain at all times the closest liaison with the battalions in the line. Section Commanders to visit Company Commanders, and Machine Gun Coy. Commander to visit Battalion Commander daily.

R.M. Barrington-Ward
Captain,
Brigade Major,
174th. Infantry Brigade.

6th March, 1918.

APPENDIX "A". SECRET.

174th. Infantry Brigade.

SIGNAL COMMUNICATIONS.

BARISIS SECTION.

Ref. Map 70 D N.W. 1/20,000.
Attached diagrams A and B.

1. Telegraphic and Telephonic Communication.

(a) To Division, Infantry Brigade on left, French Regiment on right and R.F.A. Group by overhead or staked lines. Alternative routes to Division available.

(b) Forward of Brigade H.Q. through sub-exchanges

at H.25.b.3.4. (Brigade Advanced Exchange).
at each Battalion H.Q.
and in BERNAGOUSSE QUARRIES.

(c) Existing lines are mainly French staked cable routes. Alternative routes to Forward and Battle Zones Battalion Headquarters.

Lateral communication to right and left on the Battalion H.Q. level, and, except on our left boundary on the Company H.Q. level also.

(d) A buried cable route is under construction which will give communication between Brigade and Forward and Battle Zone Battalions, and also lateral communication between the latter two headquarters and those of the corresponding units in the 175th Infantry Brigade section.

(e) Artillery liaison lines - from Forward Zone Battalion to Artillery exchange direct, from Battle Zone Battalion via Brigade Advanced exchange.

(f) Telegraphic communication from Infantry O.P's is being prepared.

(g) Fullerphones exclusively employed for telegraphic purposes forward of SINCENY. Telephonic communication for officers, and in no case in advance of Battalion Headquarters.

(h) A bombardment signal office at Brigade Headquarters is under preparation.

2. Visual Communication.

(a) Divisional Advanced Central Visual Station at H.2.a.●2 receives from Forward Zone Battalion, and sends to Brigade Visual Station, SINCENY. Both visual stations have telegraphic communication to Brigade.

(b) Visual to Forward Zone Battalion from

All three Outpost Company Headquarters.

Platoon H.Q. at H.23.a.8.8.

Hill 89.

and French Company at LE CROTOIR.

(c) Backward signalling only, except during active operations.

(d) The shell-proofing of visual stations is being proceeded with.

(e) For the purpose of testing visual communications a period of two hours daily is set apart during which all telegrams must be sent by visual where such exists.

3. Wireless and Earth Induction Communication.

(a) A wireless station at Brigade H.Q. in communication with Division and 173rd Infantry Brigade.

(b) A Power Buzzer works from the keep on Hill 89 to the central Amplifier station at LA FORTELLE (175th Infantry Brigade area.)

4. Pigeons. One pair per 48 hours to Forward Zone Battalion, for use from keep at Hill 98.

5. Runners.

Brigade relay post at ROND D'ORLEANS. Mounted men and cyclists largely employed. Two cyclist orderlies from 174th Infantry Brigade are attached to the Headquarters of the French Divisional Infantry at FOLEMBRAY, and two French cyclists in return attached to 174th Infantry Brigade for liaison duties.

6. S.O.S. Rocket System.

In addition to the system established by the R.F.A., the Central Visual Station on LES BUTTES DENROUY is fitted as an S.O.S. relay post, continual watch being kept, both over the front line and towards Battalion relay posts. Diagram A shows the complete system.

7. <u>Alarm Warnings</u>. are forwarded as signal service messages on the basis of the most speedy distribution to companies, machine gun sections, etc. The report "preparations complete" is forwarded, both to Brigade by the same system, and via the usual unit headquarters.

Diagram . B shows the system of distribution.

8. Diagram A, attached, shows the line, visual, earth induction, pigeon and S.O.S. rocket systems of communication.

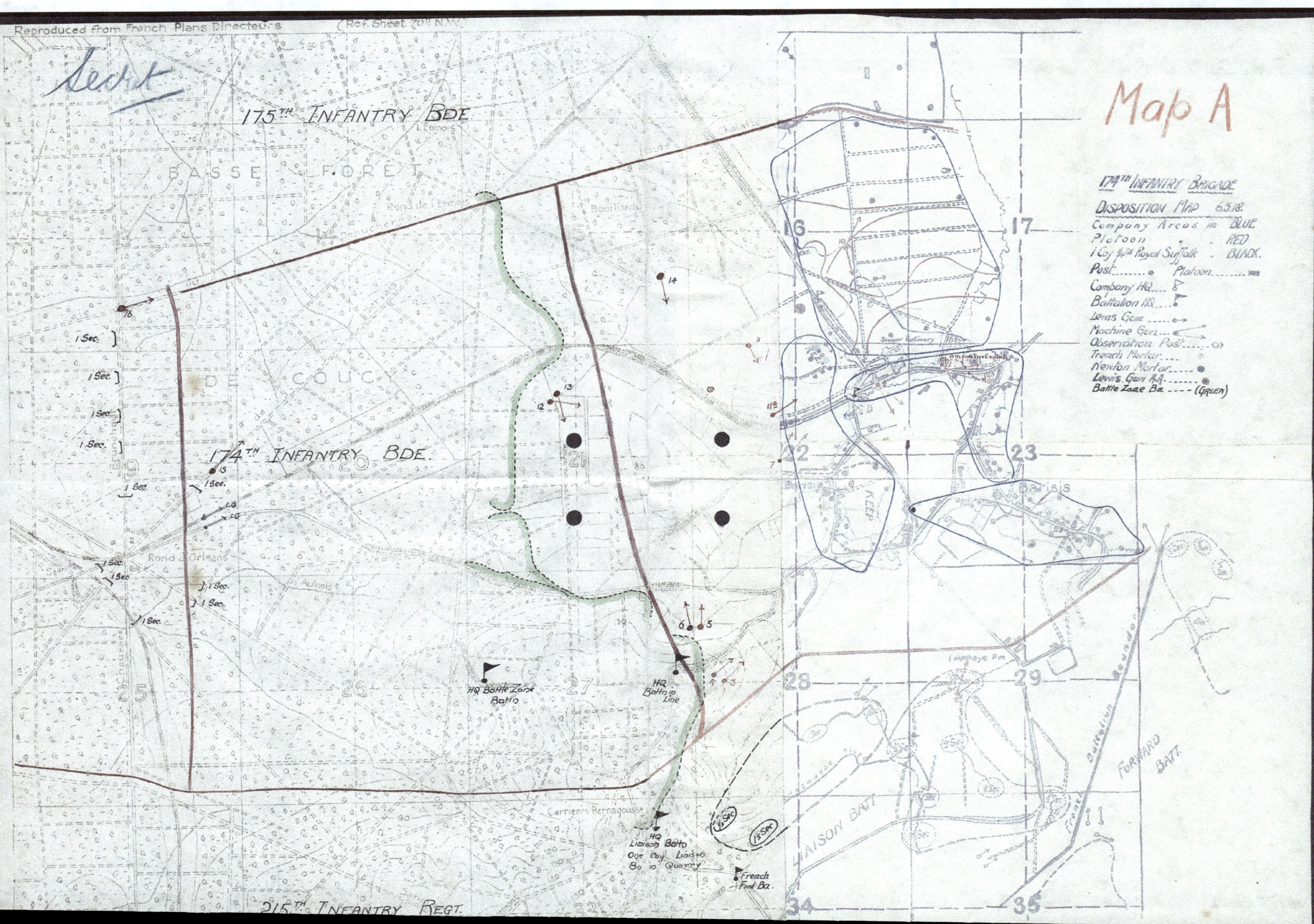

Reproduced from French Plans Directeurs
(Ref. Sheet 70a N.W.)
Secret
Map A
174TH INFANTRY BRIGADE
DISPOSITION MAP 6.5.18.
Company Areas in BLUE
Platoon . RED
1 Coy 4th Royal Suffolk . BLACK.
Post
Platoon
Company HQ.
Battalion HQ.
Lewis Gun
Machine Gun
Observation Post
Trench Mortar
Newton Mortar
Lewis Gun A.A.
Battle Zone Bz. ---- (GREEN)
175TH INFANTRY BDE.
174TH INFANTRY BDE.
215TH INFANTRY REGT.
BASSE FORET
DE COUCY
1 Sec.
HQ Battle Zone Battn
HQ Battn in Line
HQ Liaison Battn
One Coy Liaison Bn in Quarry
French Fwd Bn.
KEEP
Barisis
Sugar Refinery
LIAISON BATT
FORWARD BATT.
Battalion Boundary
Carrière Berragousse
Rond d'Orléans
Rond de l'Ecrevisse
16
17
22
23
28
29
34
35
20
21
25
26
27

35.Æ.A.33.
62ᴰD.13 b. E 8c.14a.
16·7·18–3 P.M.
F=10"

WO95/3006
35.Æ.A.35.
62D E14.
16·7·18-3 P.M.
F=10"

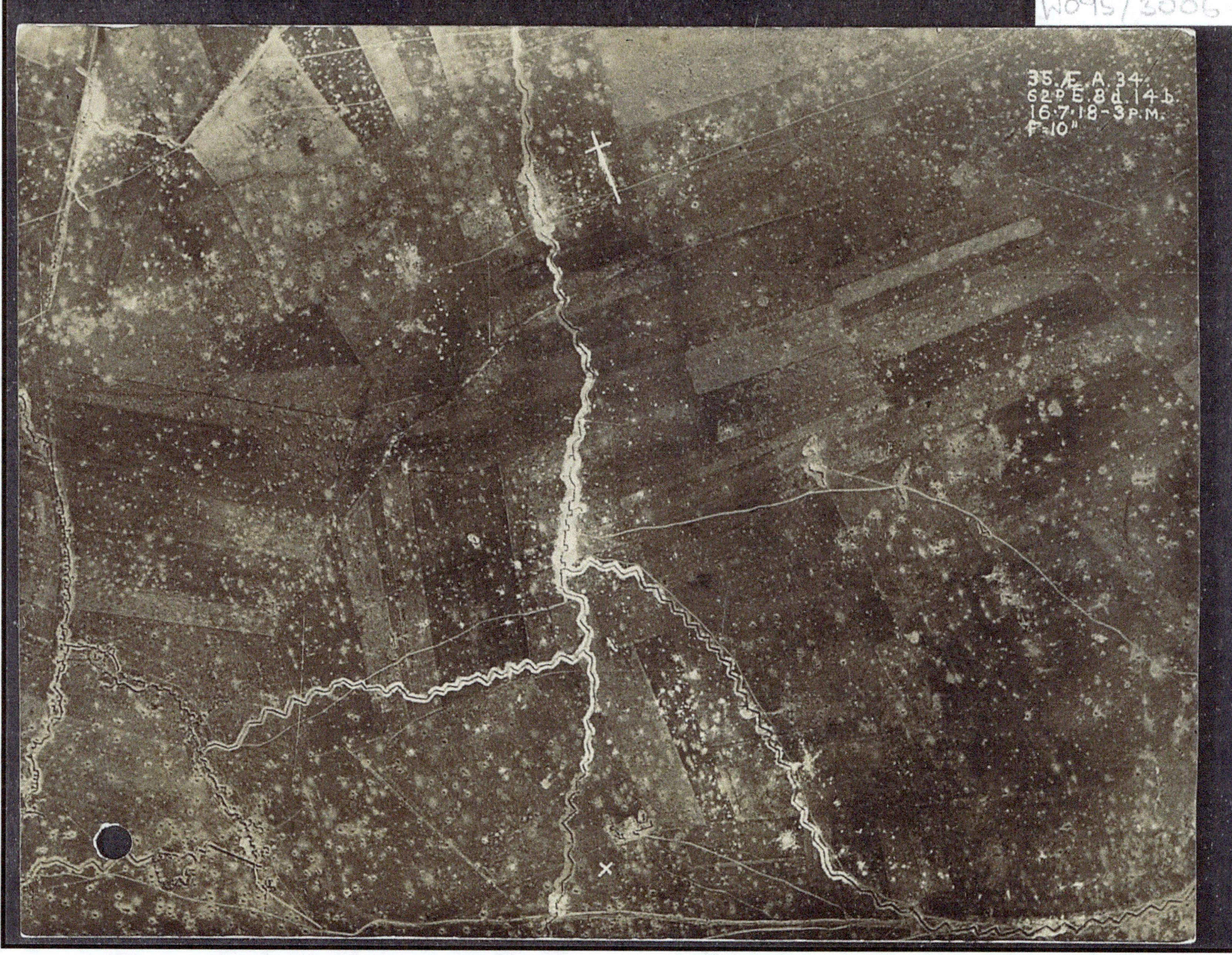
35.F.A.34.
62D.E.8d.14b.
16.7.18-3P.M.
F=10"

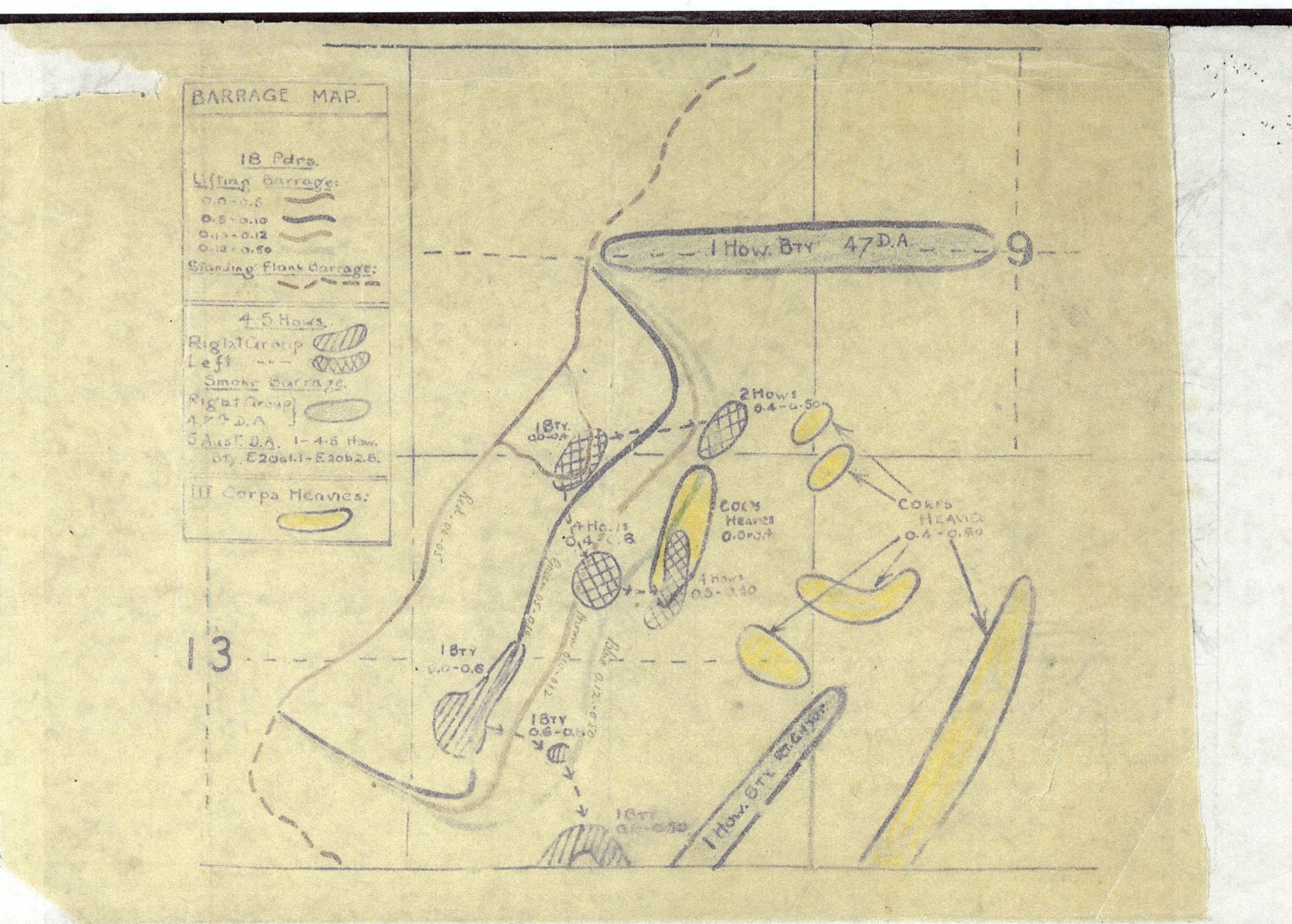
BARRAGE MAP.
18 Pdrs.
Lifting Barrage:
0.0 - 0.5
0.5 - 0.10
0.10 - 0.12
0.12 - 0.50
Standing Flank Barrage:
4.5 Hows.
Right Group
Left
Smoke Barrage.
Right Group
47th D.A.
5 Aust. D.A. 1 - 4.5 How.
Bty. E20a1.1 - E20b2.8.
III Corps Heavies:
1 How. Bty 47 D.A.
9
13
2 Hows
0.4 - 0.50
18 Bty.
Corps Heavies
0.4 - 0.50
Corps Heavies
4 Hows
18 Bty
0.0 - 0.6
18 Bty
Red. 0.0 - 0.5
1 How. Bty

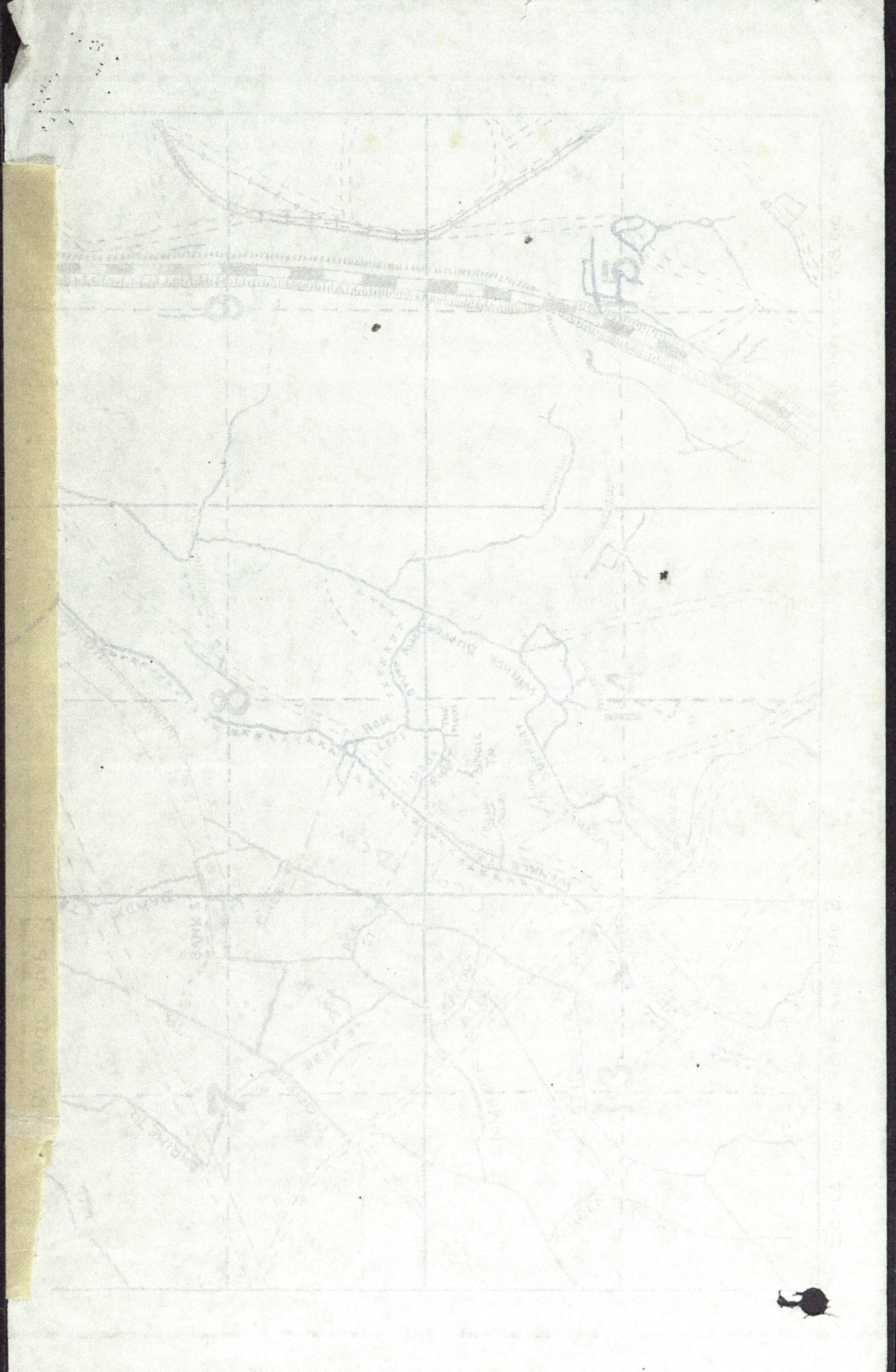

TOPO. SECTION (No 80)
ROUTES FOR EVACUATION No1 (WOUNDED)
AND ADMINISTRATIVE ARRANGEMENTS
23.6.18
REFERENCE
Trenches corrected to 22.6.18
Headquarters
Tracks
Old British Camps
Foot Bridge
FOR REFERENCE SEE OVER.
ALBERT
Méaulte
Diggers Avenue
Dirty
Trench
Square Tr.
Crater
Pioneer
Beer St.
Don St.
Dublin
Ditch
RAP
Reserve Stretchers
Relay Stretcher Post.
Ethel
Polly
Mine
Diamond
Duke
Dingo
Bingo Ditch
Welch Trench
A.D.S.
Dugouts
Cutlery
Screens
Crossing
13
7
8
9
10
14
15
16
18
19
20
21
22
24
100
90
80
70
60

REFERENCE.

ROUTES.

WALKING WOUNDED

STRETCHERS.

DUCKBOARD BRIDGES.

R.A.P.
A.D.S.

RESERVE STRETCHERS.

ADMINISTRATIVE ARRANGEMENTS

ADVANCED B.H.Q.

BN RENDEZVOUS

TROPHY COLLECTG. POST.

PRISONER COLLECTG POST

PRISONERS ESCORT PARTY

CONTROL POSTS.

MAP SHEWING COMPANY AREAS

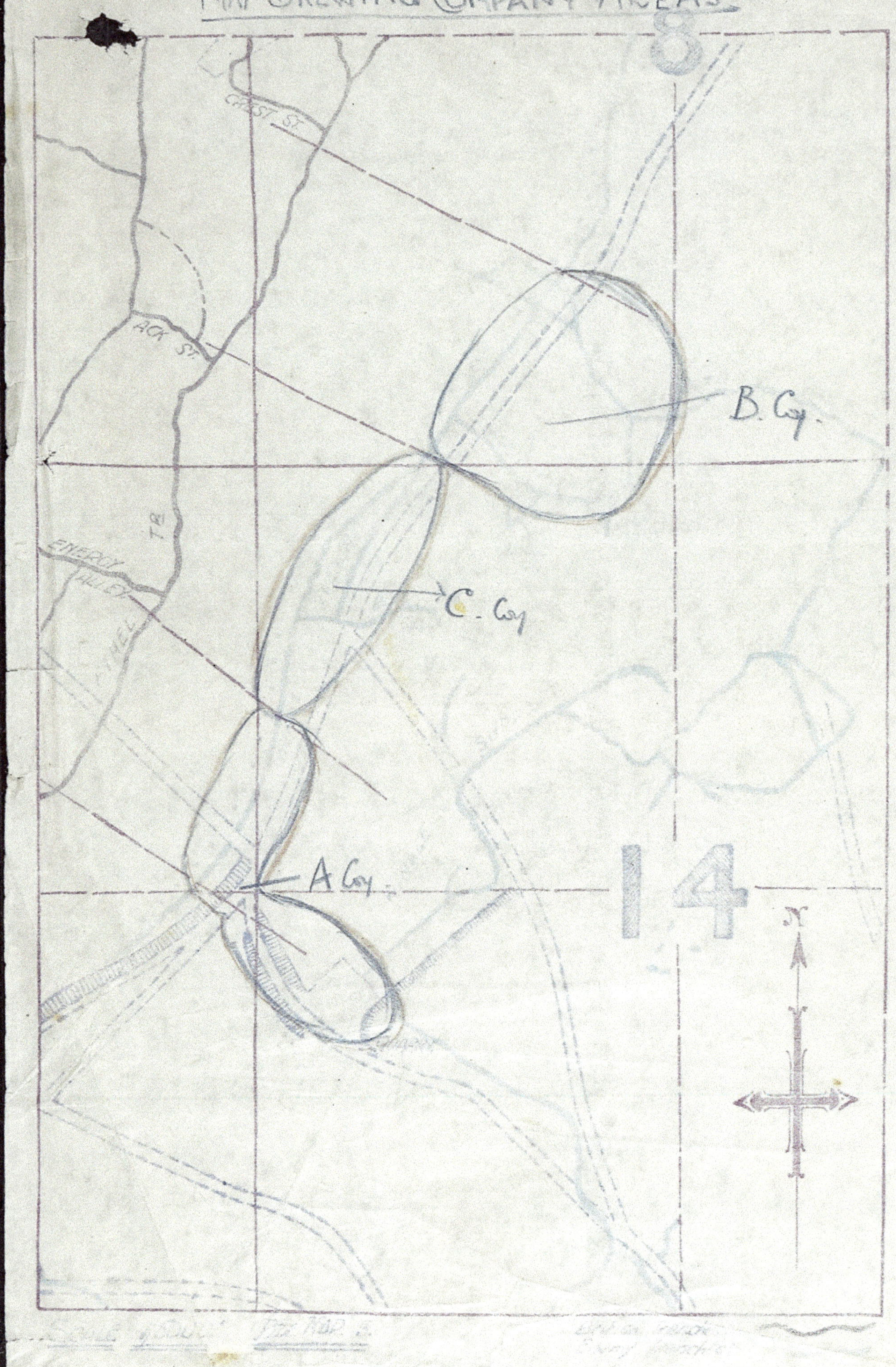

"C" Form.

MESSAGES AND SIGNALS. No. of Message

Prefix ... Code ... Words 51

£ s. d.

Charges Collect

Service Instructions. PUMU

Received. From Bde By A Norton

Sent, or sent out. At ... m. To ... By ...

Office Stamp. 41

Handed in at Bde Office 7.30 p m Received 7.45 m.

TO MOMU = 8th London Regt

*Sender's Number.	Day of Month.	In reply to Number.	AAA
QD 934	25		

Divl	Comdr	conveys	to
MOMU	his	congratulations	on
very	good	raid	carried
out	by	them	today
and	his	thanks	for
the	good	work	done
aaa	He	hopes	casualties
are	not	heavy	aaa
The	Brigadier	also	conveys
his	hearty	congratulations	and
his	warm	appreciation	to
his	comrades		

FROM Maxwell (17th Brig. Genl)

TIME & PLACE

*This line should be erased if not required.

300,000.—John Rissen, Ltd —5/17.—3280. Forms C2123.

"C" Form.

Army Form C. 2123.
(In books of 100.)

MESSAGES AND SIGNALS. No. of Message

Prefix SM Code 3.17 Words 15

£ s. d.

Charges to Collect

Received. From PUMU By Pte Norton E.

Sent, or sent out. At m. To By

Office Stamp. 7th CITY OF LONDON REGT.

Service Instructions. PUMU

Handed in at PUMU Office 4.30 m Received 7.28 p

TO MOMU - 8 London Regt

*Sender's Number.	Day of Month.	In reply to Number.	AAA
QD935	25		

PUSU = 173 Bde.	writes	aaa	best
Congratulations		on	success-
ful	show	this	morning

FROM TIME & PLACE PUMU - 174 Inf Brigade

*This line should be erased if not required.

300,000.—John Rissen, Ltd —5/17.—3280. Forms C2123.

Dîner de la FERME de la TOURETTE. 17/11/18
BAUFFE

F. Leroy
Bourgmestre.

Cecil R. Crossland M.C. 2/Lieut.

A. L. Frost Lieut.

E. Haynes Président de la
Commission for Relief in Belgium.

Thomas Fulton 2nd Lt.

[illegible], Fonctionnaire au Ministère de la Justice.

A. D. Derviche-Jones. Lt. Col. 8th London Regt.

L. Leroy

H. W. Kelly 2/Lt

Jules Haynes Etudiant

Harold Fenwick 2/Lt

E. Marlaix – Instituteur.

J. Middleton Barratt.
Capt.

à M. le Colonel du 8me R[illegible] Londr[illegible]

Au nom de la Commune de Bauffe j'ai l'honneur de vous présenter nos félicitations de bienvenue les plus sympathiques et les plus cordiales.

Je vous prie de bien vouloir accepter nos vifs et sincères remerciements pour l'insigne honneur que vous daignez nous faire en venant réinstaller nos festivités Communales.

Honneur et Gloire aux armées Britanniques et à toutes les armées Alliées qui nous ont si vaillamment délivrés de la tyrannie Allemande.

Jamais nous n'oublierons cette fameuse journée du 11 novembre 1918 marqué par l'entrée dans notre commune de ces nobles et courageux soldats, couverts de lauriers, bravant la mort et poursuivant l'ennemi pas à pas pour notre délivrance.

Tous nos remerciements, toute notre reconnaissance et tous nos souhaits de bonheur s'adressent à nos glorieux défenseurs.

Hourrah! aux vaillantes armées Britanniques et Alliées.

A notre Chère Belgique, tous nos cœurs et nos vœux.

Vive la liberté! Vive la Paix!
Vive le Roi! Vive la Belgique!
Vivent les Alliés!

Bauffe 17 nov. 1918.

SECRET.

Copy No. ....

174th Infantry Brigade Defensive Arrangements.

B.M./7/73/28.

RESERVE LINE - BOIS L'ABBE Sector.

Ref. maps,
62 D 1/40,000.
62 D S.E. 1/20,000.

12th April, 1918.

FRONTAGE. 1. The Brigade Front extends from the GENTELLES - CACHY Road (exclusive) to the AMIENS - VILLERS BRETONNEUX Road (inclusive). 173rd Inf. Brigade is on the right (H.Q. - Quarry in T.1.a.) - 15th Inf. Brigade A.I.F. is on the left (H.Q. - Chateau BLANGY TRONVILLE).

DESCRIPTION. 2. The front held constitutes a Reserve line to the front line positions on the line HANGARD - E. of VILLERS BRETONNEUX - VAIRE SOUS CORBIE. The front line positions are the Main Defensive Line on the Corps Front.

The Reserve Line defends the plateau GENTELLES - CACHY - BOIS L'ABBE, possession of which would give the enemy almost complete observation of the eastern approaches to AMIENS. Its retention is therefore of vital importance to the defence of AMIENS.

DISTRIBUTION OF TROOPS. 3. The Brigade Front is held by two Battalions with one Battalion in support.

Right Battalion. Right Brigade Boundary to O.32.a.5.4. Three coys. (= 1 Battn.) in Front and Support Lines. H.Q. T.11.d.7.3.

Left Battalion. O.32.a.5.4. to Left Brigade Boundary. Three coys. in Front Line and Posts. One coy. in support. One coy. (of Support Battn.) in reserve. H.Q. O.25.d.8.3. Railway Cutting.

Support Battalion. (less 1 coy. attached Left Battn.) Defences (part of the BOIS Line) on the Eastern slope of the BOIS DE BLANGY. H.Q. Bridge O.25.c.1.1., moving to N.30.d.8.0.

Trench Mortars. Four mortars in the line of posts, Left Battalion, covering valley in O.32.b. Alternative positions in rear of Front Line. (Under construction).

Machine Guns. 12 guns 58th M.Gun Battn. See attached tracing.

PRINCIPLES OF DEFENCE. 4. The Front Line is the Main Line of Resistance. It will be sufficiently garrisoned to ensure that it can be strongly defended throughout. It will be held at all costs, and reserves in the hands of Battalion and Company Commanders will be used for the reinforcement or recovery of any part of it as the situation may demand.

In the BOIS L'ABBE posts are sited (one section per platoon) forward of the Front Line with the mission of breaking up a hostile attack coming through the wood. These will be held to the last.

The Support Battalion (less 1 coy.) is in Brigade Reserve and available for reinforcement or recovery of any part of the Reserve Line on the Brigade Front. Officers and N.C.O's of the Support Battalion will reconnoitre this line throughout.

In the event of attack Support Battalion will send a liaison officer to H.Q. of Left and Right Battalions to keep touch with the situation.

/WORK. 5.

WORK. 5. Right and Left Battalions will organize and concentrate available labour primarily on the defences (wire and trenches) of the Front Line. This is already a continuous trench line on the Right Battalion front and will be made deep and continuous as raidly as possible in the BOIS L'ABBE.

The erection of a solid and continuous wire obstacle is of first importance. All wire will be traced by the R.E.

The detail and dimensions of the defences to be constructed have been issued to all concerned and will be strictly adhered to.

The infantry are responsible for the erection and construction of obstacles and defences. R.E. are principally employed on making Battalion and Company H.Q.

COMMUNICATIONS. 6. Direct Lines from Brigade Exchange M.36.central to Battalion H.Q. Runner and mounted orderly from Brigade H.Q. T.6.c.4.7.

ESTABLISHMENT AND SUPPLY OF S.A.A. 7. (a) Establishment.

on the man 120 plus 50	-	170 rounds S.A.A. per man.
In posts	-	100 rounds per man of garrison.
At Battalion H.Q.	-	20,000 rounds.
Per Lewis Gun	-	2,000 rounds.
Per Machine Gun	-	10,000 rounds (Supplied under arrange-ments made by O.C. M.Gun Battn.).

NOTE - S.A.A. in excess of this Scale now in line will not be withdrawn.

(b) Supply. Requirements - wired to Brigade H.Q. - are sent up by transport from CAGNY.

MEDICAL ARRANGEMENTS. 8. (a) SICK.

(i) From Forward Area to Divl. Sick Collecting Station BOVES, thence to C.C.S. NAMPS.

(ii) From back areas to Walking Wounded Collecting Station at Rue PORTE PARIS near Railway Station, AMIENS, thence to C.C.S. NAMPS.

(b) WOUNDED.

Lying Wounded from Forward Area to A.D.S., St.ACHEUL, thence to C.C.S. NAMPS.

Lying Wounded from Rear Area to :

(i) Walking Wounded Station, Rue PORTE PARIS, AMIENS.

(ii) A.D.S., Boulevard de BAPAUME, AMIENS.

Walking Wounded from Forw--ard Area to

(i) ST. NICOLAS, BOVES.

(ii) Walking Wounded Post, Road Junction S.E. of LONGEAU.

Walking Wounded from Rear Area to

(i) Corps Walking Wounded Post - Rue PORTE PARIS, AMIENS.

(ii) A.D.S., Boulevard de BAPAUME, AMIENS.

Walking Wounded from AMIENS are conveyed by Lorry or Train to C.C.S., NAMPS.

(c) French Wounded or Sick (Soldiers or Civilians) to Divl. Sick Collecting Station, BOVES, thence by Red Cross Ambulance to C.C.S. NAMPS.

(d) DENTAL TREATMENT. Cases requiring Skilled Dental Treatment sent by Fd. Ambcs. to Dental Centre, No.12 C.C.S. LONGPRES-LES-CORPS-SAINTS. Dates to be notified later.

(e) OPHTHALMIC TREATMENT. Cases will be sent as in para. 4. Arrangements regarding attendance will continue as before.

(f) MOTOR AMBULANCE CONVOYS.

No. 10 M.A.C.) At DOCK d'ARTILLERIE Rue l'ESSCOUE
No. 24 M.A.C.) at West End of BOULEVARD BAPAUME
No. 31 M.A.C.)

9. Please acknowledge.

Captain,
Brigade Major,
174th Infantry Brigade.

DISTRIBUTION.

Copy No. 1 G.O.C.
2 4th Suffolk Regt. (Pioneers).
3 7th London Regt.
4 8th London Regt.
5 Brigade Signal Officer.
6 511th Field Coy. R.E.
7 Staff Captain.
8 Brigade Int. Officer.
9 18th Division.
10 58th Division "G".
11 58th Division "Q"
12 173rd Inf. Brigade.
13 175th Inf. Brigade.
14 15th Inf. Brigade A.I.F.
15 War Diary.
16 File.

ADMINISTRATIVE ARRANGEMENTS
in connection with
B.M.7/75/19 dated 14th.May, 1918.

---

1. TRANSPORT. The following Transport will be kept by Units in some position near their present locations

Each Battalion. 6 Pack Ponies (loaded with 2,000 rounds each.)
1 S.A.A. Limber (less team) (loaded with 18,000 rounds.)
6 Lewis Gun Limbers (less teams) (carrying 4 Lewis Guns & 13,372 rounds each. limber
2 Tool Limbers. (less teams)(loaded with (full complement of tools.)
1 Bomb Limber (less team) (loaded with Mobile Reserve of bombs 8th. Battalion only.

174th.L.T.M.Btty. 2 Limbers (6th. and 7th. Battalion Bomb Limbers) complete with teams and loaded as follows :-

(a) 8 Mortars and 50 Rounds.
(b) 150 Rounds.

2. STAND TO. On receipt of order "STAND TO" the teams for above transport will at once proceed from MIRVAUX to report to Units.

Lewis Gun Limbers will be under the orders of Commanding Officers.

The following Transport will be brigaded in Valley C.4.b.8.8. under orders of Brigade Transport Officer, and will thereafter be under Brigade control :

1 S.A.A. Limber per Battalion.
1 Bomb Limber (8th. Battalion only.)
2 Tool Limbers per Battalion.
2 Limbers 174th. L.T.M.Battery (only until O.C., 174th. L.T.M.Battery receives other orders.)

3. DRESS. Battle Order. Greatcoats and haversacks will be dumped and stored under Unit arrangements before moving off. Packs will be carried.

Contents of Pack will be strictly limited to necessaries authorised less great coat.

4. RATIONS. Rations to be carried are unexpended portion of day's ration - haversack ration - and emergency iron ration.

5. WATER. All water bottles to be full.

6. MOVE. On receipt of the order "MOVE" the 6 Pack Ponies per Battalion will accompany Battalions, the Lewis Gun Limbers will accompany Battalions or not at the discretion of Commanding Officer.

The B.T.O. will report to Staff Captain for orders.

7. MEDICAL ARRANGEMENTS. These have already been circulated under this office No. SC12/430 dated 8.5.1918.

7

Instructions regarding War Diaries and Intelligence Summaries are contained in F. S. Regs., Part II. and the Staff Manual respectively. Title pages will be prepared in manuscript.

WAR DIARY
~~or~~
~~INTELLIGENCE SUMMARY.~~

(Erase heading not required.)

Army Form C. 2118.

Vol 17

Place	Date	Hour	Summary of Events and Information	Remarks and references to Appendices
			8th London Regiment May 1918	

D. D. & L., London, E.C.
(A5001) Wt. W1771/M2031 750,000 5/17 Sch. 52 Forms/C2118/14

Army Form C. 2118.

Instructions regarding War Diaries and Intelligence Summaries are contained in F. S. Regs., Part II. and the Staff Manual respectively. Title pages will be prepared in manuscript.

WAR DIARY
or
~~INTELLIGENCE~~ SUMMARY.
(*Erase heading not required.*)

Place	Date	Hour	Summary of Events and Information	Remarks and references to Appendices
NEUF MOULIN	1st May 1918	—	Following officers were with Battalion on 1st May. Major C.E. JOHNSTON (C.O.) Major P.G. EDWARDS M.C. (Sec in Command) Sec Lt J.M. BARRATT (Act/Adjt) Sec Lt E.C. KNELL (I.O.) Sec Lt P.E. D'ARCY (L.G.O.) Capt T.A.B. PURKIS (T.O.) Lt W.B. MACDEAN (M.O.) Capt A.J. JAMES (C.F.) Capt R. FAIRLEY M.C. (QM.) A Coy Sec Lt R.R. POULTON (O.C.) Sec Lts F.W. KNIGHT, J.W. SEATON, B.C. DAVIS. B Coy Capt H.H. KING (OC) Sec Lts R.F. ROTHWELL, C.R. CROSSLAND, Lt R.H.A. NEWSOME M.C. C Coy Sec Lts H. BOOTH M.C. (OC) Sec Lts C.F. YOUNGMAN, A.J. HARRIS, R.N. JOHNSON. D Coy Capt G.E. GUNNING M.C. Sec Lts W.E. CONSTANCE, A.E. MASON, E.D. JONES. Training carried out by Companies on Batt[n] Parade Ground 10 am – 12 NOON. Sec Lts A.F. MORTON, E.J. ROFT, H. ORCHARD, A.G. TAFNER, R.B. PATTISON, H. PEACOCK, R.W. PERRY, H.J. ALEXANDER, L.W. EVERETT joined Battalion as Reinforcements.	[initials]
– do –	2nd		Company training from 9.15 am to 12 NOON. Lecture to all officers by Major C.E. JOHNSTON O/C. Lt L.E.B. JACOB joins Battn & assumes duties of act/adjutant. Sec Lt J.M. BARRATT asst/adjt.	[initials]
– do –	3rd		Company training 9.15 am to 1 pm.	[initials]
– do –	4th		Battalion paraded & marched off at 9.30 am for firing on PONT REMY Range. Shooting was very good. Battalion arrived back at 6.30 pm.	[initials]
– do –	5th		Battalion proceeded by Coys to VAUCHELLES-LES-QUESNOY for testing box respirators in Bde Gas Chamber. Sec Lts BARRATT, DAVIS, MORTON, ROTHWELL, ALEXANDER, C.F. YOUNGMAN, HARRIS, JOHNSON, CONSTANCE, MASON & 70 other ranks proceeding on Battle Surplus left at 2.30 pm. Transport left at 9.0 am for MOLLIENS AU BOIS Area doing the journey in two stages.	[initials]
NEUF MOULIN — MIRVAUX	6th		Battalion embussed on main road near NEUF-MOULIN at 10 am, debussed at MOLLIENS AU BOIS & marched to MIRVAUX arriving at 6 pm. Bn H.Q. billetted in the village & Coys under canvas on the outskirts.	[initials]

C.E. Johnston Lt Col

D. D. & L., London, E.C. (A8001) Wt. W1771/M2031 750,000 5/17 Sch. 52 Forms/C2118/14

Instructions regarding War Diaries and Intelligence Summaries are contained in F. S. Regs., Part II. and the Staff Manual respectively. Title pages will be prepared in manuscript.

WAR DIARY

or

~~INTELLIGENCE SUMMARY.~~

(Erase heading not required.)

Army Form C. 2118.

Place	Date	Hour	Summary of Events and Information	Remarks and references to Appendices
MIRVAUX	MAY 7th		Companies inspected in organisation by the Commanding Officer in the morning. Battalion was practised in attack formation in the afternoon.	
– do –	8th		Battalion attack was again practised	
MIRVAUX – COPSE U29C NEAR WARLOY	9th		Battalion moved to COPSE halfway between CONTAY & WARLOY leaving at 11 am & arriving at 1·30 pm. Canvas was erected in the copse. The role of the 58th Division, while Battalion remained here, was that of counter attack division in case of serious penetration of front line system. Following awards were made for gallantry in action. D.C.M. 13765 Sgt W.W. PALMER. Bar to the M.M. 370772 Sgt C.R. HAYWARD MM. M.M. 370419 Cpl S.J. CARROLL 371055 L/Cpl G.W. REYNOLDS & 372011 Pte R.D. EVANS	
– do –	10th		Battalion worked on digging trenches in the WARLOY SECTOR from 10 am to 1 pm. Companies practised attack formations going to & returning from work. Lt R.N. SHAPLEY (Sig Officer) rejoined Battn from Hospital. Draft 8 O.R. received.	
– do –	11th		Work as above continued	
– do –	12th		Work continued. Capt H.H. KING to Hospital. Capt FABER rejoined Battn & proceeded to Battle Surplus. Draft of 34 O.R. received	
– do –	13th		Work continued. Capt A.S. THOMAS MC rejoined Battn from 6 months tour of duty at home & took command of "B" Coy.	
– do –	14th		Work continued. C.O., Adjt & Coy Cmdrs visited RESERVE BN, MILLENCOURT SECTOR prior to taking over. 371304 L/Cpl A. TAGGART awarded the M.M. for gallantry in action.	
– do – MILLENCOURT SECTOR	15th		Battalion relieved 17th Bn London Regt (47th Division) in Reserve MILLENCOURT SECTOR. Relief complete 11.40 pm. HQ A & B Coys at HENENCOURT, C Coy at MILLENCOURT, D Coy in MELBOURNE TR in front of MILLENCOURT. HQ officers were Lt Col JONHSTON (C.O), Capt JACOB (Adjt) Lt SHAPLEY (Sig O)	

D. D. & L., London, E.C. (A8001) Wt. W1771/M2031 750,000 5/17 Sch. 52 Forms/C2118/14

Army Form C. 2118.

WAR DIARY

~~or~~

~~INTELLIGENCE SUMMARY.~~

(Erase heading not required.)

Instructions regarding War Diaries and Intelligence Summaries are contained in F. S. Regs., Part II. and the Staff Manual respectively. Title pages will be prepared in manuscript.

Place	Date	Hour	Summary of Events and Information	Remarks and references to Appendices
			Sec Lt Knell (I.O.) Sec Lt D'ARCY (L.G.O) + Lt MACBEAN (M.O.). Sec Lt POULTON was commanding "A" Coy, Capt THOMAS M.C. "B" Coy, Sec Lt BOOTH M.C. "C" Coy + Capt GUNNING M.C. "D" Coy.	
			Major P.G. EDWARDS M.C. left Battalion for 6th month tour of duty in England. Sec Lt SEATON appointed Town Major of WARLOY. Ration Strength 24 officers 612 ORs.	
RESERVE MILLENCOURT SECTOR	16th		a quiet day. The Battalion worked during night 16/17th on MELBOURNE TR.	[initials]
do	17th		MILLENCOURT was heavily shelled in the morning. 1 OR. killed + 1 OR. wounded. Battalion redistributed as follows:- A + B Coys MELBOURNE TR + C + D Coys HENENCOURT	[initials]
do	18th		a fairly quiet day. A + B Coys worked on MELBOURNE TR, C + D Coys worked on forward trenches. Battalion patrol of 16 ORs formed under Sec Lt PEACOCK	[initials]
do	19th		a quiet day. Sec Lt BOOTH to Hospital. Lt R.H.A. NEWSOME assumed command of "C" Coy. Battalion relieved 7th London in Left Sub Sector. "A" Coy on Right Front "D" Coy Left Front, "B" Coy Counter attack Coy. "C" Coy Reserve. 1 OR. Killed + 2 OR. wounded.	[initials]
LEFT SUBSECTOR MILLENCOURT SECTOR	20th		a quiet day except that hostile artillery was active against our forward trenches in the early morning	[initials]
do	21st		Enemy attack expected at dawn but this did not mature. Heavy British artillery fire from 2 am. to 4.30 am. Sec Lt A.G. TAFNER assumed command of Battalion Patrol. Sec Lt PEACOCK returned to B Coy. 8 ORs. wounded.	[initials]
do	22nd		A fairly quiet day. The new Divisional Commander Major General SMYTHE V.C. CB visited the line.	[initials]
do	23rd		"B" Coy relieved "D" Coy on the left. Bn HQ moved to MELBOURNE TR.	[initials]
do	24th		Fairly quiet. During a raid by the British on our left, the enemy opened a light barrage on our lines. 1 OR. wounded. Sec Lt ORCHARD proceeded on a L.G. Course.	[initials]
do	25th		Enemy fired short bursts of light gun fire on front + support lines during the day. 1 OR. Killed	[initials]

D. D. & L., London, E.C.
(A8001) Wt. W1771/M2031 750,000 5/17 Sch. 52 Forms/C2118/14.

[signature] Lt Col

Instructions regarding War Diaries and Intelligence Summaries are contained in F. S. Regs., Part II. and the Staff Manual respectively. Title pages will be prepared in manuscript.

WAR DIARY

~~or~~

~~INTELLIGENCE~~ SUMMARY.

(Erase heading not required.)

Army Form C. 2118.

Place	Date	Hour	Summary of Events and Information	Remarks and references to Appendices
			4 ORs wounded. Bn Patrol reconnoitred the ~~[illegible]~~ QUARRY but were fired on. Useful information was obtained.	
LEFT SUBSECTOR MILLENCOURT SECTOR	26th		Quiet day. Capt E.C.K. CLARKE (Inns of Court O.T.C.) joined Battn for duty. Sec Lt SCARTH rejoined Battn & posted to "C" Coy.	[initials]
-do- WARLOY	27th		Battalion relieved by 12th Bn London Regt & moved into Divisional Reserve WARLOY. Relief Complete 1.0 am 28th. 1 OR. wounded.	[initials]
WARLOY	28th		Major J VENNING joined Battn ~~for duty~~ & assumed duties of Sec. in command. Capt Clarke assumes command of C Coy	[initials]
WARLOY	29th		Bn passed through Bde Gas Chamber. Lecture to all officers & senior NCO. by Bde Signalling officer. Lecture to all officers by the C.O. Lt Col R E WILLIS British West India Regiment joined Battalion for instruction. Sec Lt DAVIS left Battn to join 22nd London Regt.	[initials]
~~W~~ -do-	30th		Bn practised new attack formation at 11.30 am. Coys training in Lewis guns. Sec Lt BOOTH M.C. rejoined Battn from Hospital	[initials]
-do- BAIZIEUX SYSTEM	31st		Bn training carried out in the morning. 58th Divisional Relief by 18th Division commenced. Battalion relieved in WARLOY by 6th Northants at 6 pm. & relieved 8th EAST SURREYS in BAIZIEUX SYSTEM RIGHT. Relief complete 9 pm. Ration Strength. 27 officers 550 ORs.	[initials]

[signature] Lt Col
Cmdg 8th London Regt
(Post Office Rifles)

D. D. & L., London, E.C. (A8004) Wt. W1771/M2031 750,000 5/17 Sch. 52 Forms/C2118/14

20.5.18

SECRET

B.M.7/75/45.

File

174th Infantry Brigade.

DEFENSIVE ARRANGEMENTS - MILLENCOURT SECTOR.

1. **Front, Dispositions and Flank Dispositions.**

As on attached map. There is a counter-attack Brigade in Divisional Reserve, and a counter-attack Division in Corps Reserve.

2. **Principles of Defence.**

(a) Main line of resistance is the front line. In the right sub-section this is protected by a line of posts in front which is being linked up.

(b) This line will be held at all costs and Battalion Commanders will each use their support Coys to restore the situation by an immediate counter-attack should the enemy succeed in penetrating a part of it. Counter-attacks of this nature, however, in the event of our front line being broken by a heavy general attack along the Brigade front will probably not offer much prospect of success. In this event these companies are at the disposal of their C.O's for holding their present positions, forming a defensive flank or reinforcing.

(c) MELBOURNE Trench (Reserve Line) is held by one Coy. right Battn. and 2 coys. Reserve Battn. as a permanent garrison.

These coys. will not move forward from this line until relieved. Touch will be maintained on the flanks of the Brigade.

(d) It must be clearly impressed on all ranks that positions will be held on to whether flanks are turned or not. Any party of the enemy which has penetrated our positions will be counter-attacked from the flanks, the senior officer on the spot taking command of all troops immediately available for the counter-attack of whatever arm or unit.

The plan of every counter-attack will be, wherever possible, to take the enemy on the flanks.

. **Action in case of attack.**

(a) **Support Battn.**

Battn., less 2 coys., is in Brigade reserve and will be prepared to move as soon as a general bombardment opens, to WALLABY Trench.

Battn. H.Q. moves to V.30.a.0.9.

(b) **Trench Mortar Battery.**

2 reserve mortars are placed at disposal of O.C. Support Battn.

(c) **Working parties.**

Working parties, if the situation permits, will be marched to their own battle stations.

If the situation is such that they are likely to become involved in the fighting almost immediately, O.C. party will at once report to the nearest Battn. or Coy. H.Q. and man defences in the immediate neighbourhood. Fact to be reported as soon as possible to Brigade H.Q.

R.E. and Pioneers will act on the principle laid down above.

All working parties moving forward to work in the Brigade area will be fully armed and equipped.

4. Machine Guns.

See map attached for dispositions.

Machine Gun Officers will maintain close liaison with Company and Battalion Commanders in whose area they are.

5. Artillery.

The front is covered by 290th Bde. R.F.A. (3 18-pounder batteries and 1 4.5. how. battery). S.O.S. lines are shown on attached map.

Two anti-tank guns are in position on the Brigade front.

6. Tanks.

One forward section of tanks (2 male, 1 female) are in the Brigade area.
Their instructions are to move forward at once

(a) if hostile tanks are reported, in order to engage them as soon as possible.

(b) if the enemy are threatening the HENENCOURT - LAVIEVILLE Ridge.

Otherwise their role is to assist a counter-attack by the Brigade in Divisional Reserve.
Presence of hostile tanks will be reported by the quickest available means to this office.

7. Communications.

See attached Appendix "A" for detailed statement.
The following important points are emphasized :-

(a) Frequency of reports to Bde. H.Q. from all units. Negative information is valuable. Situation reports every half-hour from opening of bombardment.

(b) Important messages to be sent by two or more alternative routes.

(c) Economy in runners by whom only very urgent messages should be sent. Proper use to be made of wireless and visual.

(d) All messages to be brief and timed.

8. Administrative Instructions.

See attached Appendix "B".

J. Bryant Major
for Brigade Major,
174th. Infantry Brigade.

20th May, 1918.

Distribution :-

G. O. C.	"C" Coy. M.G.Bn.	175th Inf. Bde.
6th London Regt.	Bde. Signal Officer.	55th Inf. Bde.
7th London Regt.	Staff Captain.	511th Fd. Coy. R.E.
8th London Regt.	58th Division "G"	290th Bde. R.F.A.
174th L.T.M.B.	58th Division "Q"	War Diary.
"B" Coy. M.G.Bn.	173rd Inf. Bde.	File.

SECRET.   B.M.7/75/10.

174th. Infantry Brigade - DEFENSIVE ARRANGEMENTS.

Ref. Sheets 57 D)
               62 D) 1/40,000.   15th May, 1918.

1. LOCATIONS. 58th Division - MOLLIENS AU BOIS.
175th. Inf. Bde.- C.17.a.8.8.
173rd. Inf. Bde.- C.20.c.9.8.
174th. Inf. Bde.- U.29.c.central.
Units of 174th. Inf. Bde. - In woods in U.28.d., U.29.c. and a.

2. ROLES of BRIGADES.

175th. Inf. Bde. to hold the WARLOY SECTOR and BAZIEUX SYSTEM.

173rd. and 174th. Inf. Bdes. to counter-attack or to reinforce the WARLOY SECTOR and BAZIEUX SYSTEM.

Four For counter-attack purposes "C" Coy. 58th. M.G.Bn. is affiliated to this Brigade. They are located at C.8.a.

3. GENERAL PRINCIPLES OF DEFENCE. It is the intention of the Higher Command to retain all positions already held by our troops in the Corps Area. All available troops will be used if necessary for this purpose.

In the event of any part of our front being penetrated, it is the intention of the Divisional Commander if possible to employ the 173rd. Inf. Bde. in the 18th (Right) Divisional Area, and the 174th. Inf. Bde. in the 47th (Left) Divisional Area, for counter attack.

4. WORKING PARTIES. These will proceed to and from work fully armed and equipped. In case of attack all working parties will rejoin their units forthwith.

5. STATE of READINESS and PRECAUTIONARY MEASURES. The Brigade will remain in a state of readiness to move at 1 hour's notice.

6. ACTION IN CASE OF ATTACK. (i) In the event of attack or threatened attack the message "STAND TO" will be sent by Priority wire from these Headquarters to all units of the Brigade and "C" Coy. 58th M.G.Bn.

(ii) On receipt of this message each unit will send an officer to Brigade H.Q.

(iii) The message "STAND TO" will be followed by a second message "MOVE". On receipt of this message Units of the Brigade will move to positions that will be selected according to the tactical situation at the time when known.

7. COUNTER-ATTACK. In the event of this Brigade being ordered to counter-attack -

(i) The Brigade will normally attack with 2 Battalions in Front Line and 1 in reserve.

(ii) The formations already practised by units will be adopted.

(iii) The Brigade Intelligence Officer will show the Taping Officers of each unit the tape line selected and the Battalion frontages.

(iv) The route of the approach march and the place where guides are to meet units will be given from this office.

/8. ANTI-GAS MEASURES.

8. ANTI-GAS MEASURES. The following are the Precautionary and Alert Zones in the present Area :-

(a) PRECAUTIONARY ZONE.

East of the RAINNEVILLE - RUBEMPRE Road (Road inclusive) and West of the "ALERT" Zone.

Box Respirators will be carried within this area.

The III Corps are arranging to mark all Roads and Tracks leading into this Zone from the West.

(b) ALERT ZONE.

East of the line - D.19.central - Cross Roads D.14.c.5.8. - D.9.c.4.4. - D.3.b.5.5. - Cross Roads HENENCOURT Village - V.16.d.5.0.

Box Respirators will be worn in the ALERT POSITION East of the line.

The above mentioned Points are being marked by III Corps with "ALERT ZONE" Notice Boards, intermediate Points being marked by the Divisions in line.

9. TANKS. These will be used in co-operation with the Infantry in a counter-attack. The British Mark V Tanks and Whippets can be distinguished by the following markings on either side and the rear of each Tank :-

WHITE	RED	WHITE

10. COMMUNICATIONS. Brigade H.Q. (U.29.c.central) is in direct telephonic communication with the three Battalions at U.29.d.3.0. - U.28.d.4.4. - U.29.c.8.5., S.A.A. Section at C.3.d.5.7., Divisional Report Centre at C.14.c.5.5. and 3rd. Cavalry Division at U.27.a.4.9., and to 173rd. and 175th. Inf. Bdes. via Divisional Report Centre, and to "C" Coy. 58th M.G.Bn. via 175th. Inf. Bde.

In the event of Brigade H.Q. moving to V.20.d.2.2., lines to Headquarters of Division in the Line will be found there.

On the order "STAND TO" being given two mounted D.R's. from each Battalion and two from Brigade will report to and remain at Brigade H.Q.

11. ADMINISTRATIVE ARRANGEMENTS are attached.

12. ACKNOWLEDGE.

R.N. Barrington-Ward
Captain,
Brigade Major,
174th. Infantry Brigade.

Distribution :-

6th London Regt.	Bde. Signal Off.
7th London Regt.	Staff Captain.
8th London Regt.	War Diary.
174th. Inf.T.M.B.	File.
"C" Coy. M.G.Bn.	Spare.

APPENDIX "A".

SIGNAL COMMUNICATIONS.

Ref. maps 62 D)
57 D) 1/20,000.

1. TELEGRAPH and TELEPHONE.

Lines from Brigade H.Q. - HENENCOURT CHATEAU - to :-

58th Division (2 lines.).
58th Division Advanced H.Q.
Infantry Brigade on Right (2 lines.).
Infantry Brigade on Left (2 lines.).
Artillery Group.
58th Division H.G. Exchange.
89th Bde. R.G.A. (via R.G.A. O.P.)
Left Battalion.
Right Battalion rear and battle Headquarters.
Reserve Battalion.
Brigade O.P.
Divisional O.P. (V.24.d.05.08.).

Each Battalion has an omnibus circuit to the companies; in the case of the Reserve Battalion this is direct only from their battle headquarters.

Liaison line from Artillery exchange to Battle H.Q. of line Battalions (joint to both.

The Brigade to Battalion lines pass through a test point - V.22.d.0.0. - which is Brigade Emergency Headquarters.

Fullerphones used forward of Bde. H.Q. except for O.P's.

2. VISUAL.

To Brigade from each line Battalion H.Q. and from Brigade O.P. Battalions in line have visual from the front line.

3. WIRELESS.

(a) "Trench set" from Brigade to Division.
(b) "Loop set" from Brigade to Battalion - V.30.b.0.7. - via the Brigade test point.

4. MESSAGE ROCKETS.

Posts at - (a) E.2.a.2.2. firing to (b).
(b) V.30.b.5.4. firing to (f).
(c) V.24.c.9.0. firing to (f).
(d) Brigade O.P. firing to (f).
(e) HAM REDOUBT firing to (f).
(f) Watching post at Bde. H.Q.

5. PIGEONS.

Two pairs with right line Battalion.
One pair with left line Battalion.

6. DESPATCH RIDERS.

Direct - to Division by Motor Cyclist,
to Rear Brigade H.Q. by mounted Orderly,
to flank Brigades and all Battalions and companies by cyclist and runners.

7. S.O.S. ROCKET POSTS.

At Infantry and Artillery Bde. O.P's, in V.29.b.

File

APPENDIX "B", to B.M/7/75/45 dated 20/5/1918.

DEFENSIVE ARRANGEMENTS.

MILLENCOURT SECTOR.

1. S.A.A. The following establishment of S.A.A. is maintained on ground in Posts, in addition to 120 rounds plus 50 rounds, total 170 rounds carried on the man :

100 rounds per man of Garrison.
2,000 rounds per Lewis Gun.
20,000 rounds Battalion Reserve at Battalion H.Q.

Reserve on Wheels of S.A.A. is at Brigade Transport Lines, VADENCOURT WOOD, U.22.d.

Divisional Dump and S.A.A. Section, D.A.C.) C.3.d.5.5.

2. RESERVE RATIONS and WATER. Reserve Rations and Water are stored in Line as shown below.
Water requires turning over every three days.

Location of Dump.	Responsible Unit.	Contents of Dump: Reserve Rations.	Contents of Dump: Water.
Bde. Headquarters. V.27.b.5.1.	Brigade Guard.	500	40 galls.
Right Battn. H.Q. (Temp. Battle H.Q.) V.30. ~~a.9.9.~~ a.9.9.	Right Battn.	500	100 galls.
Left Battn. H.Q. V.30.b.6.7. (In dug-out.)	Left Battn.	96	32 galls.
Dump at V.30.b.5.4.	Left Battn.	404	200 galls.
Company H.Q. MELBOURNE TRENCH. W.25.a.5.3.	Support Battn.	Nil.	50 galls.
Company H.Q., MELBOURNE TRENCH. W.25.c.3.8.	Support Battn.	Nil.	50 galls.

3. TRENCH MORTAR AMUNITION. Trench Mortar Ammunition is in Line as shown below :

Location.	Whether Gun Actually mounted & No. of Gun.		Number of Rounds.
E.2.a.00.25.	Yes.	No. 1.	54
W.26.c.33.70.	Yes.	No. 2.	60
W.26.c.30.80.	Yes.	No. 3.	64
W.26.a.00.00.	Yes.	No. 4.	60
D.6.a.35.80.	Yes.	No. 6.	60
D.6.a.35.85.	Yes.	No. 6 .	60

3. (Contd.)

Location.	Whether Gun actually mounted & No. of Gun.	Number of Rounds.
D.5.c.20.50.	No. Reserve Position.	110.
D.4.b.35.05.	No. Reserve Positions	101.
V.29.d.80.20.	No. Reserve Dump only	180.
	TOTAL.	749

4. R.E.MATERIAL. There are no Forward Dumps of R.E. Material. This is drawn every night from R.E. Dump at BAISEUX or HENENCOURT and sent up by Transport.

5. SUPPLIES. Cookers are kept at WARLOY.
Hot meals are taken up in hot food containers every night.
Limbers can proceed as far as D.6.b.6.4. on Right and V.25.a.7.3. on Left. Pack Ponies can go right up to Company H.Q., or Front Line if required.

6. TRANSPORT LINES. Transport Lines of Units of the Brigade are at VADENCOURT WOOD, U.22.d.

7. PRISONERS of WAR. Cage at No. 58 Billet, WARLOY.
Corps Cage at MONTIGNY.

8. STRAGGLER POSTS. In the event of active operations Straggler Posts will be posted as shown below, under Divisional arrangements :

BAIZIEUX	-	C.6.d.5.9.
WARLOY	-	V.25.b.1.6.
WARLOY.	-	V.19.a.1.4.

Straggler Collecting Station at A.D.S., at WARLOY.

On commencement of active operations, 1 Officer, 1 N.C.O. and 1 man from Battalio n in Support will remain at A.D.S., WARLOY, to take over all Stragglers of the Brigade and escort them to their Transport Lines.

2nd. SYSTEM.

CONTAY	-	U.21.a.6.1.	Sheet 57 D.
		U.22.c.2.3.	
		C.3.a.7.5.	Sheet 62 D.

Straggler Collecting Station - CONTAY.

3rd. SYSTEM.

CONTAY	-	U.21.c.8.2.
		U.27.a.2.6.

9. SALVAGE. Headquarters Salvage Company at WARLOY.

Main Salvage Dump. WARLOY, Billet No. 14.

Advanced Salvage Dump. HENENCOURT.

Units return all Salvage to the nearest dump.

10. **BURIAL ARRANGEMENTS.** The following is a list of Cemeteries in or near the Divisional Area :

HENENCOURT Communal Cemetery Extension - V.28.c.5.4.
HENENCOURT WOOD Military Cemetery. - V.26.b.1.5.
ALBERT ROAD Military Cemetery. - D.17.a.5.4.
WARLOY Communal Cemetery Extension - U.24.b.9.3.
CONTAY British Cemetery - U.27.c.6.4.
BAVELINCOURT. - C.7.
FRECHENCOURT. - B.29.
FRANVILLERS. - C.29.b.1.1.

The following plot, though prepared as such, is not used as a Cemetery :
62 D / B.18.a.3.7. (MONTIGNY.)

Burials from MONTIGNY Dressing Station take place either in MONTIGNY or BEAUCOURT Communal Cemeteries.

Isolated Burials, are as far as possible, avoided.

The O.C., G.R.U. 1 is located at VIGNACOURT.

11. **HORSE BURIALS.** Brigade Transport Officer is responsible for all burials in the Brigade Area, West pf BRESLE - HENENCOURT SENLIS Road.
The Artillery are responsible for the Area West of above Road, except burials in Transport Lines for which Units are responsible.

12. **MEDICAL ARRANGEMENTS.** R.A.Ps. W.25.b.3.7., W.19.c.6.7., V.30.d.2.8.

Relay Posts. V.30.a.8.8., V.24.b.3.0.

Collecting Post. HENENCOURT. V.27.d.6.9.

H.Q., Fd. Ambce. WARLOY.

Main Dressing Station. VADENCOURT.

Corps Walking Wounded Collecting Post. BEAUCOURT.

13. **BATHS.** There are Baths (in Tubs) in Stables, HENENCOURT CHATEAU, adjoining Brigade Headquarters.
Capacity - 40 men per hour.

Water obtained from deep well pump in CHATEAU grounds, and heated in Soyer Stoves.

Copies to : All Recipients B.M/7/75/45.

Instructions regarding War Diaries and Intelligence Summaries are contained in F. S. Regs., Part II. and the Staff Manual respectively. Title pages will be prepared in manuscript.

8th Battalion London Regt.

WAR DIARY
or
~~INTELLIGENCE SUMMARY.~~

(Erase heading not required.)

June 1918.

Army Form C. 2118.

Vol 18

Place	Date	Hour	Summary of Events and Information	Remarks and references to Appendices
BAIZIEUX SYSTEM near BAIZIEUX.	June 1st 1918		The following Officers were with the Battn on June 1st 1918:- Lt Col JOHNSTON. M.C. (C.O) Major J. VENNING (2nd in Command) Capt L.G.B. JACOB. (A/Adjt) Lt R.N. SHAPLEY. (S.O) 2nd Lt E.C. KNELL (I.O) Sec Lt P.E. D'ARCY. (L.G.O) Capt T.A.B. PURKIS. (T.O)	
			Attached. Lt Col. R.E. WILLIS. British West Indies Regt. Lt W.B. MACBEAN. USMRC (MO) Rev. JAMES. (Chaplain) C.F.	
			A. Company Capt. R.R. POULTON. (OC) 2nd Lt F.W. KNIGHT. 2nd Lt ROFT.	
			B. Company Capt. A.S. THOMAS (MC) (OC). 2nd Lt R.F. ROTHWELL. 2nd Lt W.B. SCARTH. 2nd Lt C.R. CROSSLAND. 2nd Lt A.G. TAFNER.	
			C. Company Capt E.C.K. CLARKE. (OC) Lt R.H.A. NEWSOME MC. 2nd Lt C.F. YOUNGMAN. 2nd Lt A.J. HARRIS. 2nd Lt R.W. PERRY. 2nd Lt L.W. EVERETT. 2nd Lt H. BOOTH. MC.	JMB.
			D. Company Capt G.E. GUNNING MC. 2nd Lt W.E. CONSTANCE. 2nd Lt A.E. MASON. 2nd Lt H. PEACOCK. 2nd Lt R.B. PATTINSON.	
			OTHER RANKS. 550	
		7.30pm	Capt G.C. FABER, 2nd Lt J.M. BARRATT, 2nd Lt R.N. JOHNSON. 2nd Lt H.J. ALEXANDER and 46. ORs rejoined Battalion from Battle Surplus.	
			2nd Lt L.C. HATCHER and 67 ORs joined Bn. as reinforcements.	
		8.30 to 10.30 Am	WORK Work on improving shelters and trenches generally was carried out in the morning, with a view to protection from shelling and bombing.	
		11 Am to 1 Pm	TRAINING Lewis Gun and Rifle Grenade classes under Company Arrangements Officers LG class under Bn. LG Officer.	
			A percentage of men per Company inoculated by MO.	

(A8004) Wt W1771/M2031 750,000 5/17 Sch. 52 Forms/C2118/14 D. D. & L., London, E.C.

Instructions regarding War Diaries and Intelligence Summaries are contained in F. S. Regs., Part II, and the Staff Manual respectively. Title pages will be prepared in manuscript.

WAR DIARY
or
INTELLIGENCE SUMMARY.
(*Erase heading not required.*)

Army Form C. 2118.

Place	Date	Hour	Summary of Events and Information	Remarks and references to Appendices
BAIZIEUX SYSTEM near BAIZIEUX.	2nd		Quiet day, bright and hot. WORK TRAINING. 8.30 to 10.30 Am. Companies work on "Stand to" positions and improvements to trenches. 11-1 pm and 1 hour in the afternoon. LG Classes under Company Arrangements, Musketry, Bayonet fighting, Saluting, Sentry groups – – for Officers under Bn. LGO. Instruction in Grenades and Rifle Grenades. Night patrols. Signallers pigeon class at Brigade HQ. S. Bs: under MO. Voluntary Church Services were held during the day. Regimental Brass Band played Selections in the evening.	JmB
– do –	3rd		Hot day, very quiet. WORK 8.30 to 10.30 Am Work on trenches. 11 to 1.0 pm. Musketry, rapid loading, fire orders, extended order drill. Section tactics, use of ground. Officers instructed in Wiring under REs. Afternoon Grenade classes, LG firing on ranges. Night Patrols. Evening. Inter Company football matches. Regt. Band played selections.	JmB
– do –	4th		Dull morning, bright and hot later. WORK. 8.30 am to 10.30 Am. Companies working on 'Stand to' positions.	

Army Form C. 2118.

Instructions regarding War Diaries and Intelligence Summaries are contained in F. S. Regs., Part II. and the Staff Manual respectively. Title pages will be prepared in manuscript.

WAR DIARY
or
INTELLIGENCE SUMMARY.
(Erase heading not required.)

Place	Date	Hour	Summary of Events and Information	Remarks and references to Appendices
BAIZIEUX SYSTEM. NEAR. BAIZIEUX.	4th (contd).		TRAINING 10-0 Am. Platoon Commanders Wiring Classes, supervised by Div. R.E's. Company & platoon training in Co-operation in the attack, Work on defensive position. Commanding Officer, and Company Commanders attended "Stokes Gun" demonstration. Evening. Football match, Officers v. Sergeants. Regimental Band played Selections.	JmB.
			2nd Lt A. BUCK and 32 OR's joined Battalion as reinforcements.	
-do-	5th		Bright Warm Day.	
			WORK Improvements to Defensive positions. (WIRING)	
		11.0 Am	TRAINING. 11-0 AM Battalion practice training in the "attack"	
			Capt. R. R. FAIRLIE. MC. QM. rejoined Battalion from short leave in England	JmB.
			2nd Lt R. B. PATTINSON proceeded to III Corps School for Course in Rifle Grenades.	
DAILY MAIL WOODS Nr MIRVAUX.		4-0 pm.	Battalion moved off by Companies to new Area - DAILY MAIL WOODS (near MIRVAUX) route via AGNICOURT and EBARTS. FM arriving 7.30 pm, and was accomodated under Canvas.	

D. D. & L., London, E.C.
(A3004) Wt W1771/M2031 750,000 5/17 Sch. 52 Forms/C2118/14

Instructions regarding War Diaries and Intelligence Summaries are contained in F. S. Regs., Part II. and the Staff Manual respectively. Title pages will be prepared in manuscript.

WAR DIARY
or
INTELLIGENCE SUMMARY.
(Erase heading not required.)

Army Form C. 2118.

Place	Date	Hour	Summary of Events and Information	Remarks and references to Appendices
DAILY MAIL WOODS Near MIRVAUX.	6th		Bright, Warm Day. Training. Companies inspected by Commanding Officer. 11.0 Am Battn Mass Parade, Bn practice in the 'Attack'. 2nd Lt A.F. MORTON rejoined Bn from III Corps School. L.T.M Course.	JmB.
-do-	7th		Bright, Warm Day Training. 9.0 Am 10.0 Am Company training. P.T. & B.F. 9.0 Am Company Officers and unemployed NCOs instruction under the Commanding Officer. 4-0 pm 8-0 pm Firing on Range. AWARDS. Lt Col. C.E. JOHNSTON (Officer Commanding 8th Bn) awarded Military Cross for gallantry in action. Capt R.R. POULTON proceeded on Course at IV Army School. Lt C.T.A. WILKINSON and 6. ORs joined Battalion as reinforcements.	JmB
-do-	8th		Warm and bright, slight Showers in the afternoon. Training. 9-0 Am. Battalion attack practise. Enemy positions represented by Signallers with flags. Work criticised by Major VENNING (2nd in Command) as very good, but very weak in the "Scouting". 6-0 pm. Battalion route march (8 miles) Practice in Advance & ~~Rear~~ Rear-Guard actions. Enemy represented by cyclist Signallers with flags.	JmB

D. D. & L., London, E.C.
(A8004) Wt. W1771/M2031 750,000 5/17 Sch. 52 Forms/C2118/14

Instructions regarding War Diaries and Intelligence Summaries are contained in F. S. Regs., Part II. and the Staff Manual respectively. Title pages will be prepared in manuscript.

WAR DIARY
or
INTELLIGENCE SUMMARY.
(*Erase heading not required.*)

Army Form C. 2118.

Place	Date	Hour	Summary of Events and Information	Remarks and references to Appendices
DAILY MAIL WOODS near MIRVAUX.	8th		The "Commanding Officer" Capt. G.C. FABER, and 2/Lt E.C. KNELL reconnoitred Trench Area S. of AMIENS, returning 7.15 pm. CAPT. H.W. PRIESTLEY, MC. rejoins Battalion from Hospital in England 20 ORs reinforcements.	JmB.
-do-	9th		Bright, Warm, day. (Sunday) Parades 10.15 Am. The Brigade, in column of route, marched past the Corps Commander on its way to Church Service. 10.15. Am. Brigade Church Service just outside and S. of DAILY MAIL WOODS. Capt A. THOMAS. MC. Lt R.H.A. NEWSOME. MC. and 2nd Lt CONSTANCE, reconnoitred Trench Area S. of AMIENS, returning 7.15 pm. 2nd Lt A.F. MORTON proceeded to join 174th L.T.M.B. for duty. EVENING Inter-Company football, Regimental Band played Selections.	JmB
-do-	10th		Bright, and Showery at Intervals. Battalion paraded 9.15 Am and marched to Embussing point at junction of roads between PUCHEVILLERS and RUBEMPRÉ en route for PICQUIGNY (N.W of AMIENS) The embussing was carried out with smoothness, and the Brigade Convoy moved off at 12.5 pm; and proceed via; - RUBEMPRÉ, -	JmB.

D. D. & L., London, E.C.
(A8004) Wt W1771/M2031 750,000 5/17 Sch. 52 Forms/C2118/14

Instructions regarding War Diaries and Intelligence Summaries are contained in F. S. Regs., Part II. and the Staff Manual respectively. Title pages will be prepared in manuscript.

WAR DIARY
or
INTELLIGENCE SUMMARY.
(Erase heading not required.)

Army Form C. 2118.

Place	Date	Hour	Summary of Events and Information	Remarks and references to Appendices
~~St Ricq~~ PICQUIGNY. NW of AMIENS.	10th		VILLERS-BOCAGE, - VIGNACOURT, - LA CHAUSSÉE, arriving at PICQUIGNY at 4.15 pm. ~~being~~ the Battalion being accomadated in billets in the town. The Battalion Transport travelled by road under Brigade arrangements, arriving about 6.30 pm.	JMB
-do-	11th		Dull morning, bright and warm later. Training. Companies paraded 9.0 Am, and marched up to training ground for Company training. Company Officers under "Commanding Officer" Observers class under "Intelligence Officer". Company Signallers under Sig. Officer. Major. T. VENNING. (2nd in Command) Capt E.C.K. CLARKE, and 2/Lt. E.J. ROFT, Lt C.T.A. WILKINSON, reconnoitred part of French Area S. of AMIENS returning 3.0 Am.	JMB
- do -	12th		Bright, warm day. Training. Morning. Coy. training in PT & BF. Company Officers under "Commanding Officer" Junior NCOs' class under Regtl S.M. Musketry on range. Afternoon L.G. classes. Companies at disposal Company Commanders.	JMB

D. D. & L., London, E.C. (A8001) Wt. W1771/M2031 750,000 5/17 Sch. 52 Forms/C2118/14

Instructions regarding War Diaries and Intelligence Summaries are contained in F. S. Regs., Part II. and the Staff Manual respectively. Title pages will be prepared in manuscript.

WAR DIARY
or
INTELLIGENCE SUMMARY.

(Erase heading not required.)

Army Form C. 2118.

Place	Date	Hour	Summary of Events and Information	Remarks and references to Appendices
PICQUIGNY.	12th.		Evening. Bathing under Company arrangements. Regtl. Band played Selections.	
			2nd Lts. R.N. JOHNSON, C.F. YOUNGMAN, A.W. MASON, reconnoitred part of French Area S. of AMIENS.	JmB
			2nd Lt. H. ORCHARD rejoined Battn from III Corps "Stokes Gun" Course.	
- do.	13th.		Bright, warm day.	
			Training. 9.30 Battn. practice in the 'Attack', assistance by 17th Bde T.M.B. enemy represented by Signallers with flags.	JmB.
			2 pm to 8.0 pm. Musketry on ranges (firing)	
			Bathing under Company arrangements.	
			Evening Regtl. Band played Selections.	
			2/Lt. H. PEACOCK proceeded on III Corps 'Stokes Gun' Course.	
- do -	14th.		Dull morning, brighter later in the day.	
			Training. Morning Musketry on Range (Firing) 8 Am to 1 pm.	JmB.
			Evening Battalion Route March, advanced & rear guards Enemy represented by Signallers with flags.	
			2nd Lt. ROTHWELL R.F. proceeded on 14 days leave to England	

D. D. & L., London, E.C. (A8001) Wt. W1771/M2031 750,000 5/17 Sch. 52 Forms/C2118/14

Instructions regarding War Diaries and Intelligence Summaries are contained in F. S. Regs., Part II. and the Staff Manual respectively. Title pages will be prepared in manuscript.

WAR DIARY
or
INTELLIGENCE SUMMARY.
(Erase heading not required.)

Army Form C. 2118.

Place	Date	Hour	Summary of Events and Information	Remarks and references to Appendices
PICQUIGNY	15th		Bright Warm day.	
			Training. Morning. Battalion Outpost Scheme.	JmB
			Battalion inspected at work by Divisional Commander	
			Afternoon 1pm - 6pm. Musketry on Range (Firing)	
			6-0pm. Performance by the "Goods", Divisional Concert Party.	
			Lt. C. T. A. WILKINSON, proceeded to Hospital (P.U.O)	
- do -	16th		Bright. Warm day.	JmB
			Battalion Church Parade 9.30 Am, Regimental Band accompanied the service.	
			Afternoon. Cricket match against 17th Brigade Headquarters.	
			Evening Demonstration by Aeroplane for the general instruction of troops in "Flying at different Heights"	JmB
			2nd Lt. H. BOOTH proceeded to BOUCHON for III Corps Gas Course.	
- do -	17th		Fine day, rather cool, very cold night.	
			The Battalion "roused" at 3.45 Am, and paraded on PICQUIGNY - BREILLY Road ready to move to embussing point on SOUES - PICQUIGNY Road at 5-10 Am.	Appendix (A)

D. D. & L., London, E.C. (A8001) Wt. W1771/M2031 750,000 5/17 Sch. 52 Forms/C2118/14

Army. Form C. 2118.

Instructions regarding War Diaries and Intelligence Summaries are contained in F. S. Regs., Part II. and the Staff Manual respectively. Title pages will be prepared in manuscript.

WAR DIARY
or
INTELLIGENCE SUMMARY.
(Erase heading not required.)

Place	Date	Hour	Summary of Events and Information	Remarks and references to Appendices
PICQUIGNY.	17th		order of move on embussing:- C.O. Cyclists Signallers, Band, H.Q. D Coy. C. B. A. Coys. Battle Surplus. Embussing was reported complete at 7.15 Am, and the 174th Brigade Convoy moved off at 7.47 Am, en route for Debussing point which was ~~at~~ on CONTAY - FRANVILLERS Road. Route taken:- PICQUIGNY - AILLY-SUR-SOMME - DREUIL - AMIENS - BEAUCOURT - CONTAY. - DEBUSSING POINT (CONTAY - FRANVILLERS RD. REF. SENLIS SHEET. C.3.d)	JmB
VILLA SECTOR REAR. FRANVILLERS.	-	12 Noon	The Battalion (less Battle surplus, which debussed independantly at near MIRVAUX) on debussing, moved up to relieve the 20th Londons in Reserve line just behind FRANVILLERS (SENLIS Sheet C 21 b.) relief complete just after 12 noon. The Battalion being accomodated under canvas.	
			Evening The Commanding Officer and Company Commanders reconnoitred Support line near BRESLE (SENLIS. D16 and 22) occupied by 21st Londons. Proceeded to Battle Surplus at MIRVAUX;- Capt. H.W. PRIESTLEY. MC, 2nd Lts P.E. D'ARCY, W.F. KNIGHT, R.W. PERRY, L.W. EVERETT, C.R. CROSSLAND, A. BUCK, and 48 other ranks.	JmB
	18th		Bright day, very cool breeze. The Battalion relieved the 21st London Regt. in Right Brigade Support line	

D. D. & L., London, E.C.
(A8001) Wt. W1771/M2031 750,000 5/17 Sch. 52 Forms/C2118/14

Instructions regarding War Diaries and Intelligence Summaries are contained in F. S. Regs., Part II. and the Staff Manual respectively. Title pages will be prepared in manuscript.

WAR DIARY
or
~~INTELLIGENCE SUMMARY.~~
(Erase heading not required.)

Army Form C. 2118.

Place	Date	Hour	Summary of Events and Information	Remarks and references to Appendices
RIGHT BRIGADE SUPPORT SE. BRESLE	18	9.30p	South East of BRESLE. Companies took over from Corresponding Companies – A Company. Capt G.C. FABER. Right B – – Capt. A. THOMAS Right Centre C – – FCK CLARKE Left Centre D – 2Lt. W.E. CONSTANCE. LEFT.	JmB Appendix (B)
		12.10Am	Relief was reported Complete 12.10 Am, without Casualties. The 4th Battn London Regt took over from the Battn in VILLA SECTOR REAR. Major J. VENNING (2nd in Command) and 2nd Lt. J.M. BARRATT (Asst Adjt) proceeded to join DETAIL Camp at CONTAY.	JmB
– do –	19.		Very Changeable, Sunshine & Showers alternately In the line. Working parties on trenches and shelters, general improvement on living places. Major J. VENNING proceeded from Details to take over Command of the 7th Batt London Regt in the line.	
– do –	20.		Very changeable, showers. In the line 2 Companies working on new DOLLY ~~[illegible]~~ trench, deepening and building firesteps. 2 Companies wiring trench. ~~[illegible] to Right Battns, left Brigade Sector to reconnoitre front and enemy's [illegible].~~	JmB

D. D. & L., London, E.C.
(A5001) Wt. W1771/M2031 750,000 5/17 Sch. 52 Forms/C2118/14

Instructions regarding War Diaries and Intelligence Summaries are contained in F. S. Regs., Part II. and the Staff Manual respectively. Title pages will be prepared in manuscript.

WAR DIARY
or
INTELLIGENCE SUMMARY.
(Erase heading not required.)

Army Form C. 2118.

Place	Date	Hour	Summary of Events and Information	Remarks and references to Appendices
Right Brigade Support. SE. BRESLE	21.		Fine but dull. misty at night. In the line 2 Companies (C & D) working on DOLLY TRENCH, deepening and building firesteps, 2 Companies (A & B) wiring. A patrol consisting of 2nd Lt HATCHER (C. Coy) and 12 other ranks went forward the right Battn Sector of the 6th Brigade to reconnoitre enemy wire in E 8. c. & E 14 a (SENLIS map). The patrol was not successful owing to mist. Another patrol consisting of 2nd Lt KNELL (Bn I.O) and one OR went out on same front, and took up a position in no-mans land in growing corn, remaining there till 12. Noon 22nd. Valuable information gained.	JWB
- do -	22.		Dull day, some showers. In the line Work carried on by Companies as per previous night. A patrol consisting of 2nd Lt SCARTH (B Coy) and 12 OR's. as per previous patrols, went out to reconnoitre enemy wire at E 8. C. (SENLIS), but moon too bright.	JWB
- do -	23.		Dull Day. Lt Col R E WILLIS (attached) and Capt LEB JACOB proceeded to 'details' Sick 2nd Lt. J.M. BARRATT rejoined Battn from 'details'. In the line Work carried on by Companies as on previous nights. A patrol consisting of 2nd Lt PATTINSON (D Coy) and 12 OR's. carried out patrol of previous nights, examining enemy wire at E 8. C. No information	JWB

D. D. & L., London, E.C. (A8001) Wt. W1771/M2031 750,000 5/17 Sch. 52 Forms/C2118/14

Instructions regarding War Diaries and Intelligence Summaries are contained in F. S. Regs., Part II. and the Staff Manual respectively. Title pages will be prepared in manuscript.

WAR DIARY
or
INTELLIGENCE SUMMARY.
(Erase heading not required.)

Army Form C. 2118.

Place	Date	Hour	Summary of Events and Information	Remarks and references to Appendices
RIGHT BRIGADE SUPPORT S.E. BRESLE	23.		was gained as this patrol came into contact with enemy and were fired on, one OR being wounded.	JmB.
do	24		Fine, bright day, cold night. The Battn was relieved in Brigade Support line by the 12th Battalion London Regt. Relief complete 11.35 pm. On relief proceeded by Companies to VILLA SECTOR REAR, near FRANVILLERS, arriving about 1 pm. The Battalion was accommodated under canvas. The role of the Brigade was now "Brigade in Divisional Reserve". Capt L E B JACOB evacuated sick to Hospital.	Appendix (C) JmB
VILLA SECTOR REAR. near FRANVILLERS.	25.		Morning was spent in cleaning up generally. The Commanding Officer saw all Company Commanders at 10.30 am. Afternoon. Regimental Band played Selections. Night. The Battalion was ordered to work in conjunction with RE. on LAVIÉVILLE SYSTEM of trenches, moving off from Camp 8.30 pm returning 4 am. CAPT H H KING joined Battle Surplus from Hospital	JmB

D. D. & L., London, E.C.
(A8001) Wt. W1771/M2031 750,000 5/17 Sch. 52 Forms/C2118/14

Army Form C. 2118.

Instructions regarding War Diaries and Intelligence Summaries are contained in F. S. Regs., Part II. and the Staff Manual respectively. Title pages will be prepared in manuscript.

WAR DIARY
or
INTELLIGENCE SUMMARY.
(Erase heading not required.)

Place	Date	Hour	Summary of Events and Information	Remarks and references to Appendices
			Fine bright day.	
VILLA SECTOR REAR.	26.		Orders were received ~~that~~ during the night 25th/26th that the Battalion should move over by 2 pm and take up position in BAZIEUX SYSTEM. The Battalion accordingly moved off from VILLA SECTOR REAR at 11.30 am, arriving in new Area 1.45 pm. 5.30 pm. All Officers and NCOs assembled under the Commanding Officer, who explained the proposed Raid scheme, after which a taped area representing the scheme was reconnoitred.	Appendix (D) JMB
BAZIEUX SYSTEM near BAZIEUX.	27		Fine, bright day. Training 8.30 am to 1 pm. Companies practiced - bayonet fighting, bombing squads, movement over ground in attack formation. Companies practiced in [illegible] formation and movement over ground taped out by R.E. for special scheme. 8.30 pm. Battalion practiced special scheme on ground taped out. CAPT. H. H. PRIESTLEY M.C. rejoined Battalion from Battle Surplus.	JMB
-do-	[illegible]		2nd Lt. E.C. KNEAN (Bn. Intell. Officer) and one O.R. went out on patrol from Right Batt. Left Brigade Sector E.8.c. object being to gain any information of enemy dispositions and wire. Valuable information was procured.	
-do-	28		Fine, bright day. Training for special scheme as on previous day. Extra practice 2.30 am. MAJOR J. VENNING rejoined details from 7th Batt. London Regt.	JMB

A5834 Wt. W4973/M687 750,000 8/16 D. D. & L. Ltd. Forms/C.2118/13.

Instructions regarding War Diaries and Intelligence Summaries are contained in F. S. Regs., Part II. and the Staff Manual respectively. Title pages will be prepared in manuscript.

WAR DIARY
or
INTELLIGENCE SUMMARY.
(Erase heading not required.)

Army Form C. 2118.

Place	Date	Hour	Summary of Events and Information	Remarks and references to Appendices
BAZIEUX SYSTEM near BAZIEUX	29.		Bright Warm Day. Morning training. Classes in bombing + bayonet fighting. During this practice, a shell fell amongst "D" Company, causing casualties to be suffered to the extent of 4 Killed 18 wounded, all other ranks. Evening Battalion practice of special scheme. Brigadier General C G HIGGINS, Commanding Brigade, witnessed the practice.	JMB
"	30		Bright, Hot day. 6.30 pm. Battalion training in Special Scheme, witnessed by G.O.C. 58th Division. 11.30 Am The Commanding Officer and Company Commanders reconnoitred the positions held by 3rd London Regt in the Support Bn, Left Brigade Sector, with a view to taking over. The following Officers were with the Battalion on June 30th. 1918:— Lt Col. C. E. JOHNSTON MC. (CO) MAJOR J. VENNING. (2nd in Command) 2nd Lt J. M. BARRATT (A/ADJT) Lt R. N. SHAPLEY. (S.O.) 2nd Lt E. C. KNELL (IO) Capt. T. A. B. PURKIS. (T.O.) CAPT H. W. PRIESTLEY. MC. HON CAPT. R. R. FAIRLIE (QM) MC. Attached. Lt COL R. E. WILLIS. MC. British West Indies Regt. Lt W. B. MACBEAN (USMRC) (MO) REV. C. F. JAMES (Chaplain)	JMB

A5834 Wt. W4973/M687 750,000 8/16 D. D. & L. Ltd. Forms/C.2118/13.

1918 JUNE

Instructions regarding War Diaries and Intelligence Summaries are contained in F. S. Regs., Part II. and the Staff Manual respectively. Title pages will be prepared in manuscript.

WAR DIARY
or
INTELLIGENCE SUMMARY.
(Erase heading not required.)

Army Fo[rm] C. 2118.

Place	Date	Hour	Summary of Events and Information	Remarks and references to Appendices
	30th		A. Company. Capt. G.C. FABER (OC) 2nd Lt. ROFT. 2nd Lt. R.N JOHNSON 2nd Lt. A.J. HARRIS.	
			B. – Capt. A.S THOMAS MC (OC) 2nd Lt. W.B. SCARTH. 2nd Lt. H ALEXANDER, 2nd Lt. A.G. TAFNER.	[illegible]
			C – Capt. E.C.K CLARKE (OC) 2nd Lt. C.F. YOUNGMAN, 2nd Lt. L.C. HATCHER.	
			D. – 2nd Lt. W.E. CONSTANCE (OC) 2nd Lt. A.E MASON. 2nd Lt. R.B. PATTINSON 2nd Lt. H. ORCHARD	
			and 616 Other Ranks.	[illegible] Lieut Col Commanding 8 Bn [illegible]

A5834 Wt. W4973/M687 750,000 8/16 D. D. & L. Ltd. Forms/C.2118/13.

23.6.18

SECRET. Copy No. 22

174th. INFANTRY BRIGADE.

PROVISIONAL DEFENCE INSTRUCTIONS.

Right Subsector - Right Sector - III Corps.

DISTRIBUTION OF TROOPS. 1. The Divisional Front is held with two Brigades in the Line and one in Divisional Reserve.

The Brigade Front is held with two Battalions in the Line and one in Brigade Reserve and one Company of Pioneers disposed as garrisons of defensive positions.

Boundaries and dispositions in detail are shown on attached Map "A".

GENERAL DESCRIPTION OF LINE. 2. The Brigade front line is sited along the higher slopes of the spur running E. to the ANCRE Valley, S. of ALBERT. The enemy's forward system follows the lower slopes of the Spur.

On the right both trench systems descend to the Valley of the ANCRE, W. of DERNANCOURT to the point of junction with the Australians on our right.

On the left the convex slopes of the spur deny direct observation of the enemy's forward system. This is partially obtained from the high ground held by the Division on our right.

On the right observation is good.

A deeply marked valley W. of the Forward System runs N. and S. across the Brigade Area. The Westerly portion of this Valley and the Spur West of it are under the full observation of the enemy from the high ground opposite the Division on our right.

From the Spur on which our Forward System is sited we enjoy excellent observation of the enemy's back areas on the E. and S.E. slopes of the ANCRE Valley.

PRINCIPLES OF DEFENCE. 3. (a) The existing Front Line is the Brigade Line of Resistance. It will be maintained at all costs. Ground will be held whether flanks are turned or not, and, if necessary, flanks reinforced. The retention of the spur along which it runs and the line of the AMIENS - ALBERT Road is essential for the maintenance by flanking Divisions of their present forward positions about VILLE-SUR-ANCRE and across the MILLENCOURT - ALBERT Valley respectively.

(b) Four "Russian Saps", designed to give observation of the hostile forward system, are under construction from the front line (Map "A".)

(c) Each Battalion is disposed in depth. Each Company will have a platoon earmarked for counter-attack in the event of the enemy achieving a minor penetration of our line.

(d) Each Battalion will have a counter-attack Coy in Battalion Reserve available to counter-attack - in a situation warranting the employment for this purpose of one Company - to reinforce, or to form a defensive flank.

Right Battn. will be prepared to form a defensive flank if required along the line DOG Trench WELCH Trench and Left Battn. along the line ENERGY ALLEY - EMMA Trench.

Positions to be reconnoitred and selected.

(e) Strong Points.

(i) Strong Point in E.13.a. Garrison one platoon. (Left Battalion.)

(ii) " " " D.24.a. One Coy less 2 platoons (Pioneers.)

(iii) Trench running N. and S. in D.23.a. Garrison 2 platoons. (Pioneers.)

The function of all the above Strong Points is to hold on and, by breaking up any hostile advance, facilitate the counter-attack.
Strong Points Nos. (i) and (ii) above will be of special value in the event of a refusal of the left or right flank as indicated in para 3 (d).
The role of the two platoons in (iii) is to defend the spur on which they are placed and to prevent by fire a northward advance by the enemy up the spur in D.24.a. and b. or westwards into the Valley in D.23.b.

(f) The Battalion in Brigade Reserve may be employed to reinforce or extend a flank or to counter-attack.
For reinforcing or extending a flank this Battalion may be required and will be prepared to carry out the movement indicated in para 3 (d).
The Trenches DARWIN Reserve - DARLING Reserve now occupied by this Battalion are defensive positions with, generally, a limited field of fire. As the role of this Battalion is above al-l to deny ground to the enemy and to hold up his advance they will be prepared to leave their present trenches and take up other positions, not necessarily entrenched, which the needs of the situation may demand for the fulfilment of this role. Except in the case of a serious emergency this Battalion will not move unless ordered by Brigade H.Q.

(g) Battalion Commanders have a direct call on Stokes Mortars in their Area. Stokes Mortars will respond to an S.O.S. call on their normal lines, but at least 50 rounds must be retained with each Mortar for the purposes of fire on visible targets.

(h) Working Parties in case of alar-m will report to nearest Coy. or Battn. H.Q. Whenever situation permits they will be directed (in case of Infantry) to rajoin their Units, or (in case of Field Coys. or Tunn. Coys. R.E.) to their Battle Stations in BAIZIEUX Line.

(i) All H.Q. down to Coy. H.Q. will be organised for defence, and allotted Battle Stations.

MACHINE GUNS. 4. Guns of two Coys. Divl. M.G. Battn. cover the Front. See Map "A" for emplacements and S.O.S. Lines.

NEWTON MORTARS. 5. There are six 6" Newton Mortars covering the Front. (See Map "A".)

ARTILLERY. 6. Field Artillery. Right Group R.F.A. (5 - 18 pds. and 2 - 4.5" How. Batteries.)

Heavy Artillery. 76th. Bde. R.G.A. (1 battery each of 9.2", 8" and 6" Hows. 2 batteries 60 pds. (See Map "A".)

There is a Liaison Officer at each Front Line Battn H.Q. and a Senior Liaison Officer at Brigade H.Q.

TANKS. 7. (i) One Section "B" Coy 2nd Tank Battalion with 2 male and 1 female tank (Mark V) is stationed in D.21.a.

(ii) In the event of Battle, O.C. Section will order his Section to Stand to and will himself report to Bde. H.Q.
(iii) Normal Line of advance would be north of ALBERT - AMIENS Road crossing to D.17. Central and thence to D.18 or D.24 according to situation.
(iv) The first role of the Tanks is to engage any hostile Tanks.
(v) If no hostile Tanks appear, the Tanks will move forw-ard and engage any hostile Infantry who are threatening the imtermediate System.
(vi) Each Tank is provided with a Very Pistol and White Lights which will be used to signal to the Infantry, if the enemy are seen advancing or massing, the light being fired in the direction in which the enemy is seen.
(vii) British Tanks <u>returning from Action</u> fly a flag, (red, white, blue - vertical stripes). Other signals by flag from Tanks to Infantry are :

GREEN and WHITE - Come on.
RED and YELLOW - Go on. I am broken down.

S.O.S. 8. S.O.S. Signal on III Corps Front is a Rifle Grenade Rocket breaking into THREE RED Stars.

<u>COMMUNICATIONS</u>. 9. See Appendix I and Plan.

<u>WORK POLICY.</u> 10. See Appendix II.

<u>ADMINISTRATIVE ARRANGEMENTS.</u> 11. See Appendix III.

R.N. Barrington-Ward
Captain.
Brigade Major.

23rd. June, 1918.

DISTRIBUTION :

1. G.O.C.
2. 6th. London Regt.
3. 7th. London Regt.
4. 8th. London Regt.
5. 174th L.T.M.Btty.
6. Bde.Signal Officer.
7. Bde. Intell.Officer.
8. Staff Captain.
9. 58th. Division "G".
10. 58 th.Division "Q".
11. 173rd. Inf. Bde.
12. 175th. Inf. Bde.
13. 15th. Aust. Inf. Bde.
14. "D" Coy. 58th.M.G.Bn.
15. "B" Coy. 58th.M.G.Bn.
16. 511th. Field Coy. R.E.
17. C.R.E.
18. Right Group R.F.A.
19. 76th. Bde. R.G.A.
20. "B" Coy.2nd Tank Bn.
21. War Diary.
22. File.
23. 1/4th Suffolk Regt (Pioneers)

APPENDIX I.

SUMMARY OF COMMUNICATIONS.

LINES. 1. To Division. ... 1 Direct.
... 1 Via Adv. Division.

To Left Brigade.	...	1 Direct.
To Brigade on Right.	...	1 Direct.
To Artillery.	...	1 to Rt. Group Arty. 1 to Battery.
To Div. O.P.	...	1 Direct.
To Right Battn.	...	1 Direct.
To Left Battn.	...	1 Direct.
To Support Battn.	...	3 Lines with M.G.Coy. and Pioneer Battn. teed on respectively.
To Bde. Central Visual Station.	...	1 Direct.
To Brigade O.P.	...	1 Via Right Battn.

LATERALS. 2. (i) Left and Right Battalions.
(ii) Support Battalion to Left and Right Battalions.

BATTALION LINES. 3. All Companies on Omnibus Line in each case. Left Battalion also has direct earth Fuller Line to Left Company. Companies without Fullerphones send in code on D 3's with Microphone Capsules removed.

VISUAL. 4. From all Battalions to Brigade Central Visual Station at D.16 .d.4.4. also from Brigade O.P.

POWER BUZZER. 5. From Left and Right Battalions to Brigade.

WIRELESS. 6. From Brigade to Division and Left Brigade.

RUNNER. 7. From all Units to Brigade direct.

ROCKET. 8. From Right Battalion to Brigade.
From Left Coy. Rt.Battn. to Right Battalion.
From Left Coy. Right Battn. to Forward Battalion Left Brigade.

PIGEONS. 9. Left and Right Battalions to Corps.

------ -

APPENDIX II.

WORK POLICY.

TROOPS AVAILABLE. 1. One Field Company R.E. (less two Sections), Units of Brigade, and proportion on one Company Pioneers occupying positions in Brigade Area (for work on those positions.)

METHOD OF EMPLOYMENT. 2. (a) Principal tasks and priority of completion laid down, and R.E. assistance allotted by Brigade H.Q.

(b) Arrangements detailed by Brigade H.Q. or made direct between Infantry and R.E. according to convenience for particulat task.

(c) Front Line work normally to be carried out by Infantry unaided.

(d) R.E. responsible for trace of new work. Infantry Commander solely responsible for work done.

(e) Brigade Reserve Battalion employed on special tasks, e.g. DOLLY Trench.

PRINCIPAL WORK IN PROGRESS, OR PROPOSED. 3.

Ø (a) Wiring, firestepping ..... and erection of shelters in DOLLY Trench.

Ø (b) Wiring (especially on Left Battn. front) and additional fire-bays and shelters in front line.

Ø (c) Firestepping of Communication Trenches especially DOG Tr., WELCH Tr., ECHUCA and ENERGY.

(d) Improvement of NINE ELMS Trench.

Ø (e) Completion of Russian Saps

Ø (f) Firestepping and extension of Strong Point in D.24.a.

Ø (g) Improvement of DARWIN Reserve.

(h) Completion of covered approach to Line via line of AMIENS - ALBERT Road. (Road ditch to be dug out - more camouflage erected.)

(i) New Wire round Strong Point in E.13.a.

Ø (k) Salvage of timber in RIBEMONT.

Ø (l) Crop Cutting.

N O T E. As the nights are at present extremely short, at least two hours task by day as well as by night will be carried out by troops, wherever possible, on their own positions. Work may be digging, construction, carrying, cleaning or salvage according to the degree of movement visibility allows.

ALL WORK WILL BE SET BY TASK - except in case of work requiring continuous shifts.

Ø IN PROGRESS.

APPENDIX III

ADMINISTRATIVE ARRANGEMENTS.

AMMUNITION. 1. The Main Divisional Dump is at C.3.Central.

S.A.A. Section, D.A.C. is at BEAUCOURT.

S.A.A. Supply. 3 G.S. Limbered wagons, each ready loaded with 32,000 rounds S.A.A. are kept brigaded at Transport Lines under orders of the B.T.O.

BATHS. 2. There is an open bath at D.21.a.3.6. for Units and Details in Right Brigade area.

Capacity 50 per hour.

Clean clothes are supplied by Brigade, and drawn from Divisional Baths Officer.

There is a bath for Officers.

Personnel in charge - 1 N.C.O. and 1 man.

WATER POINTS.

3. BRESLE, BAIZIEUX, AGNICOURT.

S.A.A. IN LINE.

4. See TABLE "A"

RESERVE RATIONS AND WATER.

5. See TABLE "B"

STRAGGLER COLLECTING POSTS.

6. In the event of Active Operations, the following Straggler Posts to be manned as shown:

Right Bn. 1 Offr. and 1 man to D.19.d.5.4. 1 N.C.O. to C.6.Cen
Left Bn. 1 N.C.O. and 1 man to C.6.Central.
Support Bn.1 N.C.O. and 1 man to C.6.Central.

This personnel is responsible for taking over all Stragglers and escorting them to their own Transport Lines.

MEDICAL ARRANGEMENTS.

7. R.A.Ps.	D.24.a.1.3.	D.18.d.0.5.
Bearer relay posts.	D.17.b.0.5.	D.15.a.5.4.
Walking wounded collecting post.		D.16.d.5.4.
Car collecting post. FRANVILLERS.		

The car collecting post was at D.15.d.9.3. and will be re-established at this point as soon as dug-out at present in course of construction is completed.

R.E.DUMP. 8. BAIZIEUX.

P.O.W.CAGE. 9. BAIZIEUX.

SALVAGE. 10. Main Divisional Dump - BEHENCOURT - B.18.d.5.1.

RATIONS. 11. Rations are delivered by transport to Battalions by night and to Brigade Hdqrs. by day.

Q.M.STORES.12. Battalions and T.M.Battery. - No. 1 Billet, CONTAY.
Brigade Hdqrs. No.33 Billet, CONTAY.

TRANSPORT LINES.

13. Transport lines of all Units are situated at C.8.a.3.3.

TABLE "A"

AMMUNITION.

The following figures are the approximate amounts in Line:-

Description.	Left Battn.	Right Battn.	Support Battn.	T.M.B.	Bde. H.Q.	Total.
S.A.A.	107000	168000	122000	-	14000	411000
Grenades No. 5	1153	728	1524	-	-	3405
" No.23	706	952	996	-	-	2654
" No.24	146	-	-	-	200	346
" No.36	-	336	-	-	-	336
" Smoke.	-	21	-	-	-	21
Very Lights, 1-in						
White	1254	534	728	-	300	2816
Green	-	55	-	-	-	55
S.O.S.	32	32	32	-	26	122
Red flares.	225	68	140	-	-	433
Stokes shells, 3-in.	-	-	-	1058	-	1058

TABLE "B"

RESERVE RATIONS.

Description.	Left Battn. at Keep E.13.a.60.40.	Right Battn. at D.18.d.30.15	Support Battn. at D.17.b.2.2.	Total.
Biscuits.	250lbs.	250lbs.	-	500lbs.
Bully beef.	200 tins	118 tins	43 tins	361 tins
Grocery rations.	-	118 tins	-	118 "
Reserve water.	60 galls.	70 galls.	144 galls.	274 gall

Note :- Most of the biscuits are loose and in sandbags. A representative of the A.S.C. has already inspected these but his suggestions as to disposal have not yet been received

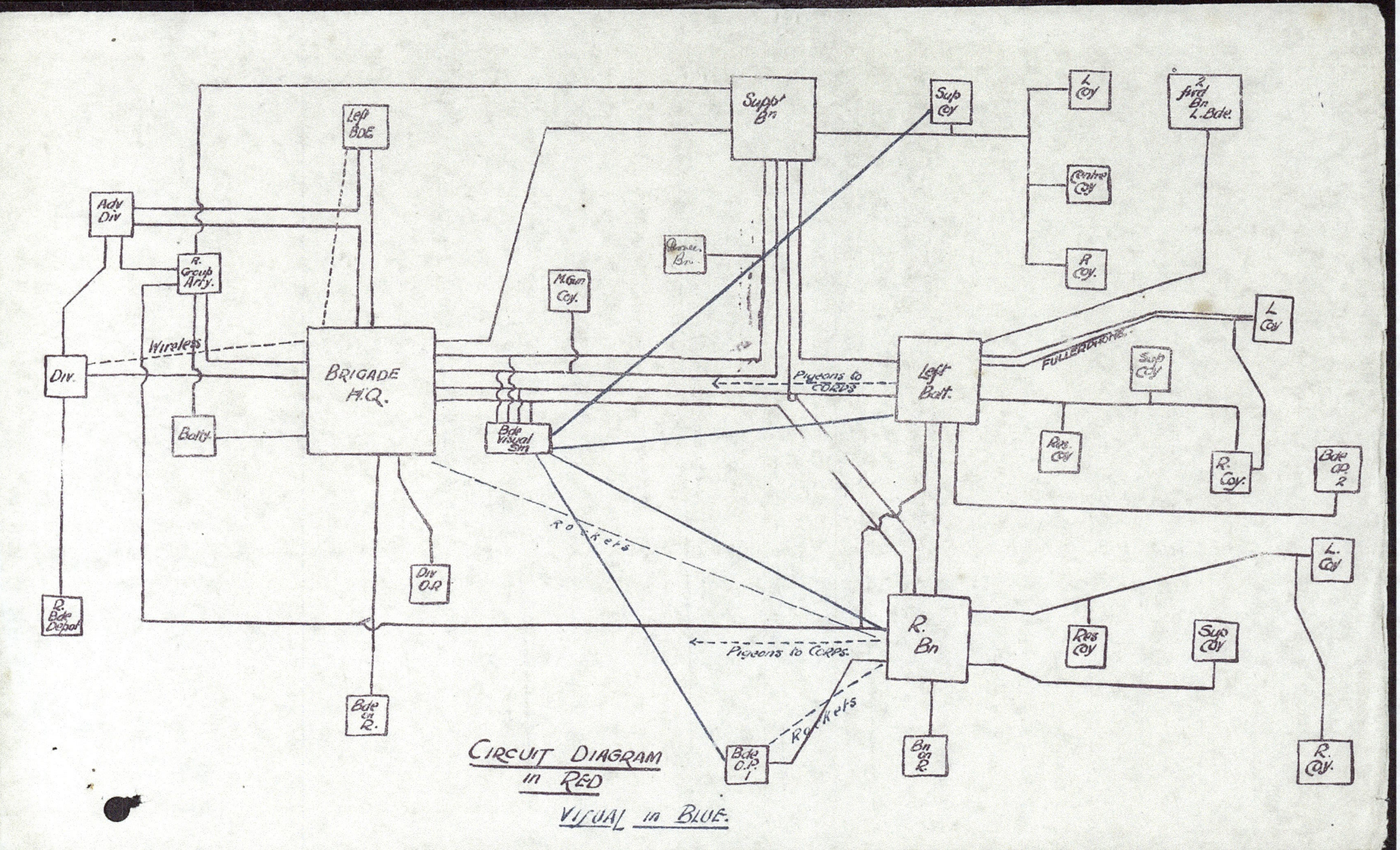

CIRCUIT DIAGRAM
in RED
VISUAL in BLUE.
BRIGADE H.Q.
Adv Div
Div.
R. Group Arty.
Left BDE
Batty
R. Bde Depot
Bde on R.
Div O.P.
Supp' Bn
Sup Coy
L Coy
Centre Coy
R Coy.
2 Fwd Bn L.Bde.
M.Gun Coy.
Bde Visual Stn
Left Batt.
Sup Coy
Res Coy
R. Coy.
L Coy
Bde O.P. 2
FULLERPHONE.
Pigeons to CORPS
R. Bn
Res Coy
Sup Coy
L Coy
R. Coy.
Bn on R.
Bde O.P. 1
Rockets
Pigeons to CORPS.
Wireless

File

MAP TO ACCOMPANY

174th Infantry Brigade Defence

SCHEME.

Coy Areas :-
Batt HQ :-

L.T.M.B. : (in Red) -
Newton Mortars :(") -
Lewis Guns. AA. -
Machine Gun Bn : A. Coy
B. Coy
D. Coy
} In Green

6th London Regt (R. Bn) Red.
7th " (L. Bn) Black.
8th " (Supp Bn) Green.
Pioneer Bn. 2 Coys in [illegible]

Artillery Barrage Lines.

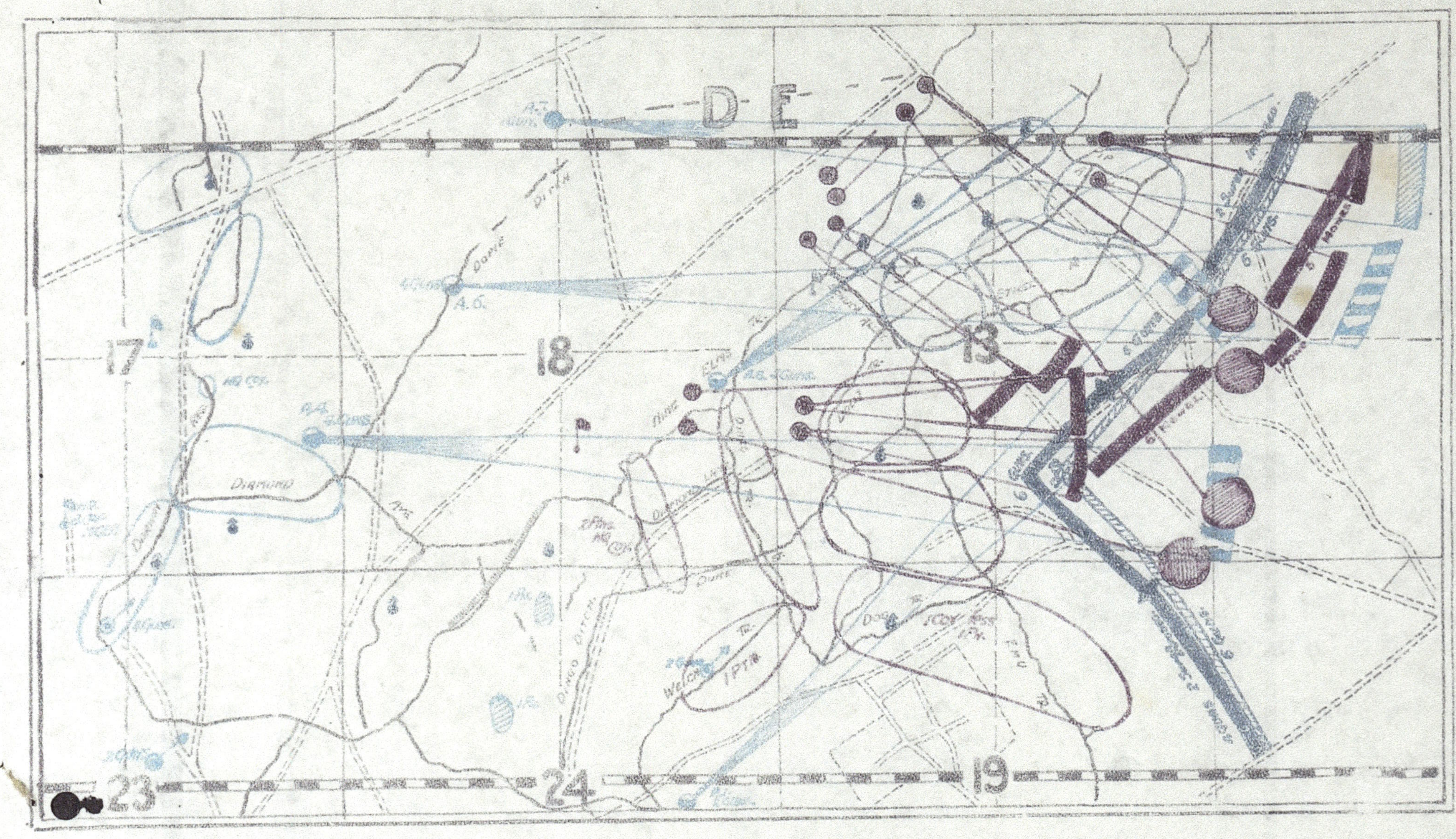
D E
17
18
13
23
24
19
A.6.
DIAMOND

(B)

SECRET. | **8TH BATTALION LONDON REGIMENT.** | Copy No. 2
Order No.61.

Reference SENLIS Sheet. | 18th June, 1918.

INFORMATION. 1. The Battalion will be relieved by 4th London Regt. today.

INTENTION. 2. The Battalion will relieve 21st London Regt. in Brigade Support today.
Companies will take over from corresponding Coys. of 21st London.

INSTRUCTION. 3. (a) Companies will move off from this Camp as corresponding Coys. of 4th London arrive, except that no Company will leave the camp before 9.30 pm.
100 yards between platoons.
(b) Guides. 1 per Platoon and 1 for Bn.H.Q. will be at Cross Roads D.21.a.8.7. at 10.30 pm.
(c) Route. AMIENS - ALBERT ROAD.
(d) Transport. 1 Limber will report to each Coy. and 1 limber and M.O. Cart to Bn.H.Q. at 8.30 pm. to convey Lewis Guns (with 24 drums per gun), dixies and Mess and M.O. Stores to the line.
(e) Rations. will be delivered before moving at about 4 pm.
(f) Officers Valises. Mens greatcoats and haversacks and all stores for return to Transport Lines will be dumped near Guard Shelter by 3 pm.
(g) Receipts given for trench stores will be in Orderly Room at 10 am 19th inst.
(h) Completion of Relief to be notified to Bn.H.Q. by wire and by runner.
Code word "SQUARE."

REPORTS 4. To Bn.H.Q. D.17.a.7.1.

Issued at 11.0 am.

L.E.B. JACOB,
Lieut. & A/Adjutant.

Copies to:-
1. File.
2. War Diary.
3. C.O.
4. 2/in/Command.
5. O.C. "A" Co.
6. O.C. "B" Co.
7. O.C. "C" Co.
8. O.C. "D" Co.
9. Headquarters.
10. Q.M.
11. T.O.
12. O.C. 21st Londons.

SECRET. **OPERATION ORDER.** JUNE 23rd, 1918. 1

8th Bn LONDON REGT.

Ref;-
57 d.
62 d. 1/40,000.

Following Provisional Order No 40 attached.

1. Unchanged.
2. ~~Instructions.~~ Intention.
   ~~(a)~~ On relief the Battalion will move into Dvl. Reserve at Camp in C.[illegible].b.
3. (a) Unchanged.
   (b) One guide per platoon and one per Coy H.Q. one BHQ report BHQ at [illegible] pm. They will meet 18th London at D.17.c.2.2. Officer from A Coy holds good.
   (c) Unchanged.
   (d) do.
   (e) do.
   (f) do.
   (g) do.
   (h) do.
   (i) An advance party consisting of 2/Lt TAFNER, and a Sergeant from each Coy and HQ, will report to BHQ at 6 am, in the morning, ready to move to take over new area.
   (j) Trench store receipts to reach BHQ by 12 noon, 25th.

J M BARRATT.
2/Lt A/Adjt.

SECRET. 8TH BATTALION, THE LONDON REGIMENT. (A) Copy No.,....

Order No. 60.

16th June, 1918.

... Sheets AMIENS and LENS. 1/100000.

INFORMATION. 1. Brigade will move by bus and route march to Reserve Line, 47th Division Area, tomorrow.

INTENTION. 2. Battalion will move to position occupied by a Battn. of 141st Infantry Brigade in C.21.b.

INSTRUCTION. 3. (a) Parade PICQUIGNY - BREILLY ROAD facing N.W.

(b) Order. Battle Surplus, A. B. C. D. H.Q. Band Cyclists.

(c) Head of Column. Orderly Room.

(d) Time. 5.10 am.

(e) Embussing point. SOUES - PICQUIGNY ROAD.

(f) Debussing point. CONTAY - FRANVILLERS ROAD.

(g) Battn. Embussing Officer. 2/Lt. J.M. BARRATT.

(h) Mess Kit, Dixies and Field Officers valises will be at Q.M. Stores at 4.45 am.

(j) Receipts for stores taken over will be at Bn.H.Q. by 6.0 pm 17th inst.

REPORTS. 4. Head of 8th Battalion busses.

Issued at 10.30 pm.

L.E.B. JACOB,
Lieut. & A/Adjutant.

Copies to:-

No.1. File.
2. War Diary.
3. C.O.
4. Second-in-Command
5. H.Q. Mess.

Nos. 6 - 9. O.C. Coys.
10. Headquarters.
11. Q.M.

S E C R E T. (C) No 7

8th Battalion LONDON REGT.

PROVISIONAL ORDER NO. 46

Ref;- SENLIS. 1/20,000 June 23rd 1918.

1. INFORMATION. The Battalion will be relieved by 12th LONDONs tomorrow the 24th inst. Companies will be relieved by corresponding companies of the 12th.

2. INTENTION. On relief the Battalion will move back, destination later.

3. INSTRUCTION.
(a) Companies will move off from their positions independently, on being relieved. Relief will be reporð to BHQ by runner, code word for relief, --GOTHIM---,
(b) GUIDES. One guide per platoon, and one for BHQ. will report to RSM at BHQ, time to be stated later. OC A Company will detail an Officer who will take guides to Cross Roads at D.21.a.6.7, where incoming Battalion will be met. He will stay at Cross Roads until the last platoon of relieving Battn has passed.
(c) TRANSPORT. One limber will report to each Coy, and one limber and MO's cart to Bn HQ, at 11 pm, to convey Lewis guns and drums, dixies, Officers Mess stores and MO's stores to the new area.
(d) RATIONS will be dumped at new area.
(e) VALISES etc. Officers valises and mens greatcoats and haversacks, and surplus stores will be dumped at new area, arrangements by T.O.
(f) COOKERS and WATER-CARTS will be moved to new area, arrangements by T.O.
(g) OFFICERS CHARGERS. at Cross Roads :-

Company Commanders	11-30 pm.
Commanding Officer.	12- mnt.

(h) C Q M Ss from details will proceed to new area with rations, and will report to their respective Coys on arrival.

J M BARRATT.
2/Lt Asst Aj

COPIES TO.
1. War Diary.
2. File.
3. C O.
4. - 7, OC COMpanies.
8. QM.
9. TO.
10. R S M.

(D)

SECRET. 8th BN. LONDON REGIMENT. Copy.....

Order No 62. 26th June 1918.

1. INSTRUCTION. (a) Bn. will move off from present area at 11.30 a.m. Order of move, H.Q., C.D.B.A. 100 yards between Platoons.

(b) Positions in new area. H.Q., C. & D. Coy. Valley about C.18.c.9.0. B. Coy. BAIZIEUX SYSTEM, same position as last occupied. A. Coy. Bank in Valley C.24.c. same as last occupied.

(c) Loading party. Each Coy will leave behind a loading party of 1 N.C.O. and 2 men, who will proceed with Limber as soon as last stores have been loaded.

(d) Mess Stores, will be packed at once and will go with next Limbers.

(e) Officers Valises. will be dumped near H.Q. immediately.

(f) Water Carts and Cookers ready to move immediately under arrangements by T.O.

Issued at 10.30 a.m.

J.M.BARRATT.
2/Lieut. & Asst. Adjt.

Copy to No.1. File.
2. War Diary.
3. C.O.
4-7. O.C. Coys.

27.6.18

SECRET.

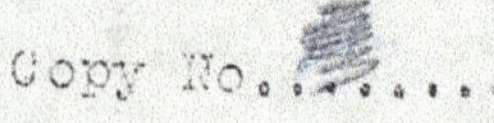

Copy No.........

174th. Infantry Brigade.

Reserve Brigade - Right Sector - III Corps.

DEFENCE SCHEME.

ROLE OF THE BRIGADE. 1. The Brigade is responsible for the defence of the LAVIEVILLE System on the Divisional Front and may, subsequently to its occupying the LAVIEVILLE System be required to counter-attack to restore the situation in the Intermediate System.

Battalions will work on LAVIEVILLE System and communications forward to the Intermediate System under the C.R.E.

Garrisons not detailed for work under C.R.E. will be employed by night on improvement of their positions and crop cutting.

4th. Suffolk Regt. (Pioneers) less 1 Coy is attached to the Brigade for the defence of the LAVIEVILLE System.

DISPOSITIONS and BOUNDARIES. 2. The LAVIEVILLE System is held by two Battalions and the Pioneer Battalion (less 1 Coy.)

The Pioneer Battalion lives in its positions. Each of the other two Battalions has two Companies accommodated in the BAIZIEUX Line.

See Map "A" attached.

MACHINE GUNS and TRENCH MORTARS. 3. See Map "A" attached.

GENERAL POLICY. 4.(a) Battalions holding the LAVIEVILLE Line will carry out at least once during the Brigade Tour in reserve a practice manning of the Line, time of which will be reported to Brigade H.Q.

(b) All Commanders down to Platoon Commanders will reconnoitre approaches to

(i) Flank Divisional Areas.

(ii) Intermediate System, with a view to the recapture of any part of it if ordered.

(c) Liaison Posts under an Officer will be found

(i) by Pioneer Battalion, with Australian Corps D.22.a.6.0. in case of attack.

(ii) by Left Battalion with Northern Divn., III Corps, D.5.d.0.6. permanently.

(d) Likely targets for hostile gas shelling are

BRESLE VALLEY (D.4.c. - D.21.)

LAVIEVILLE.

VALLEY in D.18.c. and b.

Schemes will be drawn up allotting to Units (down to Platoons) in case of an intense gas bombardment, two or more alternative positions to a flank or forward (according to the direction of the wind) for occupation.

Reserve Coys of Forward Battalions and all Coys of the Reserve Battalion will be allotted alternative localities and will be practised in moving quickly to them to facilitate clearing their normal areas in the event of these being subjected to a gas bombardment.

ACTION IN CASE OF ATTACK. 5. On the first indication of a serious hostile attack or on receipt of a telegram from Brigade H.Q. "MAN BATTLE STATIONS AAA Report Compliance AAA ACKNOWLEDGE " Units will take action as follows :

(a) Pioneer Battn (less 1 Coy.) will stand to arms in its positions. Battn. H.Q. will be established at H.Q. Right Forward Bde. Liaison Post at D.22.a.6.0. (see para. 4 (c) (i).)

(b) Centre and Left Battalions, will move up their Coys from BAIZIEUX System to reinforce the LAVIEVILLE System. In each case one Coy will be detailed to occupy the Support Line and will form the Battalion Reserve.

Positions in the Front Line for Lewis Guns of all three Coys in each Battalion must be selected beforehand.

H.Q. for Left Battalion - D.9.b.5.6.
H.Q. for Right " - with Left Battalion, until completion of new H.Q. at D.9.d.8.4. (approx.)

(c) Battalion in Valley C.18.d. and C.24.b. will fall in on its Alarm Post in the valley and await orders to move. A Liaison Officer will be sent to Brigade H.Q.

(d) Machine Guns in position will be fully manned. Machine Gun section in reserve will stand to arms and will send an Officer to report to Brigade H.Q.

(e) Trench Mortars in position will be fully manned. Two Trench Mortars in Brigade Reserve with 20 rounds per Mortar on pack mules will report to O.C. Battalion in Brigade Reserve and be placed under his orders.

(f) Advanced Bde. H.Q. will open at C.17.a.7.8.

(g) Working Parties in advance of the LAVIEVILLE Line will immediately report to the nearest Coy or Battn. H.Q. Whenever the situation permits they will be directed

(i) In the case of Field or Tunnelling Coys R.E. - To their Battle Stations in the BAIZIEUX System.

(ii) In the case of other parties - to rejoin their Units.

If the situation urgently demands their co-operation or renders their withdrawal impossible they will be told off to man defences as required. All working parties in rear of LAVIEVILLE System will rejoin Units immediately.

(h) It will be impressed on all Commanders, and especially Company Commanders in the Front Line of the LAVIEVILLE System that it is their duty to keep themselves informed at all times by means of patrols of the situation on their front or flanks. Touch will be maintained with troops of the two forward Brigades. The situation will be frequently reported to Bde. H.Q.

COUNTER - ATTACK. 6. In the case of a counter-attack by the Brigade there will be no creeping barrage, but if the attack is over 500 yards a half way standing barrage will be put down. The barrage will then lift on to the final objective and subsequently to a protective line beyond it.

Two Sections, Divl. M.G. Battn. will probably be attached to the Brigade for counter-attack. The remainder of Guns in Divl. Reserve will be available for barrage and covering fire.

APPENDICES. 7. I - TANKS.
II - SIGNAL COMMUNICATIONS.
III - ADMINISTRATIVE ARRANGEMENTS.

R. Barrington-Ward
Captain.
Brigade Major.
174th. Infantry Brigade.

27th. June, 1918.

By Wire to (LONU (LOKU (LOSU (GIGE (DODI

Q.D. 795 15 AAA

Reference Defence Scheme para 5 (c) AAA On MAN BATTLE STATIONS Liaison Officer from Reserve Battn will at once proceed to Advanced Bde H.Q. C.17.a.7.8. to receive messages and await arrival Bde representative AAA All messages from Battalions will be sent to Adv. Bde. H.Q. and repeated Rear Bde H.Q. until other orders are issued AAA Addsd Bns and GIGE by Wire reptd All other Recipients Defence Scheme by D.R.

WUSU
12.30am

Captain,
Brigade Major.

G.S. 3298.

173rd Inf. Bde.
174th Inf. Bde.
175th Inf. Bde.

The G.O.C. approves Reserve Brigade Defence Scheme as compiled by 174th Inf. Brigade (BM/7/77/72, dated 27th June) which will constitute the Defence Scheme for the Reserve Brigade and will be handed over on each Inter-Brigade relief.

R H Mangles Colonel,
General Staff 58th (London) Division.

30th June 1918.

Bde. Maj.

All Recipients. B.M.7/77/72.

The attached Defence Scheme supersedes all previous instructions issued for the Brigade in Divisional Reserve, Right Sector, III Corps.

Previous defence instructions should be destroyed.

Please acknowledge.

R. Darrington Ward
Captain.
Brigade Major.
27th. June, 1918. 174th. Infantry Brigade.

SECRET.

AMENDMENT to 174th. Inf. Bde. DEFENCE SCHEME.

APPENDIX 1. (TANKS.)

Delete first four lines and substitute the following :-

1. "B" Coy. No. 2 Tank Battn. (Mark.V Tanks) has been detailed to co-operate with the Division

The Company is divided into four sections -

Coy. H.Q. and 3 Reserve Sections (2 consisting of 2 males and 1 female and 1 of 1 male and 2 females) is located at C.12.b.3.7.

One forward Section (2 male and 1 female) is located at V.28.a.

Captain.
Brigade Major.
174th. Infantry Brigade.

16th. July, 1918.

Copies to : All Recipients of Bde. Defence Scheme.

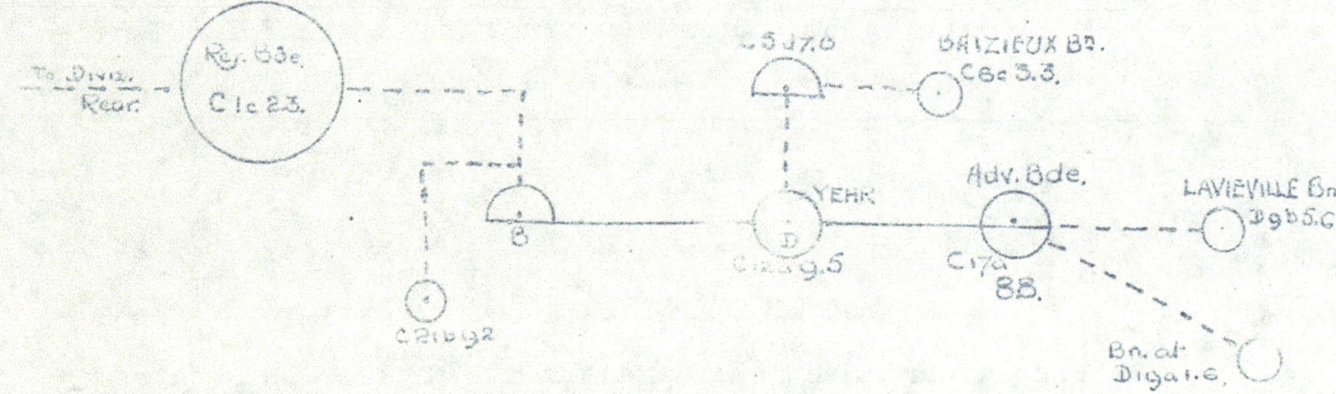

LINE DIAGRAM: RESERVE BRIGADE.

A P P E N D I X   I.

T A N K S.

1. [illegible] Coy., [illegible] 2 Tank Battalion (Mark V Tanks)., H.Q. S. end of [illegible] Wood (C.11.[illegible]) has been detailed to co-opera[illegible] with the Division.x Sections are located V.28.[illegible]. and C.11.[illegible].

Cancelled
See [illegible]

Mark V British Tanks are distinguished by having WHITE - RED - WHITE in broad lines on extreme front of sides of Tanks and on back of Rear Turrets.

German Tanks have the IRON CROSS in BLACK on a WHITE background.

British Tanks returning from Action fly a flag (RED - WHITE - BLUE Vertical Stripes). Other Signals by Flag from Tanks to Infantry are -

GREEN and WHITE	-	COME ON.
RED and YELLOW	-	GO ON. I AM BROKEN DOWN.

2. The role of the Tanks is to deal with hostile tanks, and to prevent any hostile penetration of the Intermediate Systems.

3. A hostile Smoke Barrage, especially if placed on the LAVIEVILLE - MILLENCOURT Line is a probable indication of a coming hostile attack with tanks. All concerned will therefore be warned to report enemy Smoke Barrages by the quickest available means to the nearest Tank Commander and to Brigade H.Q.

4. C Coy. No. 2 Tank Battn. (H.Q. Wood, C.3.b.) is in Corps Reserve and available to operate independently or with Reserve Troops as may be ordered by Corps H.Q.

A P P E N D I X II.

SUMMARY of COMMUNICATIONS.

LINES. 1. To Division Rear. 1 pair Poled.

To Battalions :

The Line to Battalions is an omnibus Line running by poled cable to B Test Point on bury, through Advanced Division at C.12.a.9.5. to Test Point at C.5.d.7.0.

From this Test Point a Line runs to Battalion holding BAIZIEUX Line at C.6.c.3.3.

The Line runs to Test Point at C.17.a.8.8. and is continued by poled cable to Battalion holding LAVIEVILLE Line at D.9.b.5.6. and ground line to Battalion at D.19.a.1.6.

The Advanced Signal Office will be at C.17.a.8.8. through which Battalion Lines and lines to Division and Rear Units run.

Each Battalion has lines to Companies.

VISUAL. 2. From Battalions to Brigade Visual Station at C.17.a.8.8.

APPENDIX III.

ADMINISTRATIVE ARRANGEMENTS.

AMMUNITION. 1. The following are the approximate amounts of Ammunition in the Line :

6th. London Regt. (Right)	193,000 rounds.
7th. London Regt. (Left)	97,500 rounds.
8th. London Regt. (Support)	26,000 rounds.
	316,500 rounds.

WATER. 2. Water is available at the following points :

Horse Watering Point - C.2.a.3.6.
Drinking Water - CONTAY.

STRAGGLERS POSTS. 3.

Location.	Strength.
C.6.d.5.9.	1 N.C.O. 6 men.
C.12.b.1.5.	1 N.C.O. 6 men.
D.16.c.7.5.	1 N.C.O. 6 men.

Collecting Station for Stragglers and Prisoners of War Cage - C.6.d.4.9.

BATHS. 4. AGNICOURT - Capacity 40 men per hour.
C.10.b.(near BOIS ROBERT - Capacity 50 men per hour.

Q.M.STORES.5. All Units - Billet No. 1. CONTAY.
Bde. H.Q. - Billet No.38. CONTAY.

TRANSPORT LINES. 6. All Units - C.2.a.2.2.

MAPA.

REFERENCE.

To be superimposed on
SENLIS Special Sheet. Ed. 2A.
SCALE 1/20,000.

	Accommodation	Battle
A. Battn. [RED]	H.Q. BAIZIEUX: 2 Coys. BAIZIEUX 2 Coy LAVIEVILLE LINE	LAVIEVILLE LINE
B. Battn.		
C. Battn.		

PIONEER BN. [BROWN] LAVIEVILLE LINE

L.T.M. Bty. [RED] HQ at BAIZIEUX Guns:--- ⊙

47 ... " [RED] .... "

DIVISIONAL BOUNDARY

A Bn. Battle H.Q.

47 Div M.G.

A BATT. BATTLE

1 Bn. 2 Coys Accommodation

H.Q.

Battle HQ

Liaison Post.

13 14 15 19 20 21 22 25 26 27 28 29 30 1 2 3 4 5 6

C D I J

DIVISIONAL BOUNDARY.

DIAGRAMS of COMMUNICATIONS. Reserve Bde. Centre Div. III Corps.

Normal Circuits.

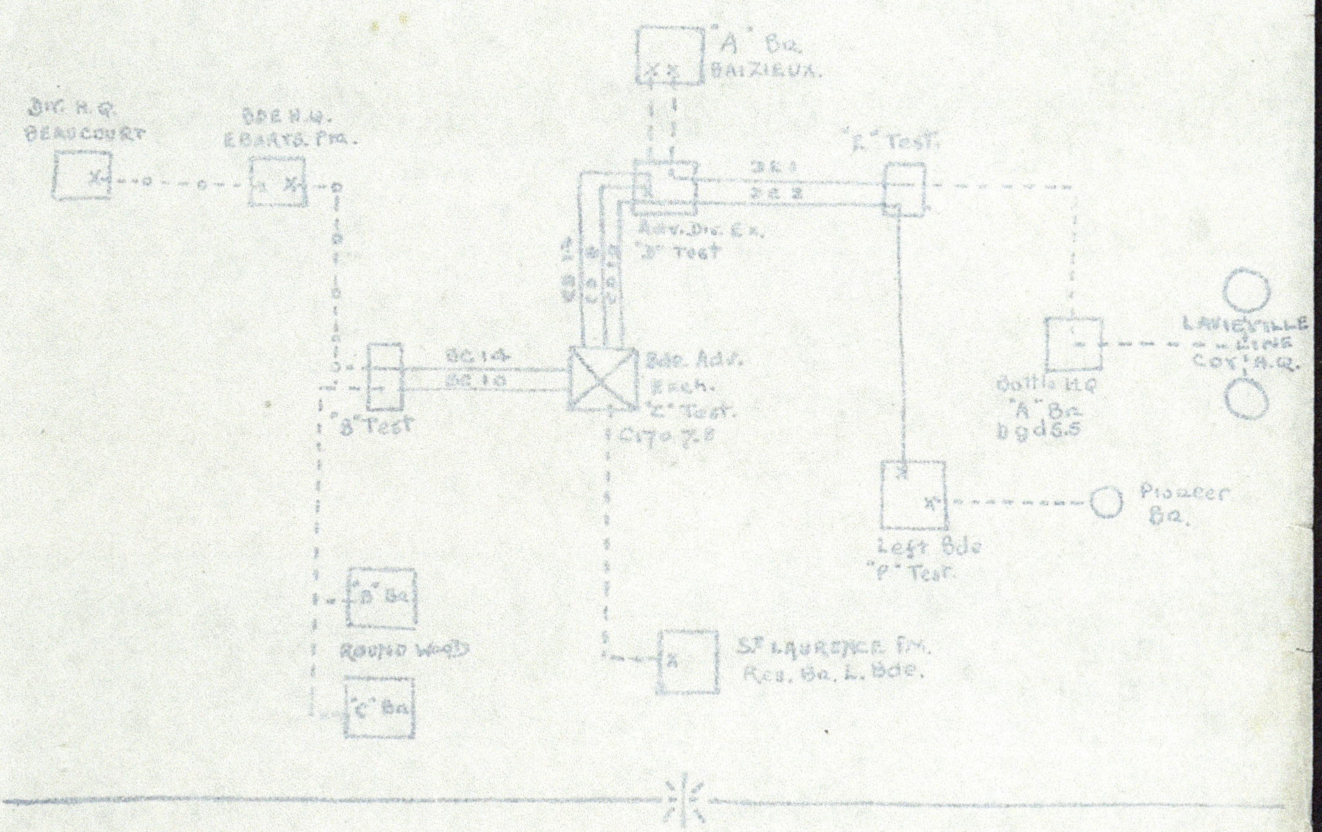

Battle Circuits

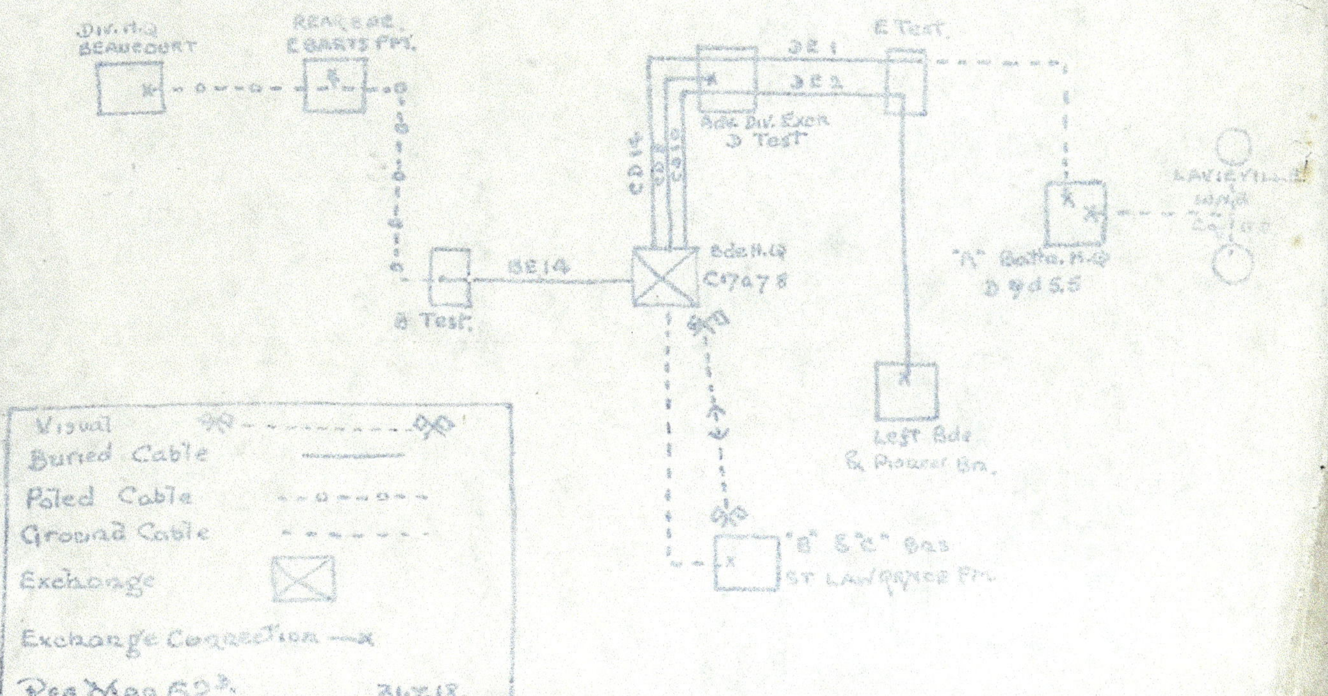

Army Form C. 2118.

Instructions regarding War Diaries and Intelligence Summaries are contained in F. S. Regs., Part II. and the Staff Manual respectively. Title pages will be prepared in manuscript.

WAR DIARY
or
INTELLIGENCE SUMMARY.

(Erase heading not required.)

Place	Date	Hour	Summary of Events and Information	Remarks and references to Appendices
			8th Bn. London Regiment – War Diary – Period July 1st to 31st 1918.	

D. D. & L., London, E.C.
(A8001) Wt. W1771/M2031 750,000 5/17 Sch. 52 Forms/C2118/14

Instructions regarding War Diaries and Intelligence Summaries are contained in F. S. Regs., Part II. and the Staff Manual respectively. Title pages will be prepared in manuscript.

WAR DIARY
or
INTELLIGENCE SUMMARY.
(*Erase heading not required.*)

Army Form C. 2118.

Place	Date	Hour	Summary of Events and Information	Remarks and references to Appendices
	1918 July 1st		The following Officers were with the Battalion July 1st 1918.	
BAIZIEUX SYSTEM NEAR BAIZIEUX.			Lt Col. C.E. JOHNSTON MC. (CO) Major J. VENNING (2nd in Command) Capt. H.W. PRIESTLEY MC.	
			2Lt. J.M. BARRATT (Actg/Adjt) Lt R.N. SHAPLEY (S.O) 2/Lt. E.C. KNELL (IO)	
			Capt T.A.B. PURKIS (T.O) Hony Capt. R.R. FAIRLEY. MC. (QM)	JmB
			Attached Lt Col R.E. WILLIS. British West Indies Regt. Lt W.B. MACBEAN USMRC (MO)	
			Rev. A.J. JAMES (Chaplain)	
			A. Company Capt. G.C. FABER. (OC) 2Lt E.J. ROFT. 2Lt R.N. JOHNSON - 2Lt A.J. HARRIS.	
			B. - Capt. A.S. THOMAS. MC (OC) 2Lt W.B. SCARTH. 2Lt H. ALEXANDER - 2Lt A.G. TAFNER.	JmB
			C. - Capt. E.C.K. CLARKE (OC) 2Lt C.F. YOUNGMAN. 2Lt L.C. HATCHER.	
			D. - 2Lt W.E. CONSTANCE (OC) 2Lt A.E. MASON.. 2Lt R.B. PATTINSON. 2Lt H. ORCHARD. and 616 other ranks.	
			Bright, Hot day.	
			Brigadier General C.J. HIGGINS: DSO. retired from Office and proceeded to ENGLAND for rest, Brig. Genl. A. MAXWELL D.S.O took over the Command of the Brigade.	app. 1.
			Capt. G.C. FABER evacuated Sick to Hospital	
			Capt. R.R. POULTON rejoined Battn from Battle Surplus & took command of 'A' Coy.	
			R. A. [illegible]	1st Coy

A5834 Wt. W4973/M687 750,000 8/16 D. D. & L. Ltd. Forms/C.2118/13.

Army Form C. 2118.

Instructions regarding War Diaries and Intelligence Summaries are contained in F. S. Regs., Part II. and the Staff Manual respectively. Title pages will be prepared in manuscript.

WAR DIARY
or
~~INTELLIGENCE~~ SUMMARY.

(*Erase heading not required.*)

Place	Date	Hour	Summary of Events and Information	Remarks and references to Appendices
BAIZIEUX SYSTEM NR BAIZIEUX	July 1st		The Battn relieved the 3rd LONDON REGT in SUPPORT, left Brigade front; A Coy in DODU TRENCH, B. Coy in HILL ROW, C. DARLING RES. LEFT, D, DARLING RES. RIGHT. BHQ on track D 5 d, 0.1 (SENLIS) just EAST of LAVIEVILLE. relief complete 12.5 am. The 2/4 Bn LONDON REGT took over position in BAIZIEUX SYSTEM.	App 2
SUPPORT BN. LEFT BRIGADE	2nd		Bright, hot day, cold at night. Working and wiring parties on SHRINE and PIONEER TRENCHES. 2Lt R.N. JOHNSON took out patrol from Right Bn front, good information obtained. Lt Col. R.E. WILLIS proceeded to ENGLAND for S.O.S. ALDERSHOT. Hon Capt. R.R. FAIRLEY MC (2M) transferred & proceeded for duty in ENGLAND.	JmB
— do —	3rd		Cool, dull at intervals. Work on repairs to own trenches during day. Working and wiring in forward areas at night. 2Lt ALEXANDER took out patrol from Right Bn front.	JmB

R. D. Deroiche[?] Comdg
Lt Col.

D. D. & L., London, E.C.
(A8001) Wt. W1771/M2031 750,000 5/17 Sch. 52 Forms/C2118/14

Instructions regarding War Diaries and Intelligence Summaries are contained in F. S. Regs., Part II. and the Staff Manual respectively. Title pages will be prepared in manuscript.

WAR DIARY
or
INTELLIGENCE SUMMARY.
(Erase heading not required.)

Army Form C. 2118.

Place	Date	Hour	Summary of Events and Information	Remarks and references to Appendices
SUPPORT BN. LEFT BRIGADE.	July 4th		Bright day, much warmer.	
			G.O.C visited the line	
EAST of LAVIEVILLE.			"CO" and Company Commanders reconnoitred front line held by 7th LONDON.	
			Battalion worked on SHRINE + PIONEER TRENCHES.	JmB
			2Lt C. F. YOUNGMAN took out patrol from Right Bn front, good information obtained.	
-do-	5th		Changeable, dull + bright at intervals.	
LEFT FRONT BATTN.			The Battn relieved the 7th Bn. London Regt in the front line, left Bn	JmB
LEFT BRIGADE SECTOR.			left Brigade Sector. C. Coy. Right front, D. Coy. left front, B. Coy Support, A Coy Reserve. Relief complete 12 mnt.	App. 3
			2Lt P. D'ARCY proceeded to ENGLAND from Battle Surplus on 14 days leave.	
			2Lt C F YOUNGMAN ~~[illegible]~~ evacuated sick to Hospital.	
			2Lt D GRANT (INTELLIGENCE CORPS) Joined the Bn for 1 months instructions.	
			2Lt H ORCHARD took out patrol from Bn front, no important information gained.	
			A D Derviche-Jones Lt Col.	

D. D. & L., London, E.C. (A8001) Wt. W1771/M2031 750,000 5/17 Sch. 52 Forms/C2118/14

Instructions regarding War Diaries and Intelligence Summaries are contained in F. S. Regs., Part II. and the Staff Manual respectively. Title pages will be prepared in manuscript.

WAR DIARY
or
INTELLIGENCE SUMMARY.
(Erase heading not required.)

Army Form C. 2118.

Place	Date	Hour	Summary of Events and Information	Remarks and references to Appendices
LEFT BN. FRONT. LEFT BRIGADE SECTOR	July 6th		Bright, warm day. Line very quiet. Work in trenches, wiring at night. 2Lt A E MASON took out patrol. Enemy reported working in no mans land not proved	JmB
— do —	7th		Bright warm day, very quiet. Usual work and wiring. 2Lt H. ORCHARD took out patrol with intention of surprising enemy working party. Enemy patrol seen, but our patrol failed to get into contact.	JmB
— do —	8th		Warm weather still holding. Line very quiet. Usual work and wiring. Lt R H A NEWSOME MC rejoined from leave in FRANCE, and took command of D Coy. 2Lt L G HATCHER took out patrol. Enemy party seen but made off before our patrol could get into touch. Lt W B. MACBEAN proceeded on leave to ENGLAND — Capt R BARWICK (RAMC) joined as relief	JmB
— do —	9th		Dull showery day, very quiet. Inter ~~Battalion~~ Company relief carried out during evening; new positions B. Coy Right front, A. Coy left front, C Coy Support D Coy Reserve. relief complete 11.20 pm. The enemy put a light barrage on our Support line while the relief was in progress. There were no casualties. 2Lt A T[illegible] took out patrol but patrol was held up by enemy barrage and object had to be abandoned	JmB Appen 4.

[illegible signature]

Army Form C. 2118.

WAR DIARY
or
~~INTELLIGENCE SUMMARY.~~
(Erase heading not required.)

Instructions regarding War Diaries and Intelligence Summaries are contained in F. S. Regs., Part II. and the Staff Manual respectively. Title pages will be prepared in manuscript.

Place	Date	Hour	Summary of Events and Information	Remarks and references to Appendices
LEFT FRONT BN. LEFT BRIGADE SECTOR.	10th.		Changeable, fine & dull at intervals. Quiet day. Enemy TMs slightly active on Right Cy. Usual work and wiring. Enemy Artillery slightly active early night. Patrol by 2Lt ROFT, effort to get into touch with enemy parties still unsuccessful. 2Lt C F YOUNGMAN returned from Hospital.	JmB
– do –	11th.		Warm & bright, cold night. Enemy very Quiet except for few TMs on right Company. Patrol by 2Lt ALEXANDER. No signs of enemy. Patrol had unusual experience of being shelled by enemy 77-mm, about 100 yds from his line, no casualties were sustained.	JmB
– do –	12th.		Very dull day. Enemy Quiet, usual TM activity. Battn relieved in line by 7/10th LONDON REGT., very slow relief by this Regt. not complete till 1.37 am. On relief Battalion moved back & took up old positions in BAIZIEUX SYSTEM, near BAIZIEUX. Capt. H. W. PRIESTLEY MC rejoined Battn from Delarlo Camp.	JmB App 5
BAIZIEUX SYSTEM NR BAIZIEUX	13th.		Dull, but fine. Morning spent in cleaning up generally. Commanding Officer's Conference for Company Commdrs 11.30 am, discussion on proposed raid on Enemy trenches. Capt. L.E.B. JACOB rejoined from Hospital and resumed duties of Adjutant.	JmB

A.D. Derviche-Jones Lt Col.

D. D. & L., London, E.C.
(A8001) Wt. W1771/M2031 750,000 5/17 Sch. 52 Forms/C2118/14

Instructions regarding War Diaries and Intelligence Summaries are contained in F. S. Regs., Part II. and the Staff Manual respectively. Title pages will be prepared in manuscript.

WAR DIARY
or
INTELLIGENCE SUMMARY.
(Erase heading not required.)

Army Form C. [illegible]

Place	Date	Hour	Summary of Events and Information	Remarks and references to Appendices
BAIZIEUX SYSTEM Near BAIZIEUX	July 14th		Showery day. Companies practiced special scheme for raid. 9am to 1pm and 2pm to 4pm also in bayonet fighting – P.T. – Bombing Etc.	JmB
–	15th		Fine bright day. Morning, practice by Companies of special scheme, Evening – – Battalion – – – witnessed by Brigadier General.	JmB
–	16th		Dull & showery. Battalion training as on previous days.	JmB
–	17th		Thunderstorms. Commanding Officer inspected Battalion by Companies.	
		3AM	3 Bombs dropped by Enemy Aircraft near 'B' Company cooker, causing 5 casualties, 3 killed and 2 badly wounded.	JmB
SUPPORT BATTALION. RIGHT BRIGADE E. of BRESLE.	18th		Bright fine morning, showers later. Battalion relieved 2/4th London Regt, in support Right Brigade, order of Companies A.B.C.D. right to left. Relief complete without casualties about 12.30 Am. Capt. G.C. FABER rejoined Battn from Hospital	JmB App. 6

R. D. Derrick. [illegible] 1st [illegible]

D. D. & L., London, E.C. (A8001) Wt. W1771/M2031 750,000 5/17 Sch. 52 Forms/C2118/14

Instructions regarding War Diaries and Intelligence Summaries are contained in F. S. Regs., Part II. and the Staff Manual respectively. Title pages will be prepared in manuscript.

WAR DIARY
or
~~INTELLIGENCE SUMMARY.~~
(Erase heading not required.)

Army Form [illegible]118.

Place	Date	Hour	Summary of Events and Information	Remarks and references to Appendices
SUPPORT BATT^N RIGHT BRIGADE E. of BRESLE	19th		Changeable, Some thunder storms. Usual work in trenches, working parties for REs. Capt F. T. CHAPMAN joined the Battalion as Quarter Master. Capt. G. C. FABER proceeded to Battle surplus. 25 ORs joined Bn in the line as reinforcements.	JmB
— do —	20th		Changeable, Some thunderstorms. Usual work in trenches working parties for REs. 2Lt. P. E. D'ARCY transferred to MGC whilst on leave in ENGLAND, and struck off strength of Battalion.	JmB
— do —	21st		Bright warm day, cloudy at intervals. Usual work in trenches, working parties for REs. 46 ORs joined Battalion in the line as reinforcements.	JmB
— do —	22nd		Fine, bright day. Work as usual. Lt R. N. SHAPLEY proceeded on leave to ENGLAND	
~~— do —~~	~~23rd~~		~~Showery~~ The Battalion was relieved in Support by the 2/2nd London Regt. on being warned to carry out a Raid on the enemy trenches on the morning of the 25th inst. On relief the Battalion moved back to ROUND WOOD (C 20, BEHENCOURT — FRANVILLERS RD) for rest + preparation.	JmB App. 7

A. S. Derwick-Jones Lt Col.

D. D. & L., London, E.C. (A8001) Wt. W1771/M2031 750,000 5/17 Sch. 52 Forms/C2118/14

Army Form C. 2118.

Instructions regarding War Diaries and Intelligence Summaries are contained in F. S. Regs., Part II. and the Staff Manual respectively. Title pages will be prepared in manuscript.

WAR DIARY
or
~~INTELLIGENCE SUMMARY.~~
(Erase heading not required.)

Place	Date	Hour	Summary of Events and Information	Remarks and references to Appendices
ROUND WOOD (BEHENCOURT FRANVILLERS ROAD)	23d.		Showery. Part of the day was spent in rest and preparation for the raid, in the evening the Battalion finally practised the proposed raid over ground specially laid out at near St LAURENCE FARM, C 18.	J.m.B.
— do —	24th		Fine, Some showers. The day was spent partly in resting, and partly in equipping for the Raid, and at 11 pm the Battalion moved off from ROUND WOOD in busses to take up positions in front line before dawn. The following took part in the operation.	J.m.B.
			HQ Lt Col. C.E. JOHNSTON MC (Comdg officer) Capt. H.W. PRIESTLEY MC. (2nd in Command) Lt L.E.B. JACOB (Adjt) Capt R.W. BARWICK. RAMC (M.O) 2Lt E.C. KNELL (B.I.O) 2Lt D. GRANT – INTELLIGENCE CORPS – [attached] (INTERROGATOR). and 60. ORs.	App Special
			A. Company Capt. R.R. POULTON. (OC) 2Lt E.J. ROFT. (Quarry Party) 2Lt R.N. JOHNSON (Support to Quarry party) and 116 ORs	
			B. Company Capt. A.S. THOMAS. MC. (OC) 2Lt W.B. SCARTH (Right Hook party) 2Lt A.J. ALEXANDER (Left Hook party) 2Lt A TAFNER and 90. ORs.	

C. E. Johnston
Lt Col.

D. D. & L., London, E.C.
(A5001) Wt. W1771/M2031 750,000 5/17 Sch. 52 Forms/C2118/14

Army Form C. 2118.

Instructions regarding War Diaries and Intelligence Summaries are contained in F. S. Regs., Part II. and the Staff Manual respectively. Title pages will be prepared in manuscript.

WAR DIARY
or
~~INTELLIGENCE SUMMARY.~~
(Erase heading not required.)

Place	Date	Hour	Summary of Events and Information	Remarks and references to Appendices
	25th	10 Am	C. Coy Capt. E.C.K. CLARKE (OC) 2/Lt C.F. YOUNGMAN. 2/Lt L.C. HATCHER and 95 ORs D. Coy Lt R.H.A. NEWSOME MC (OC) 2/Lt R.B. PATTINSON. 2/Lt H. ORCHARD. and 92 ORs. Attached full account of Operation, Operation & Administration orders etc. (See appendix SPECIAL) After the raid, the Battalion collected at Rendez-vous just behind NINE ELMS ref SENLIS. D18.d.1.8, and at night were conveyed by busses back to ROUND WOOD; arriving 11.30 pm to 12 Mnt. The number to leave ROUND WOOD for the Raid was 19 Officers and 453 ORs and the number to return was 13 Officers 338 ORs. A. D. Derwicke-Jones Lt Col	JmB.

D. D. & L., London, E.C.
(A8004) Wt. W1771/M2031 750,000 5/17 Sch. 52 Forms/C2118/14

Army Form C. 2118.

Instructions regarding War Diaries and Intelligence Summaries are contained in F. S. Regs., Part II. and the Staff Manual respectively. Title pages will be prepared in manuscript.

WAR DIARY
or
INTELLIGENCE SUMMARY.
(Erase heading not required.)

Place	Date	Hour	Summary of Events and Information	Remarks and references to Appendices
ROUNDWOOD (BEHENCOURT-FRANVILLERS-ROAD)	26th		Bright and dull at intervals, Some thunder storms. The day was spent in resting, and enquiries reference to casualties, during the morning the Battalion was visited by the "Divisional Commander," who expressed himself very pleased with the operation. The men were in excellent spirits even before this expression was repeated to them.	JmB
-do-	27th		Showery all day. The Battalion "paused" fairly late, and the day was spent in re-organising and refitting. Capt E. C. K. CLARKE proceeded to IV Army, Company Commanders Course.	JmB
-do-	28th		Fine & bright, much warmer. Morning Short spell of PT under Company arrangements. Voluntary Church Service 11.0 Am.	JmB
BAIZIEUX SYSTEM NR BAIZIEUX.			4pm. The Battalion paraded and moved off to old camp at St. LAURENCE FARM C.18, and were accomodated under canvas in valley, HQ. North End of Valley just SE of BAIZIEX C Coy and D Coy, just S, and B. Coy. A. Coy, South end of valley just below St. LAURENCE FARM, arriving about 3.30 pm	app. 7

[illegible signature]

D. D. & L., London, E.C. (A8004) Wt. W1771/M2031 750,000 5/17 Sch. 52 Forms/C2118/14

Instructions regarding War Diaries and Intelligence Summaries are contained in F. S. Regs., Part II. and the Staff Manual respectively. Title pages will be prepared in manuscript.

WAR DIARY
or
~~INTELLIGENCE SUMMARY.~~
(Erase heading not required.)

Army Form C. 2118.

Place	Date	Hour	Summary of Events and Information	Remarks and references to Appendices
St LAURENCE FARM CAMP NEAR BAIZIEUX.	28th	6pm	Company Commanders Conference by "CO," Subject. "Reorganisation". Capt G C FABER rejoined Battalion from Battle Surplus and resumed command of "A" Company. Lt C. T. A. WILKINSON rejoined Battalion from Battle Surplus. Lt W. B. MACBEAN (MO) rejoined Battalion from leave in ENGLAND.	JmB
– do –	29th		Bright warm day. Companies re-organising & training 9am to 12.30pm. "CO" and Adjutant reconnoitred left Brigade front, left Divisional Sector. Lt R H A NEWSOME MC proceeded to GHQ LG Course.	JmB
– do –	30th		Bright hot day. Battalion relieved by 12th London Regt in St LAURENCE FARM CAMP, and relieved the 9th LONDON Regt in LAVIEVILLE LINE — HQ, A – B – Coys billetted in BAIZIEUX VILLAGE, C Company LAVIEVILLE LINE Right, D Company, LAVIEVILLE LINE Left. Line Companies reported relief complete 11.53 pm.	JmB App. 8

A. D. Derviche-Jones
Lt Col

D. D. & L., London, E.C.
(A8001) Wt. W1771/M2031 750,000 5/17 Sch. 52 Forms/C2118/14

Army Form C. 2118.

Instructions regarding War Diaries and Intelligence Summaries are contained in F. S. Regs., Part II. and the Staff Manual respectively. Title pages will be prepared in manuscript.

WAR DIARY
or
~~INTELLIGENCE SUMMARY.~~

(*Erase heading not required.*)

Place	Date	Hour	Summary of Events and Information	Remarks and references to Appendices
BAIZIEUX and LAVIEVILLE	31.		Bright, hot day. A + B Coy & HQ use of Baths at BOIS ROBERT, carrying on with training on return. Lt Col. A. D. DERVICHE-JONES. D.S.O. MC. rejoined and re-assumed Command of the Battalion. Lt Col. C. E. JOHNSTON relinquished Command of the Battalion and proceeded to Command 7th Batt. London Regt. The following were with the Battalion July 31st 1918 Lt Col. A.D. DERVICHE-JONES D.S.O. MC (CO) Capt. H.W. PRIESTLEY MC (2nd in Command) Lt L.E.B JACOB (actg adjt) 2Lt J.M. BARRATT (Asst Adjt) 2Lt E.C. KNELL (B.I.O) Lt W.B. MACBEAN (MO) Capt T.A.B. PURKIS (T.O) Capt. W.J. CHAPMAN (QM) Rev. JAME (C.F.) Attached 2Lt D. GRANT. Intell Corps. A Coy Capt. G.C. FABER (OC) Capt R.R. POULTON. 2Lt A.J. HARRIS. B Coy Capt A.S. THOMAS-MC (OC) 2Lt C.R. CROSSLAND. 2Lt W. KELLY. C Coy 2Lt C.F. YOUNGMAN (OC) 2Lt R.W. PERRY. 2Lt A.E. MASON. D Coy Lt C.T.A. WILKINSON (OC) 2Lt R.B. PATTINSON. and 630. Other ranks A. D. Derviche-Jones Lt Col	JWB

D. D. & L., London, E.C. (A8094) Wt. W1771/M2031 750,000 5/17 Sch. 52 Forms/C2118/14

— APPENDIX —

SPECIAL.

REPORT ON SPECIAL OPERATION
BY 8TH BATTALION LONDON REGIMENT,
on 25/7/18.

---

1. BARRAGE.

(i) The barrage came down punctually. Two batteries were slightly ahead of time.

(ii) Some Field Guns fired very short, shells falling in and behind our front line and inflicting casualties on our own men in "No Man's Land". The Northern Smoke barrage was poor and our Left flank suffered severely from Machine Gun fire, being in full view from across the ALBERT ROAD.

(iii) Apart from these points the barrage was very good and our men were able to get up under it to within 30 yards of the enemy front line trench.

(iv) The barrage inflicted casualties on the enemy in the front line principally in front of the HOOK. Little damage had been done to the enemy wire which did not however present much obstacle: no damage by Newton Mortars was observable.

2. ENEMY BARRAGE.

The first enemy shell fell at Zero + 4.27 but the barrage did not begin to thicken un til Zero + 6 mins. and was never very effective, our casualties mainly being caused by Machine Gun fire. Many shells fell in rear of EMMA TRENCH and did no damage.

3. ASSAULT.

Right Company. (Captain R.R.POULTON.)

(i) Parties for the front line trench, namely, No.3 and 4 platoons, got well under the barrage and had no difficulty in crossing the enemy wire and entering his trench N. of DERNANCOURT ROAD. Two

~~(ii)~~ Light machine guns here were captured and 3 prisoners taken and 4 enemy killed.

(ii) The parties detailed to assault the QUARRY did not achieve their object. They came under flanking machine gun fire and the O.C. No.1 Platoon (2/Lieut. E.J.ROFT.) was killed and the O.C. No.2 Platoon (2/Lieut. R.N.JOHNSON.) severely wounded in crossing "No Man's Land." These Platoons failed to get up to the barrage before it lifted and came up against frontal fire from two machine guns and a strong defence by bombs which prevented them crossing the enemy wire.

Centre Company. (Captain E.C.K.CLARKE.)

This Company lay well up under the barrage and rushed into the enemy trench without difficulty and captured or killed those that were in the trench which was in a poor state for defence: 13 enemy killed in the trench. They captured and brought back two light machine guns and 14 prisoners. They rendered assistance to Companies on their flanks. This Company had the easiest role but carried it out with great success.

Left Company. (Captain A.S.THOMAS, M.C.)

(i) The leading wave, No.8 Platoon, lay well up under the barrage and got into the enemy front line without difficulty. The enemy in the front line trench were killed. No prisoners were taken in this sector; at least 10 enemy left dead in front line.

(ii) The party assaulting the Right HOOK, No.5 Platoon, (2/Lt. W.B.SCARTH) reached their objective and had some tough hand to hand fighting and bombing. Two Mills bombs and a smoke bomb were thrown down a single entrance dugout at the apex of THE HOOK: enemy had been heard calling "Kamerad" from down the dugout: none came out afterwards and there was no time left to examine further. Other enemy took refuge in SINGLE TRENCH which was bombed out. Estimated enemy killed by this Platoon - 40. 2/Lieut. W.B.SCARTH was wounded in the foot but fought on with his Platoon and brought them out of action.

(iii) The party assaulting the Left HOOK, No.7 Platoon (2/Lieut. A.J.ALEWANDER) reached their objective but suffered very heavily from machine gun fire from the flank. 2/Lieut. A.J.ALEXANDER was killed and only 5 men of the Platoon returned unscathed. Six enemy left dead in KOOK LEFT.

This Company had the hardest fighting and accounted for most enemy.

4. RESERVE COMPANY, (Lieut. R.H.F.Newsome, M.C.) did less conspicuous but excellent work in providing relays of Stretcher Bearers, Control Posts, Escorts etc. essential to the success of the operation.

5. GENERAL.

Along the whole enemy front line as soon as the barrage lifted, the enemy left their trenches and tried to escape to the rear. Rapid fire was brought to bear upon them by our men from the enemy front line, and considerable casualties inflicted but it is difficult to estimate the exact number. Those surprised in the front line had evidently been asleep for they were in soft caps and without equipment.

No Trench Mortars were found. A light machine gun which could not be brought back was blown up with bombs.

No heavy machine guns were found. The rope taken over for dragging back heavy trophies was therefore not used, as the light machine guns were carried.

The demolition parties of R.E. had little opportunity of fulfilling their role but did damage in blowing in shelters and would have been most useful with better opportunities.

6. WITHDRAWAL was effected under flanking machine gun fire which caused casualties in "No Man's Land". On our withdrawing and our barrage slackening, the enemy pushed forward troops to reoccupy his trenches.

7. ENEMY LIGHTS.

A single green from the HOOK when our barrage opened.

Frm 10.15 onwards double orange lights (3 or 4 from time to time) were sent up from WINKLE SUPPORT.

A message rocket about 10.20 from behind the HOOK. This is conjectured to have brought down the barrage on "No Man's Land" which fell soon after.

A message rocket beyond our right and a split green light from behind the HOOK after our withdrawal began.

8. CASUALTIES.

	Killed.	Wounded.	Wounded at Duty	
Officers.	2	4	1	
Other Ranks.	10	50	6	55x

x unaccounted for of whom 9 believed Killed and 16 believed wounded and not missing

After the barrage on both sides had died down, parties went out under the Red Cross Flag into "No Man's Land" and brought in all wounded they could discover. The enemy did not molest these parties and was himself engaged on similar work.

7th London Regiment, 2/10th London Regiment and 1/132rd American Infantry Regiment rendered valuable assistance in bringing in and carrying back wounded.

9. ENEMY CASUALTIES.

Prisoners brought in - 17.
Estimated killed - 100.

10. TROPHIES brought in - 3 Light Machine Guns.

11. ENEMY DEFENCES. In general poor.

(i) WIRE. A single belt of concertina. Very weak in places and here and there cut by the barrage. No damage by our T.M's reported.

Some concertina wire in disused front trench in centre Company objective where trench was double.

(ii) TRENCHES. Front line trench throughout poor. Shallow (not more than 5 ft. deep) and narrow (about 3 ft. wide at top). Not properly made up for defence. Shelters dug into the bank forward. No dugouts proper in the front line.

Right and Left HOOK. C.T. from front line 6 ft. deep by 3 ft. wide (E.8.c.55.75. to E.14.a.7.0.).

Old dugout partly blown in at E.14.a.70.85.(a forret bomb was discharged here).

Dugout at apex of THE HOOK (E.14.a.9.9.) (bombed with Mills and "P" bombs).

These were the only dugouts proper found. The old part of THE HOOK trenches are shallow and not in good condition: small shelters dug off the trench.

(iii) M.G. EMPLACEMENTS. Only earth emplacements were found.

(iv) T.M's. No guns or emplacements were found.

(v) SHELTERS. Poor and little head cover.

12. NO MAN'S LAND. Condition good. A little old wire in places but low and no obstacle by daylight.

13. CONCLUSION.

With the exception of the QUARRY parties who were unfortunate in losing both their Officers, before they got across No Man's Land, all ranks carried out their tasks with dash and energy.

All 3 Company Commanders did well especially Capt. A.S. THOMAS, M.C. commanding Left Company. Of the subaltern Officers I specially mention 2/Lieuts. SCARTH, YOUNGMAN and HATCHER. I also bring to notice the fine work of the Medical Officer (Capt. BARWICK, R.A.M.C.) and his assistants in bringing wounded from "No Man's Land" by daylight. Recommendations will be sent in in due course.

Casualties were unfortunately heavy, but the Battalion is in great heart at the success of the operation.

(Signed) C.E. JOHNSON MC.

Lieut. Colonel.
Commanding 8th Bn. London Regiment.

26/7/18.

Appendix I

SPECIAL ORDER
by
Brigadier General C.G. HIGGINS. D.S.O.
Commanding 174th. Infantry Brigade.

On handing over the Command of the 174th. Inf. Brigade I wish to express to all ranks in it my great appreciation of the unvarying loyal support they have always given me, and of the splendid work they have always done.

For nearly fifteen months I have had the honour of commanding this Brigade and on every occasion the Brigade has been in action it has fought with great courage and skill and earned the praise of all the Higher Commanders.

At BULLECOURT, YPRES and VILLERS-BRETONNEUX - places historical now as having been at different times the storm centres of the battle front, the 174th. Inf. Brigade have particularly distinguished themselves. Their work on field defences has been of a high level and has been always carried out in the most cheerful spirit, even under the most adverse conditions. In this connection I would notice the fine work done in the depths of winter in the crater area of FLANDERS by this Brigade.

I am greatly indebted to the Commanding Officer and all ranks of the 511th. Field Coy. R.E. for the great help they have given me and for the devotion to duty they have shewn at all times when attached to my Brigade.

I am convinced that the Brigade, which has earned for itself such splendid traditions in its first year of war, will not look back and that my successor will have every reason to be as proud of the Brigade as I have been.

C.G. Higgins
Brigadier General.
Commanding 174th. Infantry Brigade.

July 1st. 1918.

SECRET. 8th Battalion London Regiment. Copy No....

OPERATION ORDER No.63

Ref. SENLIS 1/20,000. 30th June, 1918.

APPENDIX 2

~~XXXXXXXX~~ INFORMATION. 1. The Battalion will relieve the 3rd London Regiment in Left Brigade Support tomorrow, July 1st.

INTENTION. 2. (a) Companies will take up positions as reconnoitred to-day: viz:-

"A" Coy. relieve "B" Coy. 3rd London DODO TRENCH.
"B" " " "C" " " " HILL ROW.
"C" " " "A" " " " DARLING RESERVE LEFT.
"D" " " "D" " " " DARLING RESERVE RIGHT.

R.A.P. in DARLING RESERVE RIGHT.

(b) Brigade L.G. A.A. Post will be relieved by 1 L.G. Crew from "D" Coy., who will proceed with Signallers at 2 pm. Report to Sigs. Officer at Battn.H.Q.

(c) Observers Section will relieve Brigade O.P. and Battn.O.P. in the afternoon at 4 pm. Brigade H.Q. D.4.c.2.3. Battn.H.Q. D.5.d.0.1.

INSTRUCTIONS. 3.(a) Coys. will move off from present positions as follows :-

H.Q. 9.25 pm.
"B" Company 9.30 pm.
"A" " 9.30 pm.
"D" " 9.35 pm.
"C" " 9.35 pm.

200 yards distance between platoons to be maintained.

(b) Route. AMIENS - ALBERT Main Road.

(c) Guides. 1 guide per platoon, 1 per Coy.H.Q. and 1 for Battn.H.Q. will be met on ALBERT Main Road where DARLING TRENCH meets road in D.17.b. at 10.30 pm.

(d) Transport. 1 Limber will report to each Coy. and 1 Limber to Battn.H.Q., and M.O. Cart to R.A.P. not later than 8.30 pm to convey L.G's and drums, three dixies per Coy. and H.Q.,Officers' Mess Stores and M.O. Stores to the new line.

(e) Advance party. An advance party of Sgt GURNEY for H.Q. and 1 Officer and 1 N.C.O. per platoon will assemble at Battn.H.Q. at 10.30 am ready to move to take over new sector.

(f) Rations. Rations for 2nd July will proceed along with Coys. to new line: arrangements by Transport Officer. Coys. will detail an unloading party, who will unload limbers immediately on arrival.

(g) Valises, spare mess stores, etc. Officers' valises, spare mess stores and men's greatcoats and haversacks will be dumped before 10.30 am in the morning as follows :-

H.Q. & "C" Coy. at Battn.H.Q.
"A" & "D" Coys. at one Dump mutually arranged by O.C. "A" and "D" Coys.
"B" Coy. at "B" Coy. Dump.

(h) Cookers and Water Carts will be moved to Transport Lines: arrangements by T.O.

(j) Officers' Chargers. Coy. Officers' Chargers to be at respective Coy.H.Q. at 9.15 pm.

(k) Water. Thirty cans of water will be supplied to each Coy., and 1 Water Cart for H.Q., after arrival at new area tomorrow night. Arrangements by T.O. All empty tins to be returned immediately.

(3) C.Q.M.S's. "B" and "D" Coys. will each have their C.Q.M.S's with the Coy. in the line.
C.Q.M.S's of "A" and "C" Coys. and Storemen of "B" and "D" Coys. will proceed to Details.

REPORTS. (4) Completion of Relief to be reported to Battn.H.Q. by Code Word "COMPLETION."

ACKNOWLEDGE.

J.M.BARRATT,
2/Lieut. & A/Adjutant.

Issued at 11.45 pm.

Copies to :-
1. File.
2. War Diary.
3. C.O.
4. 2nd in Command.
5. Adjutant.
6. O.C. "A" Coy.
7. O.C. "B" "
8. O.C. "C" "
9. O.C. "D" Coy.
10. Sigs. Officer (for H.Q.)
11. T.O.
12. Q.M.
13. O.C. 2nd London Regt.
14. R.S.M.

Appendix 3

SECRET. **8th Battalion London Regiment.** Copy No. 2....

OPERATION ORDER No.64.

Reference SENLIS. 5th July, 1918.

INFORMATION. 1. The Battalion will relieve the 7th Battalion London Regiment in the Left Battalion, Left Brigade, Sector to-day.

INTENTION. 2. (a) The Battalion will relieve as per table below :-

"C" Coy. 8th	will relieve	"B" Coy.7th	-	Right Front Coy.
"D" " "	" "	"C" " "		Left Front Coy.
"B" " "	" "	"A" " "		Support Coy.
"A" " "	" "	"D" " "		Reserve "

(b) The 7th Battalion after relief will occupy our present positions and will take over from Companies as table below :-

"D" Coy. 7th Battn.	take over from	"A" Coy. 8th.
"A" " "	" " "	"B" " "
"C" " "	" " "	"D" " "
"B" " "	" " "	"C" " "

INSTRUCTION. 3. (a) Guides. (I) Guides will be provided, 1 per Platoon, and 1 per Coy.H.Q. as follows :-

Guides for "A"	at "A" Coy.H.Q.	10. 0 pm.
" " "B"	" 7th Bn.H.Q.	10.15 pm.
" " "C"	" " "	10.30 pm.
" " "D"	" " "	10.30 pm.

(II) No guides will be found by us for 7th Battalion.

(b) Companies will move off as per "Guide" table, distance of not less than 200 yards being maintained between platoons.

(c) Rations. I. Rations for the 6th inst will be delivered to new Sector, cooked, as follows :-

"B", "C", and "D" Coys. at junction of DIGGER and PIONEER TRENCH at E.1.d.8.2.

"A" Coy. at junction of DIRTY TRENCH and SUNKEN ROAD at D.6.d.4.2.

Battn.H.Q., to Battn.H.Q. at D.7.d.75.85.

II. All dry rations delivered to Dump with "A" Company rations.

III. Tea will be made for Companies and Battn.H.Q. as follows :-

"C" and "D" Coys. at Cookhouse E.7.a.5.5.
"A", "B" and H.Q. " " D.6.d.5.1.

"A" Company will supply parties to carry tea to front line Companies; and O.C. "A" Coy. will detail an Officer who will be responsible that these parties are properly organised and carry out their work properly.

IV. Companies will send to Details tonight 2 cooks each and 1 from Battn.H.Q.

V. 2 Dixies per Company will be dumped on track at "C" Company H.Q. They will be picked up by H.Q. limber on return journey, and conveyed to details.

VI. Coys. will convey their own Mess Stores. One limber (empty) to report to Battn.H.Q. at 10 pm to convey bombs and trench stores to new Battn.H.Q.

(d) Water. 2 Water Carts will be sent up each night (after tonight) and will be emptied into dixies at Cookhouse in SUNKEN ROAD ("A" Coy.)

Petrol Cans. 17 per Coy. to be handed over to 7th Battn., remainder to be dumped at "C" Coy.H.Q. to be collected and taken to Transport Lines.

(e)

(e) Receipts for stores handed over to and taken over from 7th Battalion will be rendered in <u>duplicate</u> to Battn.H.Q. by 12 noon, 6th instant.

REPORTS. 4. Completion of relief will be notified by wiring to Battn.H.Q. Surname of Company Commander: confirmed by runner.

J.M. BARRATT,
2/Lieut. & A/Adjutant.

Issued at 7.30 am.

Copies to :-

1. File.
2. War Diary.
3. C.O.
4. 2nd in Command.
5. O.C. "A" Coy.
6. O.C. "B" "
7. O.C. "C" "
8. O.C. "D" "
9. Sigs. Officer (for H.Q.)
10. Q.M.
11. T.O.
12. O.C. 7th Battn. London Regiment.
13. R.S.M.
14. Spare.

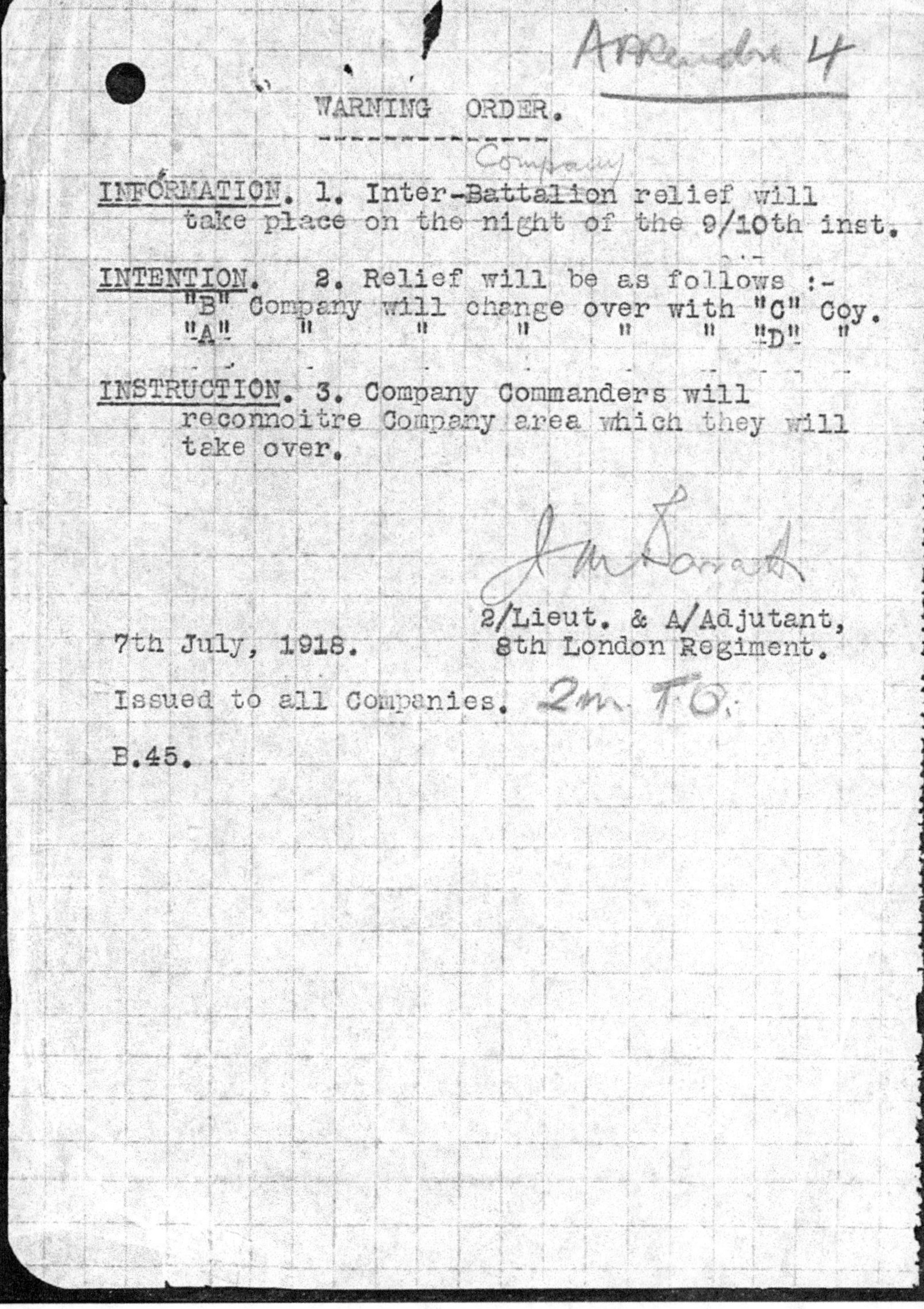

Appendix 4

WARNING ORDER.

INFORMATION. 1. Inter-~~Battalion~~ Company relief will take place on the night of the 9/10th inst.

INTENTION. 2. Relief will be as follows :-
"B" Company will change over with "C" Coy.
"A" " " " " " "D" "

INSTRUCTION. 3. Company Commanders will reconnoitre Company area which they will take over.

J. M. Farrah [signature]
2/Lieut. & A/Adjutant,
8th London Regiment.

7th July, 1918.

Issued to all Companies. 2m. T.O.

B.45.

Appen…

8th Battalion London Regiment.

After Order for Inter-company relief.

9th July, 1918.

TRENCH STORES.

Receipts for trench stores handed over and taken over will be in Battn. Orderly Room by 12 noon tomorrow.

J.M. BARRATT,
2/Lieut. & A/Adjutant.

Issued at 4.5 pm.

Copies to all recipients of Operation Orders.

SECRET. 8th Battalion London Regiment. App 4 Copy No....

Operation Orders for Inter-Company Relief.

9th July, 1918.

I. Following the Warning Order No.B.45, issued 7th inst., inter-Company reliefs tonight will take place as per time table below:-

(a) i. 5 pm - 6 pm.
Two (or three) platoons of "B" Company will relieve 2 (or 3) platoons of "C" Company (as decided by Company Commanders.)
ii. Only one front line platoon to be relieved at this hour, and a short period must elapse between the relieving platoon going in and the relieved platoon coming out.

(b) 6 pm - 9 pm.
Lewis Gun Sections of "A" Company will relieve L.G. Sections of "D" Company.
For the purpose of this relief, Sections to be numbered 1 to 7 in the order in which they are going to move, and to ensure a minimum of movement in DIGGERS AVENUE, the following table must be adhered to :-
No.1 of "A" Coy. moves at 6 pm.
No.2 " " " " " 6.30 pm.
and sections following every half-hour.
No.1 of "D" Coy. to move down DIGGERS AVENUE, immediately after, but not before, No. 2 of "A" Coy. has passed junction of DIGGERS AVENUE and PIONEER TRENCH.
No. 2 of "D" Coy. after No.3 of "A" Coy., and so on.

(c) 9 pm.
Remainder of "B" Company move forward to relieve remainder of "C" Company.
Complete by 10 pm.

(d) 10 pm.
Remainder of "A" Company move forward to relieve remainder of "D" Company.

(e) All reliefs complete by 10.45 pm.

(f) Relief complete will be wired to Bn.H.Q. code word name of Company Commander, stating time.

(g) i. All platoons relieving by daylight will move in small parties, with interval between each party.
ii. It must be impressed upon all men how important it is that they should move so as not to be visible to the enemy.
iii. Lewis Guns must be carried in such a way that no part of them can be seen above the parapet.
iv. No movement over the top until after 10 pm.

J.M. BARRATT,
2/Lieut. & A/Adjutant.

Issued at 12.20 pm.

Copies to All Companies.
War Diary.
File.

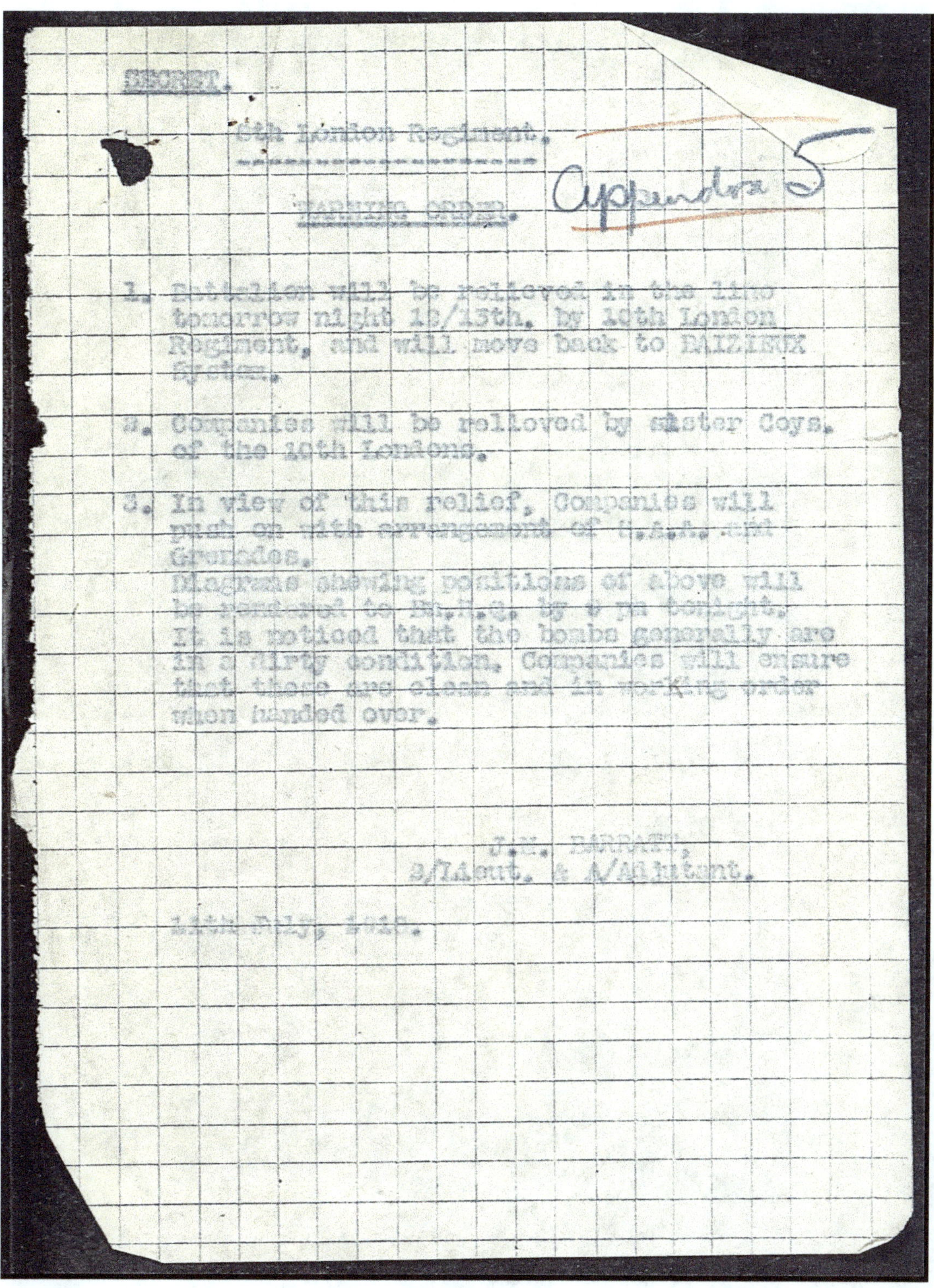

SECRET.

8th London Regiment.

WARNING ORDER.

Appendix 5

1. Battalion will be relieved in the line tomorrow night 12/13th. by 10th London Regiment, and will move back to BAIZIEUX System.

2. Companies will be relieved by sister Coys. of the 10th Londons.

3. In view of this relief, Companies will push on with arrangement of S.A.A. and Grenades.
Diagrams shewing positions of above will be rendered to Bn.H.Q. by 6 pm tonight.
It is noticed that the bombs generally are in a dirty condition. Companies will ensure that these are clean and in working order when handed over.

J.N. BARRATT,
2/Lieut. & A/Adjutant.

11th July, 1918.

Appendix 6

SECRET. Copy No: 1

8th Bn., The London Regiment.

ORDER No: 67. d/18/7/16.

---

1. INTENTION. 8th Bn., The London Regiment will relieve 2/4th Bn., London Regiment in Reserve Right Sub-sector tonight 18/19th July as follows.-

A. Co. 8th Ldn.	- C. Co. 2/4th Ldn	RIGHT.
B. Co. " "	- D. Co. " "	Rt. CENTRE.
C. Co. " "	- B. Co. " "	LEFT CENTRE.
D. Co. " "	- A. Co. " "	LEFT.

2. INSTRUCTIONS.
   (1) ORDER. A. D. B.C. H.Q.
   (2) STARTING POINT. - Junction of track and road D.20.c.4.7.
   (3) TIME. 9.30. p.m.
   (4) DISTANCE BETWEEN PLATOONS. 100 yds.
   (5) GUIDES. 1 per platoon and 1 for H.Q. at 2nd barrier D.17.a.2.2. at 10.p.m.
   (6) TRANSPORT.
      (a) 1 limber per company and 2 for H.Q. will report at respective H.Qrs to convey L.G.s. & Stores to the line. They will move with their companies.
      (b) Watercart will be at new Bn. H.Q at 11:30, p.m. and will remain there.
      (c) Company Officers chargers will be at respective H.Qrs. at 9. p.m.
   (7) TRENCH STORES. Receipts will be sent in duplicate to Bn. H.Q. by 12 noon tomorrow the 19th inst.
   (8) CODE-WORD. for relief complete "67 acknowledged".

3. REPORTS. Bn. H.Q. D.17.b.0. 2.

Lieutenant & A/Adjutant.
8th Bn., The London Regiment.

Issued at 1:23. p.m.

Copy No. 1. War Diary.
2. File.
3. 2/4th.
4. C.O.
5. 2nd in command.
6. O.C. A.
7. B.
8. C.
9. D.
10. H.Q.
11. Transport.Officer.

Appendix 7

SECRET. 8TH BATTALION LONDON REGIMENT. Copy.........

ORDER NO. 67. 28/7/18.

Ref. SENLIS SHEET.

1. INTENTION. Battalion will move to-day to ST. LAURENCE FARM and will be disposed as follows:-
H.Q., B. C. and D. Coys in vicinity of C.18.b.2.2
A. Coy at D.19.a.4.0.2

2. INSTRUCTIONS. (1) Order of march - H.Q. A.B.C.D. Coys. 200 yards between platoons.
(2) Starting point. Cross track near Orderly Room.
(3) Time. 2.0 p.m.
(4) Route. Road through C.21. a and b and C.22.a. thence by track through C.22.b. to the Camp.
(5) Officers kits will be dumped at Bn. H.Q. by 11.30 a.m.
(6) Limbers for Lewis Guns, Stores etc. will report to each Company and H.Q. by 1.0 p.m.
(7) Cookers will be ready for removal at 1.30 pm.

3. REPORTS. To head of column.

Lieut. & A/Adjutant.
8th Bn. London Regiment.

Issued at..11 am..

Copy No. 1. War Diary.
2. File.
3. C.O.
4. Sec. in Command.
5. A. Company.
6. B. Company.
7. C. Company.
8. D. Company.
9. M.O.
10. T.O.
11. Q.M.
12. Spare.

Appendix 8

SECRET. 8th BATTALION, LONDON REGIMENT. Copy No...2...

ORDER NO. 62.

Ref. SENLIS SHEET. 30th July 1918.

1. INFORMATION. 12th London Regiment will relieve 8th London Regt. this evening.

2. INTENTION. 8th London Regiment will relieve 9th London Regt. as follows:-

8th London.	9th London.	Position.
C. Coy.	A. Coy.	LAVIEVILLE SYSTEM RIGHT. D.16.b.
D. "	B. "	LAVIEVILLE SYSTEM LEFT. D.10.d. & D11
B. "	C. "	BAIZIEUX VILLAGE.
A. "	D. "	-ditto-
H.Q.	H.Q.	-ditto-

3. INSTRUCTIONS. (a) Companies will move when relieved, except that there will be no movement EAST of a line N. & S. through ~~BAIZIEUX~~ BRESLE before 9.30 p.m.

(b) Transport. Four Limbers will report to C. & D. Coys at 8.15 p.m. for conveyance of Lewis Guns, Officers valises, Mess Stores and Dixies. G.S. Wagon will be utilised to take stores ~~xxxxxxxxx~~ of H.Q., A. & B. Coys to BAIZIEUX. Lewis Guns of A. & B. Coys will be carried.

M.O. Cart will report AID POST at 6.0 p.m.

(c) Greatcoats and Haversacks of C. & D. Coys will be dumped ready for removal by 3.0 p.m. A G.S. Wagon will collect and dump them at BAIZIEUX.

H.Q., A. & B. will retain their greatcoats and haversacks.

(d) Cooking. C. & D. Coys will take Dixies with them. 30 cans of water will be sent to each Coy nightly. Cookers of A. & B. Coys and 1 watercart remain in BAIZIEUX. To-nights rations for these Coys and H.Q. will be delivered to BAIZIEUX.

(e) Tentage and Trench stores will be carefully handed and taken over. Duplicate copies of receipts will be sent to Bn. H.Q. by 12 noon 31st inst.

(f) Completion of relief will be notified by Code Word "NOT SO BAD."

4. REPORTS. To Battalion H.Q., BAIZIEUX, C.6.c.45.38.

[signature]
Lieut. & Adjutant.
8th Battalion London Regiment.

Issued at..11.25 am

Distribution.

1. File.
2. War Diary.
3. C.O.
4. Sec. in Command.
5. O.C. A. Coy.
6. O.C. B. "
7. O.C. C.Coy.
8. O.C. D.Coy.
9. Headquarters.
10. T.O.
11. Q.M.
12. Spare.

SECRET.

Copy No. 2....

War Diary

8th Battalion London Regiment.

OPERATION ORDER No.65.

Reference SENLIS. 12th July, 1918.

INFORMATION. 1. The Battalion will be relieved in the line tomorrow night, 12/13th, by 10th Battalion London Regiment.
Companies will be relieved by sister companies of 10th Londons.
Order of relief - H.Q., "B", "A", "C", "D" Coys.

INTENTION. 2. (a) On relief the Battalion moves back and takes up position in BAIZIEUX SYSTEM. Companies same position as before.
(b) Route. H.Q. and "C" Coy. via cross country tracks.
"A", "B" and "D" Coys. via ALBERT-AMIENS Main Road.
200 yards distance between platoons to be maintained.

INSTRUCTION. 3. (a) Guides. Guides will be provided by us as follows :-
Battn.H.Q. 1, each Coy.H.Q. 1, each Platoon 1, and will meet incoming Battalion :-
H.Q.) On Main ALBERT-AMIENS Road, just below
"B" Coy.) Battn.H.Q. at 10.30 pm.
"A" Coy.)

"C" Coy.) At Cross Roads, D.5.d.4.4. near Support
"D" Coy.) Battn.H.Q. at 10 pm.
(b) An advance party of 1 N.C.O. from Battn.H.Q. and C.Q.M.S. or Storeman from each Company will report to Captain PRIESTLEY at 2 pm tomorrow at Battn.H.Q. C.18.d.

REPORTS. 4. (a) Relief complete to be reported to Battn.H.Q. by wiring surname of Company Commander.
(b) Receipts for Trench Stores, handed over and taken over, will be rendered in duplicate to Battn.H.Q. by 12 noon 13th inst.

TRANSPORT and Q.M. ARRANGEMENTS. 5.
(a) Limbers. H.Q. and M.O. 1 Limber at Battn.H.Q. at 10.45 pm.
"A" Coy.) One limber per Coy. to be at
"B" Coy.) junction of DARLING RESERVE
"D" Coy.) TRENCH and ALBERT Main Road
) D.17.b.40.75. (12.30 am).
"C" Coy. One Limber at D.5.d.4.4.(12.30 am).
Cookhouses. One Limber to collect Dixies and empty cans 10.45 pm.
(b) Chargers. C.O., 2nd in Command, Adjutant at D.17.b.40.75 at 1.0 am.
"A", "B" and "D" Coys. at D.17.b.40.75 at 12.30 am.
"C" Coy. at D.5.d.4.4. Cross Roads at 12.30 am.
(c) Kits. Officers' Valises and mens' kits to be at new area.
(d) Cookers, and spare mess stores to be at new area.

J.M.BARRATT,
2/Lieut. & A/Adjutant.

Issued at 4.0 am.

Copies to :-
1. File.
2. War Diary.
3. C.O.
4. 2/Command.
5. Capt.H.W.PRIESTLEY.
6 - 9. O.C. Companies.
10. Headquarters.
11. T.O.
12. Q.M.
13. O.C. 10th Londons.
14. Spare.

SECRET. **8TH BATTALION LONDON REGIMENT.** Copy..........

OPERATION ORDER NO. [illegible].

[illegible] SHEET [illegible] 1/20,000 and SKETCH MAP.

INTENTION. 1. The Battalion will raid enemy trenches from N.13.b.90.00 to N.8.c.80.35 at a day and hour to be notified later.

INSTRUCTIONS. 2. (i) COMPANY DISPOSITIONS AND OBJECTIVES.

Right. "A" Company.

1st Objective.

[illegible] TRENCH from N.13.b.90.00 to N.14.a.05.40

No.4 Platoon – leading wave.

No.3 Platoon (Less 1 Section) 2nd wave.

1 Section No.3 Platoon act as covering party in "No Man's Land."

Right Section of No.4 Platoon double block in [illegible] TRENCH 50 yards S.W. of DERHANCOURT ROAD.

2nd Objective.

QUARRY at N.14.c.35.35.

No.1 Platoon to assault.

No.2 Platoon (Less L.G. Section) in SUPPORT.

L.G. Section of No.2 Platoon (2 guns) protect flanks.

Centre. "C" Company.

Objective.

[illegible] TRENCH from N.14.a.05.40 to N.8.c.45.00. and BLIND ALLEY.

Three Platoons.

No. 12 Platoon – leading wave.

No. 11 and 9 Platoons – 2nd wave.

1 Section No 12 Platoon – covering party in "No Man's Land."

Left. "B" Company.

1st Objective.

(Leading Wave)

[illegible] TRENCH from N.8.c.45.00. to N.8.c.80.35.

No. 6 Platoon.

1 Section No.6 Platoon form double block [illegible] TRENCH 50 yards North of HOOK LEFT.

2nd Objective.

(2nd Wave)

(i) HOOK RIGHT and SINGLE TRENCH.

No. 8 Platoon.

(ii) HOOK LEFT.

No. 7 Platoon.

1 Section No.6. Platoon in Support.

L.G. Section (2 guns) No.6 Platoon form protective flank on left in "No Man's Land.

1 Section No. 10 Platoon form covering party.

RESERVE COMPANY. "D" Company.

Provide Control Posts – checking posts – prisoners escorts and guards.

(ii) ASSEMBLY POSITIONS. In [illegible] TRENCH.

"A" Company 100 yards South of DERHANCOURT ROAD in N.13.b. to head of [illegible] ALLEY.

"C" Company from [illegible] ALLEY to ACK STREET.

"B" Company from ACK STREET to L.G. Post in sap at N.8.c.90.50.

(iii) FORMATIONS.
Each assaulting Company in two waves, as follows.-

Leading wave. 1 Platoon extended across Company front.
2nd Wave. Sections in single file.
25 yards between waves. One section per platoon will be organised as a bombing section and no company will carry more than 2 Lewis Guns to the enemy trenches.
A squad in the platoons assaulting the QUARRY and [illegible] will be equipped as Rifle Grenadiers.

(iv) DEMOLITION PARTIES.
4 R.E.s for demolition purposes will go with each assaulting Company. Two with each of the following Platoons.- 1, 3, [illegible], 11, 6, 7.

(v) TIME.
Zero day and hour will be notified later.
Duration of operation - 30 minutes from Zero.
Assaulting Companies will be in their assembly positions at Zero minus 15 minutes and will move forward under the barrage at Zero plus 15 seconds.
"D" Company will be at their posts by Zero minus 15 minutes.

(vi) BARRAGE. As per Barrage table.

(vii) SILENCE.
All ranks will be warned that absence of noise and avoidance of unnecessary movement in assembling and whilst waiting in assembly positions are essential to the success of the operation.

(viii) COMMUNICATION.
(a) Across "No Man's Land" through covering parties.
(b) By Runners from head of [illegible] ALLEY and ACK STREET.
(c) By wire from Advanced Battalion H.Q. to Brigade H.Q.

(ix) SYNCHRONIZATION OF WATCHES.
Each Company will send an Officer to Advanced Battalion H.Q. at 3 hours before Zero and again at 1 hour before Zero to synchronise watches.

(xi) ~~(x)~~ RECALL SIGNAL. will be a red rocket breaking into three.

(x) ~~(xi)~~ ADVANCED BATTALION H.Q. will be established at Company H.Q. at junction of [illegible] ALLEY and [illegible] TRENCH.

(xii) WITHDRAWAL.
On the recall signal being fired and at Zero plus 30 minutes in any case, assaulting platoons will withdraw independently by sections bringing with them all casualties, prisoners and trophies not already evacuated.
Parties in enemy front line trench will not withdraw until ground in front of them is clear of our own troops.

Covering parties will not withdraw until the assaulting Platoons have reached our own front line.
Companies will rendezvous at D.18.d.1.8.

(xiii) ADMINISTRATIVE INSTRUCTIONS will be issued later.

REPORTS. 3. To Advanced Battalion H.Q.

Lieutenant & A/Adjutant.
6th Bn., The London Regiment.

Issued at ....

Copies.
1. War Diary.
2. File.
3. C.O.
4. 2nd in command.
5. M.O.
6. A. Company.
7. B. Company.
8. C. Company.
9. D. Company.
10. Q.M.
11. I.O.
12. S.O.
13. R.E.
14. R.A.
15. 174th Inf. Bde.
16. Spare.
17. Spare.

List of Code Names Used

GEORGE - OBJECTIVE. gained

HENRY - PRISONERS. taken.

WILLIAM - ALL CLEAR.

MATTHEW - our CASUALTIES HEAVY.

MARK - our CASUALTIES SLIGHT.

LUKE - FIRST OBJECTIVE. (Enemy front trench)

JOHN - SECOND OBJECTIVE. (Quarry. R and L. Hook)

War Diary.

SECRET.

ADMINISTRATIVE INSTRUCTIONS
in Connaction with
OPERATION ORDER No:66.

%%%

1. DRESS and EQUIPMENT.

EACH MAN.

Belt, Braces and pouches.
S.B.R., Waterbottle (full) on left, haversack on right side.
120 ~~100~~ rounds S.A.A.
Entrenching tool slung in front.
Mess tin strapped on back of belt by a valise strap.
Two No:23 Grenades in haversack.
One sandbag for the collection of trophies.
Breakfast ration in mess tin and emergency ration of one tin of Bully Beef and 2 biscuits in haversack.
All identification marks to be removed.
Special numbered identity discs will be issued.
All ranks engaged will wear a band of left arm above the elbow.-

A. Company YELLOW.
C. Company RED.
B. Company GREEN.

EACH LEWIS GUN SECTION.
8 Magazines - Flanking Lewis Guns 12 magazines.

EACH MAN BOMBING SECTION.
6 No:23 Grenades in haversack.

EACH MAN RIFLE GRENADE SQUAD.
Extra haversach with 6 No:23 and 6 No:24 Grenades and Grenade Cup.

BLOCKING SECTION will be equipped as Bombing Sections and will carry also 6 sandbags per man and 2 shovels and 1 pick.

EACH SECTION OF LEADING WAVE. carry ~~XXXXXX~~ 4 wire cutters and 2 mats.

EACH ASSAULTING PLATOON will carry 10 "P" Bombs and 2 electric torches.

EACH COMPANY will carry four 12 ft. lengths of rope.

ALL RANKS will leave Camp for the operation equipped ready for the raid.

SURPLUS EQUIPMENT will be stored in Company lines under Guard.

2. PAPERS. No papers or maps of any kind will be carried during the operation.
These will be collected by Companies by 6.0 p.m. on the afternoon preceding Zero, and a certificate from Company Commanders that all have been collected will be sent to Bn. H.Q. by 7.0 p.m.
They will be left with the surplus equipment in Camp.

3. OFFICERS will wear Soldiers Service Dress with badges of their rank on shoulder straps. Not more than 3 Officers per Company will take part in the operation.

4. NOMINAL ROLLS of all Officers and Other Ranks participating will be prepared, and copies will be furnished to parties who check in at the Rendezvous after the operation.

5. CHECKING-IN PARTIES will be formed from Company Signallers who will check casualties as they pass, and Platoons as they come in.
Companies will report to Bn. H.Q. as early as possible the names of any men unaccounted for.

6. MARKING of Assembly positions and gaps in wire will be carried out by the Bn. Intelligence Officer.

7. GAPS in our own wire, 6 per Company, will be cut by Bn. Observers under direction of Bn. Intelligence Officer, in consultation with Company Commanders concerned, the night before Zero.

8. HOT TEA will be supplied for breakfast at 5 hours before Zero and again at 1 hour before Zero.
The 2nd in Command will arrange for the establishment of a Cookhouse near the Rendezvous and for the organisation of carrying parties from Reserve Company.

9. CASUALTIES. (i) R.A.P. at junction of EMMA TRENCH and NINE ELMS TR.
(ii) A.D.S. at D.18.d.0.0.
(iii) EVACUATION ROUTES.
(a) Stretcher Route. Along "No Man's Land" to head of ENERGY ALLEY - line of ENERGY ALLEY and track in rear of EMMA TRENCH to R.A.P.
(b) Walking Wounded. As for Stretchers and also line of ACK STREET to EMMA TRENCH and along rear of EMMA TRENCH to R.A.P.
(iv) BRIDGES. Duckboard bridges will be placed across ETHEL TRENCH and EMMA TRENCH just N. of ENERGY ALLEY to facilitate passage of stretchers.

10. STRETCHER PARTIES.
(a) Each assaulting ~~party~~ Company will carry 4 stretchers with them.
(b) Reserve Company will furnish 32 extra S.B's as follows:-
8 men and 4 stretchers to go with No.2 Platoon.
8 men and 8 stretchers in ETHEL TRENCH near ENERGY ALLEY - to act as a relay post from front line. This party will place the bridge over ETHEL TRENCH in position at Zero plus 1 minute.
16 men and 12 stretchers at R.A.P. 2 men from this party will place the bridge over EMMA TRENCH in position at Zero plus 1 minute.
(c) 4 stretchers will be deposited with control post at head of ACK STREET.
(d) 8 men with 4 stretchers will be supplied by Battalion Pioneers as a reserve in case of emergency. They will be stationed in NINE ELMS TRENCH near R.A.P. and will be at the disposal of the M.O.
(e) D. Company and Battalion Pioneers will draw their Stretchers and duckboards from the Rendezvous.

11. BUGLERS. One bugler will go with each assaulting Company and 1 at Bn. H.Q.
They will sound the Battalion call followed by 3 "G" on the recall signal being fired or in any event at Zero plus 30 minutes. This will only be done under orders of an Officer.

12. PRISONERS. will be escorted across "No Man's Land" and handed over to collecting party at E.13.b.2.8. furnished by D. Company who will escort them to the collecting station near the Battalion Rendezvous D.18.d.1.8.
Escorting parties will be kept to a minimum.
Slightly wounded men can be employed on this duty.
The O.C. Battalion H.Q. Personnel will supply a guard of 1 Officer and 12 Other Ranks over the collecting station.

13. RESERVE COMPANY will supply the following parties:-
(a) 6 CONTROL POSTS of 2 Other Ranks at
Head of ENERGY ALLEY.
Head of ACK STREET.
Junction of ACK STREET with EMMA TRENCH.
Junction of EMMA TRENCH and NINE ELMS.
Junction of ENERGY ALLEY and DOLLY TRENCH.
Junction of ENERGY ALLEY and EMMA TRENCH.
to control traffic, to direct casualties and escorts and withdrawing parties.
(b) One party of 1 Officer and 12 Other Ranks at EMMA TRENCH about E.13.b.2.8. to take over and escort prisoners back to the collecting station.
(c) 4 N.C.O's. and 24 Other Ranks as carrying parties from Cookhouse.
(d) 32 extra S.B's. as detailed under para. 11.

14. TROPHIES will be collected at a trophy post to be established near Battalion Rendezvous. H.Q. Signallers will provide 1 N.C.O. and 2 men in charge of this post.

15. BATTALION RENDEZVOUS at D.18.d.1.8. will be provided with notice boards indicating the re-assembly position of each ~~boards~~ Company, the trophy post and collecting station for prisoners.
Major VENNING will be in charge of all arrangements at Rendezvous and will be responsible for providing all notice boards in trenches for the operation.

16. EMBUSSING. The Battalion will be conveyed in busses from D.20.c.4.7. to D.17.b.5.8. on the night before Zero.
Capt. PRIESTLEY, M.C. will be in charge of embussing arrangements.
Embussing orders will be issued separately.

17. GUIDES. The S.O. will arrange for guides to be stationed at points between DEBUSSING POINT and junction of EMMA TRENCH and NINE ELMS TRENCH to direct Platoons to the trenches.

L.E.B.JACOB.
Lieut. & A/Adjutant.

EMBUSSING ARRANGEMENTS.
8th Bn., The London Regiment. 4/24.7.18.

1. The Battalion will embus at ROUND WOOD, tail of column at G.30.d.8.3. facing E.

2. The busses will be divided into five groups.

Group 1. leave 10. 0.P.M.
(5 busses) 1st bus. "D" Co. Control Posts. Gap cutting party under I.O.

Other buses. "B" Company.

Group 2. – 10.30.P.M. "C" Company.
(5 busses)

Group 3. – 11. 0.P.M. "A" Company.
(5 busses)

Group 4. – 11.30.P.M. "D" Company.
(5 busses)

Group 5. – 12 MN H.Q.
(3 busses)

Companies will tell off the men to their busses before embussing.
Companies will embus in the order they are going into the trenches.

3. Sec. Lieut. J.H. BARRATT will be embussing officer.
Sec. Lieut. A.E. MASON will be debussing Officer.
An officer of 6th London will control busses at G.30.d.6.7.

4. Each group will return immediately it has debussed. unloaded

5. Route from debussing point.-
Main Road to D.15.c.8.1. thence by track to junction of NINE ELMS TR and EMMA TR - EMMA TRENCH - EMERY ALLEY.
The route ACK ST - EMMA TR & SHRINE TR. will be reserved for out-going troops of 175th Inf. Bde.
Standing Guides will be stationed on road D.15.c.8.1.
Junction of Tracks at D.15.b 31
do. D.15 b 88
Junction of NINE ELMS TR. and EMMA TR.

Lt. and A/Adjt.,
8th.London Regt.

Copies to:-
O.C.Companies.and H.Q.
Embussing Officer.
Debussing Officer.
File.

G.O.C.

ADMINISTRATIVE ARRANGEMENTS
Issued with Brigade Provisional Defence Scheme.BM/7/141

1. LOCATIONS.
Transport and Detail Camp at MOISLAINS.

511 Coy. A.S.C. - VILLE WOOD.

Supply refilling point - D.15.b.0.4.

2. AMMUNITION.

(a) In Line:-
S.A.A. 170 rounds per man
Lewis Gun Magazines 24 per gun.
Bombs 1 No. 23 Rifle-Grenade per man.

(b) Dumps -
Divisional Grenade Dump - D.15.a. central.
Bde Dump at E.24.a.5.7., contains
S.A.A. - 30,000 rounds
No.23 R.G. - 400

(c) Bde. Flying Column under command of B.T.O. at LIERAMONT.

3. TOOLS.
Units mobile reserve with Flying Column.

4. WATER.

(a) Drinking.
The following water points are available for filling petrol tins and water bottles in the forward area.
*E.[illegible].d.7.6.
*E.27.b.9.1.
*E.30.c.0.9.
F.13.a.9.9.
F.20.a.3.5.
Water cart refilling points *.

(b) Horse watering points.
Forward - E.[illegible].d.7.3. TROUGHS.
Rear - MOISLAINS C.18.d.55 TOUGHS
- LIERAMONT E.13.a.4.4 "
E.14.b.9.4. "

Water for troops in the line is delivered with rations in patol tins.

5. RATIONS.
Rations are delivered to Units Q.M.Stores by A.S.C., H.T. Thence by 1st Line Transport to Cookers for Left and Centre battalions at E.23.b. & d., for Right Battn at L.2.b.4.5.
From this point by limber to Battn. H.Q.

6. TRANSPORT ROUTES.
Left and Centre Battalions:-
From railway crossing E.23.d. to Battn H.Q. via, Ste. EMILE - F.19.b.6.9., F.20.a.3.5. - E.20.c. F.21.c.3.10. RONSSOY LEMPIRE Road.
Right Battalion:-
From railway crossing E.23.d. E.29.b.2.3. - E.30.c. & d. F.25.c. - L.1.b. to Cookers L.2.b.2.3.
Thence F.26.d., F.27.c.6.9., via track through F.27 cent and to Battalion H.Q.

- 2 -

Transport may use these routes to Bn. H.Q. by day.

7. SALVAGE.

To Brigade Dump - MOISLAINS by returning ration limbers

8. MEDICAL.

A.A.P. at Battalion H.Q.

Bearer Squads - 3 Bearer Squads R.A.M.C. personnel are attached to each Battalion.

CAR POST - F.21.a.8.6. for Left and Centre Battalions
For Right Battalion Cross roads F.31.d.7.2.
Thence to A.D.S. Ste. EMILIE.

9. P.O.W.

Divisional Cage - E.8.a.5.7.

10. BATTLE SURPLUS.

Div. Reception Camp - MARICOURT A.22.b.6.3.

H. J. [illegible]
Lieut.
Actg. Staff Captain.
174th. Infantry Brigade.

23.9.18.

PROVISIONAL DEFENCE SCHEME

SUPPORT BRIGADE LEFT DIVISION.

III CORPS.

References 57.c S.E.)
32.c. N.E.) 1/20,000
Bde. map attached.

1. In the event of hostile attack the 174th Infantr Brigade Group, composed as under, will man and hold at all costs the trench system from Southern Divisional Boundary at E.10.c.2.0 through E.10.a., E.9.b., E.3.d., E.3.b and W.27.d., W.28.a to Northern Divisional Boundary at W.22.c.4.0.

<u>174th Infantry Brigade GRoup</u>

6th London Regiment.
7th London Regiment.
8th London Regiment.
1/4th Suffolk Regiment.
"B" Coy., 58th M.G.Bn.
174th. L.T.M.Battery.

2. The tactical features of this area are the ridge extending north-east from GUYENCOURT, the GUYENCOURT PLATEAU the valleys in E.2 and W.27 and in E.4 and W.28., and the low undulating country east of SAULCOURT.

There are many sunken roads and banks under cover of which the enemy could approach the line almost unobserved, whilst CHAUFFEURS WOOD constitutes a screen behind which he could form up for an attack.

The trenches defending this locality are in fair condition and the wire is on the whole good. There are however, numerous gaps, and Battalion Commanders will reconnoitre these on their respective fronts and take steps to protect them.

The dominant positions of the line are:-

(1) The high ground about E.3.d.1.7. which covers a greater part of the ridge N.E. of GUYENCOURT, the sunken road and the valley in E.4.a. and W.28.c and a., also the ridge in E.4.b, W.28.d.

(2) The junction of sunken roads in E.10.a from which locality are commanded the approaches North and South-west of CHAUFFEURS WOOD and the greater part of the GUYENCOURT PLATEAU.

(3) The nose of the small salient in E.10.c.4.4., from whence the western edge of CHAUFFEURS WOOD is enfiladed and the South and South Eastern sides, together with the road passing through E.10.b., d and c and the high ground in E.17.a and E.11.c can all be covered by fire.

(4) The high ground E.9.b.1.6 from which SAULCOURT WOOD and the valley in E.9.c. and 14.b are commanded.

3. On receipt of the command "MAN BATTLE STATIONS" the following positions will be taken up.

(a) The Brigade front will be held by the 6th Londons on the left and the 8th Londons on the right, the inter-battalion boundary being an E. & W. line through E.3.c.0.7.

A joint liaison post will be established at about E.3.d.2.7., the actual site being selected by Battalion

/Commanders in

Commanders in consultation.
(b) The 7th Londons will take up a position in E.2.b and d and will be held in readiness for counter-attack. No counter-attack will, however, be launched without orders from Brigade unless in the opinion of the Battalion Commander the situation demands immediate action.
(c) The 1/4th Suffolk Regiment will be concentrated in the sunken roads in E.7.d where they will await orders from Brigade.
(d) "B" Coy. 58th M.G.Bn., will take up the positions shown on the attached map "A".

4. The dispositions of Battalions on manning their battle position are shown on the attached map "A"

5. 174th. L.T.M.Battery will attach two guns to each of the forward Battalions.

6. Brigade Headquarters will remain at W.25.c.2.5.
Advanced Report Centre will be established at E.3.c.1.5.

7. Administrative and Signal Instructions in connection with the scheme will be issued separately.

8. ACKNOWLEDGE.

[signature]

Captain.
Brigade Major.
13th. September, 18. 174th Infantry Brigade.

Distribution: -

G.O.C.
6th Londons
7th Londons
8th Londons
174th.L.T.M.B.
"B" Co., 58th M.G.Bn.
1/4th Suffolks (Pioneers)
Bde. Signal Officer.
Staff Captain.
58th Division.
Right Flank Bde.
Left Flank Bde.
173rd Infantry Bde.
175th Infantry Bde.
War Diary.
File.

BM/7/141

S E C R E T.

AMENDMENT No.1
to
174th. Infantry Brigade Provisional Defence Scheme
for Green Line, 58th Divisional Front.

Ref. sheet 62c. N.E. 1/20,000.   23rd September, 19.

1. The Green Line now extends from F.10.c.4.7. to L.4.b.1.4. (about)

2. Inter-Battalion boundaries, Liaison Posts, dispositions and Headquarters are shown on attached map "A".

The Provisional Defence Scheme (B.M.7/141) of 22nd September will be amended accordingly.

[signature]

Captain.
Brigade Major.
174th. Infantry Brigade.

APPENDIX II.

SIGNAL COMMUNICATIONS.

Reserve Brigade - Centre Sector - III Corps.

Ref. 62 D. 1/40,000. July, 31st. 1918.

1. Normal Communication. Brigade H.Q., EBARTS FARM.

   Lines thence to Divisional H.Q. and Brigade Forward Exchange C.17.a.7.8.

   Lines from Brigade Forward Exchange to Adv. Div. Exchange, BAIZIEUX.

   to "A" Battalion H.Q. BAIZIEUX, party line to "B" and "C" Battalions ROUND WOOD, and to Left Brigade H.Q.

   "A" Battalion have a party line to the Companies in LAVIEVILLE LINE.

   Communication with the Pioneer Battalion through Left Brigade.

2. Battle Communications. Battle Brigade H.Q. at C.17.a.7.8.

   Lines thence to Division, Rear Brigade H.Q., (EBARTS FARM,) Adv. Divl. Exchange, "A" Battalion, D.9.d.8.5., "B" Battalion and "C" Battalion, ST. LAWRENCE FARM and Left Brigade. Pioneer Battalion with Left Brigade.

   "A" Battalion have line to two Company H.Q. in LAVIEVILLE Line.

   Visual between ST. LAWRENCE FARM and Battle Brigade H.Q.

3. Diagrams attached.

APPENDIX III

ADMINISTRATIVE ARRANGEMENTS.

AMMUNITION. The following is the approximate amount of ammunition in the line:-

8th London Regiment. 47000 rounds

The two Battalions (6th and 7th Battalions) in Camp in ROUND WOOD, C.20.b. have only the ammunition carried on the man.

WATER. Water is obtained at the following points:-

Horse watering point,	C.2.a.3.6.
Drinking water.	BOIS ROBERT, C.10.b.5.5.
" "	CONTAY.

Also numerous wells in the area. 1 scoop of chlorination required.

STRAGGLERS' POSTS.

Location.	Strength.
C.6.d.5.9.	1 N.C.O. 3 men.
C.12.b.1.5.	1 N.C.O. 3 men.
D.16.c.6.6.	1 N.C.O. 6 men.

For the first two mentioned posts 3 additional men are earmarked for duty in the event of battle.

Collecting Station for Stragglers and P.O.W. Cage, C.6.d.4.9.

BATHS.

AGNICOURT.
BEAUCOURT.
BEHENCOURT.
BAIZIEUX. (P.O.W. Cage).

Capacity of baths, 40 per hour.
Arrangements for the bathing and reclothing of gassed cases have been made at the BEAUCOURT baths, where a reserve of clothing is maintained.
The FODEN lorry is at BEAUCOURT.

Q.M.STORES.	All Units.	Billet No. 1, CONTAY.
	Bde. H.Q.	" " 38 "
TRANSPORT LINES.	All Units.	C.2.a.3.2.

File

Reference Reserve Brigade Defence Scheme.

1. Cancel heading and substitute the following :

Reserve Brigade - Centre Sector - III Corps.

---

2. Cancel Appendix II and substitute the enclosed Appendix II in its place.

3. Cancel Appendix III and substitute the enclosed Appendix III in its place.

D C Henryht for
Captain.
Brigade major.
174th. Infantry Brigade.

31st. July, 1918.

Copy to : All recipients
Reserve Brigade Defence Scheme.

PROVISIONAL AMENDMENTS and ADDENDA

to

D E F E N C E   S C H E M E

Reserve Brigade - Centre Sector - III Corps.

Cancel para. 2 and substitute the following :

2. The Reserve Brigade is disposed as under :

"A" Battalion - (2 Companies LAVIEVILLE LINE.
(2 Companies BAIZIEUX.
(H.Q. BAIZIEUX.

"B" and "C" Battalions - ROUND WOOD, C.20.b.

The Pioneer Battalion lives in its Battle Positions in the LAVIEVILLE Line.
(See Map "A" attached.)

Amend para.4 as follows :-

Sub-para (a) line 1 for "Battalions" read "The Battalion".
Sub-para (c)
(i) for "Australian Corps" read "Right Flank Brigade".
(ii) For "D.5.d.0.6." read "D.11.a.4.0."

add

(e) C's.C. "B" and "C" Battalions will select alarm posts at their camps, and will practise their Battalions in falling in upon such alarm posts and marching to their Battle Positions by night at least once during each tour in Reserve. The times of carrying out this practice will be reported to Brigade H.Q.

Cancel para.5 Sub-paras (a), (b) and (c), also amendments B.M.618 of 22nd. July issued by 173rd. Inf. Brigade, and also provisional amendments B.M.F.26/186/2 of 27th. July issued by 175th. Inf. Brigade, and substitute the following :

(a) The Pioneer Battalion (less one Company) will stand to arms and will hold the LAVIEVILLE System from the inter-Brigade Boundary to the AMIENS - ALBERT Road. Battalion H.Q. will be opened at H.Q. Left Forward Brigade. The Liaison Post at D.22.a.6.0. (see para 4 (c) (i))will be established.

(b) "A" Battalion will reinforce its two Companies in the LAVIEVILLE System with the two Companies at BAIZIEUX, and will hold the LAVIEVILLE System from the ALBERT - AMIENS Road to the Northern Divisional Boundary. Battalion H.Q. will be established in Tunnelled Dug-out D.9.d.8.5.

(c) "B" and "C" Battalions will take up positions in the Valley W. of ST. LAURENT Farm and will open a Joint Battalion H.Q. at D.19.a.2.3. A liaison officer will at once be sent to Brigade H.Q. from each Battalion.

[signature]
Captain,
Brigade Major,
174th. Infantry Brigade.

31st. July, 1918.

Copies to : All recipients of
Defence Scheme - Reserve Brigade
- Centre Sector - III Corps.

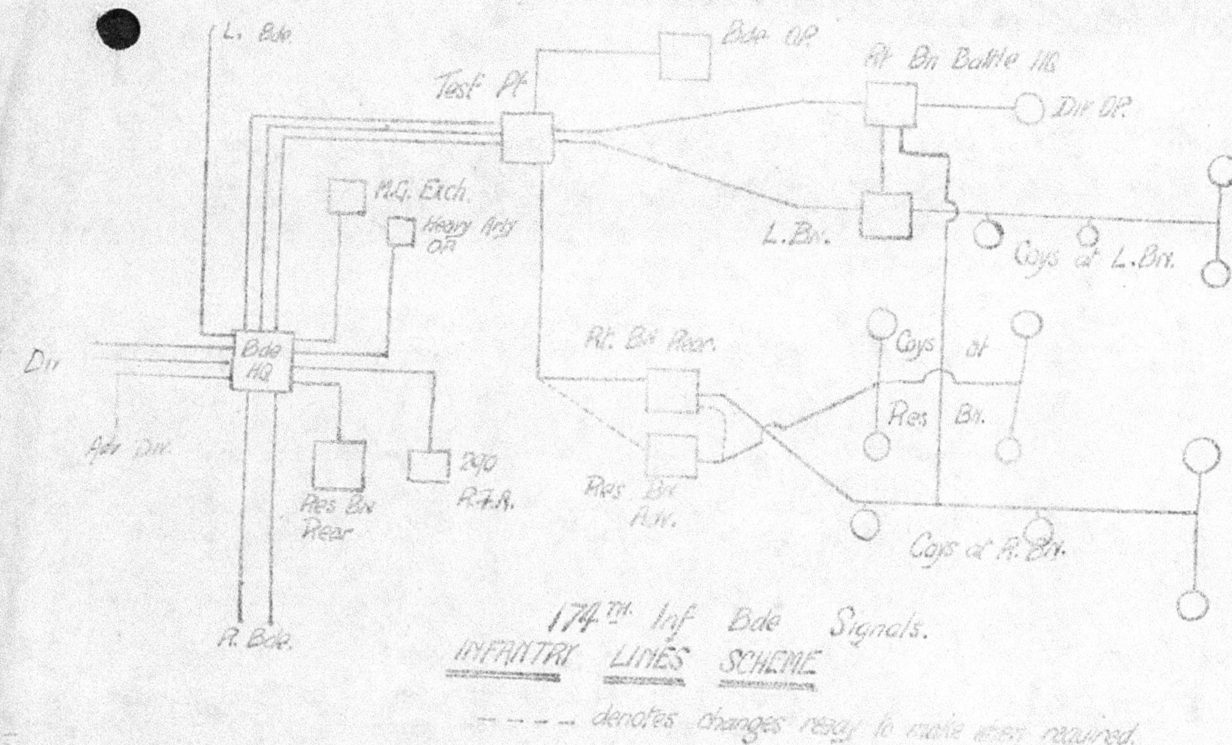

174th Inf Bde Signals.

INFANTRY LINES SCHEME

- - - - denotes changes ready to make when required.

VISUAL COMMUNICATION.

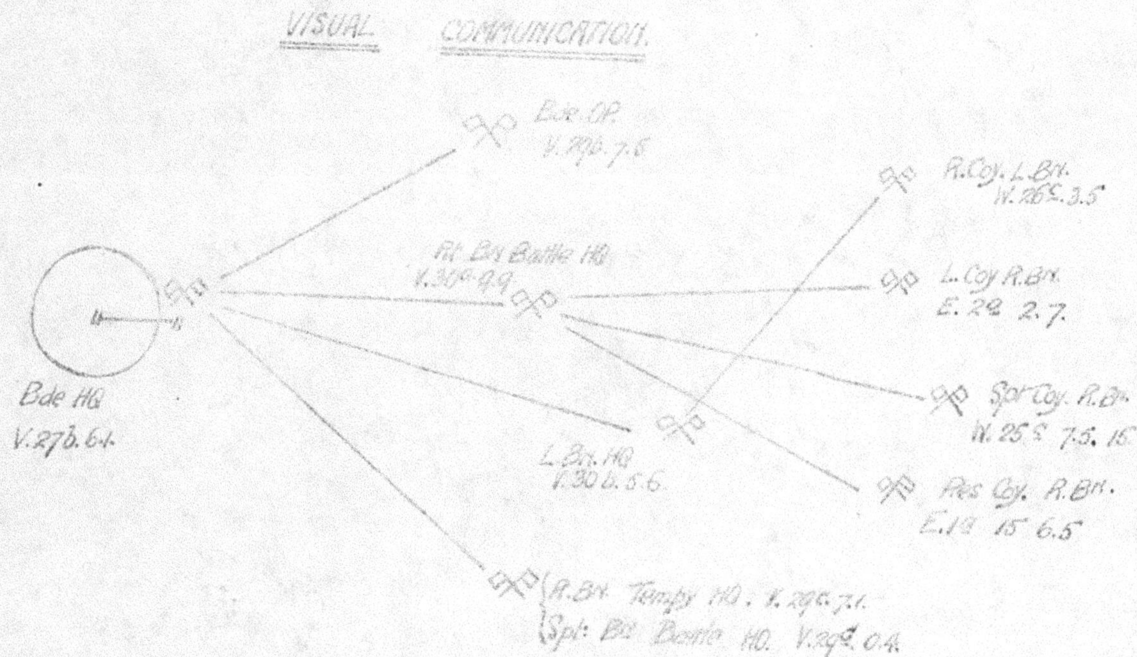

Locations of Visual Stns (not of Hqrs necessarily) given.

Visual Comn in battle position of Support Bn is possible & will be established as neces

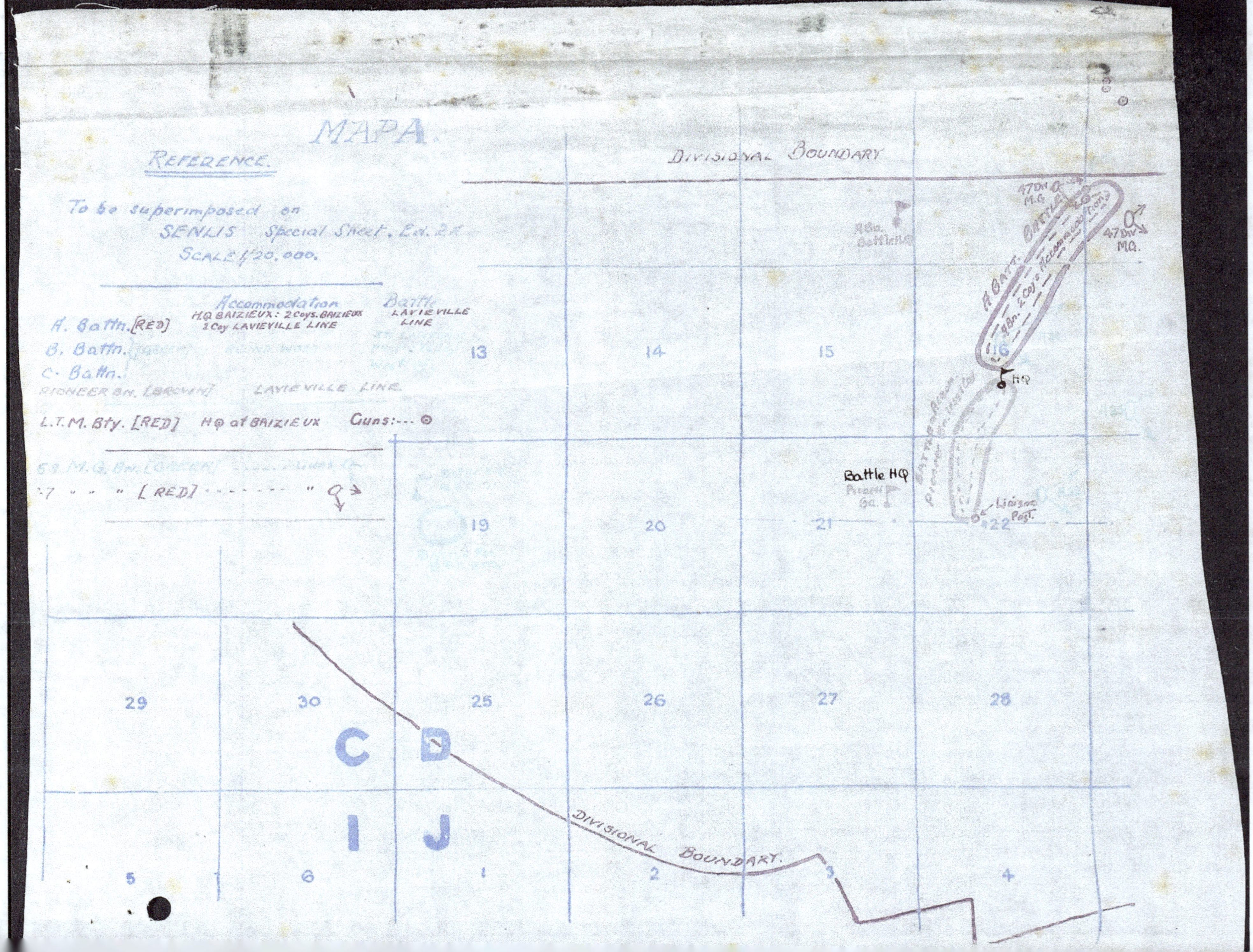

MAPA.

REFERENCE.

To be superimposed on
SENLIS Special Sheet. Ed. 2A
SCALE 1/20,000.

	Accommodation	Battle
A. Battn. [RED]	H.Q. BAIZIEUX: 2 Coys. BAIZIEUX 2 Coy LAVIEVILLE LINE	LAVIEVILLE LINE
B. Battn.		
C. Battn.		
PIONEER BN. [BROWN]	LAVIEVILLE LINE.	

L.T.M. Bty. [RED] HQ at BAIZIEUX Guns:--- ⊙

" " " [RED] -------- "

DIVISIONAL BOUNDARY

47 Div M.G.

A BATT. BATTLE

4 Bn. 2 Coys Accommodation

47 Div M.G.

HQ

Battle HQ

Liaison Post.

13 14 15 16

19 20 21 22

29 30 25 26 27 28

C D

I J

5 6 1 2 3 4

DIVISIONAL BOUNDARY.

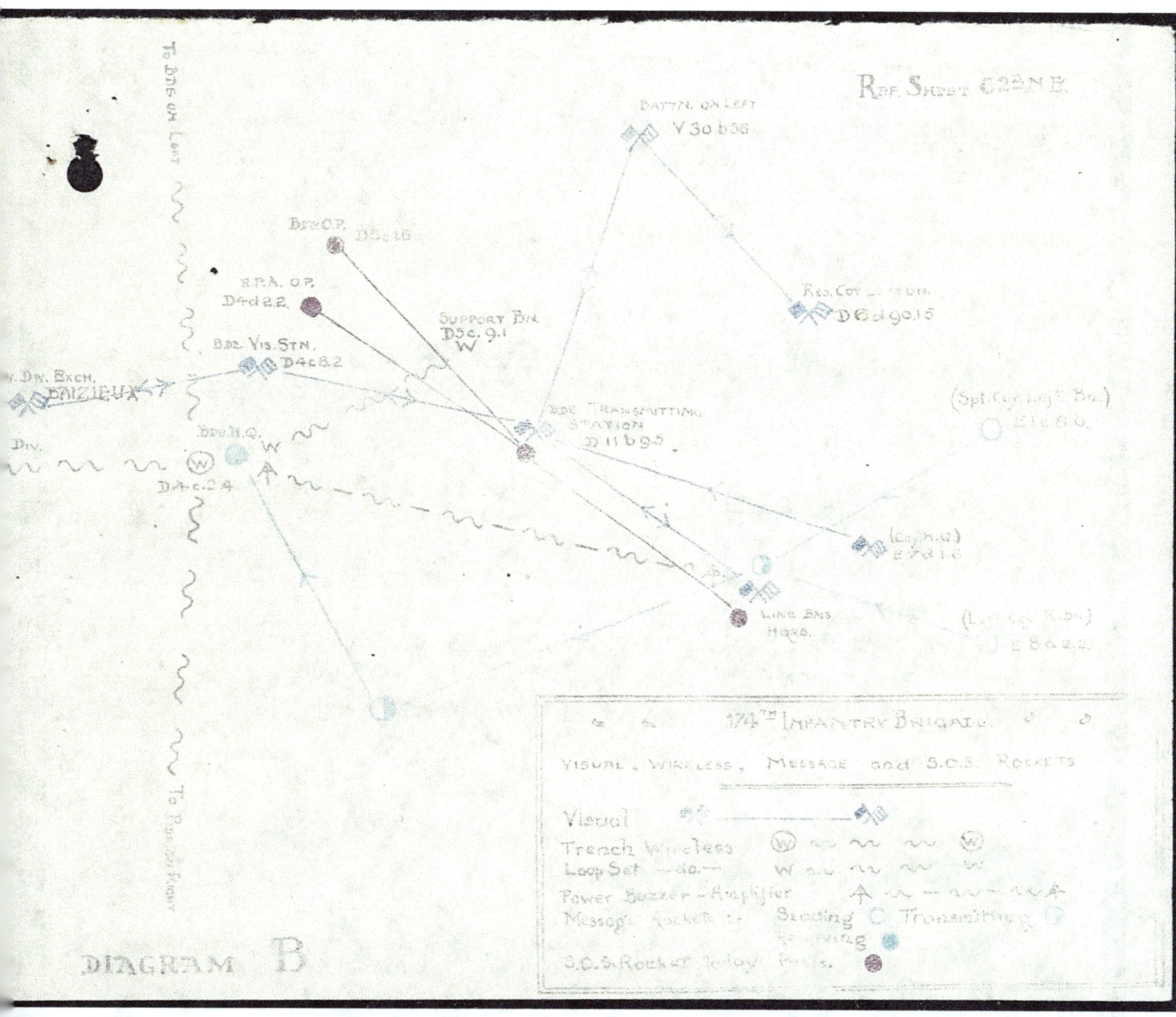

BATT'N. ON LEFT
V 30 b 56
SUPPORT BN.
D5c. 9.1
W
R.F.A. O.P.
D4d 2.2.
BDE. VIS. STN.
D4c8.2
DIV. EXCH.
BAIZIEUX
DIV.
BDE. H.Q.
D4c.2.4
BDE TRANSMITTING STATION
D 11 b 9.5
LINE BNS HQRS.
E 8 a 2.2
174TH INFANTRY BRIGADE
VISUAL, WIRELESS, MESSAGE and S.O.S. ROCKETS
Visual
Trench
Loop Set —do.—
Power Buzzer - Amplifier
Sending
DIAGRAM B

APPENDIX II.

SIGNAL COMMUNICATIONS.

Reserve Brigade - Centre Sector - III Corps.

Ref. 62 D. 1/40,000. July, 31st. 1918.

1. Normal Communication. Brigade H.Q., EBARTS FARM.

Lines thence to Divisional H.Q. and Brigade Forward Exchange C.17.a.7.8.

Lines from Brigade Forward Exchange to Adv. Div. Exchange, BAIZIEUX.

to "A" Battalion H.Q. BAIZIEUX, party line to "B" and "C" Battalions ROUND WOOD, and to Left Brigade H.Q.

"A" Battalion have a party line to the Companies in LAVIEVILLE LINE.

Communication with the Pioneer Battalion through Left Brigade.

2. Battle Communications. Battle Brigade H.Q. at C.17.a.7.8.

Lines thence to Division, Rear Brigade H.Q., (EBARTS FARM,) Adv. Divl. Exchange, "A" Battalion, D.9.d.8.5., "B" Battalion and "C" Battalion, ST. LAWRENCE FARM and Left Brigade. Pioneer Battalion with Left Brigade.

"A" Battalion have line to two Company H.Q. in LAVIEVILLE Line.

Visual between ST. LAWRENCE FARM and Battle Brigade H.Q.

3. Diagrams attached.

DIAGRAMS of COMMUNICATIONS. Reserve Bde. - Centre Div. III Corps.

Normal Circuits.

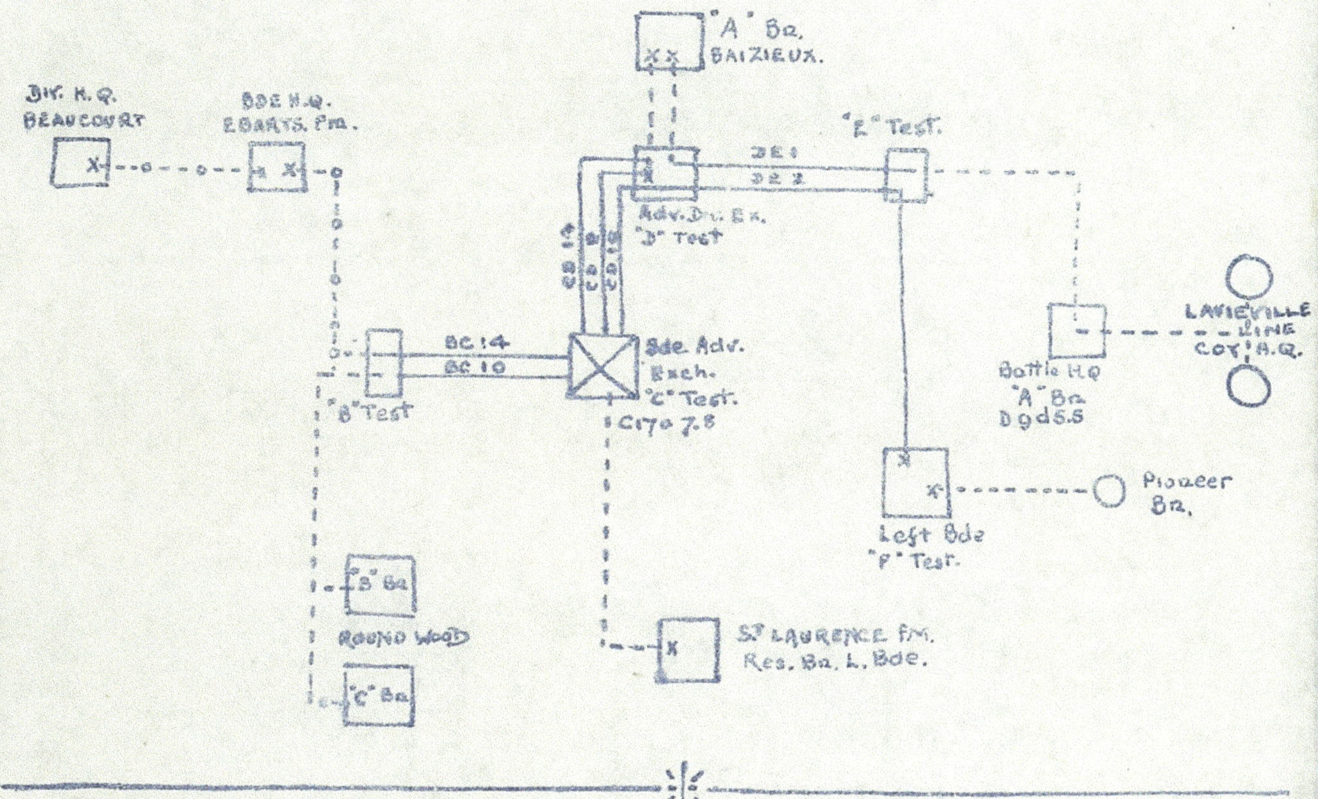

Battle Circuits

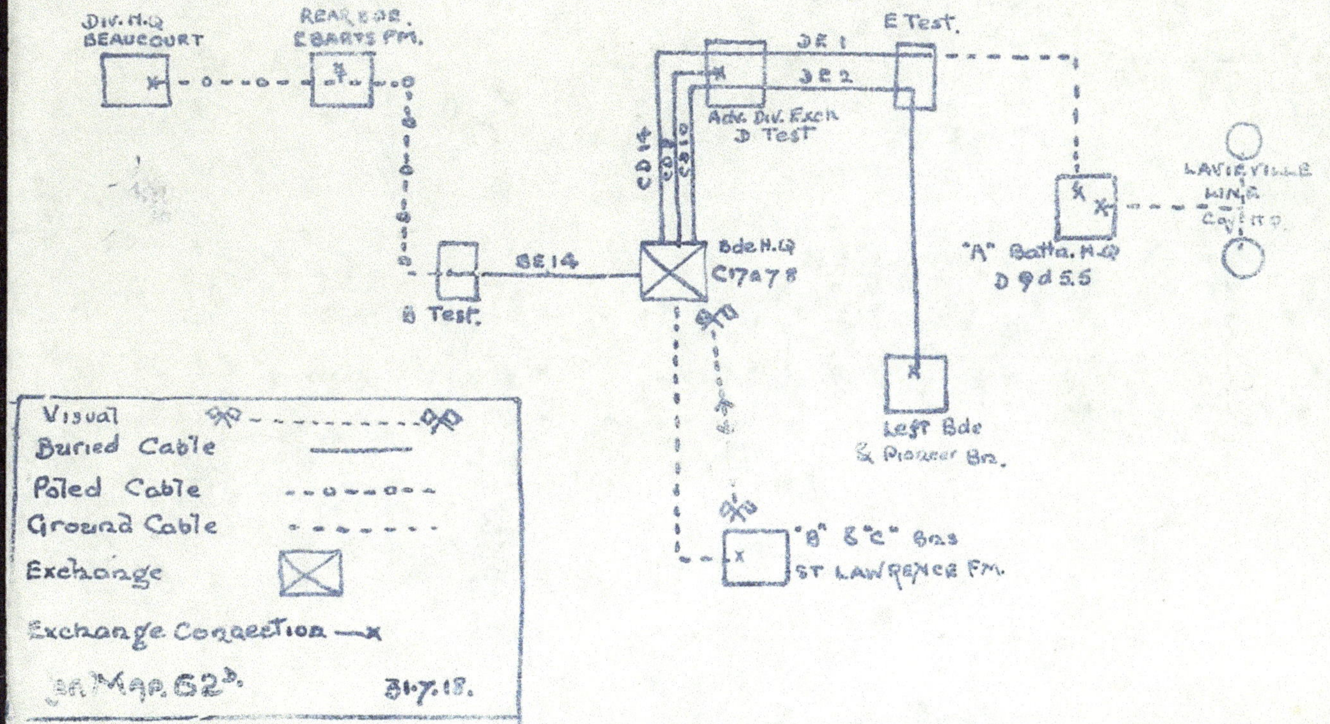

APPENDIX III

ADMINISTRATIVE ARRANGEMENTS.

AMMUNITION. The following is the approximate amount of ammunition in the line:-

8th London Regiment. 47000 rounds

The two Battalions (6th and 7th Battalions) in Camp in ROUND WOOD, C.20.b. have only the ammunition carried on the man.

WATER. Water is obtained at the following points:-

Horse watering point.	C.2.a.5.6.
Drinking water.	BOIS ROBERT, C.10.b.5.6.
" "	CONTAY.

Also numerous wells in the area. 1 scoop of chlorination required.

STRAGGLERS' POSTS.

Location.	Strength.
C.6.d.5.9.	1 N.C.O. 3 men.
C.12.b.1.5.	1 N.C.O. 3 men.
D.16.c.6.6.	1 N.C.O. 6 men.

For the first two mentioned posts 3 additional men are earmarked for duty in the event of battle.

Collecting Station for Stragglers and P.O.W. Cage, C.6.d.4.9.

BATHS.

AGNICOURT.
BEAUCOURT.
BEHENCOURT.
BAIZIEUX. (P.O.W. Cage).

Capacity of baths, 40 per hour.

Arrangements for the bathing and reclothing of gassed cases have been made at the BEAUCOURT baths, where a reserve of clothing is maintained.

The FODEN lorry is at BEAUCOURT.

Q.M.STORES.	All Units.	Billet No. 1, CONTAY.
	Bde. H.Q.	" " 38 "
TRANSPORT LINES.	All Units.	C.2.a.2.2.

APPENDIX III

ADMINISTRATIVE ARRANGEMENTS.

AMMUNITION. The following is the approximate amount of ammunition in the line:-

8th London Regiment. 47000 rounds

The two Battalions (6th and 7th Battalions) in Camp in ROUND WOOD, C.20.b. have only the ammunition carried on the man.

WATER. Water is obtained at the following points:-

Horse watering point.	C.2.a.3.3.
Drinking water.	BOIS ROBERT, C.10.b.5.5.
" "	CONTAY.

Also numerous wells in the area. 1 scoop of chlorination required.

STRAGGLERS' POSTS.

Location.	Strength.
C.6.d.5.9.	1 N.C.O. 3 men.
C.12.b.1.5.	1 N.C.O. 3 men.
D.18.c.6.6.	1 N.C.O. 6 men.

For the first two mentioned posts 3 additional men are earmarked for duty in the event of battle.

Collecting Station for Stragglers and P.O.W. Cage, C.6.d.4.9.

BATHS.

AGNICOURT.
BEAUCOURT.
BEHENCOURT.
BAIZIEUX. (P.O.W. Cage).

Capacity of baths, 40 per hour.
Arrangements for the bathing and reclothing of gassed cases have been made at the BEAUCOURT baths, where a reserve of clothing is maintained.
The FODEN lorry is at BEAUCOURT.

Q.M.STORES.

All Units.	Billet No. 1, CONTAY.
Bde. H.Q.	" " 38 "

TRANSPORT LINES. All Units. C.2.a.2.2.

6.7.18

SECRET.

Copy No. 19

B.M./7/77/33.

174th. Infantry Brigade.

DEFENCE SCHEME.

LEFT SUBSECTOR - RIGHT SECTOR - III CORPS.

DISTRIBUTION OF TROOPS. 1. The Divisional Front is held with two Brigades in Line and one Brigade in Divisional Reserve.

The Brigade Front (Left Brigade) is held with two Battalions in Line and one in Reserve.

Each Battalion in Line has two Coys in front and Support Trenches, one Coy in Support and one in Battalion Reserve. The Reserve Coy in either case mans the intermediate Line.

The Battalion in Brigade Reserve mans part of the Intermediate Line with two Coys and has two Coys in rear of it.

Boundaries and Infantry dispositions in detail are shown on attached Map A.

NOTE.

The dispositions indicated above, in the case of Reserve Coys of Battalions in Line and the leading Coy of the Battalion in Brigade Reserve, are battle positions. As soon as the condition of the Intermediate Line permits these positions will be permanently occupied by the garrisons allotted to them.

GENERAL DESCRIPTION OF THE LINE. 2. The Brigade Front Line follows the higher slopes of the spur running East to the ANCRE Valley South of ALBERT. A small well defined re-entrant runs Westward into the forward positions about the centre of the Front.

The hostile forward system runs obliquely down the forward slopes of the main spur from the high ground about our right boundary to the lowlying ground immediately W. of ALBERT.

On the extreme right and on the left the convex slope denies direct observation of the enemy's forward system. In the centre we have good observation across the re-entrant mentioned above of his Line where it descends the lower slopes N.E. towards ALBERT.

From our front line we have excellent observation of the enemy's back areas across to the further slopes of the ANCRE Valley.

With the exception of a limited area E.7.c. - D.12.b., c. and d. - the whole of the plateau East of LAVIEVILLE and consequently all approaches to the sector are under observation from the high ground held by the enemy opposite the Divisions on right and left.

PRINCIPLES OF DEFENCE. 3.(a) The existing Front Line is the Brigade Line of resistance and on this line the Brigade will fight. It will be maintained at all costs. All Commanders will know that ground is to be held whether flanks are turned or not and, if necessary, flanks reinforced.

The retention of the high ground in the subsectors held by the right and left Battalions is essential for the maintenance of these positions by flanking Brigades on our right and left respectively.

(b.) Each Coy in the Line will have one Platoon ear-marked for immediate counter-attack in the event of the enemy achieving a local penetration of the Company Front, as the result of a minor enterprise.

(c) The Support Coy of either Battn is available to reinforce or counter-attack or extend a flank as the situation demads.

The Reserve Coy of t-he Right Battalion is available to counter-attack or entend a flank. The reserve Coy of the Left Battalion will not be employed withoutx reference to Brigade H.Q. Should the Reserve Company of the Right Battalion be employed Brigade H.Q. and Reserve Battalion will be at once informed by the quickest available means by O.C., Battalion concerned and O.C., Reserve Battalion will immediately replace the Company so employed by his Company from HILL ROW.

The Support or Reserve Coys will only be employed for reinforcement or counter-attack in a situation warranting the use for this purpose of so limited a force. In the first stages of a general attack on the Front of the Brigade and Flanking Brigades, counter-attacks by one or two Coys on the Front System will either be impossible to launch or will offer little prospect of success. In the event of a serious attack, therefore, support and reserve Coys will garrison and maintain at all costs their Battle positions or will be employed to entend a flank along the line DIGGERS AVENUE or BEER STREET - SHRINE TRENCH if the situation demands.

(d) The tw-o Coys of the Battalion in Brigade Reserve (Counter-attack Battalion) allotted to the Intermediate System will maintain their positions in case of attack. The counter-attack Battalion (Less 2 Coys) is available fo-r counter-attack under the orders of Brigade H.Q., to recapture any part of the Front.

In the event of a general attack how-ever, the role of the Counter-attack Battalion, will be the maintenance of the Intermediate Line (MELBOURNE - DITTON - DARWIN Trenches) and the Battalion will be prepared to recapture any portion of this Line on the Brigade Front if ordered.

(e) Battalions and Coys will be in possession of written Defence Schemes. Coy Defence Schemes will be approved by Battalion Commanders. Battalion Defence Schemes will be submitted to Brigade H.Q. for approval.

(f) All Commanders down to Section Commanders of the Support and Reserve Coys and Platoons and the Counter-attack Battalion will reconnoitre lines of approach and positions of assembly for the co-unter-attacks they may be called upon to carry out as outlined in paras (b) (c) and (d) above.

(g) Personnel of Coy. Battalion and Brigade H.Q. will be organised for defence and allotted Battle Stations.

ACTION IN CASE OF ATTACK.

4. In the event of a hostile attack opening on the Brigade Front or of warning being received that an attack is imminent the messagey "MAN BATTLE STATIONS AAA REPORT COMPLIANCE AAA ACKNOWLEDGE" will be sent out from Brigade H.Q. On receipt of this message the following action will be taken unless alrea-dy taken on the initative of local Commanders :

(a) Reserve Coys of Forward Battalions man their Battle Stations in the Intermediate Line.

(b) 2 Coys of Counter-atta-ck Battalion man their Battle Stations in the Intermediate Line.

2 Coys of Counter-attack Battalion stand to arms in their positions and remain ready to move when required. O.C. Counter-attack Battn will assume command of the Intermediate Line and all troops manning it on the Brigade Front.

He will make arrangements to collect all stragglers on each Company front and will ensure that these are organised and allotted fire stations in the Intermediate System under Company Commanders responsible for the defence of their System.

(c) Liaison Officers will be found as follows :

(i) From Right Battn with Battn on Right Flank.
(ii) From Counter attack Battn with Forward Battalions.
(iii) From Counter attack Battn with Brigade H.Q.

(d) Situation reports will be rendered to Brigade H.Q. at least once every half hour until further orders.

(e) Working pa-rties w ill report to nearest Coy or Battalion H.Q. Whenever situation permits they will be directed (In case of Infantry) to rejoin their Units or (in case of Field Coys or Tunnelling Coys R.E.) to their Battle Stations in the BAIZIEUX LINE.

MACHINE GUNS. 5. Map "B" shows emplacements and S.O.S. Lines of Guns in the Brigade Sector. One Coy (less 1 section) is located in the Line. One Section is in Brigade Reserve at Brigade H.Q.

NEWTON MORTARS. 6. There are two 6" NEWTON MORTARS covering the Front (See Map "B".)

STOKES LIGHT TRENCH MORTARS. 7. Six Stokes Guns are located in the Line, tw-o are held in reserve at D.9.b.9.9. (See Map "B".)
Battalion Commanders have a direct call on Stokes Mortars in their Area. Stokes Mortars will respond to an S.O.S. call on their normal lines, but at least 50 rounds must be retained with each Mortar for the purpo-se of fire on visible targets.

ARTILLERY. 8.(a) Field Artillery. Left Group, R.F.A. (4 18 pndrs. and 1 4.5 How Battery.)

(b) Heavy Artillery

98th. Bde. R.G.A.	76th. Bde. R.G.A.
3 - 6" How.Batteries.	1 - 9.2" How. Battery.
1 -9.2" Battery.	1 - 8" How. Battery.
1 - 6" Gun Battery.	2 - 6" How. Batteries.
1 - 12" How.	2 - 60 lbr. Gun Batteries.

There is a Liaison Officer at each H.Q. of the two Battalions in the Front Line. A Map showing locatio[n] of Batteries and S.O.S. Lines is attached. (Map "B".)

TANKS. 9.(i) One Section of "B" Coy, 2nd Tank Battalion with 2 male and one female tank (Mark V) is situated in D.21.a.

(ii) In the event of battle O.C. Section will keep in to-uch w-ith Brigade H.Q.

(iii) Normal line of advance will be North of ALBERT - AMIENS Road.

(iv) The first role of the tanks is to engage any hostile tank.

(v) If no hostile tanks appear, the tanks will advance and engage any hostile Infantry who are threatening the Intermediate System.

(vi) A hostile smoke barrage is a probable indication of a coming enemy attack with tanks. All concerned will therefore be warned to report at once to the nearest Tank Commander and to Brigade H.Q. any hostile Smoke Barrage which may be seen. Smoke Shells will be stored at Gun positions Divl. Artille[ry] to assist our own tanks by forming a smoke screen beyond the Area in which they will be operating.

(vii) Mark V British Tanks are distinguished by having WHITE - RED - WHITE in broad lines in extreme front of sides of Tanks and on back of rear Turrets.

German Tanks have the IRON CROSS in BLACK on a WHITE background.

British Tanks returning from action fly a flag (RED - WHITE - BLUE vertical stripes).

Other Signals by flag from Tanks to Infantry are :

GREEN and WHITE - Come on.
RED and YELLOW - Go on. I am broken down.

S.O.S. 10. S.O.S. Signal on III Corps Front is a rifle Grenade Rocket breaking into three GREEN stars.

DEFENCE AGAINST GAS. 11. Cylinder attacks are possible and projector attacks probable on this Front. Suitable targets for projectors in our Area include, [illegible] the H.Q., of the two Battalions in the Line.

Good targets for attack by Gas Shelling are LAVIEVILLE and the Trenches Roads and Tracks in vicinity of two Battn. H.Q., in D.12.d. Each Platoon on occupation of a Trench System must, wherever possible, have two or more alternative positions to a flank or forward for occupation (according to the direction of the wind) in the event of the normal locality occupied being subjected to a Gas attack.

COMMUNICATIONS. 12. See Appendix (1) and Plans.

WORK POLICY. 13. See Appendix (2).

The Brigade is responsible for work back to and inclusive of the Intermediate Line.

ADMINISTRATIVE ARRANGEMENTS. 14. See Appendix (3).

Ron Dannington Ward
Captain.
Brigade Major.
174th. Infantry Brigade.

6th. July, 1918.

DISTRIBUTION. Copy No. 1. G.O.C.
2. 6th. London Regt.
3. 7th. London Regt.
4. 8th. London Regt.
5. 174th. L.T.M.Battery.
6. Bde. Signal Officer.
7. Bde. Int. Officer.
8. Staff Captain.
9. 58th. Division "G".
10. 58th. Division "Q".
11. Right Flank Bde. (53rd.Inf.Bde.)
12. Left Flank Bde. (173rd.Inf.Bde.)
13. Reserve Bde. (175th.Inf.Bde.)
14. "C" Coy. 58th. M.G. Bn.
15. 511th. Field Coy. R.E.
16. 290th. Bde. R.F.A.
17. "B" Coy. No. 2 Tank Battn.
18. War Diary.
19. File.

A P P E N D I X 1.

SIGNAL COMMUNICATIONS.

Ref. SENLIS Sheet 1/20,000.

LINE COMMUNICATIONS. 1. (Diagram "A".)
Telephonic and Telegraphic communication between Brigade H.Q. and Division, Divn. Advanced Exchange and Flank Inf. Bdes. Left Group R.F.A., 270th. Battery R.G.A., Machine Gun Exchange, Right Battalion, Left Battalion, Support Battalion (with alternative routes) Divisional O.P., Brigade O.P. and Brigad-e Visual Stations, Forward Battalion Reserve Brigade.

Battalions have Lines to Coys and O.P's.

Brigade Rear H.Q., and Transport Lines connected to Divisional Exchange.

Fullerphone or ciphered messages only in front of Battalion H.Q.,

Fullerphone or Officers telephonic communications only in front of Brigade H.Q.

Lines to Division on buried cable route. Lines forward of Brigade being organized as trenched cable routes.

VISUAL COMMUNICATIONS. 2. (Diagram "B".) by Lucas Lamp working both ways between Brigade H.Q. and Advanced Division. Also via Brigade Transmitting Station to Line Battalions, Line Battalion Brigade on Left, and Coy H.Q. E.7.d.1.6; also between Coy H.Q. D.6.d.90.15. and Battalion on Left.

WIRELESS and EARTH INDUCTION COMMUNICATION. 3. (Diagram "B".)

Trench Set working to Division and Flank Brigades.
Loop Set working to Support Battalion.
Power Buzzer- Amplifier (Both way working) to Line Battalion.

PIGEONS. 4. Two pairs daily per Line Battalion located at Right Bn H.Q., and Coy H.Qs. E.8.a.2.3.,E.7.b.75.80 and E.1.d.8.0.

RUNNERS. 5. Divisional D.R.L.S. by Mounted D.R. from Advanced Divn. Exchange."Special" by Motor Cyclist.
D.R's. forw-ard of Brigadd by runner. A cross country runner track between Brigade and Battalion H.Qs. is being staked ~~[illegible]~~ out, whic-h involves the minimum enemy observation.

MESSAGE ROCKETS. 6. (Diagram "B".)

Rocket Posts at : E.1.c.8.0., E.8.a.2.2. (Sending)
Line Battn. H.Q. (Receiving & sending
D.16.d.8.6. (Forwarding Station.)
Brigade H.Q.(Receiving.)

S.O.S. ROCKET SYSTEM. 7. (Diagram "B".)

Relay Posts at : Left Battn. H.Q.
Bde.Visual Transmitting Station (D.11.b.9.5.)
Bde. O.P. No. 1 (D.5.c.1.6.)
Artillery O.P. (D.4.d.2.2.)

DIAGRAM 'A'

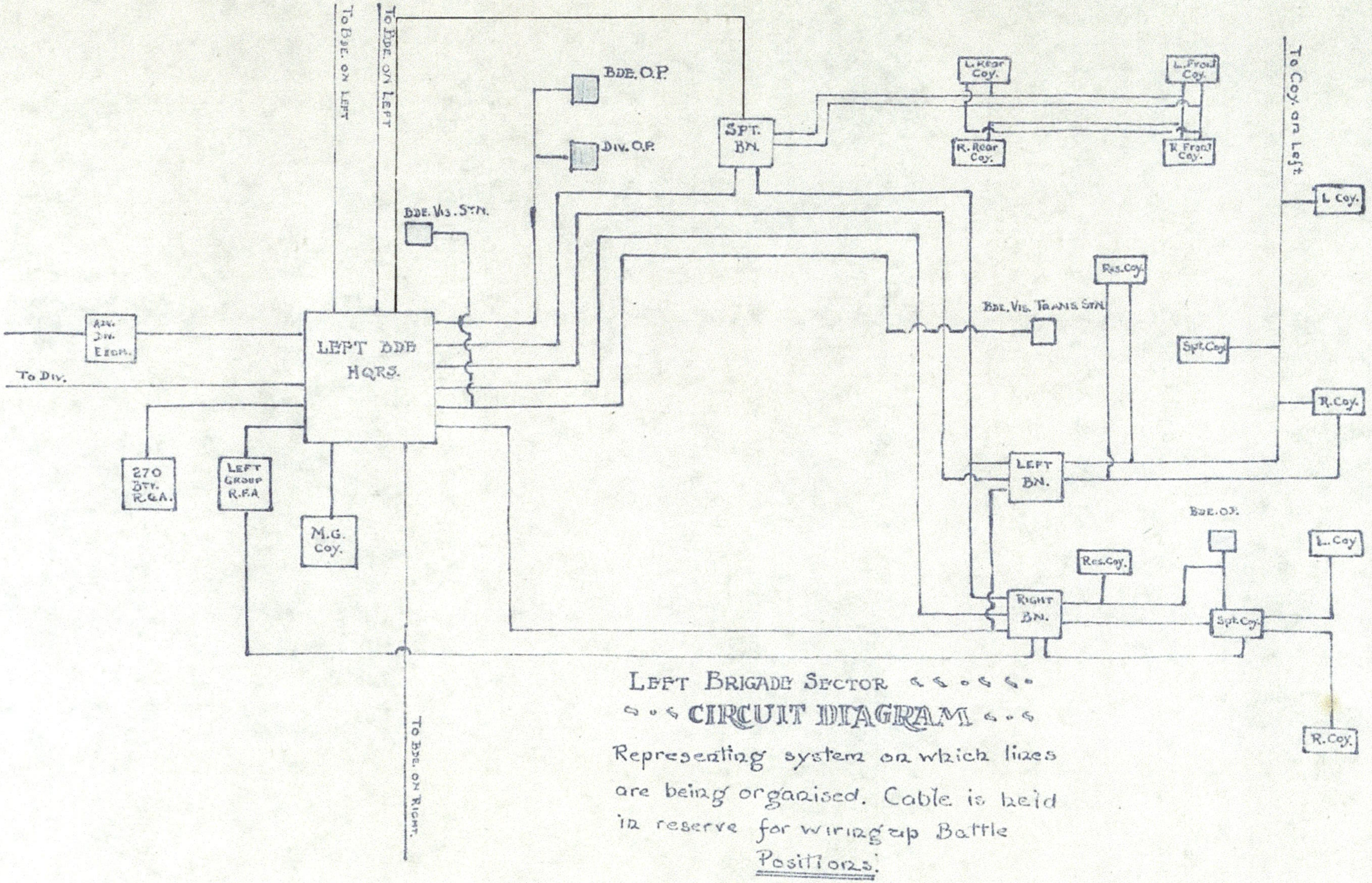

To Bde. on Left
To Bde. on Left
Bde. O.P.
Div. O.P.
Spt. Bn.
L. Rear Coy.
L. Front Coy.
R. Rear Coy.
R. Front Coy.
To Coy. on Left
L. Coy.
Bde. Vis. Stn.
Res. Coy.
Bde. Vis. Trans. Stn.
Spt. Coy.
R. Coy.
Adv. Div. Echn.
Left Bde HQrs.
To Div.
270 Bty. R.G.A.
Left Group R.F.A.
M.G. Coy.
Left Bn.
Bde. O.P.
Res. Coy.
L. Coy.
Right Bn.
Spt. Coy.
R. Coy.
To Bde. on Right.

Left Brigade Sector

CIRCUIT DIAGRAM

Representing system on which lines are being organised. Cable is held in reserve for wiring up Battle Positions.

A P P E N D I X 2.

W O R K   P O L I C Y.

TROOPS AVAILABLE. 1. One Field Coy R.E. (Less one section) and Units of Brigade. Proportion of Divisional Pioneers as may be allotted by Divisional H.Q.

METHOD OF EMPLOYMENT. 2. (a) Principal tasks and priority of completion laid down and R.E. assistance allotted by Brigade H.Q. Details issued in Brigade Table of Work.
(b) Arrangements detailed by Brigade H.Q. or made direct between Infantry and R.E. according to convenience for particular task.
(c) Front Line work normally to be carried out by Infantry unaided.
(d) R.E. responsible for trace of new work. All work task work, tasks being estimated by R.E. Infantry Commander solely responsible for work done.
(e) Bde. Reserve Battalion employed on special tasks e.g. Intermediate Line.

PRINCIPAL WORK IN PROGRESS OR PROPOSED. 3.

(x)(a) Wiring of front line especially on right of Brigade Front. Special task for Reserve Coy., Right Battn.
(x)(b) Construction of shelters and latrines in front and support Lines.
(x)(c) Crop cutting on all Battalion fronts and Reserve Lines. Every Reaping Tool to be in use nightly in the Brigade.
(x)(d) SHRINE Trench N. of ALBERT Road. Deepening, widening, firestopping and provision of shelter.
(e) BEER Trench - EMMA Trench. Trench improvement. BEER TRENCH to be stopped for fire both sides.
(f) Wiring the Line EMMA - BEER - SHRINE Trenches (Support Line). BEER Trench to be wired on both Flanks.
(x)(g) Stopping DEGGERS AVE. for fire North and North East.
(x)(h) MELBOURNE - DITTON Trenches (Intermediate Line) Deepening, firestopping and provision of shelter.
(i) HILL ROW - DARLING Trench (Intermediate Line) as for (h). Crop Cutting.
(k) Additional wiring of Intermediate Line throughout
(x)(l) New L.T.M. emplacements ACK ST. and BANK ST.

(x) I N   P R O G R E S S.

APPENDIX 3.

ADMINISTRATIVE ARRANGEMENTS.

1. LOCATIONS.

Brigade Headquarters.	-	D.4.c.2.3.
Right Battalion H.Q.	-	D.12.d.6.7.
Left Battalion H.Q.	-	~~D.12.c.5.6.~~ D.11.d.7.8
Support Battalion H.Q.	-	D.5.d.0.1.
L.T.M.Battery H.Q.	-	D.4.c.2.3.

2. TRANSPORT ROUTES. For Limbered wagons or Pack animals principally by cross country tracks to H.Q. of Battalions in Front Line.

3. AMMUNITION. Divisional S.A.A. and Grenade Dump. — C.3. Central.

3 L.G.S. wagons at Transport Lines to be kept always loaded with 22,000 rounds S.A.A. each.
Bde. Transport Officer to be responsible that these 3 wagons are always ready to be turned out at a moments notice.
The approximate amount of Ammunition held in the Brigade Sub-Sector is shown on the attached Table.

4. CLOTHING. 25 suits S.D. clothing and 25 suits underclothing are held at each Battalion H.Q., and the same quantity at Bde. H.Q. for men whose clothing has been contaminated by Mustard Gas. Clothing contaminated by Gas will be sent to Divisional Sick Collecting Station, BEAUCOURT for cleaning.

5. R.E.DUMP. BAIZIEUX.
Indents for R.E. material will reach Bde. H.Q. by 9 a.m. daily. Material will be sent up by transport the same night.

6. PRISONERS OF WAR. P.O.W. Cage. - BAIZIEUX. C.6. Central.

7. STRAGGLERS. In the event of active operations, Stragglers Posts will be established at :-

D.4.c.2.3.
D.10.c.0.9.

Battalions will each detail 1 N.C.O. and 2 men to report to Bde. H.Q. for these posts. All Stragglers will be collected at Bde. H.Q.

8. MEDICAL ARRANGEMENTS.

R.A.P's.	Front Line Battalion.	- D.12.d.5.6.
	Support Battalion.	- D.11.d.3.5.
Bearer Relay Post.		- D.17.b.0.5.
Advanced Dressing Station.		- D.15.d.9.2.
Walking Wounded Collecting Post.		- D.19.d.5.4.
Main Dressing Station. / Divisional Gas Centre.		Red Chateau, MONTIGNY.

9. RATIONS. Rations are delivered by transport to Battalions and Brigade H.Q. by night.

Q.M. Stores of the 3 Battalions and 174th L.T.M. Battery are at - No. 1 Billet, CONTAY.

Q.M.Stores of Brigade H.Q. are at No. 38 Billet, CONTAY.

10. TRANSPORT LINES. Transport lines of all Units are situated at C.2,a.2.2.

11. HORSE BURIALS. All Units are responsible for the burial of their own animals.

Battalions in the Front Line are responsible for burials in their Sections East of the N. and S. Grid Line through D.12. Central.

Support Battalion is responsible for the Area West of the above Grid Line and East of the HENENCOURT -BRESLE Road, within the Brigade Boundaries.

12. IRON RATIONS. 20 cases each containing 25 tins, - 500 rations, are in Dump at Support Battalion H.Q., D.5.d.0.1.

As the Intermediate Line is completed, these Iron Rations will be distributed throughout this line.

7th July, 1918.

Table Showing Approximate Amounts of Ammunition etc. in Brigade Sector.

Detail.	Each Platoon.				Each Company.			Each Battalion.				TOTAL for BRIGADE,
	Each Section.	4 Sections.	Platoon Reserve.	TOTAL.	4 Platoons.	Company Reserve.	Total	4 Companies	Addl. Lewis Gun.	Battalion Reserve.	TOTAL	
S.A.A. rounds.	1000	4000	2000	6000	24000	10000	34000	136000	12000 (a)	20000	168000	504000
Grenades, No. 23.	12	48	24	72	288	120	408	1632	-	240	1872	5616
S.O.S. Rifle Gde. Rockets.	-	-	1	1	4	2	6	24	-	8	32	(b, 96
V.P.A., 1" White, Cartridges (c).	-	-	-	-	-	150	150	600	-	150	750	2250
Ground flares.	-	-	-	-	-	20	20	80	-	100	180	540
T.M.Stokes, 3" Shells.	200 rounds at each Gun position in the Line. 600 rounds in two or more Dumps arranged by O.C., T.M.B.										1200) 600)	1800

NOTES. :-

(a) For 12 additional Lewis Guns, 1000 rounds per Gun, either at Gun Position or with the Gun if it is in Company or Battalion reserve.

(b) 24 additional Signals are held at Bde. H.Q. as reserve in case of emergency.

(c) Coloured V.P.A. is held at Bde. H.Q. for issue for special operations.

7th July, 1918.

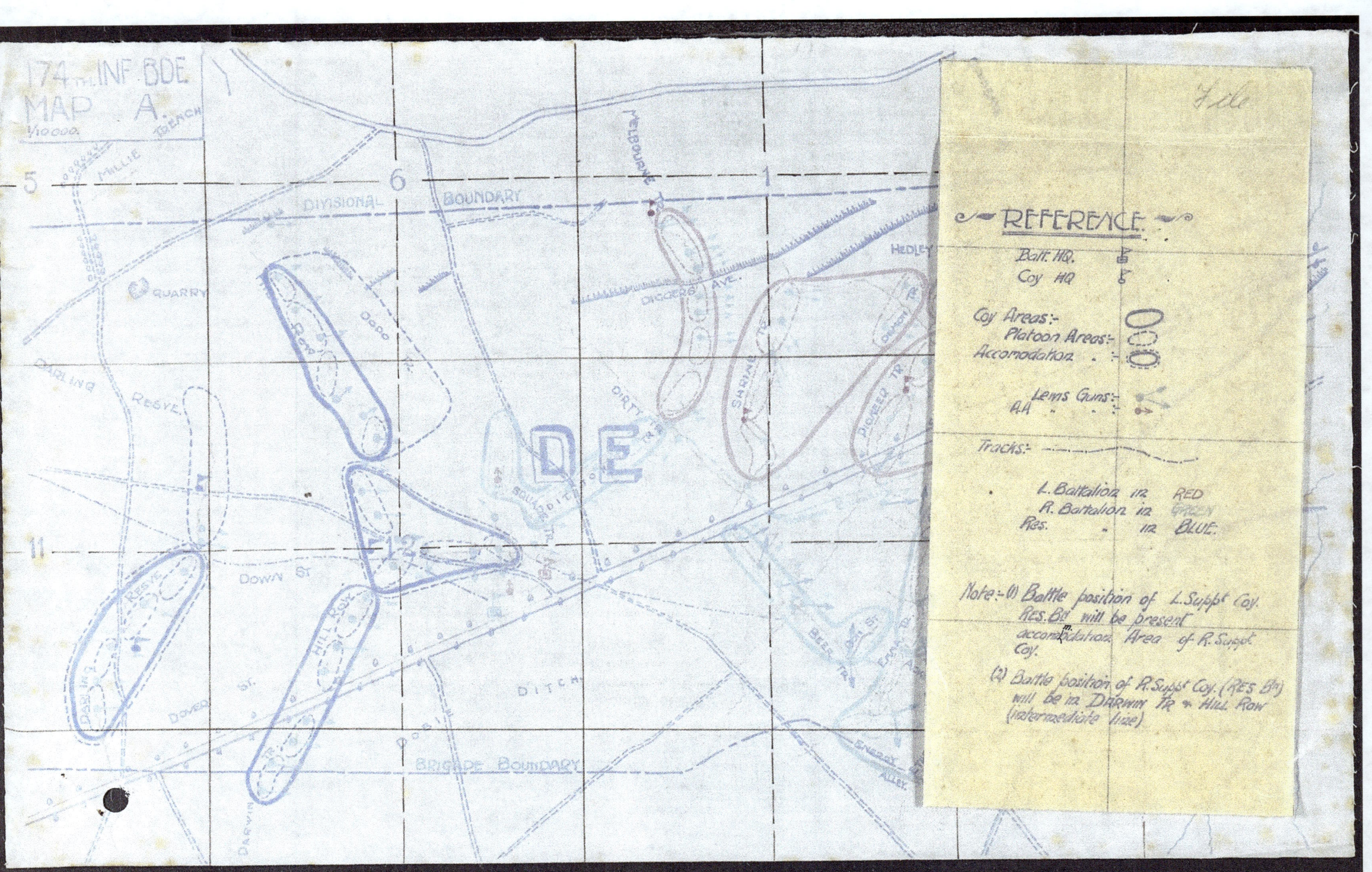

174TH INF BDE
MAP A.
1/10000
TRENCH
MILLIE
QUARRY
DARLING
RESVE.
RESVE.
DARLING
DOVER
ST.
DOWN ST
ROW
DODO TR.
HILL ROW
DARWIN TR.
DIVISIONAL BOUNDARY
BRIGADE BOUNDARY
DITCH
SQUARE
DE
E12
DIRTY TR.
MELBOURNE TR.
DIGGERS AVE.
HEDLEY
SHRINE TR.
PIONEER TR.
BEER TR.
ALLEY
5
6
1
11
REFERENCE.
Batt. HQ.
Coy HQ
Coy Areas:-
Platoon Areas:-
Accomodation
Lewis Guns:-
AA " "
Tracks:-
L. Battalion in RED
R. Battalion in GREEN
Res. " in BLUE.
Note:- (1) Battle position of L. Suppt Coy. Res. Bn will be present accommodation Area of R. Suppt Coy.
(2) Battle position of R. Suppt Coy. (RES Bn) will be in DARWIN TR & HILL ROW (intermediate line)
File

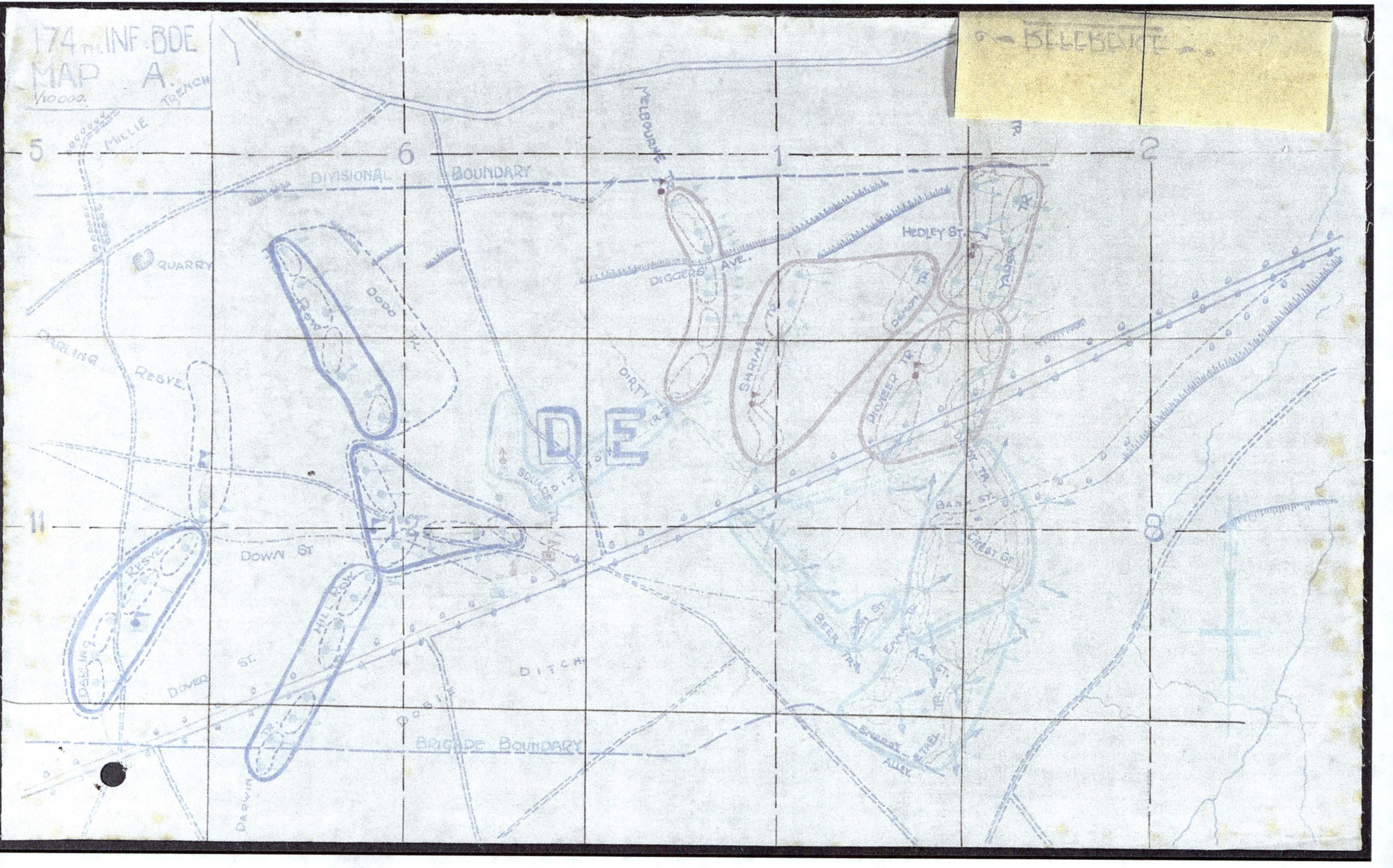

174TH INF BDE
MAP A.
1/10000.
MILLIE TRENCH
QUARRY
DARLING RESVE.
DIVISIONAL BOUNDARY
BRIGADE BOUNDARY
MELBOURNE TR.
DIGGERS' AVE.
HEDLEY ST.
DIRTY TR.
DE
E13
DODO TR.
DOWN ST.
DOVER ST.
HILL ROW
DARWIN
DITCH
BANK ST.
CREST ST.
BEER TR.
BARROW ALLEY
5
6
1
2
8
11

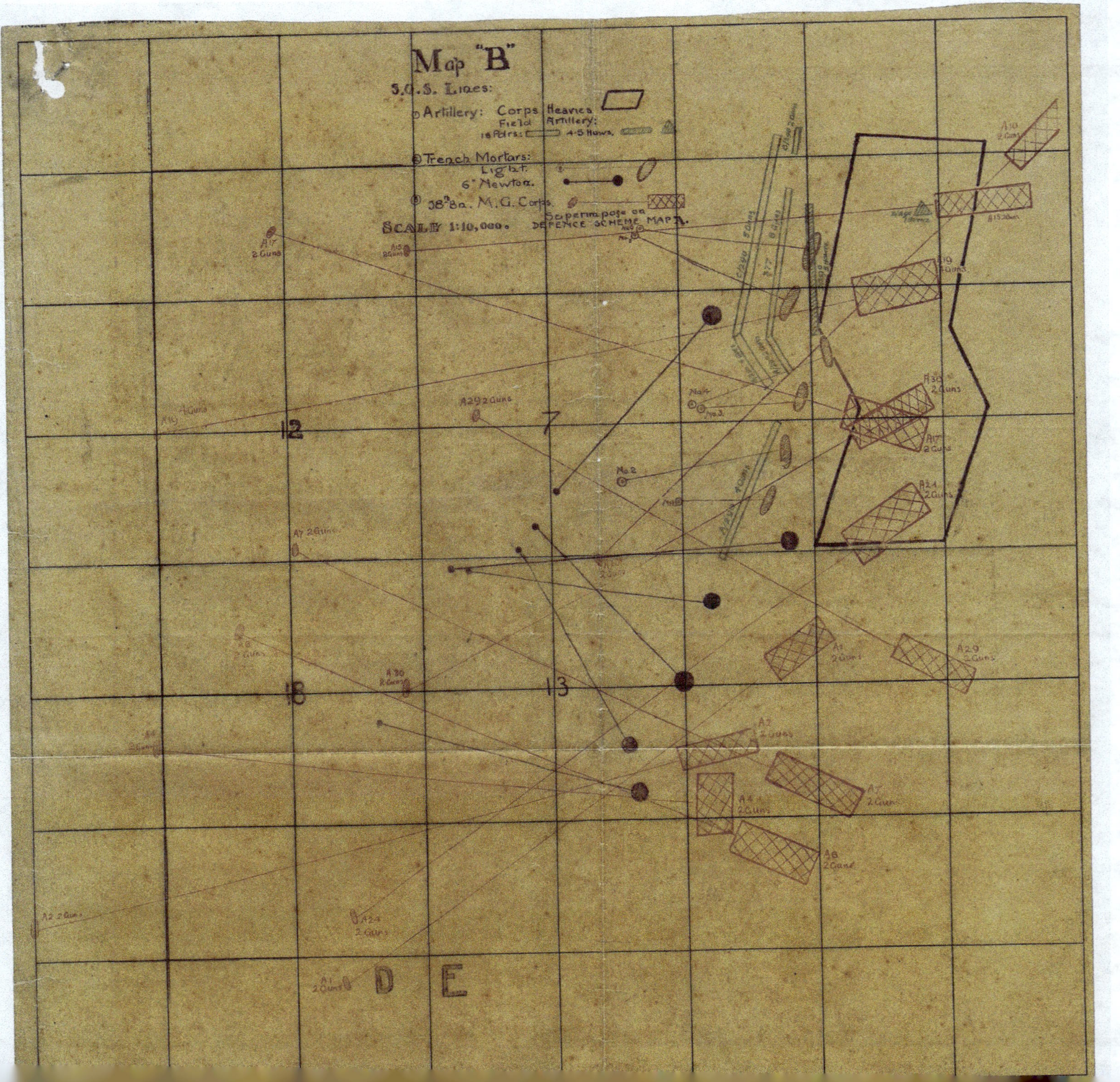

Map "B"
S.O.S. Lines:
Artillery: Corps Heavies
Field Artillery:
18 Pdrs: 4.5 Hows.
Trench Mortars:
Light
6" Newton.
38th Bn. M.G. Corps.
Superimpose on DEFENCE SCHEME MAP A.
SCALE 1:10,000.
A17 2 Guns
A29 2 Guns
A7 2 Guns
A30
A24 2 Guns
A1 2 Guns
A29 2 Guns
A7 2 Guns
A4 2 Guns
A8 2 Guns
A2 2 Guns
A24 2 Guns
A19 2 Guns
No. 2
12
7
13
18
D
E

WO95/3006
7th.
8th.
9th
10th.

174th Bde.

58th Div.

8th BATTALION

LONDON REGIMENT

A U G U S T 1 9 1 8

Instructions regarding War Diaries and Intelligence Summaries are contained in F. S. Regs., Part II. and the Staff Manual respectively. Title pages will be prepared in manuscript.

WAR DIARY
or
~~INTELLIGENCE SUMMARY.~~

(~~Erase heading not required.~~)

Army Form C. 2118.

8 London Regt

Vol 20

Place	Date	Hour	Summary of Events and Information	Remarks and references to Appendices
LAVIEVILLE LINE and BAIZIEUX.	August 1.		The following Officers were with the Battalion August 1st 1918. Lt Col. A D. DERVICHE-JONES. DSO. MC (CO) Capt. H W PRIESTLEY MC (2nd in C) Lt L.E.B JACOB (Actg adjt) 2Lt J.M BARRATT (Asst. Adjt) 2Lt E.C KNELL (IO) Lt W.B MACBEAN (MO) Capt. T.A.B. PURKIS (TO) Capt. H.T. CHAPMAN (2M) Rev AJ JAMES CF. attached – 2Lt D. GRANT. INTELLIGENCE CORPS. A. Coy. Capt. G.C FABER (OC) Capt R.R. POULTON. 2Lt A. J HARRIS. B. Coy Capt. A. S. THOMAS.MC (OC) 2Lt C.R. CROSSLAND. 2Lt W. KELLY. C. Coy 2Lt C. F YOUNGMAN (OC) 2Lt R.W. PERRY. 2Lt A.E MASON. D. Coy Lt C. T.A. WILKINSON (OC) 2Lt R.B. PATTINSON. and 655 other ranks. Bright, Hot day. Brigade role – Brigade in Divisional Reserve. Disposition of Battalion — HQ. A. B. Coys billetted in BAIZIEUX village C. Coy. LAVIEVILLE LINE Right D. Coy. LAVIEVILLE LINE left. Lt L.E.B. JACOB. proceeded on 14 days leave to ENGLAND.	JW
do	2.	2AM	Showery day. C + D Coys withdrawn from LAVIEVILLE LINE to billets in village of BAIZIEUX	Appendix I

D. D. & L., London, E.C. (A8004) Wt. W1771/M2031 750,000 5/17 Sch. 52 Forms/C2118/14

Army Form C. 2118.

Instructions regarding War Diaries and Intelligence Summaries are contained in F. S. Regs., Part II. and the Staff Manual respectively. Title pages will be prepared in manuscript.

WAR DIARY
or
~~INTELLIGENCE SUMMARY.~~
(Erase heading not required.)

Place	Date	Hour	Summary of Events and Information	Remarks and references to Appendices
BAIZIEUX	2nd		The Battalion moved by march-route and bus to WARGNIES, near CANAPES embussing on BEHENCOURT – BAIZIEUX Rd just outside BEHENCOURT, debussing at , arriving WARGNIES 10.15 pm	JMB App. No. 2
WARGNIES.	3		Showery day. The day was spent in cleaning up generally – inspection of Companies by Commanding Officer. Siting of parade + training grounds.	JMB
– do. –	4		Bright, fine day. Battalion Church Parade – Anniversary of Beginning of War Service.	JMB.
			Soon after noon Orders were received that the Battalion was to move back to the line, and at 9.0 pm the Battalion embussed near HAVERNAS, travelling during the night and debussing just before 2.0 am on ALBERT – AMIENS Rd just West of FRANVILLERS	App. No. 3

D. D. & L., London, E.C. (A8004) Wt. W1771/M2031 750,000 5/17 Sch. 52 Forms/C2118/14

Instructions regarding War Diaries and Intelligence Summaries are contained in F. S. Regs., Part II. and the Staff Manual respectively. Title pages will be prepared in manuscript.

WAR DIARY
or
~~INTELLIGENCE SUMMARY.~~
(Erase heading not required.)

Army Form C. 2118.

Place	Date	Hour	Summary of Events and Information	Remarks and references to Appendices
	5th		On debussing the Battalion proceeded by march route via LA HOUSSOYE & BONNAY to small wood on BRAY – CORBIE Rd (Ref J19. 62 D) arriving about 5 am. The weather was very bad, the day commencing with a slight drizzle developing into showers later on. The men spent the day resting. Parties of Officers and NCOs went forward to reconnoitre the part of the front line held by the 2nd BEDFORDS, and at 8.30 pm the Battalion moved forward to relieve this Regiment.	App. No 4 J.H.B.
	6th 7th 8th 9th 10th 11th		A full account of all operations undertaken by the Battalion by Lt Col. A D DERVICHE-JONES DSO MC attached, marked "APPENDIX SPECIAL."	J.H.B.
			On the afternoon of the 12th, the Battalion moved back to small copse on BRAY – CORBIE RD (ref 62 D. J24. b. 8.0) and once again came under orders of 17th Inf Brigade	

D. D. & L., London, E.C.
(A8001) Wt. W1771/M2031 750,000 5/17 Sch. 52 Forms/C2118/14

Instructions regarding War Diaries and Intelligence Summaries are contained in F. S. Regs., Part II. and the Staff Manual respectively. Title pages will be prepared in manuscript.

WAR DIARY

~~or~~

~~INTELLIGENCE SUMMARY.~~

(Erase heading not required.)

Army Form C. 2118.

Place	Date	Hour	Summary of Events and Information	Remarks and references to Appendices
COPSE J24 b.8.0.	12th		Bright – Hot day. The day was spent in cleaning & reorganising. Stragglers collected & deficiencies made up as far as possible.	JWB
COPSE. J24 b 8.0. and ROUND WOOD.	13.		The Battalion paraded and moved off by march route to ROUND WOOD (FRANVILLERS – BEHENCOURT RD.) (T20) arriving about 8-0 pm, & being accomodated in tents and bivouacs.	App. No 5. JWB
ROUND WOOD.	14th		Fine Bright Day. Reorganisation & inspection of Companies. 11-0 am. – Battalion paraded and were ~~inspect~~ addressed by the Commanding Officer – Lt Col. A.D. DERVICHE – JONES. D.S.O. MC.	JWB
-do-	15th		Bright – Hot day. 9-0 am to 12 noon. – Training. 3-0 pm Battalion paraded and were addressed by Brigadier General A. MAXWELL. DSO. Commanding 17th Inf Brigade.	JWB
-do-	16th		Lt Col. A.D. DERVICHE – JONES. DSO. MC. Cmdg – proceeded to Rest Camp, Fine – Bright Day. Training. 9-0 to 12 30 pm. Practice – Battalion in the Attack. Capt H.W. PRIESTLEY M.C. assumed command of Bn.	JWB

D. D. & L., London, E.C. (A8001) Wt. W1771/M2031 750,000 5/17 Sch. 52 Forms/C2118/14

Army Form C. 2118.

Instructions regarding War Diaries and Intelligence Summaries are contained in F. S. Regs., Part II. and the Staff Manual respectively. Title pages will be prepared in manuscript.

WAR DIARY
or
INTELLIGENCE SUMMARY.
(Erase heading not required.)

Place	Date	Hour	Summary of Events and Information	Remarks and references to Appendices
ROUND WOOD.	17.		Bright Day. Training. 9-0 to 1 pm. Musketry on range – PT and BF – Gas – Close order drill. 9 – 11 pm. Night-patrolling 2.30 pm Specialist training. Bath at FRANVILLERS. Percentage of men inoculated.	JmB
	16th		Following Officers as reinforcements:– Lts. HUMPHREYS, – E KING – T. PORTER. 2Lts TALLIN. – C.R. SMITH, – L.J. SMITH – – RIORDON – FERGUSSON. – ROSS.	JmB
-do-	18.		Fine Bright day. Brigade Church Parade 11-0 am. – also Services for other denominations.	JmB
-do-	19.		Fine – rather windy day	
			Training. 9 am to 1 pm. – Musketry on range – Close order drill, PT, BF, Coy attack practice. – Battalion drill. 2.30 to 3.30 pm Specialist training. 9 pm to 11 pm Night patrolling. Bath at FRANVILLERS.	JmB
-do-	20.		Fine – rather windy day. Lt L.E.B. JACOB rejoined from leave in ENGLAND. Capt. T.A.S. PORKIS proceeded on leave.	JmB

Instructions regarding War Diaries and Intelligence Summaries are contained in F. S. Regs., Part II. and the Staff Manual respectively. Title pages will be prepared in manuscript.

WAR DIARY
or
INTELLIGENCE SUMMARY.
(Erase heading not required.)

Army Form C. 2118.

Place	Date	Hour	Summary of Events and Information	Remarks and references to Appendices
	21st Aug to 1st Sept		See Special Narrative of Operations	Appendix 6.
			Casualties. Officers. Sec Lt H.C. GRAHAM. Killed. 26.8.18	
			Major H.W. PRIESTLEY M.C. wounded 25.8.18	
			Lt H.L. HUMPHREYS " 26.8.18	
			Lt R.H.A NEWSOME M.C. " 26.8.18 subsequently died of wounds	
			Sec Lt H. ORCHARD " 27.8.18	
			Lieut G.E. GUNNING M.C. " 27.8.18	
			Major HENNIKER M.C. " 27.8.18	
			Capt E.C.K. CLARKE M.C. " 31.8.18	
			Sec Lt R.F. ROTHWELL " 31.8.18	
			Sec Lt C.R. SMITH " "	
			" L.J. SMITH " "	
			Lt H. BOOTH M.C. " "	
			Lt T.W. PORTER " "	
			Sec Lt L.V. EVERETT "	
			Sec Lts F.A. YALE & Sec Lt C.A. BASSETT & 55 ORs joined Bn on 29.8.18	
			Draft of 236 ORs joined Battalion on 31.8.18	

[signature] Major
Cmdg 8th London Regt.

D. D. & L., London, E.C.
(A8001) Wt. W1771/M2031 750,000 5/17 Sch. 52 Forms/C2118/14

G.O.C.
174th Infantry Brigade.

NARRATIVE OF OPERATIONS
FOR THE PERIOD 22nd Augt. to 1st Sept

<u>Wednesday 21st Augt.</u> Major H.W.PRIESTLEY, M.C. in charge of the Battalion. A Warning Order was received this day that the Brigade might move that night or early next morning. Battle Surplus was detailed and all arrangements made for the move.

<u>Thursday 22nd Augt.</u> The Battalion moved off at about dawn. Route - From ROUND WOOD to Valley C.30.c and d where the day and the night were spent. Company Commanders were told that the Brigade was attached to the 18th Division for its attack on the ALBERT Sector.

<u>Friday 23rd Augt.</u> The Battalion moved up into close support to the 18th Division by march route via HEILLY - RIBEMONT - BUIRE-SUR-ANCRE up the Valley in D.17 and 23 to DINGLE COPSE in D.17.a. arriving about 8.30 a.m.

Company Commanders were told that we had been placed at the disposal of the 18th Division for active operations and would probably relieve the <u>54th</u> Brigade. (?) Instructions were given regarding the road to be taken through ALBERT. The Battalion spent the day and night in this area.

<u>Saturday 24th Augt.</u> Orders having been received for the Division to concentrate in the neighbourhood of MORLANCOURT, the Battalion moved at dawn via BUIRE and VILLE-SUR-ANCRE along Road through K.1.b and d to trenches in K.13.b. where the Battalion spent the day and the first part of the night.

<u>Sunday 25th Augt.</u> About midnight the Battalion moved by Companies via MORLANCOURT to the Railway Cutting K.5.c. where we remained until 8.18 am when we moved off at very short notice, the Companies in the following order - C.D.A.B. keeping along the Railway through K.5.d. - K.6.c and d - L.1.c and d to the Road in L.2.d. From this Road we moved forward in Artillery formation up the opposite slope in the direction of the chalk pit, three Companies in front, C.A.D. from right to left, B. Company in rear, the 7th Battalion on our Right and the 8th Battalion in Support. The Battalion H.Q. was established in the chalk pit at L.3.d. and the Battalion was disposed along the two roads running N. and S. in L.3.c and d, B. Company in the banks in L.8.e.

The day was intensely hot and the men exhausted by the heat and frequent moves and lack of sleep and water.

During the afternoon Major PRIESTLEY instructed Company Commanders that the 175th Brigade would be relieved by the 174th Brigade that night, on the line of BILLON WOOD. We were preparing to go up and reconnoitre, when these instructions were cancelled and we were told that the Brigade were to do an advance guard, passing through 175th Brigade and BILLON WOOD. We were further told that the 7th Battalion would find the advance guard for the whole Brigade front, the 6th on the Right and the 8th on the Left in the rear of the 7th. The direction of our advance was to be Northwards up the Valley in L.4.c and a.F.26.c. changing Eastwards through F.26.b. thence to BILLON WOOD. Companies were ordered to move in Artillery formation, C. and D. Coys in front, A. and B. Companies in rear and H.Q. in rear of A. and B. These were all the instructions given. The Battalion moved at 7.45 p.m.

It subsequently transpired that Major PRIESTLEY was wounded by a shell at the very beginning of the advance and this was the cause of much subsequent confusion. The night was exceedingly dark, the movement a very complicated one, the Valley up which the advance was to take place was being heavily bombarded with Blue Cross and H.E., and a violent thunderstorm did not lessen the difficulty of keeping touch, direction and control. However at about midnight I, as O.C. A. Company, reached the edge of BILLON WOOD with the greater part of my Company. I succeeded in finding Lieut. R.H.A. NEWCOMBE with D. Company and Lieut. PORTER with B. Company, both on the Western side of BILLON WOOD. We none of us had any idea of the whereabouts of Battalion H.Q. and we had lost touch with the 7th. Of C. Company I could find no trace. After 2 hours fruitless search I came across 2 Signallers who were able to direct me to Col. JOHNSTON'S H.Q. in TRIGGER WOOD where I reported at 2.15 a.m. on the 26th.

Monday.
26th Augt.

On reporting to Col. JOHNSTON I realised for the first time that Major PRIESTLEY was missing and that it was incumbent on me to take temporary command of the Battalion. It was at this moment that orders were received for an attack at 4.0 a.m. Col. JOHNSTON having explained the situation to the Brigade I returned and collected Commanders of A.B. and D. Companies and succeeded in giving instructions for the attack in time for these Companies to get into position at 4.0 a.m.

The 8th Battalion was ordered to move in close support to the 7th. I instructed Companies to form up in Battle formation along the whole Brigade front, A. on Right, B. in the Centre and D. on the Left, C. Company having during the night pushed through BILLON WOOD, it was impossible to get in touch with them in the time at my disposal.

It is impossible to give a connected account of what happened when the Battalion went forward. The 7th were not in a position to attack at all and the 8th found themselves in the front line almost from the commencement. Heavy artillery fire was encountered in the Ravine in BILLON WOOD and the advance from BILLON WOOD was held up by very strong hostile machine gun fire from the right and left flanks. Touch was never established with the 173rd Brigade on our left and our right flank was also in the air. Capt. GUNNING under my orders, established a defensive flank with D. Coy round the North of BILLON WOOD. C. Company was in advance of the WOOD in A.30.c. Portions of A and B Companies under 2/Lt. G.P.R.TALLIN and Lieut. T.W. PORTER maintained themselves in spite of heavy machine gun fire in ~~COPSE E~~ neighbourhood of COPSE E. During the morning the 7th were reorganised on our Right.

A counter-attack was reported to be developing about 11 a.m. This consisted of a few enemy machine gunners working their way up towards COPSE E. from the S.E., but nothing came of this and bar artillery fire which continued heavy the rest of the day passed quietly.

It should be pointed out that owing to the hurried move from Happy Valley on the evening of the 25th, the men were without rations and water for the 26th. The issue of rations and water during the night of the 26/27th was a matter of great difficulty and many of the troops continued up to the evening of the 27/28th without having received rations or water since the night of the 24/25th. When this fact is realised the achievement of the men in the attacks of the 27th and 28th about to be related, becomes worthy of the highest praise.

During this morning Lieut. NEWSOME, M.C. and 2/Lieut. GRAHAM were killed and Lieut. HUMPHRIES wounded.

At about 9.0 p.m. orders were received from Brigade for an attack next morning to be carried out by the 7th on the Right, the 6th on the Left and the 8th in close support. Major HENNIKER arrived during the night to take command of the Battalion but pending his arrival I gave the necessary instructions to Company Commanders.

The Battalion was to form up in the usual formation D. Company behind the 7th, C. Company behind the 6th, A. Company in rear on the Right and B. Company ditto on the Left. Major HENNIKER arrived about midnight when I rejoined my Company and took them out into assembly positions.

Tuesday 27th Augt.

The assembly of the Battalion for the attack was carried out successfully, though machine gun fire had not ceased over the area of assembly and the 6th Battn. appeared to me to be encroaching too far to the right.

As usual it it becomes very hard to say exactly what happened to the various Companies. C. Company on the Left found itself in the front wave of the attack from the commencement and under 2/Lieut. L.J.SMITH (Capt. GUNNING having been wounded) early in the attack) reached the first objective together with some men of the 6th. D. Company on the Right mopped up a portion of FARGNY WOOD where they established contact with the Australians.

B. Coy [illegible] in Road

~~Avenue~~. A. Company ended up in Ravine Avenue and Ravine Shelters. The general result was that the Battn. was disposed roughly in depth with its front on the first objective.

Casualties during the attack were light. Immediately on my arrival I made a reconnaissance of the whole position as well as I could for the enemy machine gun fire sweeping the ~~[illegible]~~ Gaps between trenches and reported to Battn. H.Q. in the RAVINE at A.30.a. where I found Major HENNIKER wounded and once more took command of the Battn. During the day Companies were reorganised, rations, water and rum were brought up and arrangements made for the continuation of the attack next morning.

Wednesday. 28th Augt.

At 11.30 a.m. I issued written orders for the attack a copy of which is attached. Considerable difficulty was experienced in getting Companies into the right assembly positions and I had myself to place A. Company in position only 30 minutes before Zero. The night was very dark and the Officers very tired and the ground very difficult owing to trenches, wire and shell holes.

The attack was carried out at 5.5 a.m. and the objective was obtained without difficulty. On going up as soon as the objective was reached, I found that the advance of

(C Coy)

the Exploitation Company, had been held up by machine gun fire from the direction of B.19.a. and the Company was lining the PERONNE ROAD and in touch with the Australians at the CRUCIFIX in A.30.b. The remainder of the 8th were consolidating along the trench from A.29.b.96.70. - through A.30.a.20.85. to A.24.a.0.0. where they were in touch with the 6th. During the morning the 8th obtained temporary possession of the machine gun positions commanding our line but were shortly afterwards bombed out. Our forward positions therefore remained along the PERONNE ROAD.

We established a Battn. Report Centre at about A.25.b.7.9 connected by wire to Battn. H.Q. which much simplified communications. Our new line was shelled all day and some casualties incurred. During the night the 8th were relieved by the 10th Londons and the Battalion concentrated in A.31.d. 32.c. and 27.b. The relief was reported complete at 4.30 a.m.

Thursday 29th Augt.

On this day re-organisation was vigorously carried out. Battle Surplus was exchanged and deficiencies as far as possible made good and the men given the maximum amount of rest.

The casualties for the three attacks above described were Killed - 2 Officers 15 Other Ranks, Wounded 8 Officers 160 Other Ranks, Missing 11 Other Ranks. Some 150 prisoners were taken and a large number of machine guns. Also 3 Field Guns and 40 German pigeons.

Friday 30th Augt.

Orders were received for the Brigade to push forward as advance guard to the Division, the 8th forming the left half of the main guard.

The Battn. embussed about 9.0 p.m. near MARICOURT and debussed about 11 p.m. on the PERONNE ROAD about 500 yards West of HEM WOOD and from thence we marched past HEM WOOD and up the Valley between HEM WOOD and HOWITZER WOOD to the cross roads at B.20.a.6.[illegible] where the men bivouacked. The Valley was somewhat heavily shelled during the night.

Saturday 31st Augt.

At about 1 a.m. orders were received from Brigade to attack at 5.10 a.m. I collected Company Commanders and gave them their instructions at 1.30 a.m. I ordered the following dispositions,- B.C.D. from Right to Left covering whole Battn. front of about 750 yards, A. Coy in support in line of platoons towards the Right flank. The forming up positions were on a line N. and S. through B.19.c.0.2. B. Company S. of AGILE AVENUE, D. Company N. of AGILE AVENUE and C. Company astride of AGILE AVENUE between A. and B. Battn. H.Q. were located in AGILE AVE. about B.17.d.9.4. The Battalion moved at 2.15 a.m. and was led by the Adjutant and myself to the forming up position. The night was again very dark and the identification of the ground selected for forming up was a matter of the greatest difficulty. The utmost care was taken to arrive at the correct position and the whole of the front three Companies were formed up ready for the attack about half an hour before Zero. As the Left Coy Company Commander was killed by one of our own 18 Pdr. shells during the subsequent advance to the WOOD and as it has been suggested that the forming up position selected was too near our own barrage I attach a Copy of the report made by the surviving Officer of the Left or D. Company.

What happened was that some of our guns, probably two guns, were firing short during the whole of the barrage. While the barrage remained stationary shells from these guns were bursting on my Battn. H.Q. which had to be hastily evacuated and was re-established at B.23.b.4.6. When the barrage lifted these guns overtook our own troops and caused the casualties inflicted by by our own barrage.

The attack was completely successful but some difficulty was experienced in keeping in touch with the 47th Division on our Left and B. Company on our Right pushed forward beyond the objective to the ridge in G.20.b. and d. The other Companies were situated as follows:- A. Company along the Ridge in G.19.b. and G.13.d. together with portions of C. Company. D. Company in AGILE AVENUE in G.13.b. from which they would be in touch with the 47th Division. The Valley between B. and A. Companies was strongly commanded by both and the situation required very little readjustment when I visited the positions in the afternoon.

The casualties in this attack were,- Killed 2 Officers 9 Other Ranks, Wounded 5 Officers 71 Other Ranks, Missing 21 Other Ranks.

Prisoners were estimated at about 230 and numerous machine guns were captured

Our troops remained in these positions until they were withdrawn on the 1st Sept. at 8.0 p.m. to the neighbourhood of HINDLEG WOOD.

3/9/18.

Addendum I

COPY.

SECRET. 8TH LONDON ORDER NO. B. 28th Aug. 1918.

Ref. Map 62C. N.W. 1/20,000

Par. 1. The Battalion will continue the attack today 28th inst. Zero hour 4.55 a.m. 6th London will be attacking on the Left and the Australians on the Right.

Par. 2. The attack will be carried out by "A" Company on the Right and B Company on the Left. D. Company will move in close support along the ~~old~~ this Battalion front. C. Coy will move behind D. Company.

OBJECTIVES. As explained verbally with following additions. A. Company will find liaison post with Australians at A.30.a.2.9. (junction of trenches) D. Company will ~~move~~ occupy trench ~~occupy~~ from A.23.d.9.0. to 8.7. in rear of A. and B. Companies. C. Company will occupy a liaison post with Australian Battn. at A.30.b.7.5. and will be in depth.

The 6th M.G. Section will assist this Post with protecting fire from the rear.

Formations as in recent attacks. Coy. Commanders will see that the front line is sufficiently strong.

JUMPING OFF POSITIONS. A. and B. Companies in front of NEW STREET. D. Company in ~~front~~ BLACK STREET. C. Coy behind BLACK STREET. The Australians are assembling on N. and S. Grid Line between A.28. and 29.

MOPPING UP. This will be done by one Platoon in each Coy. A. Company will include the trench running E. and W. across top of A.29.b.

Par. 3. The attack will be covered by Artillery barrage at the rate of 100 yards in 6 minutes, commencing at start line at Zero, and lifting at Zero plus 10 minutes at the rate named.

Par. 4. A protective barrage will search in depth for 30 minutes up to the line of exploitation.

Par. 5. ACKNOWLEDGE.

(sgd) G.C. FABER. Capt.

Issued at 12.30 a.m.

Copies to:- O.C. A. Coy.
B. Coy.
C. Coy.
D. Coy.
174th Bde.
War Diary.
C.O.

P.S. Reports to present Battn. Headquarters.

Addendum 4

To Capt. Faber. 8th London Regiment.

From 2/Lt. A. Buck.

On the morning of the 31st inst. D. Company was formed up quite 200 yards in rear of the rear edge of the barrage. The Company moved forward when the barrage lifted and had proceeded for about 400 yards when some of our shells burst among the Company. The main barrage was still well ahead and it is my opinion that at least one of our 18 Pdr. guns was faulty and so was shooting short.

So far as I know we suffered no casualties from our own barrage until we had gone forward at least 400 yards.

The guns responsible for our casualties continued firing short during the whole of our advance tot he objective.

There is no impression on my mind or on the minds of the men that the Company had formed up too near the barrage.

(sgd) A. BUCK. 2/Lt.
D. Coy. 8th London Regiment.
2/9/18.

APP No 1

OPERATION ORDERS. No:67.
8th Bn., The London Regiment.

Ref. SENLIS Map.

Aug. 1st 1918.

---

1. INFORMATION.
C. & D. Companies will withdraw tonight 1st/2nd Aug. from LAVIEVILLE LINE.

2. INTENTION.
The two companies will move back and be billeted in BAIZIEUX.

3. INSTRUCTIONS.
(a) Companies will move from LAVIEVILLE LINE at 2.30.a.m. and will be met by guides at Cross Roads D.12.b.08.60. and will be guided to billets. (List of billets attached)
(b) One limber per company will be at company dumps at 1.30. a.m. for Lewis Guns, Mess Kit, etc.
Limbers are to be loaded quickly and must not be kept waiting longer than is absolutely necessary.
(c) Company Officers chargers will be at Cross Roads D.16.c.5.5. at 2.15. a.m.
(d) All maps papers etc. taken over in line will be brought out and handed into Bn. Orderly Room by 10. a.m. tomorrow 2nd inst.
(e) Companies will report arrival to Bn. Orderly Room.

J M Bennett
2/Lieutenant & A/Adjutant.
8th Bn., The London Regiment.

Issued to runners at. 7-24

Copy 1 War diary.
2 C.O.
3 O.C. C. Co.
4. O.C. D. Co.
5 T.O.

APP. No. 2

SECRET. 8TH BN. LONDON REGIMENT.

WARNING ORDER. 1st Augt. 1918.

INFORMATION. 1. The Battalion will move by Bus and Road to the CANAPLES AREA tomorrow, 2nd August.
Embussing Orders will be issued later.
Transport will move independently, leaving Transport Lines about 6.0 a.m.

INSTRUCTIONS. 2. (i) (a) The following will be dumped outside Battalion Orderly Room by 10.0 p.m. tonight:-
Officers valises of B.H.Q., A. & B. Coys. Pioneers and Tailors Stores. Surplus Mess Stores. Orderly Room Stores. [illegible] packs, rifles and stores.
(b) The following stores of C. & D. Coys will be taken direct from the Line to Q.M. Stores:-
Officers kits. Surplus Mess Stores. Surplus Dixies.

(ii) The following Transport will remain behind and proceed to new area independently under Cpl. WAINE.
Water Cart. Officers Mess Cart. C.O's horse.

(iii) Sufficient dixies for tomorrow's breakfast and Dinners will be retained by Companies and will be conveyed to embussing point together with Officers Mess Baskets, by Officers Mess Cart.

(iv) Lewis Guns and 1,000 rounds S.A.A. per gun will be retained by Companies, and man-handled to embussing point.

(v) M.O's Cart will report at H.A.P. at 8.30 p.m. to-night to collect stores and will return to Transport Lines when loaded.

J.M. BARRATT.
2/Lt. & Asst. Adjutant.

Distribution:- Normal.

SECRET. 8TH BN. LONDON REGIMENT Copy No.........

OPERATION ORDER NO.70. 2nd August 1918.

Ref. SENLIS. LENS.

Following Warning Order issued 1st August 1918.

INFORMATION. 1. The Battalion will move by Bus and Road to-day, the 2nd inst., to WARGNIES, near CANAPLES.
Embussing point - S. ~~[illegible]~~ BEHENCOURT - BAIZIEUX RD. Head of Column facing W. at Eastern outskirts of BEHENCOURT.
~~[illegible]~~.
The Battalion will embus at 4.0 p.m.
Battalion embussing Officer - 2/Lt. E.C.KNELL.

INSTRUCTIONS. 2.(i) (a) Dinners will be at 11.30 a.m. and all dixies to be dumped outside Orderly Room by 12.30 p.m. sharp. They will be conveyed to embussing point in Mess Cart, dumped and a Water duty man left in charge.
(b) Officers Mess Stores to be dumped outside Orderly Room by 2.0 p.m. and conveyed to new area by Mess Cart.

(ii) (a) The Battalion will parade outside billets in WILSON STREET and CHURCH STREET ready to move at 2.30 p.m. Order of march - H.Q., Band, C.D. B. & A. Companies, - head of column to pass starting point on main road C.11.b.95.75 at 2.35pm
(b) 100 yards distance between Companies to be maintained.
(c) The C.O. directs that strict march discipline be maintained both to embussing point and from debussing point to new billets. No man must be allowed to drink from his water bottle until the embussing point is reached.
(d) Billets must be left in a clean condition and a certificate rendered to Adjutant by 1.30 p.m. to this effect. The C.O. will inspect billets at this hour. Men and equipment etc. must not be allowed in the billets once they are cleaned.
(e) Companies will send in detailed embussing strengths to reach Battalion Orderly Room not later than 11.0 a.m.
(f) Copies of receipts for all stores handed over by C. & D. Companies in LAVIEVILLE LINE will be rendered in duplicate to the Orderly Room by 10.0 a.m. 3rd inst.

J.W.BARRATT.
2/Lt. & Asst. Adjutant.

Distribution :- Normal.

War Diary

App. No. 3

SECRET. 8th Battalion London Regiment. Copy No.......

OPERATION ORDER NO.71.

Reference Maps - 62D N.E. & N.W. 1/40,000. 4th August 1918.

1. The Battalion will move from its present billets to-day by Bus and march route.

2. Embussing Point - HAVERNAS - CANAPLES ROAD. Head of Column facing West at N.E. Edge of HAVERNAS.

3. Battalion Embussing Officer. 2/Lieut. E.C.KNELL.

4. Debussing Point. LA HOUSSOYE, then by march route to Road junction S. of HEILLY, J.13.b.7.6. where guides will be met.

5. Starting Point. WARGNIES CHATEAU.

6. Order of March. H.Q., A. B. C. D.

7. Leading Company to pass starting point at 8.10 p.m. sharp.

ADMINISTRATIVE INSTRUCTIONS.

1. Band, Shoemakers, Tailors and Q.M. Staff will proceed to new Area by march route along with Transport under orders of T.O.

2. Surplus Stores.
A dump will be formed at Q.M. Stores for all surplus stores which cannot be carried by horse transport. Q.M. will leave two men of his staff in charge.

3. Rations.
All ranks proceeding by bus will carry tomorrow's rations cooked in addition to iron rations.
Companies will take sufficient dixies for making tea, and will carry tomorrow's tea and sugar ration inside the dixies.

4. Lewis Guns.
Eight L.G's. per Company and 24 magazines per gun will be carried The 4 Battn. H.Q. A.A. Lewis Guns will be taken to new area by Transport.
Each man in L.G. Section will carry extra 4 x 2, and sufficient rifle oil for 3 days, must be carried by each L.G. Section.

5. Officers Valises and Mess Stores.
Officers Valises and Mess Stores to be dumped at Q.M. Stores by 7.30 p.m.

J.M.BARRATT.
2/Lieut. & A/Adjutant.

Distribution - Normal.

SECRET. 8th Battalion London Regiment.

File

OPERATION ORDER NO.72.

Reference Map 62D. 5th Aug.1918.

1. The Battalion will relieve the 2nd BEDFORD Regiment in the line tonight 5/6th instant.

2. Companies will relieve as follows :-
"A" Coy. 8th will relieve "D" Coy. BEDFORDS.
"B" " " " " "B" " "
"C" " " " " "A" " "
"D" " " " " "C" " "
Battn.H.Q. at J.22.d.20.35.

3. Order of Move. A. D. B. C. Headquarters.
Distance of 200 yards between platoons to be maintained.

4. Time of Starting. "A" Company 7.15 pm.
"D" " 7.30 pm.
"B" " 7.45 pm.
"C" " 8. 0.pm.
H.Q. 8.15 pm.

5. Route. Track past Brigade H.Q. - VAUX-SUR-SOMME - SAILLY-LE-SEC Road.

6. Guides. One per Company and one per Company H.Q. and 2 for Battn.H.Q. will be met at J.28.c.6.6. at 8.15 pm.

7. Relief. Relief complete will be notified by runner to Battn. H.Q.
Code Word - NINETY-FIVE.

8. Receipts for all trench stores taken over will be rendered in duplicate to Battn.H.Q. by 12 noon 6th inst.

J.M.BARRATT,
2/Lieut. & A/Adjutant.

Distribution Normal.

ADMINISTRATIVE ARRANGEMENTS
in accordance with Operation Order No. 72. 5/8/18.

APPN [handwritten]

1. **TRANSPORT.**
   (a) **Route** LA HOUSSAYE – along main road to C.28.d.6.8. – HEILLY – Cross two streams – Cross Railway at J.7.d.5.0 – J.14.a.20.85. – follow track to Battn.H.Q. J.22.d.20.35 crossing all roads and tracks to Gully.
   (b) **Company dump.**
   2 left Companies, "A" and "D" Coys., at J.24.d.7.3.
   2 right Companies, "C" and "B" Coys., later.

2. **RATIONS.**
   (a) Rations will be delivered cooked to all Companies, uncooked to Battn.H.Q.Section.
   (b) Tea for all Companies will be made at Battn.H.Q. in Containers and sent for at nights by Companies, commencing tomorrow night 6/7th instant.

3. **WATER.**
   A pump from which drinking water may be obtained at about J. 22.c.
   Particulars of supply later.

4. **RESERVE RATIONS.**
   Battn.H.Q. 600 tins Meat.
   75 tins Water.
   Claremont Line 600 tins Meat.
   75 tins Water.

5. **RUNNERS.** 4 Battn.H.Q. Runners will proceed with "B" Coy H.Q. to form a Relay Station. Companies will send runner messages to this Station, and runners there will forward them to Battn.H.Q.

J.M.BARRATT,
2/Lieut. & A/Adjutant.

SECRET. **8th Battalion London Regiment.** Copy No.

OPERATION ORDER No.79.

Reference Map 62D. 8th Aug.1918.

1. The Battalion will relieve the 2nd BEDFORD Regiment in the line tonight 8/9th instant.

2. Companies will relieve as follows :-

"A"	Coy.	8th	will	relieve	"D"	Coy.	BEDFORDS.
"B"	"	"	"	"	"B"	"	"
"C"	"	"	"	"	"A"	"	"
"D"	"	"	"	"	"C"	"	"

Battn.H.Q. at J.33.d.90.35.

3. Order of Move - A. D. B. C. Headquarters. Distance of 300 yards between platoons to be maintained.

4. Time of Starting.

"A"	Company	7.15 pm.
"D"	"	7.30 pm.
"B"	"	7.45 pm.
"C"	"	8. 0 pm.
H.Q.	-	8.15 pm.

5. Route. Track past Brigade H.Q. - VAUX-SUR-SOMME - SAILLY-LE-SEC Road.

6. Guides. One per Company and one per Company H.Q. and 2 for Battn.H.Q. will be met at J.36.c.6.6. at 8.15 pm

7. ~~Time. 8.15 pm.~~

8. Relief. Relief complete will be notified by Runner to Battn.H.Q.

9. Code Word. NINETY-FIVE.

10. Receipts for all trench stores taken over will be rendered in duplicate to Battn.H.Q. by 12 noon 9th inst.

J.M.BARRATT,
2/Lieut. & A/Adjutant.

Distribution Normal.

SECRET Aug 15

OPERATION ORDER 7/1
8th Bn London Rgt

Adm No 5

1. The 8th Bn London Rgt will route march today to ROUND WOOD

2. Order of March H.Q. A. B. C. D

3 Time 5.15 pm (Ready to move)

4. Starting Point Cross Rds J. 18 d. 6.0. Leading Co. to pass starting point at 5.20 pm

5. Distance (later)

6. Route BRAY–CORBIE RD–HEILLY – FRANVILLERS.

7 Dress. Marching order, steel helmets to be worn

8. ADMINISTRATIVE.
(a) The following to be dumped at cookers by 4 pm.

L. Guns. Gt Coats
Panniers Offrs Kits and Mess store.

Issued at 2.15 pm

J. M. Breast.
Lt Adjutant

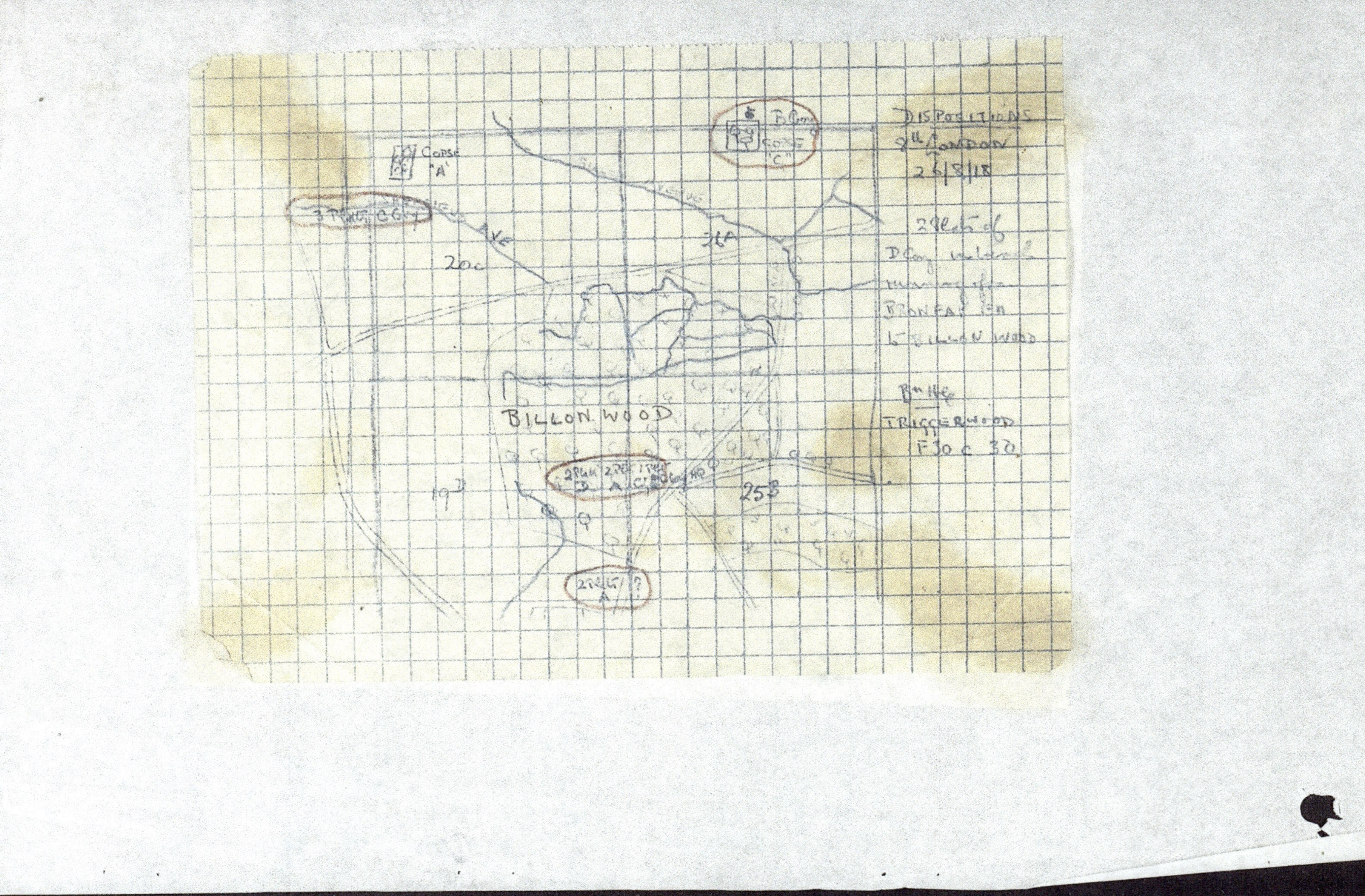
DISPOSITIONS
8th LONDON
26/8/18
2 Plts of
D Coy
BRONFAY Fm
BILLON WOOD
Bn HQ
TRIGGER WOOD
F30 c 30
B Coy
Copse 'C'
Copse 'A'
BILLON WOOD
20c
19d
25b
A

Secret.

8th London Order No. B

Ref. Map 62 C N.W 1/20000 29 Aug 1918

Par. 1. The battn will continue the attack ~~tomorrow~~ Today 28 inst. Zero hour 4.55 A.M. Sixth London will be attacking on the left, and the Australians on the right

Par. 2. The attack will be carried out by A. Coy on the right and B. Coy on the left. D Coy will move in close support along the old battalion front C. Coy will move behind D. Coy.

28th

Objectives

As explained verbally with following additions A Coy will find liason post with Australians at A ~~E~~ 30 A 29 (Junction of trenches) D ~~C~~ Coy will occupy trench from A 23 D 90 to 87 in rear of A & B. Coys. C. Coy will occupy a liason post with Australian battn at A.30 B ~~[illegible]~~ 75 and will be in depth.

The 6th M. G. Section will assist this post with protecting fire from the ~~[illegible]~~ rear

Par. 4.

A protective barrage will search in depth for 30 minutes up to the line of exploitation

Formations

Formations as in recent attacks. Coy Commanders will see that the front line is sufficiently strong

Jumping off positions

A. and B. Coys in front of New Street D. Coy in front Black, C. Coy behind Black Street. The australians are assembling on N. and S. Grid line between A.28 & 29

Mopping up

This will be done by one platoon in each Coy. A. Coy will include the Trench running E. and W. across top of A.29.B.

Par. 3.

The attack will be covered by artillery barrage at the rate of 100 yards in 6 minutes commencing at Start-line at zero, and lifting at zero plus 10 minutes at the rate named

Par. 4.

A protective barrage will search in depth for 30 minutes up to the line of exploitation

Par 5.

Acknowledge.

Signed G. C. Faber Captn

Issued at 12-30 AM. Copies to

O.C A Coy

B "

C "

D "

174 Bde

War Diary

C.O.

P.S.

Reports to present Battn

Headquarters

28/8/18 All Coys 8th London
Battalion will be relieved tonight by 10th Londons and will march ~~back to neighbourhood of BILLON WOOD via re-entrant in A23D and PERONNE ROAD aaa Companies will not strike PERONNE ROAD E of A23A52 Limbers will be at SE corner of orchard in A22B52 1 Limber to 2 companies~~ aaa For purposes of relief the right half of the garrison of Battn main line will be called A Coy the left D and B Composite Coy aaa Companies will be relieved as follows.

C Coy of the 8th by A Coy of the 10th
A Coy of the 8th by B Coy of the 10th
D and B composite Coys by C Coy of the 10th aaa D ~~Coy~~ company of the 10th will be in trench running from A23D9500 to 9070 aaa Coy Commdrs of the 10th will visit their positions during the afternoon aaa A guide for each coy will be sent forthwith to report Centre to wait their arrival aaa ~~guides will meet outgoing Coys on PERONNE ROAD at A75C20 aaa~~ A hot meal will be ready for troops in ~~BILLON WOOD VALLEY~~ aaa Completion of relief will be notified by wire and runner aaa

B Coy - under 2Lt. PEACOCK in trenches about C 21 a & b.
C Coy - under 2Lt. WILLS in AGILE AVENUE West of C 13 b 0 2
D Coy - under 2Lt. BUCK in trenches East of C 13 b 0 2.
2Lt. YALE with B Coy.
2Lt. BASSETT " C ".

All officers will on receipt of this order take immediate steps to conduct men to their ~~pap~~ company area. Owing to enemy observation all movement must be reduced to the minimum necessary.

4. Reports to Bn HQ. B 23 b 4 8.
A wire is being laid to A Coy HQ.

[illegible] Capt

8th Bn. London Regt: Warning Order

1.5.18

1. 2 Coys. of the Life Guards Battn. are taking over the line held by the 174 Bde. this evening.

2. The Battn. after relief will concentrate at a point and time to be notified later.

3. Reorganisation will be at once carried out as far as possible on the following lines.

All N.C.O.'s & men will join their now Companies as follows:

A Coy – under 2 Lt. TALLIN will concentrate on Eastern edge of MARRIERES WOOD in A 13 b.

B Coy – under 2 Lt. PEACOCK in trenches about C 21 a & b.

C Coy – under 2 Lt. WILLS in AGILE AVENUE West of C 13 b 0 2.

D Coy – under 2 Lt. BUCK in trenches East of C 13 b 0 2.

2 Lt. YALE with B Coy.

2 Lt. BASSETT " C ".

All officers will on receipt of this order take immediate steps to conduct men to their company area. Owing to enemy observation all movement must be reduced to the minimum necessary.

4. Reports to B. HQ. B 23 b 4 8.

A wire is being laid to A Coy HQ.

[illegible] Capt

Instructions regarding War Diaries and Intelligence Summaries are contained in F. S. Regs., Part II. and the Staff Manual respectively. Title pages will be prepared in manuscript.

9

WAR DIARY
or
INTELLIGENCE SUMMARY.
(Erase heading not required.)

8 London Rg

Army Form C. 2118.

174/58

21

Place	Date	Hour	Summary of Events and Information	Remarks and references to Appendices
HINDLEG WOOD NEAR HEM	SEPT 2		Day was spent in cleaning up & reorganization. Major C.H. WILD Royal West Kent assumed command of Bn. The following officers were with the Battalion on September 2nd 1918	
			Commanding Officer ~~[illegible]~~ Major C.H. WILD Sec in Command Capt G.C. FABER	
			Adjt Capt L.E.B. JACOB. Sec Lt J.F.W. KELLY (I.O) Sec Lt J.O. RIORDAN (Sig Officer) Lt W.B MACBEAN (M.O) Sec Lt H. ROSS (a/T.O) Capt H.T. CHAPMAN (Q.M)	[initials]
			A Coy Sec Lt G.P.R. TALLIN (O.C) Sec Lt S.C. FERGUSON Sec Lt V.W.G. SMITH	
			B Coy Sec Lt J.M. BARRATT (O.C) Sec Lt H. PEACOCK Sec Lt F.A. YALE	
			C Coy Sec Lt G.F. WILLS (O.C)	
			D Coy Sec Lt A. BUCK (O.C) Sec Lt C.A. BASSETT.	
			and 830 ORs.	
do	3		Reorganization carried on. Sec Lt C.F. YOUNGMAN rejoined from leave & assumed command of C Coy.	[initials]
do	4.		Company Training. Capt PURRIS (T.O) rejoined from leave & Sec Lt ROSS joined C Coy. Sec Lt R.B PATTINSON rejoined from course & took command of D Coy. Sec Lt G.F. WILLS proceeded on III Corps L.G. Course.	[initials]
do	5.		Brigade Practice attack in the morning. Extremely heavy thunderstorm in the evening, all tents & bivouacs flooded.	[initials]

D. D. & L., London, E.C. (A8001) Wt. W1771/M2031 750,000 5/17 Sch. 52 Forms/C2118/14

Instructions regarding War Diaries and Intelligence Summaries are contained in F. S. Regs., Part II. and the Staff Manual respectively. Title pages will be prepared in manuscript.

WAR DIARY
or
INTELLIGENCE SUMMARY.
(Erase heading not required.)

Army Form C. 2118.

Place	Date	Hour	Summary of Events and Information	Remarks and references to Appendices
HINDLEG WOOD Nr HEM	6		Warning order recieved Bde would move in afternoon 2nd Lt J.M. BARRATT proceeded on leave 2nd Lt Buck took command of B Co. Btn moved at 3.30 P.M. and embussed at B27 a 22 arriving at MOISLAINS at 10 P.M. Marched from here to VILLE WOOD and arrived 12.15 AM. taking over from 23rd LONDON R.	JR
VILLE WOOD MOISLAINS	7		Morning clear and warm. Men rested. Brigade ordered reconnaissance to be made around SAULCOURT. LIERAMONT + GUYENCOURT. Movement order recieved 7.30 P.M. Battn moved 10.30 P.M. VIA LIERAMONT and GUYENCOURT to sunken road E4 A+C and took over from the BUFFS	JR
SUNKEN RD before EPEHY	8 9 10		Special appendix. The following officers were present.	appendix 1
			MAJOR C H WILD (CO) CAPT L E B JACOB. (ADJ) Lt R N SHAPLEY (SIGNALS) 2Lt J F W KELLY (I.O)	
			CAPT G C FABER (2 i/c) CAPT T A B PURKIS (T.O) CAPT A H CHAPMAN (QM) Lt W MACBEAN	
			A. Co 2nd Lt G P R TALLIN (OC) 2Lt S C FERGUSON 2Lt F YALE	
			B. Co 2Lt A BUCK (OC) 2Lt H PEACOCK	
			C. Co 2Lt C YOUNGMAN (OC) 2Lt SMITH.	
			D. Co 2Lt R B PATTINSON (OC) 2Lt J L RIORDAN 2Lt C A BASSETT	JR

D. D. & L., London, E.C. (A8001) Wt. W1771/M2031 750,000 5/17 Sch. 52 Forms/C2118/14

Instructions regarding War Diaries and Intelligence Summaries are contained in F. S. Regs., Part II. and the Staff Manual respectively. Title pages will be prepared in manuscript.

WAR DIARY
or
~~INTELLIGENCE SUMMARY.~~
(Erase heading not required.)

Army Form [illegible] 2118.

Place	Date	Hour	Summary of Events and Information	Remarks and references to Appendices
" Lievramont.	11		Day fine & warm. Men rested all day	JH
	12		Weather showery. Day spent in cleaning equipment and arms for inspection by C.O. next day. The Brigade ordered a reconnaissance to be made by two officers in defensive system round Taulcourt and Guyencourt in event of attack. Result to be furnished to Brigade. At 5 P.M. Brigade ordered Battn to move to shelters in area E14B & E9C during the evening. An advance party was sent off immediately to allot ground. The night was very stormy and wet, and move was cancelled about 7 P.M. The following reinforcements joined Batt. Lt R D. ANDERSON 2Lt F.G. MACINNES 2Lt ARTHUR R. BOWDEN 2Lt JOSEPH CHARLES BATTOCK 2Lt R. REEVES-MOORE. Lt R.D. Anderson assumed command of D Coy. 18 other ranks joined Battn on this day.	JH
Lievramont	13		Morning cold and wet. Company inspected by C.O. Reorganisation and specialist training until 12.30. Baths allotted from 5AM but Battn stood by ready to move at hours notice until 11 AM when Brigade cancelled order. Baths were allotted 12.30 P.M. as arranged. Bathing to be continued on Monday.	JH

D. D. & L., London, E.C. (A5094) Wt. W1771/M2931 750,000 5/17 Sch. 52 Forms/C2118/14

Instructions regarding War Diaries and Intelligence Summaries are contained in F. S. Regs., Part II. and the Staff Manual respectively. Title pages will be prepared in manuscript.

WAR DIARY

~~or~~

~~INTELLIGENCE SUMMARY.~~

(Erase heading not required.)

Army Form C. 2118.

Place	Date	Hour	Summary of Events and Information	Remarks and references to Appendices
LIERAMONT	14		Morning fine and warm. Training carried on as usual. Coy Cmdrs made a reconnaissance ~~[illegible]~~ of trenches around Guyencourt & Saulcourt. Considerable enemy bombing by night.	JH
do	15		Morning showery. Orders received to relieve 175th Bde. in EPEHY SECTOR at night. Coy Cmdrs made reconnaissance of these positions by day. Battn moved off 8 P.M. at intervals of 10 minutes between Coys. D C & B Coys in front line A Coy in support. Relief complete at 10.15 P.M.	Appendix II JH
Before Epehy			I.O. took out patrol along Battn front. Everything very quiet.	
do	16		2nd Lt. A.M. Robinson + 2nd Lt A.R.T. Robinson joined Battn as reinforcements. Morning cold and damp. Little machine gun fire during night between and fairly heavy artillery fire during day. No casualties. Fighting patrol out at night. Brigade report enemy evacuating Epehy. At 10 P.M. three patrols sent out. Enemy still in occupation. Wire in front of [illegible] line reported strong with few gaps. Gas shells fired.	JH
do	17		Morning wet & cold. Heavy rain. Trenches waterlogged. Later sunny. Occasional artillery bombardment. Otherwise day passed quietly. Arrangements made with Cambridgeshire Regiment for relief. Brigade ordered guides for 12th Division. Battn guided into position by 12.30 A.M. Gas bombardment [illegible]	JH Appendix III B.H.P.

Instructions regarding War Diaries and Intelligence Summaries are contained in F. S. Regs., Part II. and the Staff Manual respectively. Title pages will be prepared in manuscript.

WAR DIARY
or
INTELLIGENCE SUMMARY.
(Erase heading not required.)

Army Form C. 2118.

Place	Date	Hour	Summary of Events and Information	Remarks and references to Appendices
Before Epehy	Sept 18		12th Division passed through and attacked at zero. A + C Co with view to LIERAMONT at 2 AM. B.H.Q., D + B companies following at 5 PM. C Co and A Coy had baths and issue of clean clothes during the day	[illegible]
LIERAMONT	19		Morning cold + wet. Companies cleaned up and had baths and clean issue. Fresh S.D. issued. Men rested. C.O to visit all ranks next day	[illegible]
LIERAMONT.	20		Morning clear but windy. Companies inspected and carried out Coy attack schemes for battalion attack scheme next day. At 5.10 PM order to proceed to TEMPLEUX-LE-GUERARD QUARRIES at once to act as reserve to 74th Division. Battn moved off 7.15 PM. via VILLERS FAUCON TEMPLEUX LE GUERARD to QUARRY. The night was bright and E.A bombed Bn on the way. Entering the QUARRY a bomb fell amongst B Co and it sustained four casualties. Throughout the night the battn was heavily shelled and gassed causing casualties. Battn attached to 229th Infantry Bde. 2/Lt A Buck proceeded on leave	[illegible]
TEMPLEUX	21		Morning clear. 74th Division attacked at dawn and battn received orders to move to Green Line (Reserve Line) and relieve Black Watch and 16th Devons who moved forward to support. The Battn moved at [illegible] to Harry Lane. Enemy shelled and gassed the route	[illegible]

D. D. & L., London, E.C. (A5001) Wt. W1771/M2031 750,000 5/17 Sch. 52 Forms/C2118/14

Army Form C. 2118.

WAR DIARY
or
~~INTELLIGENCE SUMMARY.~~
(Erase heading not required.)

Instructions regarding War Diaries and Intelligence Summaries are contained in F. S. Regs., Part II. and the Staff Manual respectively. Title pages will be prepared in manuscript.

Place	Date	Hour	Summary of Events and Information	Remarks and references to Appendices
TEMPLEUX QUARRY	21		The Battn held line from road junction F10c(?) to TOINE'S POST. BHQ was in HARRY LANE. The following officers were present with Battn. Major C H Wild (CO) Capt L.E.B Jacob (ADJ) Lt R N SHAPLEY (SIGNALS) 2/Lt J E W. KELLY (I.O) Lt W. MACBEAN (M.O) Capt Rev H C JAMES (CHAPLAIN) 2Lt G.P.R TALLIN (OC AC) 2Lt F G Mac Innes 2Lt E.M. Robinson B Co. 2/Lt R REEVES-MOORE (OC) 2Lt H PEACOCK C C. 2/Lt H ROSS (OC) 2Lt A.R.T. Robinson 2Lt A BOWDEN D C Lt R D ANDERSON (OC) 2Lt N. SMITH 2Lt J.C. BATTOCK	JH.
TEMPLEUX HARRYLANE	22		Morning fine & warm. Enemy shelled continually throughout the day. Men rested. Orders received remainder of 174 Bde would take over part of GREEN LINE on our left. Bde to be lent to 18th Division. 55th Bde Heavy gas bombardment at night. Several casualties. (TOINE POST F28 b inclusive to junction of DUSE TRENCH & PATRICKS AVENUE F10 c 37)	JH.
TEMPLEUX HARRYLANE	23		Morning wet & cloudy. The Battn moved to right and held sector from G in HARGICOURT to ORCHARD POST exclusive. A Co in centre C Co on left B Co on right and D C in Reserve. During night heavy gas bombardment. C Coy had a number of casualties.	appendix JH IV
do	24		Morning fine. HOSTILE AIRCRAFT flew over our lines at 300 ft sweeping our trenches with machine gun fire. One machine brought down at 11.30 a.m. Orders received Battn would be relieved by 105th American Regiment. Relief completed at 9.30 pm. Battn withdrew by Coys to ST EMELIE and embussed for HEILLY. Btn moved for HEILLY at 3.30 am.	appendices JH V & VI

D. D. & L., London, E.C.
(A8001) Wt. W1771/M2931 750,000 5/17 Sch. 52 Forms/C2118/14

Instructions regarding War Diaries and Intelligence Summaries are contained in F. S. Regs., Part II. and the Staff Manual respectively. Title pages will be prepared in manuscript.

WAR DIARY
~~or~~
~~INTELLIGENCE SUMMARY.~~
(~~Erase heading not required.~~)

Army Form C. 2118.

Place	Date	Hour	Summary of Events and Information	Remarks and references to Appendices
HEILLY	25		Battn arrived at HEILLY at 10-15 AM and were billetted around the Chateau. Men rested and cleaned up for inspection. The following officers joined the battn. 2Lt F.R. JULIAN 2Lt F. DAVIES 2Lt H. BENN 2Lt S.R. POWL 2Lt R.C. STECKLEY. Lt T.F. HANNAH Lt W.M. PETERS. Orders received battn would move to CHATEAU-DE-LA-HAIE. One officer to go on in advance with Brigade at 9. AM next morning. Train from HEILLY STATION to SAVY BERLETTE.	[initials]
do	26		All companies inspected by Coy Cmdrs. Men rested. Kit inspection. Lt COL A GROVER D.S.O. M.C. joined battn and assumed command. Battn moved with all stores & transport at 9.30 PM and entrained at HEILLY STATION.	Appendix VII
SAVY BERLETTE	27		Btln arrived at 5.30 P.M. and afterwards marched to ST LAWRANCE CAMP CHATEAU DE LA HAIE arriving at 9.30 PM. Coy Cmdrs received orders to proceed to Brigade HQ next morning at 9 AM to reconnoitre trench system near LOOS to prepare to take over from Royal Fusiliers.	[initials]
CHATEAU DE LA HAIE	28		Morning wet & cold. Companies inspected by Major Wild. Reconnoitring party went by lorry to BULLY GRENAY and arranged relief. Men rested. Deficiencies made up.	[initials]
do	29		Morning fine. Brigade Church Parade at 9.30. CO's conference for Coy Commanders at 11 AM. Orders received for battn to embus next day at 4 P.M.	[initials]

D. D. & L., London, E.C.
(A8001) Wt. W1771/M2031 750,000 5/17 Sch. 52 Forms/C2118/14

Instructions regarding War Diaries and Intelligence Summaries are contained in F. S. Regs., Part II. and the Staff Manual respectively. Title pages will be prepared in manuscript.

WAR DIARY

or

~~INTELLIGENCE~~ SUMMARY.

(*Erase heading not required.*)

Army Form C. 2118.

Place	Date	Hour	Summary of Events and Information	Remarks and references to Appendices
CHATEAU DE [illegible] HAIE	30.		Morning cold and dull. COs conference for all officers. Final arrangements as to transport. Battle surplus arranged. Men rested. Battn embussed at gates of CHATEAU at 4.15 PM and reached GRENAY at 6 PM. Guides from ROYAL FUSILIERS arrived at 7 PM and companies moved off independently. Relief complete 12.30 AM. The following officers were with the battn. LT COL A. GROVER DSO MC (CO) MAJOR C H WILD (2/c) CAPT L E B JACOB (ADJ) LT W. KENNEDY (MO) LT R N SHAPLEY (SIGNALS) 2LT J.F.W. KELLY (I.O) 2LT R. REEVES-MOORE (ASST. ADJ) Capt & REV H.C. JAMES (CHAPLAIN) CAPT T A B PURKIS (T.O) CAPT A.T. CHAPMAN (QM) A.C. 2LT G.P.R. TALLIN (O.C) 2LT H BENN 2LT E.M. ROBINSON B C 2LT J.M. BARRATT (OC) 2LT F.R. JULIAN 2LT F DANIEL C Co LT T.R HANNAH (OC) LT M PETERS 2/LT G WILLS 2LT R. STECKLEY D Co LT R.D ANDERSON (OC) 2LT J. BATTOCK 2LT S.R. POWL 2LT H PEACOCK proceeded on leave	JK

A. D. Derviche-Jones
Lt Col
Commanding 8th London Regt.

D. D. & L., London, E.C.
(A8004) Wt W1771/M2031 750,000 5/17 Sch. 52 Forms/C2118/14

Secret.

Administrative Instructions
in conjunction with
175th Infantry Brigade Order No.145.

11.9.18.

1. Dress. - Fighting Order less Overcoats; Water Bottles filled.

2. Battle Stores. - Each man will carry 170 rounds S.A.A.

S.O.S.Rockets will only be carried by Officers, W.O's, and Senior N.C.O's.

A Brigade Dump has been established at E.13.a.4.7. and contains the following :-

Water.	300 Tins.
S.A.A.(ord).	125000 rds
S.A.A. (M.G).	25000 "
V.P.A. White.	850
W.P.A.	900
Flares (red).	300
S.O.S.Signals.	9
L.G.Magazines,filled	546
Stokes Shells.	200
Gdes.No23.	600
Gdes.No.36.	900

3 limbered G.S.Wagons, 6 Mules and 6 sets Pack Saddlery are held at Bde.H.Q. to meet urgent requirements.

3. Rations. - Rations for tomorrow will be delivered to Units in the line tonight. Guides will be detailed by Units to report at Bde.H.Q. as soon as possible to guide ration limbers forward to points selected by Officers Commanding.

4. Dumps. - All Stores which cannot be carried will be dumped at the Brigade Dump E.13.a.4.7. Detailed lists should accompany them for the N.C.O. i/c.

5. Medical. - Advanced Dressing Stn. & Walking Wounded Collecting Post is established at E.14.a.8.8.
Car Post is at E.9.d.2.9.

6. Straggler Arrangements.

Posts No.1.	E.15.a.1.3.
" " 2.	E.9.b.3.1.
" " 3.	E.7.c.2.4.
Collecting Stn	E.7.c.2.4.

The above posts are manned by Traffic Control personnel and are also Traffic Control Posts.

7. P.O.W.Cage. - D.22.a.2.4.

8. ACKNOWLEDGE.

Edwin Tilbury /[illegible]

A/Staff Captain
175th INFANTRY BDE

DISTRIBUTION: Normal.

5.15pm.

Secret.

Administrative Instructions in conjunction with 175th Infantry Brigade Order No.145.

11.9.18.

1. Dress. - Fighting Order less Overcoats; Water Bottles filled.

2. Battle Stores. - Each man will carry 170 rounds S.A.A.

S.O.S.Rockets will only be carried by Officers, W.O's, and Senior N.C.O's.

A Brigade Dump has been established at E.13.a.4.7. and contains the following :-

Water.	300	Tins.
S.A.A.(ord).	125000	rds
S.A.A. (L.G).	25000	"
V.P.A. White.	850	
W.P.A.	900	
Flares (red).	300	
S.O.S.Signals.	9	
L.G.Magazines,filled	546	
Stokes Shells.	200	
Gdes.No23.	600	
Gdes.No.36.	900	

3 limbered G.S.Wagons, 6 Mules and 6 sets Pack Saddlery are held at Bde.H.Q. to meet urgent requirements.

3. Rations. - Rations for tomorrow will be delivered to Units in the line tonight. Guides will be detailed by Units to report at Bde.H.Q. as soon as possible to guide ration limbers forward to points selected by Officers Commanding.

4. Dumps. - All Stores which cannot be carried will be dumped at the Brigade Dump E.13.a.4.7. Detailed lists should accompany them for the N.C.O. i/c.

5. Medical. - Advanced Dressing Stn. & Walking Wounded Collecting Post is established at E.14.a.8.8.
Car Post is at E.9.d.2.9.

6. Straggler Arrangements.

Posts No.1.	E.15.a.1.3.
" " 2.	E.9.b.3.1.
" " 3.	E.7.c.2.4.
Collecting Stn	E.7.c.2.4.

The above posts are manned by Traffic Control personnel and are also Traffic Control Posts.

7. P.O.W.Cage. - D.22.a.2.4.

8. ACKNOWLEDGE.

Edwin Tilbury [signature] /Capt.

A/Staff Captain
175th INFANTRY BDE

DISTRIBUTION: Normal.

5.15pm.

APPENDIX TO
PROVISIONAL DEFENCE SCHEME
SUPPORT BRIGADE.LEFT DIVISION
III CORPS.
(Issued 13th September, 18)

SIGNAL ARRANGEMENTS

1. Brigade Report Centre at E.3.c.1.5 is in communication with Brigade Headquarters via Headquarters of Brigade in the Line.

On receipt of "MAN BATTLE STATIONS" -

(a) a direct line will be laid from Brigade Headquarters to the Report Centre, and thence to the Headquarters of the Right and Support Battalions, the exchange at the Report Centre being taken over by Brigade Signals.

Sufficient cable is held in reserve for this purpose part to be kept at Brigade Headquarters and part at Report Centre.

(b) Visual will be established between E.3.c.4.3 and E.1.b.1.3.

(c) Brigade Runner post will be established at Report Centre.

2. Battalions will notify the Brigade Signal Officer early what amount of cable they would require to link up company Headquarters in case of "MAN BATTLE POSITIONS". This will be held reserve at the Report Centre.

14th September, 1918.

13-9-18

PROVISIONAL DEFENCE SCHEME

SUPPORT BRIGADE LEFT DIVISION.

III CORPS.

References 57.c S.E.)
62.c N.E.) 1/20,000
Bde. map attached.

1. In the event of hostile attack the 174th Infantr Brigade Group, composed as under, will man and hold at all costs the trench system from Southern Divisional Boundary at E.10.c.8.0 through E.10.a., E.9.b., E.3.d., E.3.b and W.27.d. W.28.a to Northern Divisional Boundary at W.22.c.4.0.

<u>174th Infantry Brigade GRoup</u>

6th London Regiment.
7th London Regiment.
8th London Regiment.
1/4th Suffolk Regiment.
"B" Coy., 58th M.G.Bn.
174th L.T.M.Battery.

2. The tactical features of this area are the ridge extending north-east from GUYENCOURT, the GUYENCOURT PLATEAU the valleys in E.2 and W.27 and in E.4 and W.28., and the low undulating country east of SAULCOURT.

There are many sunken roads and banks under cover of which the enemy could approach the line almost unobserved, whilst CHAUFFEURS WOOD constitutes a screen behind which he could form up for an attack.

The trenches defending this locality are in fair condition and the wire is on the whole good. There are however, numerous gaps, and Battalion Commanders will reconnoitre those on their respective fronts and take steps to protect them.

The dominant positions of the line are:-

(1) The high ground about E.3.d.1.7. which covers a greater part of the ridge N.E. of GUYENCOURT, the sunken road and the valley in E.4.a. and W.28.c and a., also the ridge in E.4.b, W.28.d.

(2) The junction of sunken roads in E.10.a from which localit are commanded the approaches North and South-west of CHAUFFEU WOOD and the greater part of the GUYENCOURT PLATEAU.

(3) The nose of the small salient in E.10.c.4.4., from whence the western edge of CHAUFFEURS WOOD is enfiladed and the Sout and South Eastern sides, together with the road passing throu E.10.b., d and c and the high ground in E.17.a and E.11.c can all be covered by fire.

(4) The high ground E.9.b.1.6 from which SAULCOURT WOOD and t valley in E.9.c. and 14.b are commanded.

3. On receipt of the command "MAN BATTLE STATIONS" the following positions will be taken up.

(a) The Brigade front will be held by the 6th Londons on the left and the 8th Londons on the right, the inter-battalion boundary being an E. & W. line through E.3.c.0.7.

A joint liaison post will be established at about E.3.d.2.7., the actual site being selected by Battalion

/Commanders in

Commanders in consultation.
(b) The 7th Londons will take up a position in E.2.b and d and will be held in readiness for counter-attack. No counter-attack will, however, be launched without orders from Brigade unless in the opinion of the Battalion Commander the situation demands immediate action.
(c) The 1/4th Suffolk Regiment will be concentrated in the sunken roads in E.7.d where they will await orders from Brigade.
(d) "B" Coy, 58th M.G.Bn., will take up the positions shown on the attached map "A".

4. The dispositions of Battalions on manning their battle position are shewn on the attached map "A"

5. 174th. L.T.M.Battery will attach two guns to each of the forward Battalions.

6. Brigade Headquarters will remain at W.25.c.2.5. Advanced Report Centre will be established at E.3.c.1.5.

7. Administrative and Signal Instructions in connection with the scheme will be issued separately.

8. ACKNOWLEDGE.

[signature]

Captain.
Brigade Major.
174th Infantry Brigade.

13th. September, 18.

Distribution: -

G.O.C.
6th Londons
7th Londons
8th Londons
174th.L.T.M.B.
"B" Co., 58th M.G.Bn.
1/4th Suffolks (Pioneers)
Bde. Signal Officer.
Staff Captain.
58th Division.
Right Flank Bde.
Left Flank Bde.
173rd Infantry Bde.
175th Infantry Bde.
War Diary.
File.

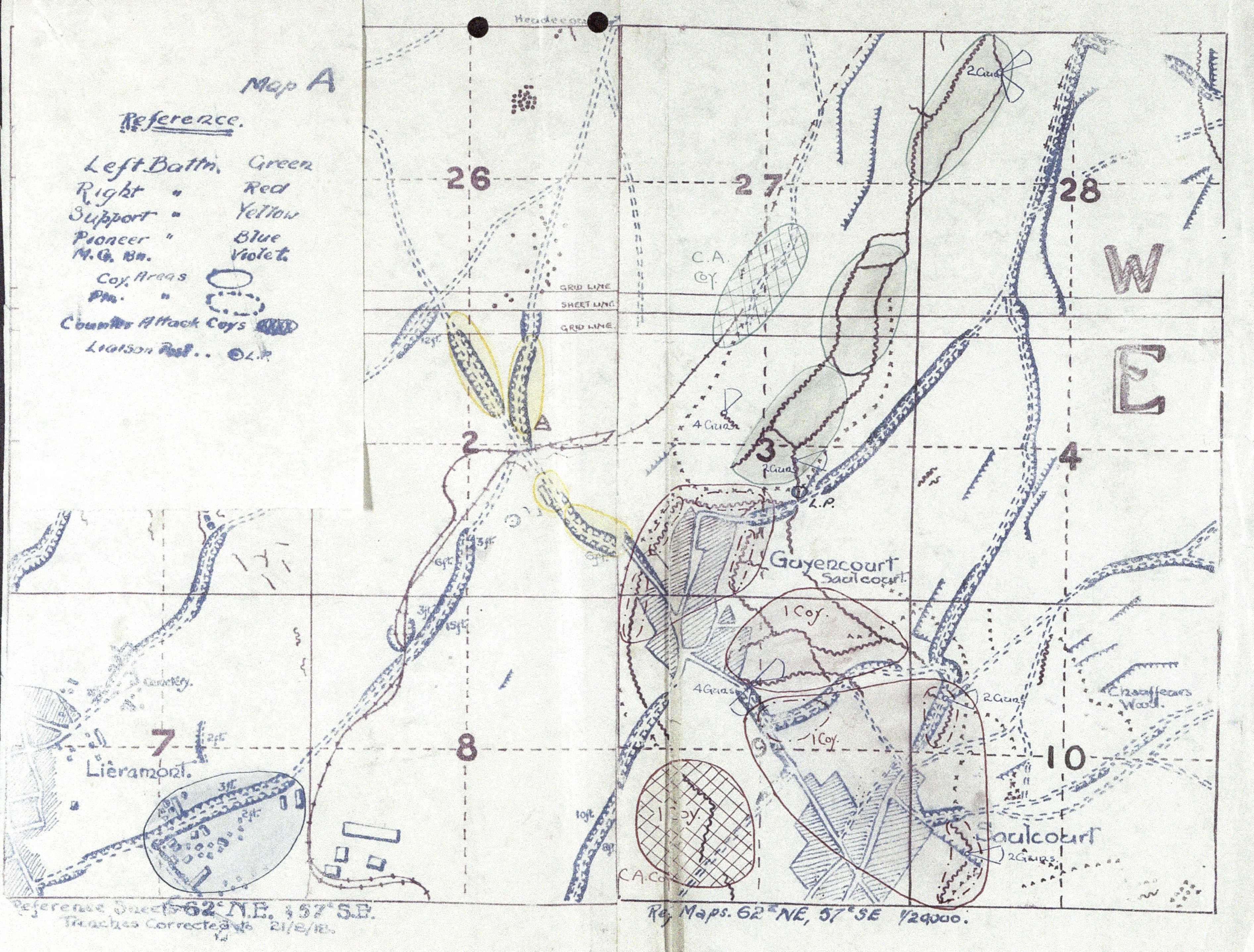

Map A
Reference.
Left Battn. Green
Right " Red
Support " Yellow
Pioneer " Blue
M.G. Bn. Violet.
Coy. Areas
Pln. "
Counter Attack Coys
Liaison Post.. L.P.
26
27
28
2
3
4
7
8
9
10
W
E
GRID LINE
SHEET LINE
GRID LINE
C.A. Coy.
4 Guns
2 Guns
L.P.
Guyencourt
Saulcourt.
1 Coy.
1 Coy.
C.A. Coy.
Saulcourt
Chauffeurs Wood.
Lieramont.
Reference Sheets 62c N.E. & 57c S.E.
Trenches Corrected to 21/2/18.
Ref. Maps. 62c NE, 57c SE 1/20000.

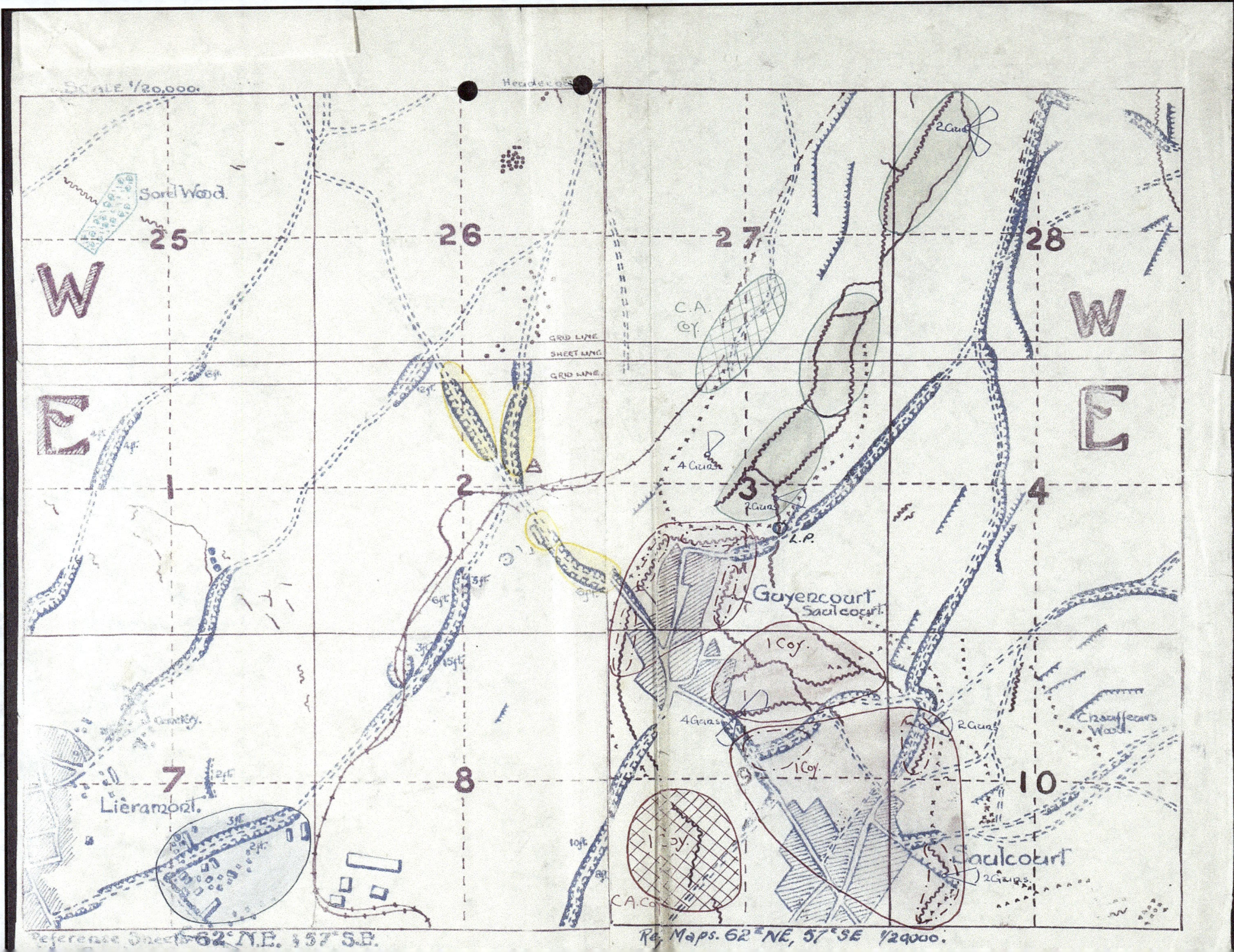

SCALE 1/20,000.
Sorel Wood.
25
26
27
28
W
E
GRID LINE
SHEET LINE
GRID LINE
C.A. Coy.
2 Guns
4 Guns
L.P.
1
2
3
4
Guyencourt
Saulcourt
1 Coy.
Chauffeurs Wood.
4 Guns
7
8
10
Lieramont.
C.A. Coy.
Saulcourt
2 Guns.
Reference Sheets 62c N.E. & 57c S.E.
Ref. Maps. 62c NE, 57c SE 1/20000.

S E C R E T.

22-9-18

Bn/7/141.

174th Infantry Brigade Provisional Defence Scheme
for Green Line, 18th Divisional Front.

Reference -
Sheet 62 c N.E. 1/20,000.

22nd September, 19[illegible]

1. The Green Line on the Brigade front extends from the junction of DOSE TRENCH and ST. PATRICKS AVENUE F.10.c.4.7 along DOSE TRENCH, THISTLE TRENCH, SHAMROCK TRENCH, ORCHARD POST, DOINE TRENCH to TOINE POST (inclusive) F.28.b.3.1.

The tactical features of the area are ST. PATRICKS VALLEY and the LEMPIRE VALLEY (separated by the RONSSOY RIDGE) on the North and the BASSE BOULOGNE - GUILLEMONT FARM Ridge crossed by the EGG POST - BENJAMIN POST Ridge on the East. Our positions in DOSE TRENCH are overlooked from the KNOLL in F.12.a. and the TOMBOYS VALLEY and TOMBOY FARM localities afford cover for the forming up of hostile forces.

2. (a) The Brigade front is held by three battalions in the line.

Inter-battalion boundaries are as follows :-

F.10.c.4.7 to COLLEEN POST (exclusive) Left Battalion.
COLLEEN POST (inclusive) to cross-roads F.22.b.4.3. Centre Battalion.
Cross-roads F.22.b.4.3. to TOINE POST (inclusive) Right Battalion.

(b) Liaison Posts will be found as under :-

By Left Battalion with 12th Division.	F.10.c.4.7.
By Left and Centre Battalions.	At COLLEEN POST
By Centre and Right Battalions.	Cross-roads F.22.b.4.3
By Right Battalion with 74th Division.	F.28.b.35.05 (South of TOINE POST)

3. Battalions will be disposed as under :-

(a) Left Battalion.

One Company in DOSE TRENCH.

One Company in THISTLE TRENCH from F.16.b.2.7 to Liaison Post with Centre Battalion.

One Company in RIDGE RESERVE SOUTH from F.16.a.1.7 to F.16.c.9.5.

One Company (for counter-attack) in the trench running between F.15.d.2.9 and F.15.d.9.3.

As many men as possible of the two support companies will be accommodated in dugouts in RONSSOY but will immediately man their battle positions in the event of hostile attack.

(b) Centre Battalion.

One Company in COLLEEN POST and BASSE BOULOGNE NORTH.

One Company in SHAMROCK TRENCH in the neighbourhood of BASSE BOULOGNE SOUTH.

Remaining two companies in dugout accommodation in RONSSOY.

In the event of hostile attack one of the remaining companies will at once occupy the trench system from F.16.c.2.1. to F.22.a.2.3. The fourth company will be held for counter-attack.

(c) Right Battalion will hold its front with three companies in the front line and one counter-attack company in the trench from F.23.a.1.6 to F.22.c.5.1.

/4. Headquarters

4. Headquarters are as under :-

174th Brigade H.Q.	E.24.a.5.7.
Advanced H.Q.	F.21.b.2.1 (moving to F.21.[illegible]
Left Battalion.	F.21.a.7.4.
Centre Battalion.	F.21.b.7.8.
Right Battalion	F.28.a.3.7.
"B" Coy. 58th M.G.Bn.)	With Brigade H.Q.
174th L.T.M.Bty.)	

5. The Machine Gun defence of Centre and Left Subsectors is as laid down by O.C. 18th M.G.Battalion. [illegible] Machine Gun defence of Right Subsector is as taken over from 74th Divisi[illegible]
Details of these defences and of artillery and Stokes Mortar defences will be issued ~~at~~ later.

6. Administrative and Signal Instructions in connection with this scheme will be issued later.

7. Acknowledge.

Captain,
Brigade Major,
174th. Infantry Brigade.

Copies to :-
G.O.C.
6th London Regt.
7th London Regt.
8th London Regt.
174th L.T.M.Bty.
"B" Coy. 58th M.Gun Bn.
Det. 1/1st Northumbeeland Hussars.
Bde. Signal Officer.
Staff Captain.
18th Division.
58th Division.
53rd Inf. Brigade.
239th Inf. Brigade.
War Diary.
File.
54th Infantry Bde
55th Infantry Bde

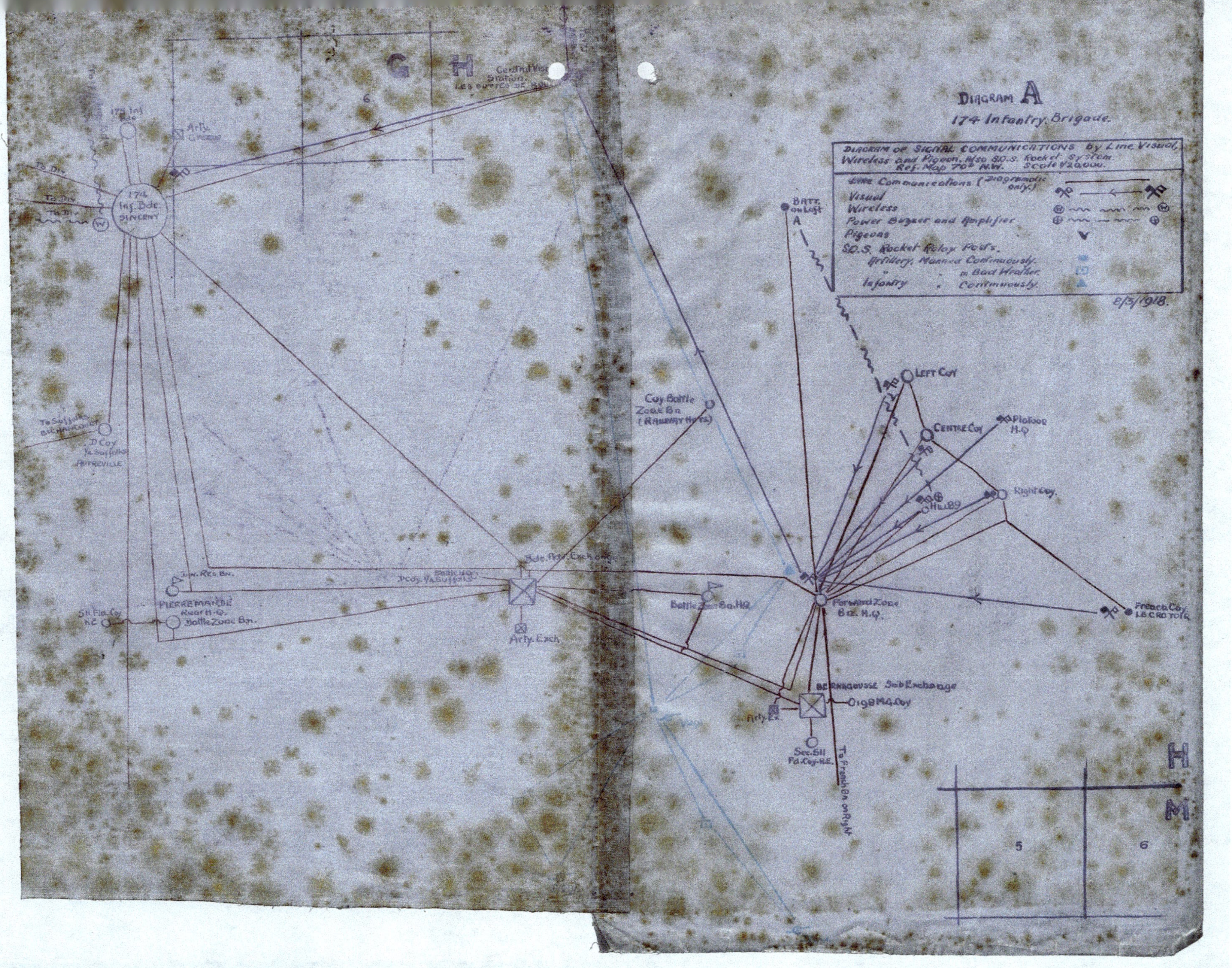

DIAGRAM A
174 Infantry Brigade.
DIAGRAM OF SIGNAL COMMUNICATIONS by Line, Visual, Wireless and Pigeon. Also S.O.S. Rocket System.
Ref. Map 70D N.W. Scale 1/20,000.
Line Communications (Diagrammatic only.)
Visual
Wireless
Power Buzzer and Amplifier
Pigeons
S.O.S. Rocket Relay Posts.
Artillery, Manned Continuously.
" " in Bad Weather.
Infantry " Continuously.
8/3/1918.
G
H
5
6
Central Visual Station.
LES BUTTES DE ROUY
173 Inf. Bde.
Arty. Group
To Div.
To Div.
To Div.
174 Inf. Bde. SINCENY
To Suffolks BICHANCOURT
D Coy 1/4 Suffolks
AUTREVILLE
1/4 W. Res. Bn.
PIERREMANDE Rear H.Q. Battle Zone Bn.
511 Fld. Coy. R.E.
Battle H.Q. D Coy. 1/4 Suffolks
Bde. Arty. Exchange
Arty. Exch.
Coy. Battle Zone Bn. (RAILWAY HUTS)
Battle Zone Bn. H.Q.
BATT. on Left
A
LEFT COY
CENTRE COY
Platoon H.Q.
Right Coy.
Hill 89
Forward Zone Bn. H.Q.
French Coy. LE CROTOIR
BERNAGOUSSE Sub Exchange
0198 M.G. Coy.
Arty. Ex.
Sec. 511 Fd. Coy. R.E.
To French Bn. on Right
H
M
5
6

DIAGRAM B

To illustrate distribution

of ALARM ~~SIGNALS~~ WARNINGS

291 R.F.A.
Warn: All Artillery concerned

Bde HQ.
Warn: Bde HQ Officers } Sec. 182 Tunn[g] Coy }

D Coy 1/4 Suff[k] Reg[t]
Warn: 1/4 Suff[k] Reg[t]

Reserve Batt[n]
Warn: All Coys

Battle Zone Batt[n]
Warn: Reserve Coy

5th Coy R.E.

S.T. Exchange
Warn: Sec. 198 M.G.C. H.19.c.95.20.

Coy. Battle Zone Batt[n] Railway Huts
Warn: Section M.G.C. H.21.a.7.9

Line Bn
Warn: All Coys 174 L.T.M.B. Sec. 198 M.G.C. H.16.d.4.7

B.J. Exchange Coy Battle Zone Batt[n]
Warn: ~~Sec. 214~~ Bde Tunn[g] Sec.

198 M.G.C.
Warn: Sec. M.G.C. H.28.d.90.51

Sec. 5th Fd Coy R.E.

War Diary.

8th Battalion London Regiment.

Appendix I.

NARRATIVE

of Operations near EPEHY from 6th - 10th September, 1918.

September 6th. Battalion moved by bus to MOISLANS in afternoon. From there marched to VILLE WOOD (62c. D.8.a.3.1) arriving about 1 am 7th Sept.

September 7th. Received orders to attack on following morning. Battalion marched from VILLE WOOD at 11 pm to SUNKEN ROAD, E. of GUYENCOURT, running from 57c. W.28.b.1.9. to 62c. E.4.c.4.4. arriving about 3 am.
Battalion here took up position of Assembly, "D" Company on right, "C" in centre, "A" on left and "B" Company in support.

September 8th. Battalion was in position by 6 am.
At 6.15 orders were received from Brigade to form up on line N. and S. grid line joining W.23.c.4.0. and E.5.c.4.0. As it was already daylight and it was impossible to move over ridge without being observed, Companies were ordered to creep forward as far as possible and then to catch up the barrage as soon as they could - the line of barrage was N. and S. grid line between W.23.d.0.0. and E.5.d.0.0.
ZERO hour was 7.30 am, barrage to rest there four minutes and then advance at intense rate 100 yards every 6 minutes to N. and S. grid line joining X.19.d.4.0 and F.1.d.4.0. Another barrage at slow rate to fall at ZERO on line joining E.6.c.4.0 and E.12.c.4.0., and rest on this line until caught up by other barrage and then proceed with it.
The barrage on the whole was very poor.
The objectives of the Brigade were KILDARE POST X.28.a.9.9. LITTLE PRIEL FARM X.28.d. through F.5.c - F.12 Central - F.12.c.9.0.
The Battalion had a frontage of 1,700 yards, their objectives being from KILDARE POST to BRERETON POST F.5.c.4.5. including the villages of PEIZIERES and EPEHY.
The 7th London Regiment was on our right and the 21st Division on our left: the 6th London Regt. in Support.
The 21st Division were to attack on our left, but did not intend to go further than 1,500 yards, unless we made our objectives and they were able to advance without fighting.
The following were in command of Companies :-
"A" Company 2/Lieut. G.P.R. TALLIN, "B" Company 2/Lieut. A. BUCK, "C" Company 2/Lieut. C.F. YOUNGMAN, "D" Company 2/Lieut. R.B. PATTINSON.

The Battalion moved forward when barrage started - "B" Company in Support 400 yards in rear. Companies were able to advance about 1,000 yards without many casualties - the enemy's barrage falling behind them. Later the Companies came under heavy machine gun fire and the attack got partially held up - "B" Company sent up a platoon to support "C" Company and 2 Sections to outflank a machine gun at WOOD FARM which was holding up the advance at that point. This operation was successfully carried out

"A"

"A" Company on right got held up by heavy M.G. fire on road running through E.6.a. About this time 2/Lieuts FERGUSSON and RIORDAN were killed and 2/Lieuts YOUNGMAN, PATTINSON and BASSETT wounded. Parties of "D", "C" and "B" Companies entered the villages of PEISIERES and EPEHY. In the former only 1 M.G. was encountered and enemy were seen retreating eastwards. As these parties were unable to get in touch with anyone on either flank and were being subjected to very considerable shelling and machine gun fire, they were compelled to fall back, and eventually all four Companies concentrated in trench running from W.29.b.8.9. to E.5.d.5.5., through TOTTENHAM POST and trenches in vicinity were held on to for a considerable time longer - one or two small parties remained in village till following morning.
About 30 prisoners were taken and several M.G's, but we were unable to get the latter away - most of them were however destroyed.
Owing to Corps on flanks not attacking, the Division altered the objectives to the line of trench X.25.a & c - F.1.b. - F.2.c. - F.8.b. - F.9.c. This message was received at 12.30 pm on the 8th. However, it was impossible owing to heavy M.G. fire to reach these objectives - my left flank were unable to get in touch with the 21st Division, who did not advance - consequently I put all my machine guns there to protect this flank.
Throughout the day and subsequent days "C" Battery of 62nd Brigade R.F.A. under Major RONEY DOUGALL rendered most efficient aid by taking on M.G's which were holding up the advance and any other targets which presented themselves, Major RONEY DOUGALL personnally at one time taking half his Battery to within 800 yards of the enemy.
Captain G.C. FABER went down sick.

<u>September 9th</u>. I went round the trenches in the morning with my Adjutant and Major RONEY DOUGALL. The trench line, though shallow, was in very fair condition and the wire in front good.
The Battalion were given orders that this line was to to held at all costs and patrols sent out to see if it was possible to advance and improve position.

<u>SEPTEMBER 10th</u>. The 173rd Infantry Brigade attacked through us at dawn - "B" and "C" Companies sending out battle patrols and making good the ground up to their line of assembly. "A" Company were ordered to report to Col. C.E.JOHNSTON, MC, Commanding 7th London Regt., to be attached to him during this operation, but owing to orders arriving late, and the very wet dark night, the Company lost its way and did not reach the 7th Londons. They subsequently were ordered back to the trenches they had left.
The Battalion was considerably shelled during the day, but suffered few casualties.
We were relieved at night by the 12th London Regt and marched back to billets at LIERAMONT, the last Coy. not getting in until after 6 am Sept. 11th.

The total casualties were 2 Officers killed and 4 wounded the 6th Officer being 2/Lieut. YALE, and 141 O.R's.
The weather for the last 24 hours was very bad - very heavy storms and high wind, and the trenches became very wet and muddy - the men suffered a good deal from exposure.

Major,
Commanding 8th London Regiment.

14th Sept., 1918.
F.O.517.

Copy No. 1

appendix II

SECRET. **8th London Regiment.**

OPERATION ORDER No. 76.

Reference 62C. N.E. 15th Sept., 1918.

INFORMATION. 1. 174th Brigade will relieve 173rd Brigade in the line tonight.

INTENTION. 2. 8th Battalion London Regt. will relieve 9th London in the Centre.
Companies will take over from corresponding Companies of the 9th London.

INSTRUCTIONS. 3. (a) Coys. will leave LIERAMONT at 10 minutes interval commencing at 8.30 pm in order H.Q., A. B. C. D. Coys.
(b) O.C. Coys. will reconnoitre the line this morning and will make own arrangements as to guides and routes.
(c) One limber will report to each Coy. and H.Q. at 8 pm to carry Lewis Guns, etc.
(d) Each man will carry one Bomb.
(e) Greatcoats and haversacks will be dumped at the Tailors Shop by 3 pm.
Officers valises will be dumped near Officers' quarters.
(f) Code Word for Relief complete "ENCORE."

REPORTS. 4. To Battalion H.Q. [illegible]. Location of Report Centre will be notified later.

[signature]
Captain & Adjutant.

Issued at 10 am.

Copies to :-
1. File.
2. War Diary.
3. C.O.
4. O.C. "A" Company.
5. O.C. "B" "
6. O.C. "C" "
7. O.C. "D" "
8. Headquarters.
9. T.O.
10. Q.M.

8th. L O N D O N R E G I M E N T

OPERATION ORDER No. 81.

1. At 0530 on 14th inst. the Battalion will make good the line of the CANAL on the whole of the Battalion Sector.
2. Artillery will co-operate.
3. O.C. A. Coy will detail a strong Fighting Patrol of one Platoon accompanied by one L.T.M. (which will deal with obstinate M.G's.) One Section (L.G.) willproceed along CANAL BANK to I 29 b. Remaining 3 Sections will move on to CANAL BANK via E. side of MARAIS WOOD.
4. Another Platoon of A Coy will follow in the same order at 200 yds distance.
5. One M.G. will cover the advance of the two Platoons until ZERO plus 35 mins when it will advance and take up a position on FOSSE 8 and protect the left flank of the Battalion.
6. On reaching the CANAL BANK A Coy will form Posts at:-
   I 30 A 0.3.
   I 30 A 7.4.
   I 30 b 9.8.
   The L.T.M. will take up a position about I 30 b 3.3.
7. When CANAL BANK is reached Patrols will be sent out to keep intouch with the enemy.
8. O.C. B. Coy willdetail a strong Fighting Patrol accompanied by a L.T.M. (which will pay special attention to the MAZE in I 36 b) The Patrol will move on to the CANAL BANK in the Coy Sector.
9. Another Platoon of B Coy will follow the Patrol at 200 yds distance to the CANAL BANK.
10. O.C. B.Coy will form Posts at :- J 25 A 5.5.
    J 25 A 9.1.
    J 25 b 3.2.
11. A Machine Gun will cover the advance of B Coy from I 36 B 9.8. aat ZERO plus 35 Mins this gun will move forward and take up aposition on the CANAL BANK about J 25 d 2.8.
12. The L.T.M. attached to B Coy will take up a position on the CANAL BANK about J 25 A 7.2.
13. O.C. B. Coy on occupying CANAL BANK will push out Patrols into OIGNIES.
14. O.C. D. Coy will send out a strong Fighting Patrol of one Platoon followed by another Platoon at 200 yds distance and make good the line of the CANAL on Coy Sector forming Posts at about:-
    J 25 d 7.0.
    J 31 b 3.4.
    J 31 d 6.2.
15. The advance of D Coy will be covered by 2 M.G's. from about O 6 c. Central At ZERO plus 35 the guns will move forward to a suitable position about P 1 A. Central.
16. O.C. D Coy on occupying CANAL BANK will push two Patrols in BOIS DES HAUTOIS.
17. The remaining Platoons of each Coy will be held as a Coy reserve to be used at Coy Commanders discretion.
18. A special report on conditions and location of bridges will be sent to B.H.Q. as soon as possible stating also if fit for foot or wheeled traffic.
19. O.C. Coys are reminded to send in dispositions as quickly as possible.

Issued at 0345 14/10/18
Copies to :- No 1. H.Q. 174 th Inf. Bde.
2 O.C. A Coy
3 O.C. B "
4 O.C. C "
5 O.C. No 7 Section M.G.
6 O.C. L.T.M.B.
7 File
8 War Diary.

Appendix IV

8th London Regt. Order No. 77.

17.9.18

—

Information 1. The 12th Div. will attack through 174 Bde at Zero hour tomorrow. 2 Coys of Cambridgeshire Regt will attack from the Battn front. 173 Bde will attack on left. 36th Bde on Right.

Intention 2. A. Coy. will withdraw from support trenches in E5a & c at 2 am. & proceed by march route to LIERAMONT. Guides will meet this Coy at LIERAMONT CEMETERY & conduct them to billet. On withdrawal of A Co. B Coy will leave 1 post per platoon and parties detailed for wire cutting (if any) and covering parties will withdraw to support trenches in E5a & c vacated by A Coy. The greatest care must be taken that the Coy on withdrawing do not pass through forming up line of Cambridge Regt. The attacking Coy of the Cambridgeshires will form up on line E5b7.4. to E5b7.9. The support Coy will assemble in trenches in E5c6. After arrival of B Coy in support trenches C. Coy. will withdraw from front line and proceed by march route to LIERAMONT. Guides will meet the Coy & conduct them to billets.

D. Coy under arrangements to be made with O/C B. Coy. will at the same time withdraw 1 platoon to trenches in E5a & c. O/C D Coy. will thin out his remaining 2 platoons in the front line, holding it with posts. The platoon (No 15) now in support line will remain there.

<u>Instructions 3.</u>

Rations for A & C. Coys will be delivered at LIERAMONT. Rations for B & D & H.Q. will come up as usual. Limbers for L.G.s of A & C. Coys will be at ~~Ration Dump~~ ~~[illegible]~~ at 2 a.m. (E4d.8.5) Care must be taken that all L.G. panniers & bombs are taken out.

OC Coy Appendix IV

1. The Battalion will extend tonight to the right along the GREEN LINE as far as L 4 B 14.

2. Half of B Coy under 2nd Lt PEACOCK will take over line from F 28 D 20 (where the road crosses trench) to Southern Boundary L 4 B 14.

3. A Coy will side step to join up with B Coy South of CONNOR POST at F 28 D 20.
A Coy's Northern Boundary will be F 28 B 1 7.

4 C Coy will side step to join up with A Coy at F 28 B 17

5. A & B Coy will reconnoitre their new line at once. Move will not take place until after 10 pm. Guides if required will be at F28c on road at F 28. c 7 8 from 10 pm onwards.

6. Names of the two Battalions holding the line to be relieved will be forwarded as soon as known. These Battalions will be in support ready to reinforce if necessary. A & B Coys will find out where these battalion HQ are & will send runners to get in touch.

7 Completion of move to be notified to Bn HQ

8 Acknowledge

4.3.23.4 22 April

Capt - Adjt

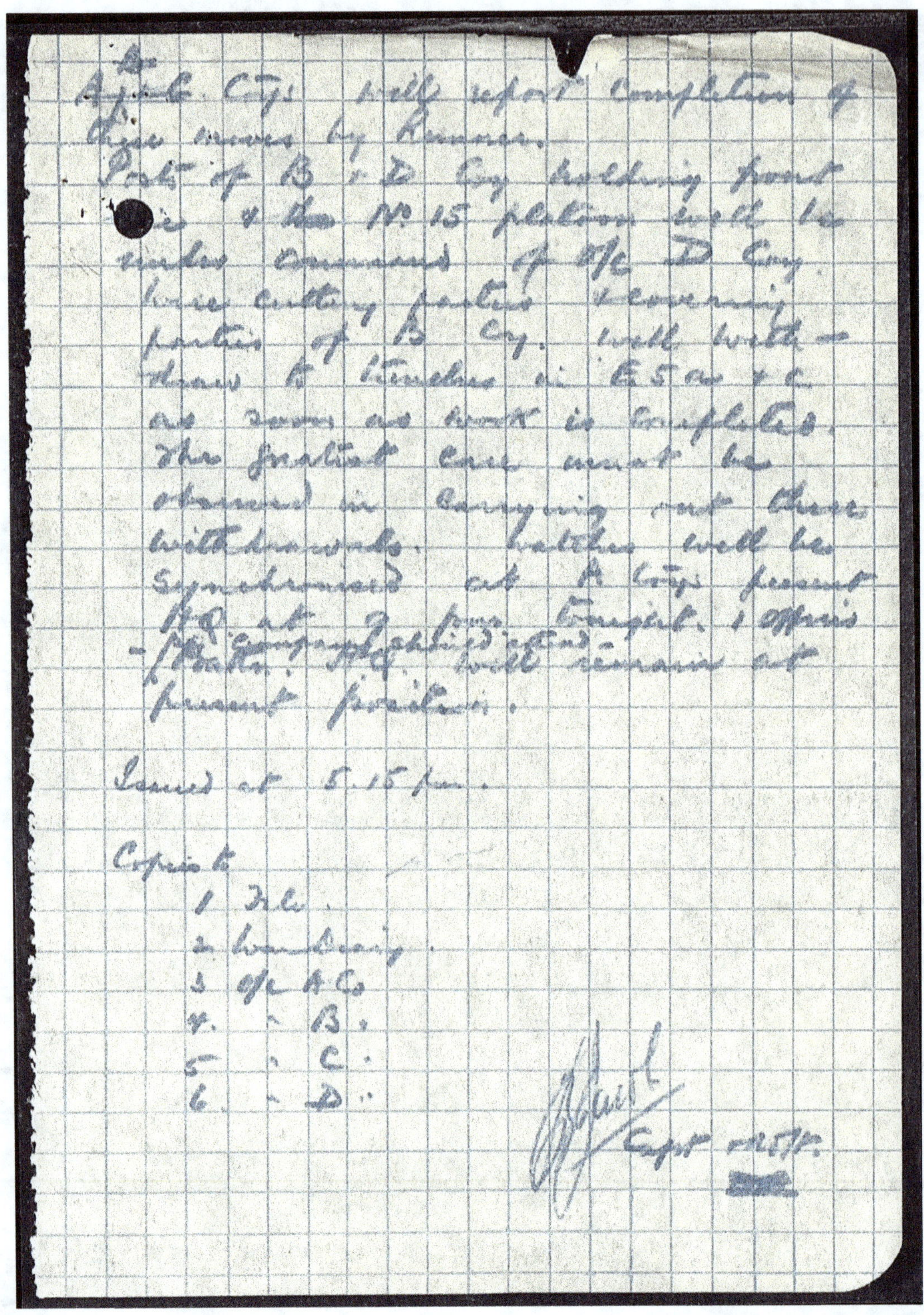

A & C Coys will report completion of these moves by Runner.
Posts of B & D Coy holding front line & the No 15 platoon will be under command of O/C D Coy.
Wire cutting parties & covering parties of B Coy. will withdraw to trenches in E5a & c. as soon as work is completed.
The greatest care must be observed in carrying out these withdrawals. Watches will be synchronised at A Coys present HQ at 7 pm tonight. 1 officer per company will attend. Battn. HQ will remain at present position.

Issued at 5.15 pm.

Copies to
1 File.
2 War Diary.
3 O/c A Co
4. " B.
5 " C.
6. " D."

[illegible]
Capt & Adjt.

O.C. Coy

Appendix V

AT STAND DOWN TO-DAY.

1. D Coy will withdraw to trenches at present occupied by B Coy from F28 c 7.7 to F28 a 4.3. on relief by 6th London

2 C Coy will hold line from F22 D 2 3 (South of ORCHARD POST) to F28 B 2 4 (North of TOINE POST) Both these posts will be exclusive to C Coy

3 A Coy will hold from TOINE POST inclusive to South of CONNOR POST inclusive at F28 D 2 0

4 B Coy will hold from F28 D 2 0 to [illegible] B 1 4.

5 Completion of move to be reported to Bn HQ by the word "WHAT AGAIN"

LJ 229

24.9.1918

A & C Coy Handed to [illegible] 3.26 [illegible]

LJ 234 Carpenter

[illegible] Capt & Adjt

8th London Regt

B & D Coys Handed to [illegible] 3.30 [illegible]

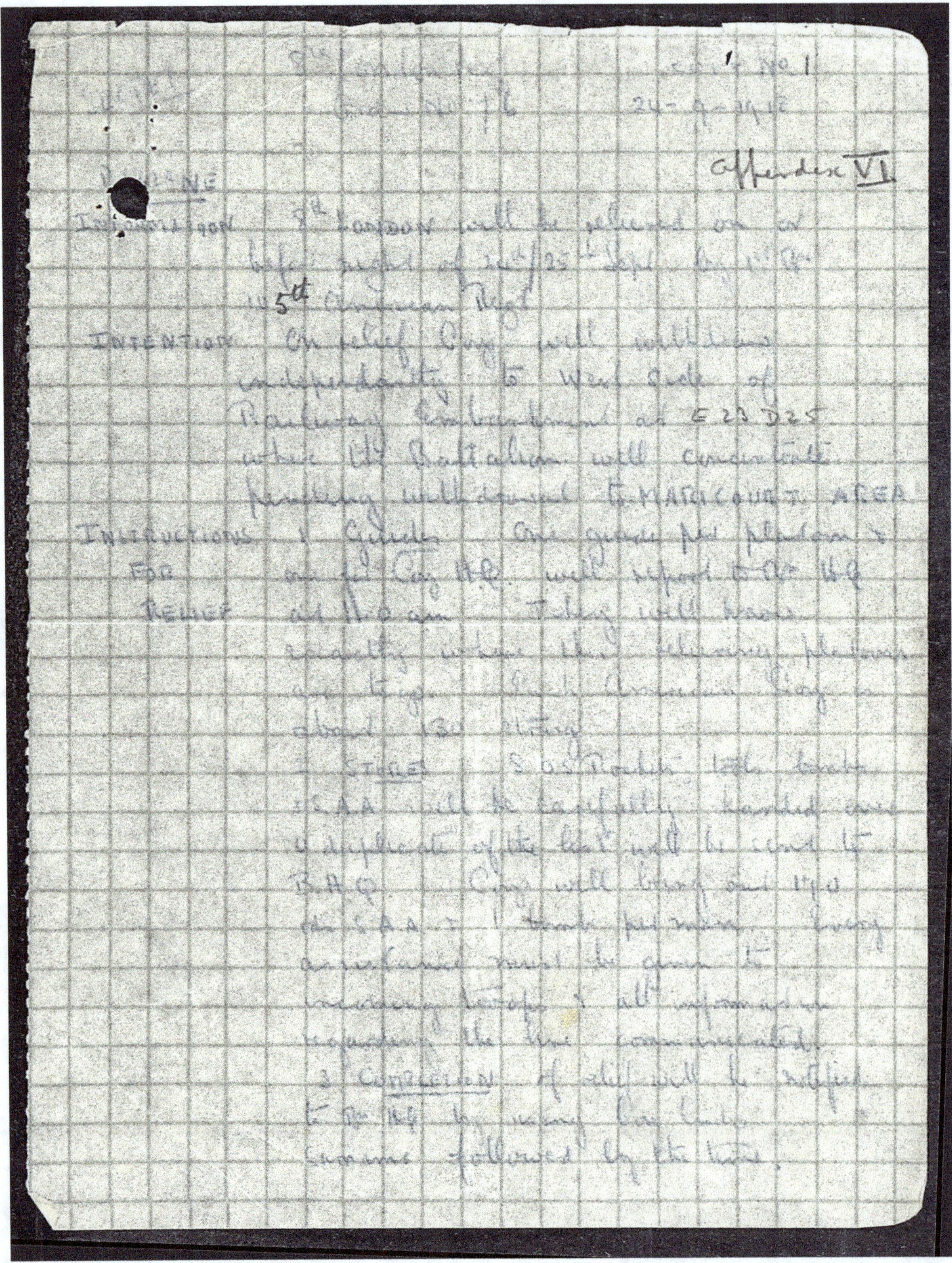

[illegible] 8th London Regt [illegible] No 1
[illegible] Order No 76 24-9-1918

Appendix VI

[illegible] LINE

INFORMATION 8th LONDON will be relieved on or before night of 24th/25th Sept by the 115th American Regt

INTENTION On relief Coys will withdraw independently to West side of Railway Embankment at E 23 D 25 where the Battalion will concentrate pending withdrawal to MARICOURT AREA

INSTRUCTIONS FOR RELIEF 1 Guides. One guide per platoon & one per Coy H.Q. will report to Bn H.Q at 11.0 am. [illegible] will know exactly where their relieving platoons are to go. Each American Coy is about 130 strong.

2 Stores. S.O.S. Rockets, [illegible] & S.A.A. will be carefully handed over & duplicate of the list will be sent to B.H.Q. Coys will bring out 170 rds S.A.A. & 1 bomb per man. Every assistance must be given to incoming troops & all information regarding the line communicated.

3 Completion of relief will be notified to Bn HQ by using Coy Code names followed by the time.

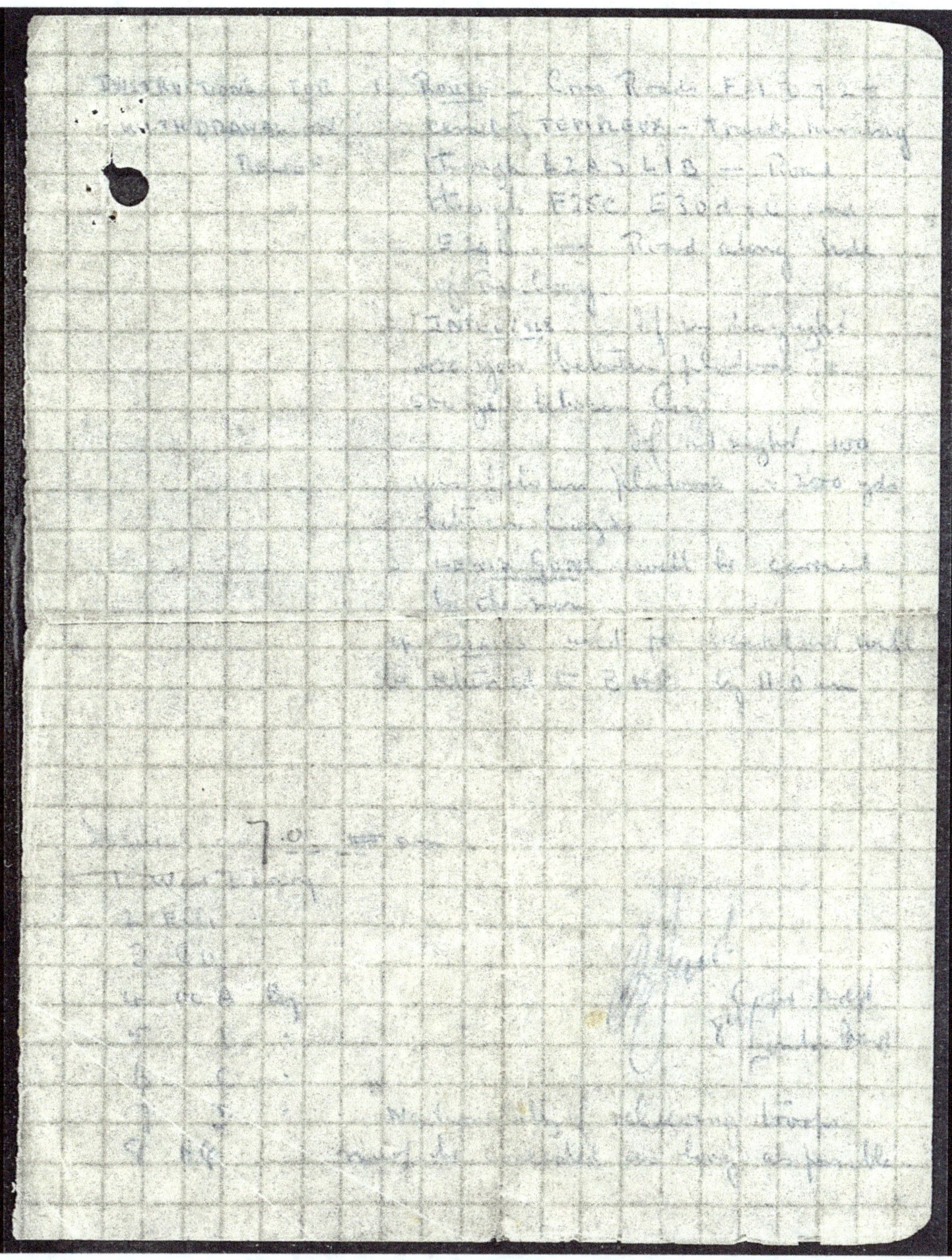

INSTRUCTIONS FOR WITHDRAWAL OF [illegible]

1. Route – Cross Roads F11 b 7.2 [illegible] TEMPLEUX – Road running through E2 [illegible] – Road [illegible] F15c E30 d [illegible] Road along [illegible]

2. INTERVALS [illegible]

[illegible] 2000 yds [illegible]

3. Heavy Guns will be [illegible]

4. [illegible] by 11.0 pm

[illegible] 7.0 pm

[illegible]

appendix 4

NARRATIVE OF OPERATIONS 13th to 18th. OCTOBER 1918.

COURRIERE 14/15 October 1918.

Orders were received to send forward two Platoons from each of the three forward Companies to secure Bridgehead at J25 D 74 and after objective was gained the remainder of the Battalion was to move up, consolidate theline of the Canal and push Patrols across

The advance commenced at 0530."A"Coy on the left,"B"Coy in the centre "D" Coy on the right. "C" Coy was in reserve at COURRIERE. "A" and"B" Coys although subjected to heavy M.G. fire reached their objective, which they were unable to hold owing to the enemy crossing the Canal and surrounding them. The Battalions on the Right and Left had not advanced and our men formed a salient in the Bosch line. "D" Coy on the right advanced through some thickly wooded ground where the enemy had some- several posts

2/Lt. POWL commanding No 13 Platoon was met by about thirty of the enemy crying "KAMERAD" and holding up their hands. He immediately ordered them to go back to his Coy H-Q. and being anxious to reach his objective, pushed forward.

As soon as he had moved theenemy went back to a gun position and opened fire. No 14 Platoon "D" Coy was also advancing 200 yds in rear of No 13. Nothing further is known of these except that bodies were found on the Canal bank and a few wounded came back. It is feared that most of the men were captured, also 2/Lt. POWL and 2/Lt. E.M. ROBINSON.

During these operations the enemy shelled COURRIERE continuously. One shell falling on "A" Coy H-Q, wounded Lieut. R.M.KELLY and 2/LT H. BENN. Later in the morning orders were received to push out Patrols and establish forward posts near the Canal. Each time, however, the patrols came under heavy M.G. fire and could not advance. The remainder of the day was passed with Patrol encounters.

During the night LIEUT. COLONEL A.D.DERVICHE-JONES. D.S.O. M.C. arrived and took command of the Battalion. LIEUT. COL. A.GROVER D.S.O. M.C. relinquished command and went to the 12th.London Regiment. That night a Company of the 7th London Regiment came up and strengthened our left flank.

The night passed quietly. Next morning at 1000 orders were received that the Battalion should push forward Patrols to the Canal and secure the near bank. "A" and "B" Coys reached objective but "D" Coy could not get forward. At 1530 MAJOR GENERAL RAMSEY and several Officers came to COURRIERE and against advice went along the road towards the Bridgehead . As they neared the Canal a sniper killed the General's A.D.C. CAPTAIN SIR WILLIAM FARQUHAR BART.

During the evening the Battalion crossed the Canal, established a line on the far side and sent out Patrols. The enemy shelled the Bridgehead during the night. Arrangements were made for the 7th LondonRegiment to push Patrols through our lines at dawn and continue the advance.

The following Officers were present.

LIEUT COLONEL A.D.DERVICHE-JONES. D.S.O. M.C.
CAPTAIN L.E.B.JACOB. (Adjutant)
2/LT. R.REEVES-MOORE (Asst.Adjt.)
2/LT.J.F.W. KELLY (Int. Officer)
LIEUT. A.KENNEDY. (Med. Officer)
LIEUT. R.N. SHAPLEY. (Sig. Off.)
CAPT.REV.H.C. JAMES. (Chaplain)

"A" COY. LT. H.L. HUMPHREYS.
2/LT. R.G. STECKLEY.
"B" " CAPT. J.M. BARRATT.M.C.
2/LT. F.DANIEL.
2/LT. F.R.JULIAN.

"C" COY. 2/LT. W.WEATHERHEAD.
"D" " CAPT. A.BUCK.
LIEUT R.D.BORRETT.

T.O. CAPT. T.A.B. PURKISS.

Q.M. CAPT. F.T. CHAPMAN

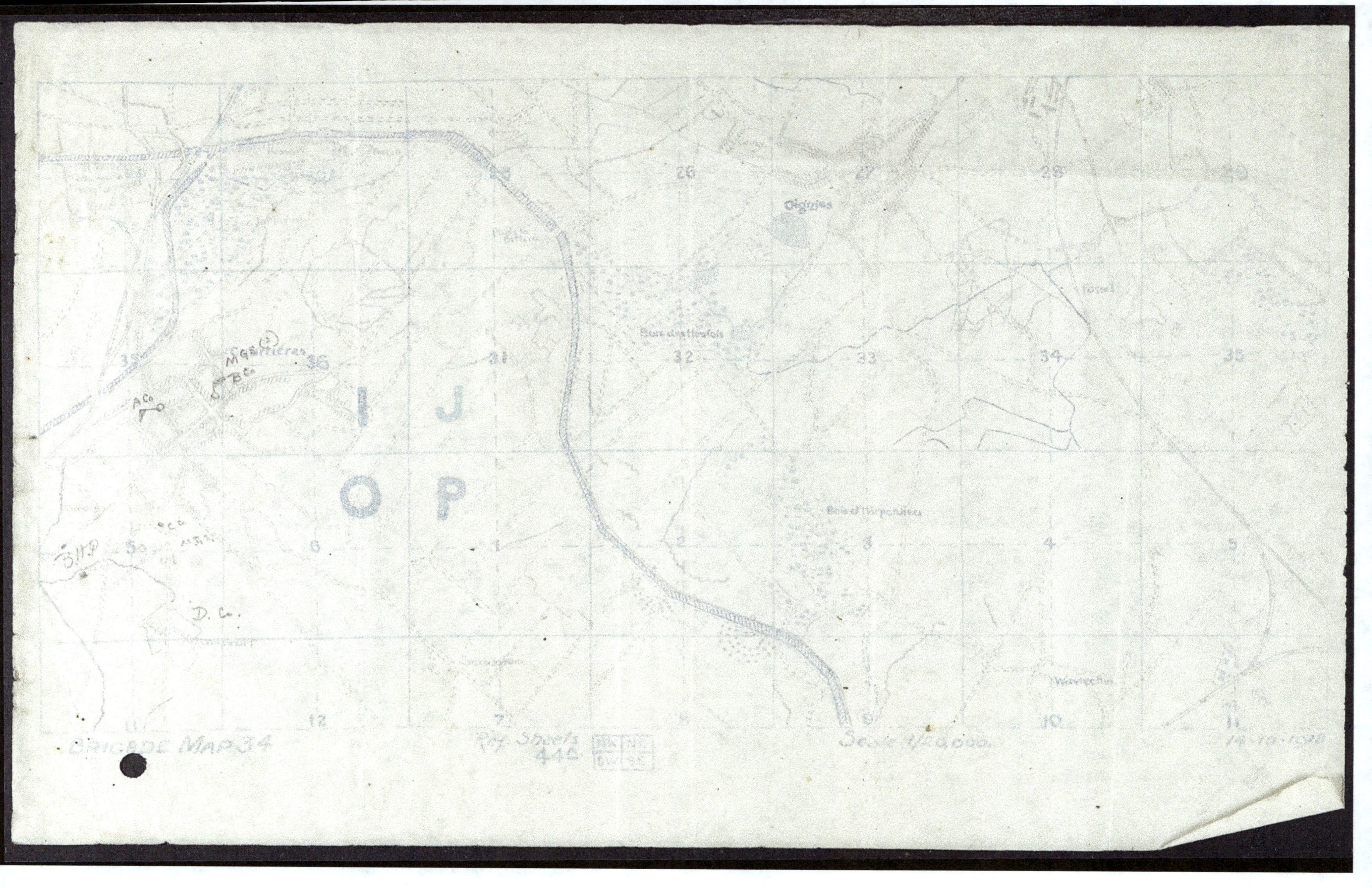

BRIGADE MAP 34
Ref. Sheets 44a
Scale 1/20,000
14-10-1918
I J
O P
A Co
B Co
D. Co.
BHQ
26
27
28
29
31
32
33
34
35
36
1
2
3
4
5
6
7
8
9
10
11
12

Appendix 5

NARRATIVE OF OPERATIONS AT BERSEE 18/19 October 1918.

At 0515 the Battalion left LA RUSHONNETTE and marched towards MONS-EN-PEVELE which was reached at 0630. The morning was misty and cold. The Battalion advanced along the road to BERSEE with two Companies in front in Battle Formation" "C" Company (LT. HALIFAX) on Right and "B" Company (Capt, J.M. BARRATT) M.C. on Left. The remainder of the Battalion with M.Gs. and a Battery of Artillery followed, along the road 1000 yards behind. Great difficulty was experienced in keeping direction owing to the wooded country and thick mist. Little opposition, however, was metwith, and BERSEE was occupied. Thee people were nearly wild with joy and gave the Battalion a magnificent reception. Coffee and food were given to the troops on all sides.

Immediately the town was passed Patrols were sent forward to hold a line outside the town, as the two reserve Companies were to pass through this line and continue the advance.

"D" and "A" Companies passed through the Outpost line at 1030, but could not get forward owing to the M.G. fire.

It was now ascertained that the Division on the Left had not advanced by the road in L 4. a. The Battalion was over a mile ahead of this Division and the Left flank was therefore in the air. The Colonel immediately informed Brigade of this and meanwhile ordered "B" Company, then in rest, to form a defensive flank to cover the ground around FARM DES MOTTES. Headquarters Company in the meantime established a post on the railway at K 4. a, 7.3. and kept in touch with the Division on the left.

Orders were then received that the left Division would go forward at 1800 and straighten the line. After "A" Company had established liason on the left "B" Company withdrew to billets as ordered. Throughout the afternoon the enemy shelled BERSEE and the country around, principally the cross roads K20 b, 4. 2. The night passed quietly, our Patrols meeting with little opposition.

18/19 At 1400 orders were received to advance on WATTINES. "D" and" B" Companies moved between 1530 and 1600. and after a sharp resistance entered WATTINES. Aline of Posts was placed in front of the village and the remainder of the men rested.

The people here were extremely glad and entertained the men with Coffee and Food. AS soon as information was received that the village had been secured, the 6th London Regiment continued the advance, passing through our Outpost line at 0700.

The Battalion then formed up on road in L 17 d. and became part of the Main Body of the 174th Brigade.

Owing to the 6th. London being held up the Battalion halted beside the road L 18, a. and rested for some hours. Later they moved forward to G 3 c 2.8. but owing to the mist returned to MAISON WATTINES where they were billetted and spent the night. The enemy caused several fires among the farms in this area and stacks of corn were destroyed.

The following Officers were present.

LIEUT. COLONEL A.D.DERVICHE-JONES. D.S.O. M.C.
CAPTAIN L.E.B.JACOB. (Adjutant)
2/LT. R.REEVES-MOORE, (Asst. Adjt.)
LIEUT. R.N. SHAPLEY (Sigs. Officer)
LIEUT. A. KENNEDY. (Med. Officer)
REV.&CAPTAIN. A.C. JAMES. (Chaplain)
2/LT. J.F.W. KELLY (Intelligence Off)

"A" Coy. LT. H.L. HUMPHREYS. LT. R.C.STECKLEY.

"B" Coy CAPT. J.M. BARRATT. M.C. LT. F.R. JULIAN.

"C" Coy LT.J.H. HALIFAX. 2/LT.W.WEATHERHEAD. 2/LT. S.G. SMITH.

"D" Coy CAPT. A.BUCK. LT. R.D. BORRETT.

T.O. CAPT. T.A.B. PURKISS.

Q-M CAPT. F.T. CHAPMAN.

SECRET. 8th Battalion London Regiment. Copy No.2...

OPERATION ORDER No.77.

Appendix VII

Ref. AMIENS & LENS Sheets. 26th Sept., 1918.

INFORMATION. 1. 174th Infantry Brigade will move by train and march route to CHATEAU DE LA HAIE Area today.

INTENTION. 2. 8th Battalion will entrain at HEILLY Station, train leaving at 12.35 am 27th, and detrain at SAUY BERLETTE.
Duration of train journey 6 hours.

INSTRUCTIONS. 3. (i) Battalion less Transport will parade at 10.30 pm on HEILLY - BONNAY Road, head of Column at Q.M. Stores.
Order H.Q. C. A. B. D Coys.

(ii) Transport will be at the Station at 9.30 pm under orders to be issued by T.O.

(iii) Battalion Entraining Officer.2/Lt R.REEVES-MOORE.

(iv) Battalion Detraining Officer.2/Lt J.F.W.KELLY.

(v) Officers Valises will be dumped at Q.M. Stores by 4.30 pm.

(vi) Cookers and Watercarts will be withdrawn to Transport Lines at 6 pm.
All waterbottles must be filled by this hour. Watercarts and petrol tins will be entrained full.

(vii) Dress. Overcoats will be worn, but will be replaced in the pack on nearing end of journey. Soft caps.

(viii) March Discipline. Strictest attention is to be paid to March Discipline.both on march to Entraining Station and march from Detraining Station.

(ix) Guards. "D" Company will provide a guard of Sergeant and 6 men at rear end of the train to prevent men detraining at halts. Regimental Police will provide similar guard at the front of the train.

(x) Train Orders. No man will ride on top of the truck or on the steps.
A N.C.O. will be placed in charge of each truck and will be responsible for the discipline of the men in that truck.
No fires are allowed in the truck. Candles must be properly protected.
Entraining and detraining will be carried out as expeditiously as possible and with the least possible noise.

(xi) Lewis Guns will be packed on limbers under instructions issued by L.G. Sergeant.

[signature] Captain & Adjutant.

Issued at 11.50 am.

Copies to :-
1. File.
2. War Diary.
3. O.C. "A" Company.
4. O.C. "B" Company.
5. O.C. "C" Company.
6. O.C. "D" Company.
7. Headquarters,
8. T.O.
9. Q.M.
10. Spare.

War Diary

Fourth Army No.G.S.2/16

58th Division.

Before the 58th Division leaves the Fourth Army I desire to place on record, my appreciation of the excellent services they have rendered, and the prominent part they have taken, both in holding the line previous to August 6th, and in the advance that has taken place since that date.

During the trying days of April they fought at and about HANGARD WOOD with a dogged determination which was wholly admirable and for which I can never thank them sufficiently.

I was well satisfied with the hard work they put in throughout the Summer in constructing defences, and holding a defensive front, West of ALBERT and the ANCRE.

From the 6th August onwards they have undertaken attack after attack with the greatest gallantry and success. The way in which they have responded to the repeated calls upon them, to undertake further offensive operations after the heavy and successful fighting on August 8th, and all along the North bank of the SOMME, is deserving of the highest praise and I offer every Officer, N.C.O. and man my warmest thanks for their indomitable spirit and endurance throughout.

Their final success in capturing KILDARE POST and DADOS LOOP after being almost continuously engaged for over 7 weeks in the line was a very fine performance, especially coming as it did so soon after their heavy fighting in capturing PEIZIERE. - next village to Epehy - adjoining.

I much regret that the Division is being transferred to another Army. I wish all ranks every possible good luck and trust that at some future time I may again be fortunate enough to find the Division once more under my command.

H Rawlinson

Adv. H.Q. Fourth Army.
25th September, 1918.

General,
Commanding Fourth Army.

8/B

WAR DIARY

D.R.L.S.

G.637 15th AAA

The following approciation of the 58th (London) Division is quoted from a Gorman document captured at HENIN LIETARD - The 58th Division woro identified on this front by 7 prisoners of 2/2nd London Regiment on 4th October. Thoy were put into the lino just North of LENS and it is not certain whothor they woro put in to strengthon the line or to relievo the 24th Division, whose Right boundary is South of AVION. The 58th Division is considered an excellent Storm Division. They woro engaged twice in the heavy fighting between the SOMME and the SCARPE last month, during which period they had exceedingly heavy casualties.
Botwoen the 23rd Septembor and the 4th October the Division was out in rest.
.... to List "C" less Corps and Flanks.
Added.

C.K. Spencer Capt.
for

58th Div.

23-00

Lt-Col.
G.S.

War Diary

58th Div.
G. S14/5

58th Division.

It is with the greatest regret that I bid "au revoir" to the 58th Division.

Throughout all the operations of the III Corps since March, 1918, the Division has not only fought with gallantry and determination, but also with that spirit of mutual co-operation and comradeship which ensures success.

I wish also to convey my personal thanks to General RAMSAY, the Staff and all ranks of the 58th Division for their loyal support and for the manner in which they have always "played up". I trust that it may be my good fortune, at no distant date, to have the Division in my command again in further victorious operations.

Sd. R. BUTLER,
Lieutenant-General,
Commanding III Corps.

III Corps H.Q.
26th September 1918.

26

Instructions regarding War Diaries and Intelligence Summaries are contained in F. S. Regs., Part II. and the Staff Manual respectively. Title pages will be prepared in manuscript.

WAR DIARY

~~or~~

~~INTELLIGENCE SUMMARY.~~

(Erase heading not required.)

Army Form C. 2118.

58

Place	Date	Hour	Summary of Events and Information	Remarks and references to Appendices
			VB 22	
			8th LONDON REGIMENT	
			" "	
			POST OFFICE RIFLES	
			" "	
			Oct 1st to Oct 31st 1918	
			"	

(A8004) D. D. & L., London, E.C. Wt W1771/M2931 750,000 5/17 Sch. 52 Forms/C2118/14

Instructions regarding War Diaries and Intelligence Summaries are contained in F. S. Regs., Part II. and the Staff Manual respectively. Title pages will be prepared in manuscript.

WAR DIARY
or
~~INTELLIGENCE SUMMARY.~~
(Erase heading not required.)

Army Form C. 2118.

Place	Date	Hour	Summary of Events and Information	Remarks and references to Appendices
LOOS	Oct. 1.		Morning dull and wet, later sunny. C.O went around line before "stand to" Men rested during the day. Occasional enemy shelling.	JK
do	2		Morning fine + clear. Orders received at 9.30 A.M. Bde would advance. Conference of Coy. Commanders. Battn moved to NOGGIN TRENCH at 12.30 A.M.	JK
Pt Auguste	3/4		See Special Appendix.	Appendix I
Loos	5		Morning dull. Men rested. Occasional shelling throughout the day.	JK
do	6.		Morning bright and fine. Bde ordered change in dispositions. MAJOR C. H. WILD proceeded on leave. 2Lt J.C. BATTOCK transferred for duty in EGYPT.	JK
do	7.		Morning sunny. Battn ordered to be ready to move immediately. Day passed quietly. Occasional shelling. Germans claim Armistice.	JK
do	8		Morning sunny + fine. Orders received Battn would be relieved by 9th London. Enemy shelled throughout the day. Aerial activity by night. Bombs dropped.	JK
do	9.		Morning fine. Day passed quietly. Battn was relieved by 9th London. Relief complete 9 pm. Battn marched to MARQUEFFLES FARM. 44 B 26A 9.3 arriving 11 ½ P.M.	JK

D. D. & L., London, E.C. (A3004) Wt W3771/M2031 750,000 5/17 Sch. 52 Forms/C2118/14

Army Form C. 2118.

Instructions regarding War Diaries and Intelligence Summaries are contained in F. S. Regs., Part II. and the Staff Manual respectively. Title pages will be prepared in manuscript.

WAR DIARY
or
~~INTELLIGENCE SUMMARY.~~

(*Erase heading not required.*)

Place	Date	Hour	Summary of Events and Information	Remarks and references to Appendices
MARQUEFFLES FARM.	Oct 10		Morning dull. Battn cleaned equipment and rifles. Divisional Cmdr visited battn. Imperial War Museum acknowledged gift of German Machine Gun by 8th London Regt. Deficiencies of kit made good. Remainder of day men rested.	JK Appendix 2
do	11		Morning dull & showery. Training under Company Commanders in the morning. Remainder of day men rested. The following officers joined the battn. CAPT G. BARNES Lt H. HUMPHREYS Lt R. BORRETT 2Lt W WEATHERHEAD. CAPT A BUCK rejoined from leave. Orders received the battn would embus to-morrow for SALLAUMINES to relieve 37th Infy Bde.	JK Appendix 3
do	12		Morning wet. Lt Col GROVER DSO MC & one officer made a reconnaissance of ground round SALLAUMINES before battn arrived. Battn embussed near camp and moved to LIEVIN where transport carried stores & LEWIS GUNS to SALLAUMINES. The day was wet and transport had great difficulty in moving. Battn arrived late at SALLAUMINES and in meantime the 7th LONDON had been sent forward to replace 8th L. Battn halted at SALLAUMINES and moved at 3 AM next morning for MONTIGNY. Rained hard throughout the night.	JK JK

D. D. & L., London, E.C. (A8004) Wt W1771/M2031 750,000 5/17 Sch. 52 Forms/C2118/14

Army Form C. 2118.

WAR DIARY
or
~~INTELLIGENCE SUMMARY.~~
(Erase heading not required.)

Instructions regarding War Diaries and Intelligence Summaries are contained in F. S. Regs., Part II. and the Staff Manual respectively. Title pages will be prepared in manuscript.

Place	Date	Hour	Summary of Events and Information	Remarks and references to Appendices
SALLAUMINES	Oct 13		Morning wet & cold. The Battn moved at 03.00. 15 minutes interval between companies. A Co arrived at MONTIGNY at 04.15. A B & C Coys held RESERVE LINE D Coy in RESERVE. AT 17.00 Battn moved to COURRIERE to relieve 7th LONDON REG. Orders received for Battn to seize bridgehead next morning	JK
COURRIERE	14/15/16		Special appendix	appendix 4 JK
do	16		Morning fine. Battn held line along canal bank. Heavy enemy shelling throughout the day. No casualties.	JK
do	17.		Morning bright. Battn received orders and moved to OIGNIES at 0900. Here the men rested and at 20.00 marched to LA RUCHONNETTE (44a 27D 7.9) via THOMERIES arriving at 23.30. The following officers joined the Battn Lt. J.H. HALIFAX. 2Lt. S.G.S. SMITH 2LT F DANIEL went sick	JK
MONS & BERSEE	18/19		Special appendix	JK appendix 5
WATTINES	20		Morning fine. Battn moved to NOMAINE with all transport. The Brigadier General took the salute as the brigade marched into the town. Men were then billeted. The remainder of the men rested.	JK
NOMAINES	21		Morning wet. Men cleaned equipment re. training under Coy Cmdrs in afternoon. Orders received to move to RUMEGIES next day. C.O's meeting for all officers & N.C.O's.	JK

D. D. & L., London, E.C.
(A8004) Wt W1771/M2031 750,000 5/17 Sch. 52 Forms/C2118/14

Instructions regarding War Diaries and Intelligence Summaries are contained in F. S. Regs., Part II. and the Staff Manual respectively. Title pages will be prepared in manuscript.

WAR DIARY
~~or~~
~~INTELLIGENCE SUMMARY.~~
(Erase heading not required.)

Army Form C. 2118.

Place	Date	Hour	Summary of Events and Information	Remarks and references to Appendices
NOMAIN	22		Morning fine and clear. Training carried on by Company Cmdrs. The Brigadier General visited the battn. Capt T.J MUMFORD MC joined battn. + assumed command of D. Coy. 2Lt H PEACOCK rejoined from leave.	
do	23		Morning fine. Training carried on by Coy Cmdrs. 2Lt J.F ROST joined battn. Enemy shelled NOMAINE during the night. No casualties	[initials]
do	24.		Morning fine & warm. Training under Coy. Commanders. Men rested in afternoon. Occasional enemy shelling by night	[initials]
do	25		Morning fine. Attack practice by companies. New system of communication to rear by means of flags. Conference for OC Companys in afternoon. CAPT G.C. FABER. and Lt C.A. MONTGOMERY joined battn.	[initials]
do	26		Morning sunny. Battn received orders to move with all transport to RONGY. Brigade starting point passed at 1015. After leaving AIX the movement order was cancelled and battn returned to billets at NOMAIN arriving 1330. Conference for officers at 1530. Men rested remainder of the day.	[initials]
do	27		Morning fine. Orders received 174 Brigade would relieve 175 Brigade on night of 27-28. Battn marched to RUE DOMPRIE with battle transport arriving 16 45. Battn billeted in the village. Coy Cmdrs made reconnaissance at MAULDE. 2Lt A BENN + 2Lt F.R JULIAN went sick.	

D. D. & L., London, E.C. (A8004) Wt W1771/M2031 750,000 5/17 Sch. 52 Forms/C2118/14

Army Form C. 2118.

Instructions regarding War Diaries and Intelligence Summaries are contained in F. S. Regs., Part II. and the Staff Manual respectively. Title pages will be prepared in manuscript.

WAR DIARY
or
INTELLIGENCE SUMMARY.

(Erase heading not required.)

Place	Date	Hour	Summary of Events and Information	Remarks and references to Appendices
RUE DOMPRIE	28		Morning fine & clear. C.O. made reconnaissance of MAULDE and area. Battn trained under Coy Cmdrs. Enemy shelled occasionally during the day, and heavily during the night the battn area. Several casualties	[illegible]
do	29		Morning fine. Training carried out under Coy Cmdrs. Reconnaissance made of route to MAULDE via LE MAROC L^T A. PETERS rejoined battn and assumed command of C Coy.	[illegible]
do	30		Morning sunny. Training by Coy Cmdrs. Enemy anti-aircraft guns very active. Day passed quietly.	[illegible]
do	31		Morning cold but bright. Training as usual. Day passed quietly. Occasional enemy shelling during the night. 2L^T V.W.G. SMITH rejoined battn. The following officers were with the battn:— L^T COL A.D. DERVICHE-JONES D.S.O. M.C. (C.O.) MAJOR C.H. WILD (2nd/c) CAPT L.E.B. JACOB (ADJT) L^T C. MONTGOMERY (L.G.O.) 2L^T R. REEVES-MOORE (ASST ADJ) L^T R.N. SHAPLEY (SIGS) L^T W. LONG (M.O.) 2L^T J.E.W. KELLY (I.O.) T.O. CAPT. T. PURKIS Q.M. CAPT F.H. CHAPMAN CHAP: CAPT H.C. JAMES A.C. CAPT G.C. FABER. L^T H.L. HUMPHREYS 2L^T R.C. STECKLEY 2L^T J. FROST B.C. CAPT J.M. BARRATT M.C. 2L^T PEACOCK C.C. L^T A.C. PETERS L^T J.H. HALIFAX 2L^T W. WEATHERHEAD 2L^T S.G. SMITH. D.C. CAPT. T.J. MUMFORD M.C. L^T R.U. BARRETT 2L^T A. BOCK 2L^T V.W.G. SMITH	[illegible] A. D. Derviche-Jones Lt Col, Cmdg 8th [illegible]

D. D. & L., London, E.C. (A8024) Wt W1771/M2031 750,000 5/17 Sch. 52 Forms/C2118/14

Appendix I

NARRATIVE OF OPERATIONS AT CITE ST AUGUSTE. 4/5 10!18.

At 0930 orders were received to advancev to CITE ST AUGUSTE and holds line from H 35 c 75 to N 5 c 63. The 7th London attacked on the left and the 2/2nd. on the Right. The attack commenced at 1600. "B" Company, (capt, J.M. BARRATT) advanced from NETLEY TRENCH, one Platoon in front as screen and remainder following at 200 yards, in Battle formation. "D" Company (Lt. ANDERSON) followed, then "A" Company (Lt. PETERS) and finally "C" Company (Lt. HANNAH) in Support. The first two Companies advanced without much opposition, but "A" Company and "C" Company were heavily bombarded by gas shells which caused a number of casualties.

The forward Companies "A" and "B" pushed forward while "D" Company cleared CITE ST. AUGUSTE. During this time they were subjected to heavy M.G. fire from Railway Embankment in H.34. and bombarded with Artillery from ANNAY on the flank. The Battalion on the Left failed to move forward so we were compelled to remain in HYMAN TRENCH until liason was established. Night came on and "A" and "D" Companies each sent two Platoons to secure the Railway Embankment in H. 34. and a place known as the COKE OVENS.

After some time touch was established with th eBattalion on the left and an arrangement was made if any forward movement was ordered each Battalion would act in unison. The Brigade ordered renewal of advance at 0445. Owing to the broken ground and wire the message was not delivered until 0600. The Left Battalion had moved earlier but the Battalion moved as soon as orders were received and at 0700 occupied the Railway Cutting H.35.c.7.5. to N.5.c.6.3. Immediately patrols were sent out but came under machine gun fire from HARNES FOSSE. The position was consolidated and men rested. "C" Company then moved to NOMAD TRENCH and remained in Support. At 1500 Lt. Col. GROVER, D.S.O., M.C. moved H.Q. to N.5.a.8.8. Furgher orders were received at 1800 to advance on ANNAY Switch Line and get in touch. The forward Companies advanced but came under heavy M.G. fire and Trench Mortars. The men stayed out until dawn and then returned. Patrols were sent out by all Companies and in every case they were attacked. It was quite clear the enemy were holding this line in strength. During one of these patrol encounters Lt. R.D. ANDERSON was wounded. The next day was fairly quiet, with the exception of M.G. fire from HARNES FOSSE and ANNAY. The Brigade ordered H.Q. to return to old H.Q. in HYMAN TRENCH at 1600 as the 6th London would relieve the Battalion that evening. The relief was complete at 0130 and Battalion marched back by Companies to Trench in front of LOOS.

The following Officers were wih the Battalion:-

Lt. Col. A. GROVER, D.S.O., M.C.
Capt. L.E.B. JACOB. (Adjutant)
Major G.H. WILD. (Second in Command)
Lieut. A. KENNEDY. (M.O.)
2/Lt. J.F.W. KELLY. (I.O.)
2/Lt. R.REEVES-MOORE. (Asst. Adjutant)

"A" Company. Lt. C.S. PETERS, 2/Lt. FOWL, 2/Lt. H. BENN.
"B" Company. Capt. J.M.BARRATT, 2/Lt. F.DANIELL, 2/Lt. F.JULIAN.
"C" Company. Lt. T.R. HANNAH, 2/Lt. R.C.STEGGLEY.
"D" Company. Lt. R.D. ANDERSON, 2/Lt. E.M.ROBINSON, 2/Lt, BATTEC

Capt. T.A.B. PURKIS. Transport Officer.
Capt. F.T. CHAPMAN. Quartermaster.

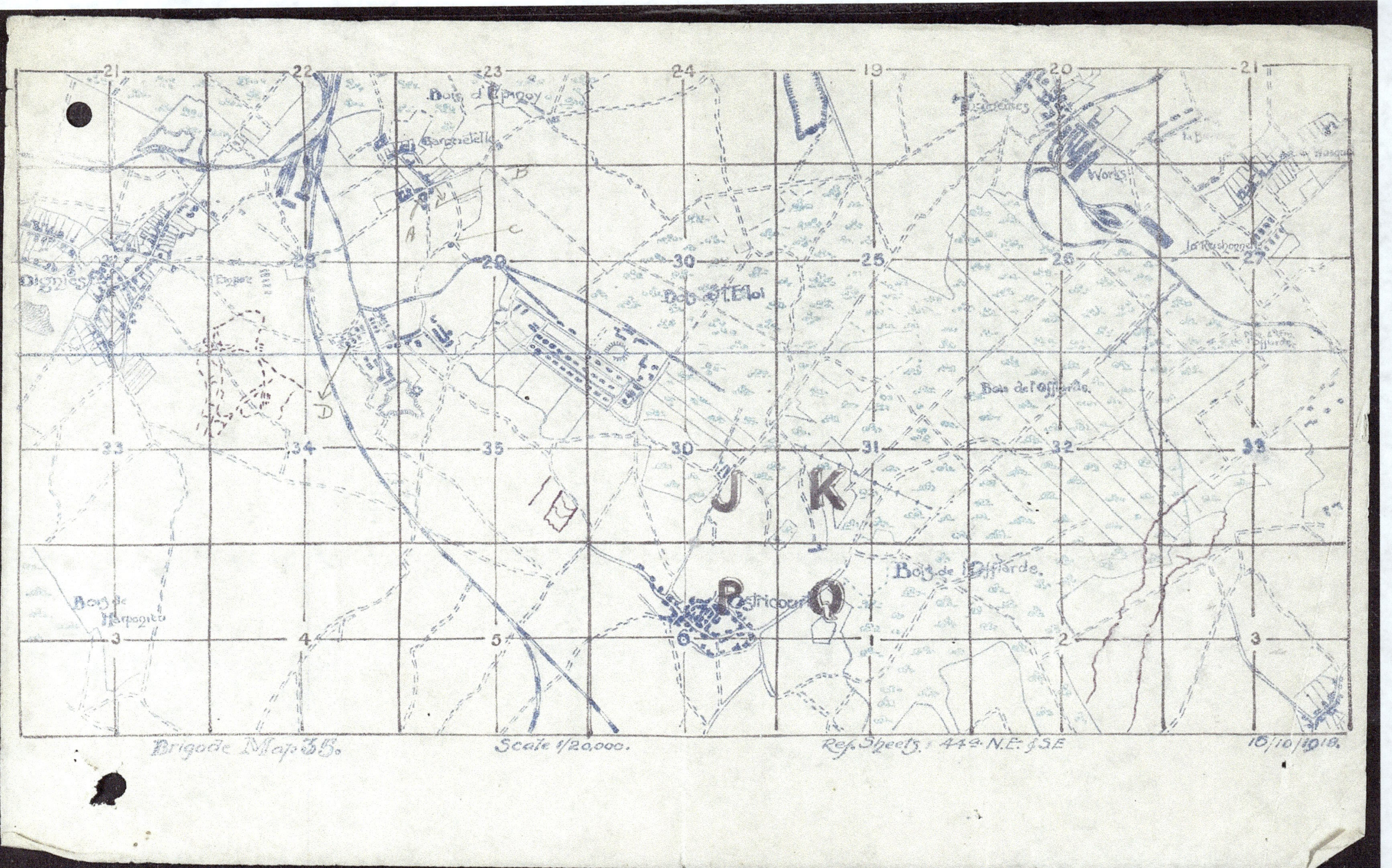

Bois d'Epinoy
Works
la Rasbonne
Bois de St Eloi
Bois de l'Offarde.
Bois de l'Offarde.
J
K
P
Q
Bois de Hargnites
Brigade Map 35.
Scale 1/20,000.
Ref. Sheets: 44a N.E. & S.E.
10/10/1918.

appendix 2

War Diary

Appendix 2

NATIONAL WAR MUSEUM.

Oct. 3. 1918.

Sir.

I am directed by the Chairman of the Committee of the National War Museum (the First Commissioner of Works) to thank you warmly on behalf of His Majesty's Government for your Gift to the National War Museum which is much appreciated and will be carefully preserved for all time as a National Relic.

Yours faithfully,

Charles ffoulkes

Curator and Secretary.

Your Gift is recorded overleaf.

O.C. 1/8th London Regt.

Machine Gun.

War Diary
Appendix 3

WARNING ORDER.

8th Battalion London Regiment.

1. Sub-paras. (2), (3), (4) and (5) of Para 2 Battalion Orders are cancelled. Dinners at 1100.

2. Battalion will move to SALLAUMINES tomorrow. Embussing at about 1330 hours.

3. Unexpended rations and rations for 13th to be carried on the man.

4. Officers Kits and all stores not needed in the line will be stacked at Guard Room by 0900 hours. Lewis Guns and Mess Boxes will be taken on the busses. Blankets will be rolled in bundles of ten and dumped in Tailors Shop by 0900 hours.

5. Dress - Full Marching Order.
Water Bottles to be filled by 1000 hours.

6. 1 N.C.O. per Company and 1 N.C.O. from H.Q. will be at Orderly Room at 0845 ready to proceed on bicycles to look out accommodation at SALLAUMINES. Remainder of day's rations will be carried.

Captain & Adjutant.

SECRET.

Copy No. 1

8th Battalion London Regiment.

OPERATION ORDER No. 80.

Reference LENS 11. 13th October, 1918.

INTENTION. 1. 8th London Regiment will move to SALAUMINES by bus and route march.

INSTRUCTIONS. 2. (i) Embussing Point BOUVIGNY - AIX NOULETTE Road near MARQUEFFLES ~~Rest~~. CAMP.

(ii) Debussing Point S.E. Corner of LIEVIN.

(iii) Parade. Companies will parade on Company Parade Grounds ready to move at 1200.

(iv) Dress. F.M.O. Jerkins will be carried under flap of packs. Caps will be carried in packs.

(v) Limbers. For Lewis Guns and Mess Stores will meet the Battalion at Debussing Point.

(vi) Huts must be cleared by 1130 and left in a thoroughly clean condition. Certificates to this effect will be handed to Orderly Room.

(vii) Rations for 13th will not be carried on the man but will be delivered to Companies at SALAUMINES.

Issued at 0930

Copies to 1. File.
2. War Diary.
3. C.O.
4 - 7. O.C. Companies.
8. Headquarters.
9. T.O.
10. Q.M.
11. R.S.M.
12. Spare.

[signature]

Captain & Adjutant.

War Diary

To O/C Coys.

(1) Battalion will be relieved to-night by the 6th London. Coys of 6th taking over from corresponding Coys 8th Bn.

(2) On relief Bn will move into Brigade support taking over positions vacated by corresponding of 6th Bn. H.Q. in HARRISON'S CRATER.

(3) 2 Guides per Coy will report at Bn H.Q. HYMAN TR at 12-30. they will then be taken to meet 6th Bn at group of trees at H.34 A 23.

(4) The N.C.O's. who preceeded in advance will meet Coys at N2A92. A tape runs across old no mans land from about H33C27 to N2A92. Coys will find out from their opposite numbers where they are grouped.

(5) Relief complete will be sent by wire or runner. Code word "STRANGE".

Captain & Adjutant.

4-10-18.

War Diary

6th Bn.	174th L.T.M.Bty.
7th Bn.	511th Fd. Coy. R.E.
8th Bn.	242nd Army Bde. R.F.A.
B Coy. M.G.Bn.	

G.893. 18. AAA

Northern Brigade Boundary is extended forward along line L.9.c.0.0. L.11.a.0.0. G.1.d.5.1. G.3.a.0.0. G.5.a.1.5. A.30.b.8.3. AAA Southern Brigade Boundary is extended along line L.22.central LE CHATELET G.13.d. Junction of Road and Railway G.11.c.5.5. ROMAIN CHURCH H.1.c.0.0. AAA Addsd. all units Brigade Group.

174th Inf. Bde.

2155.

Captain,
Brigade Major.

Recipients of O.O.132.

G.B.43. 18 AAA

Signal In tructions reference O.O.132 AAA A forward Brig de Report Centre will be established at LE NOUVEAU MONDE L.15.d.6.5. at 0600 to-morrow morning AAA All reports to Brigade should be forwarded to this station after that hour AAA The post will consist of telephone exchange on Brigade system, runner relay station and a visual station which will endeavour to obtain touch with any forward station seen AAA The station visual call will be R.C. AAA O.C. Main Body will detail from troops under his command a forward cyclist relay post of 4 men to be left at cross-roads G7.c.9.25 on passing that point: this post will work back to the Brigade report centre.

G769.2

174th Inf. Brigade.

Captain,
Brigade Major

19

174/58

CONFIDENTIAL

Army Form C. 2118

VR 23

WAR DIARY
or
INTELLIGENCE SUMMARY.
(Erase heading not required.)

Instructions regarding War Diaries and Intelligence Summaries are contained in F. S. Regs., Part II. and the Staff Manual respectively. Title pages will be prepared in manuscript.

Place	Date	Hour	Summary of Events and Information	Remarks and references to Appendices
			8th Battalion the London Regiment (Post Office Rifles) — 11 — NOVEMBER 1918 — 1 —	

D. D. & L., London, E.C.
(A8004) Wt W1771/M2031 750,000 5/17 Sch. 52 Forms/C2118/14

Army Form C. [illegible]8.

Instructions regarding War Diaries and Intelligence Summaries are contained in F. S. Regs., Part II. and the Staff Manual respectively. Title pages will be prepared in manuscript.

WAR DIARY
or
INTELLIGENCE SUMMARY.

(*Erase heading not required.*)

Place	Date	Hour	Summary of Events and Information	Remarks and references to Appendices
QUESNOY	1.11.18		8th Battalion ordered to relieve 7th London Regt in front line at MAULDE. 8 Battn moved off at 17.00 hours. relief completed 21.30 hrs	C.A.h. appendix. I
MAULDE	2.11.18 to 5.11.18		8th Battn in line. considerable enemy M G fire and shelling at night by small calibre guns. Flooded areas on our front made patrol work difficult, and L'ESCAUT river a difficult barrier to getting in close touch with enemy.	C.A.h. C.A.h. appendix II
do	6.11.18		Officers joined the battalion for duty in the line. 2nd LT. G.P.R. TALLIN 2nd LTS A.J. FISHER - H.C. FRASER - T. FULTON G.M. GARROW. C.A.h. rafts being prepared by R.E. personnel for crossing L'ESCAUT CANAL and RIVER	C.A.h. C.A.h.
do	7.11.18		Rafts carried to positions near intended crossings. Enemy still active and getting rid of spare ammunition before retiring	C.A.h.
do	8.11.18	09.00 hrs	Orders received from Brigade to carry out crossing of RIVER L'ESCAUT. Enemy still occupying MORTAGNE village until 09.45 hrs. Crossing proceeded with at 10.30 hours by means of small rafts and floats and battalion crossed RIVER L'ESCAUT by 12.30 hours. No enemy opposition as enemy had retired at 10.30 hrs. 8th Battn formed bridge head on line ROUEX - FLINES - FORT de FLINES and held position. Some enemy shelling on FLINES	C.A.h. C.A.h. C.A.h. C.A.h.
FLINES	9.11.18		8th Battn held bridge head until 10.30 hours and was relieved by brigade advance guard which passed through our posts. LT. CROSSLAND rejoined Battn. 8 Battn marched to CALLENELLE as main body of Brigade. 3 companies detailed to repair bridge at CALLENELLE over ANTOING - POMMEROEUL CANAL during night 9/10 of Nov 18. A considerable shortage of rations experienced owing to transport difficulties on the advance. C.A.h.	C.A.h. C.A.h. C.A.h.
CALLENELLE	10.11.18		8th Battalion formed main guard for Brigade and started at 06.00 hrs. Rations brought up to Battn and breakfast eaten at BRASMENIL. Inhabitants very glad to see English troops and produced coffee for all ranks. 8 Battalion marched to BELOEIL and billeted there for the night. Great welcome given by the inhabitants. Our advance faster than German retreat and expect to get in touch with enemy on 11.11.18 C.A.h.	C.A.h. C.A.h.
BELOEIL	11.11.18		8 Battalion ordered to form advance guard and proceed to CAMERON CASTEAU. Left BELOEIL at 07.30 hrs. At 11.00 hours when on outskirts of WAUDIGNIES village Armistice declared and 8th Battalion ordered to form out post line BAUFFE + East of WAUDIGNIES village. The inhabitants of WAUDIGNIES all at Mayors house to welcome English. A speech given by Mayor to the commanding officer and replied to by C.O. in French. Local band had dug up its brass instruments and played Belgian National Anthem. C.A.h.	C.A.h. C.A.h. C.A.h. C.A.h. Appendix III

A5834 Wt. W4973/M687 750,000 8/16 D. D. & L. Ltd. Forms/C.2118/13.

Army Form C. 2118.

Instructions regarding War Diaries and Intelligence Summaries are contained in F. S. Regs., Part II. and the Staff Manual respectively. Title pages will be prepared in manuscript.

WAR DIARY
or
INTELLIGENCE SUMMARY.
(Erase heading not required.)

Place	Date	Hour	Summary of Events and Information	Remarks and references to Appendices
WAUDIGNIES	12.11.18		Battalion on outpost duty on line BAUFFE - BAILLES - BOIS DE LENS. Battn. HDQ at WAUDIGNIES. Cdn.	
do	13.11.18		as for 12.11.18. Cdn.	
do	14.11.18		Battn attended thanksgiving Service (cessation of hostilities) at GROSAGE less B.C.D Coys. Cdn.	
do	16.11.18		Orders received that outpost line to be withdrawn. Battn troops remain in billets in villages on outpost line Cdn. Education sports etc. started Cdn	
do	17.11.18		Fete held at BAUFFE village in honour of arrival of English troops. C.O. 8th London invited by Burgomaster. Many speeches of welcome made to troops present and replied to in French by Lt. Col. A.D. Derviche-Jones D.S.O. M.C. Village inhabitants entertained 8th London troops. 8th London Band played National Anthems. A written address presented to Battn By Burgomaster. See Appendix. Cdn. 2/Lt. ROSS rejoined Battn for duty.	Appendix IV
do	18.11.18		Battn received orders to proceed to BELOEIL. Billeted in BELOEIL for night 18/19th.11.18 Cdn.	Appendix V
BELOEIL	19.11.18		Battn proceeded to PERUWELZ and billeted in town. all 174 Inf. Bde in PERUWELZ. Cdn.	
PERUWELZ	20.11.18		Battn. performing Ceremonial drill - Educational classes - recreation sports etc. Good billets obtained and comfort for all ranks. Cdn.	
do	21.11.18		Lieut. O.P. RAPHAEL 2/LTS J.M. MATCHAM - F.W. BUCKLAND - F. CAMPBELL joined 8th London for duty (from England) Cdn.	
do	22.11.18		Capt. F.T. CHAPMAN proceeded to England on leave. 2nd Lt. W.J. LEE reported for duty with Battn. Cdn.	
do	23.11.18		2/Lt. A.L FROST proceeded to 1st Army Musketry course. Cdn.	
do	24.11.18		Presentation of Medal ribbons in PERUWELZ SQUARE by B.G.C. to A/Col. A.D. DERVICHE-JONES. D.S.O. and bar. M.C. Capt BARRATT. M.C. Cdn	
do			M.C. and to O.R's 3 D.C.M'S. - Bar to M.M. and 8 M.M'S. 2 LT. F. CAMPBELL proceeded to England on Cdn	
			2/Lt. CROSSLAND. 2/Lt. F.G. McINNES rejoined Battn from Hospital. Lt. McBEAN. M.O. took over M.O. duties from Lt KENNEDY Cdn	
			duty.	
do	25.11.18		Capt. L.E. JACOB proceeded on duty to ABBEYVILLE. Cdn.	
do	26.11.18		Capt. M.F. BRICKDALE rejoined Battn from ENGLAND. Cdn.	
do	28.11.18		2/Lt. REEVES MOORE proceeded to England on Special leave Cdn.	

A. D. Derviche-Jones
Lt Col
2/12/18 8th London

A5834 Wt. W4973/M687 750,000 8/16 D. D. & L. Ltd. Forms/C.2118/13.

Appendix I

1/4/1918

8th Bn, London Regt.

SECRET.
Ref. Sheet. 44. Order No 89. Copy No . 1 .....

1. 8th. London Regt will relieve 7th. London Regt. in Right Section to-night as follows.

"D" Coy (with I Platoon of "C" Coy attached) 8th. Lon. will relieve "D" Coy 7th. Lon. in Forward Pos'n.

"C" Coy 8th.Lon. will relieve "A" Coy 7th.Lon. on Right.

"B" " " " " "B" " " in Centre.

"A" " " " " "C" " " on Left.

Bn, H.Q. will be at J 9 c 096
R.A.P. will be at J 9 c 79 .

2. Coys and H.Q. will pass road junction I 11 d 78 as follows.

Bn.H.Q.	1705.
"D"Coy	1715.
"A" "	1725.
"B" "	1735.
"C" "	1745.

3. Times and places of guides and routes as arranged between Coy Commanders.

4. Officers Mess, R.A.P. and Signalling Stores , Lewis Gun Reserve Ammunition will be dumped at present B.H.Q. at 1730 and will be conveyed by Limber to New Bn H.Q.

5. Code word for relief complete " COB".

Issued at 1510.

Copies:-
------
1. War Diary.
2. O.C. A.Coy.
3. " B "
4. " C "
5. " D "
6. H.Q.
7. Sec. IN Command.

[signature]

Captain & Adjutant.

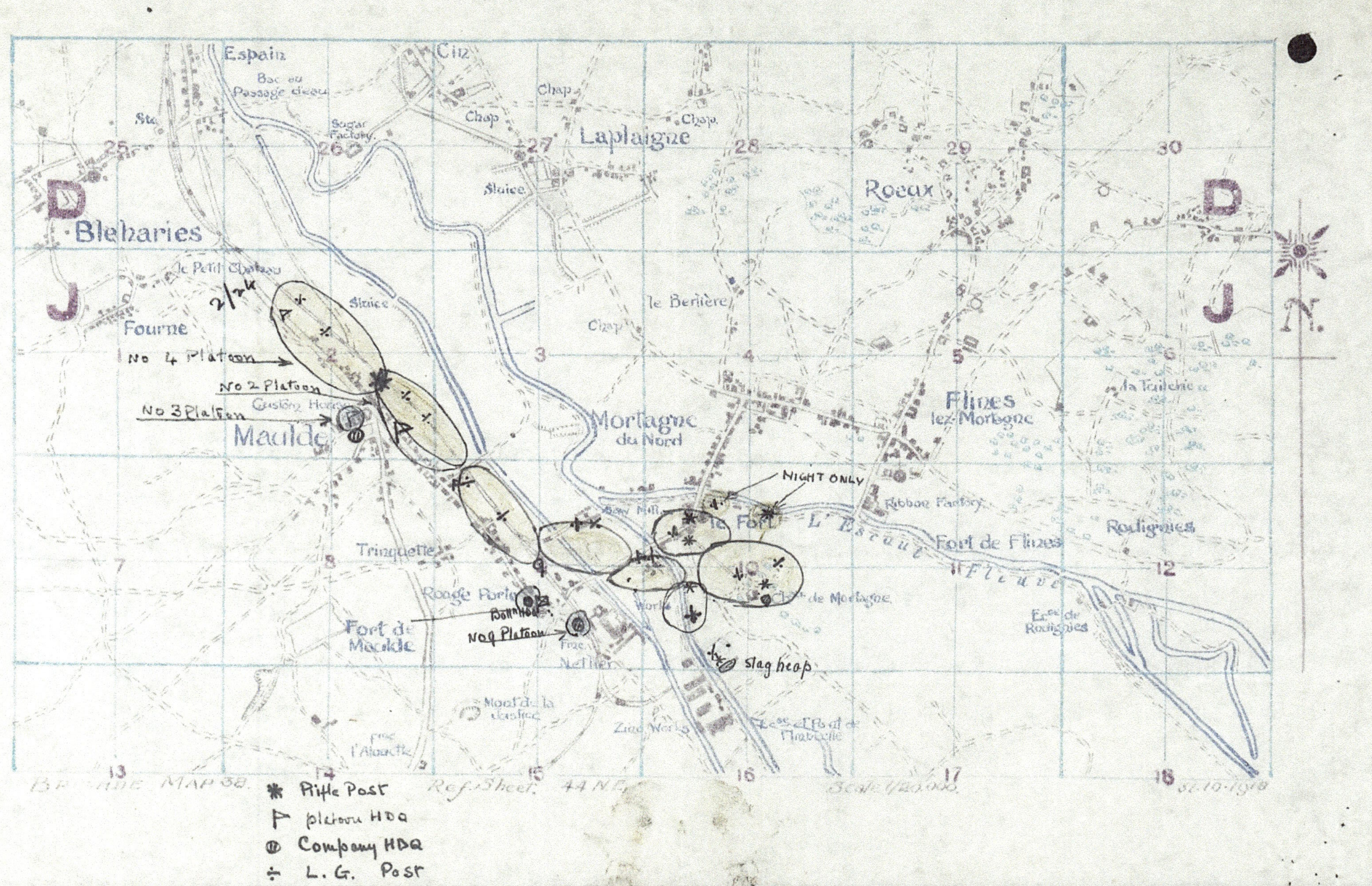

Espain
Bac ou Passage d'eau
Ciz
Chap
Chap
Sugar Factory
Laplaigne
Chap
Sluice
Roeux
Bleharies
le Petit Chateau
2/24
Sluice
le Berlière
Chap
Fourne
No 4 Platoon
No 2 Platoon
No 3 Platoon
Custom House
Maulde
Mortagne du Nord
Flines lez-Mortagne
la Tuilerie
NIGHT ONLY
Ribbon Factory
Saw Mill
le Fort
L'Escaut
Fort de Flines
Fleuve
Rodignies
Trinquette
Rouge Porte
Bn HQ
No 9 Platoon
Fort de Maulde
Works
de Mortagne
Ecluse de Rodignies
Slag heap
Mont de la Justice
Zinc Works
Fme l'Alouette
D
J
N.
BRIGADE MAP 38.
Ref. Sheet 44 N.E.
Scale 1/20,000
31.10.1918
Rifle Post
platoon HDQ
Company HDQ
L. G. Post

Secret. 8th.Bn. London Regt. Copy No. 1......

Order No. 90. 5/11/1918.

Appendix II

Ref 44 N.N. 1:20,000

5/6th Nov.

1. A small organised raid will be carried to-night by A Coy. (strength not less than one platoon).
2. The Object of the raid is :-
   (a) To secure a prisoner.
   (b) To effect a crossing of the SCHELDT.
3. The objective will be the enemy M.G. at J 3 c 70 80.
4. The raiding party will be divided as follows:-
   (a) Hut party, One officer, one Lewis Gun and L.G.Section.
   (b) POPLAR party, One Rifle Section.
   (c) Attacking party. One officer and at least one section.
   (d) Raft Party. One N.C.O. and four men.
5. (a) The raid will commence at ZERO with a T.M. demonstration on the objective, under cover of which Hut Party, followed later by the POPLAR Party will take up a position at the HUT, J3c75.50. The POPLAR Party will proceed to the POPLARS in J3c90.50 and search same for enemy sentry. The HUT and POPLARS Parties will remain in the HUT and POPLARS respectively until ZERO plus 2 hours, when there will be another T.M.demonstration accompanied by bursts of L.G.Fire from the HUT and rifle fire from the POPLARS, under cover of which the Attacking Party will proceed from Bridgehead N.W. to about J3c30,50 under cover of the Bank and thence N.E. skirting the floods and attack the M.G.position.
6. Great Care must be taken to regulate the lenght of time during which the L.G. and rifle bursts are to continue and the time of ceasing, so that the Attacking Party may not come under our own fire.
7. It is to be understood that the attack is to be pressed home in spite of opposition. It is essential to out this post if it is occupied - if it is not occupied the place must be carefully examined for traces of enemy occupation or means of crossing.
8. When this post has been outed and the men taken prisoner or killed, the Attacking Party will send a runner to the HUT & thence to the Raft Party and have the raft brought up, so that a crossing may be at once affected and the Brickstack and the Rubble on the further bank examined. For this purpose a covering party must remain by the raft to cover the withdrawal and the carrying back of the raft to the HUT where it may be left.
9. All watches must be synchronised ; an officer must be in charge of the attacking Party and one in charge of the HUT and POPLAR Parties. THe latter parties will not withdraw until the Raft and Attacking Parties have returned to the Bridge-head.
10. Lastly, the attack must be resolute and pressed home - the most careful cooperation employed and every detail thoughtout and arranged beforehand so that everyman understands what he has to do in any emergency.

THERE MUST BE NO FAILURE.

ZERO 2200

Issued at 1200 hours.

Copies
1. War Diary.
2. H.Q.174th, Inf.Bde.
3 to 6 - O.C.COYS.

Capt and Adjt.

WAR DIARY

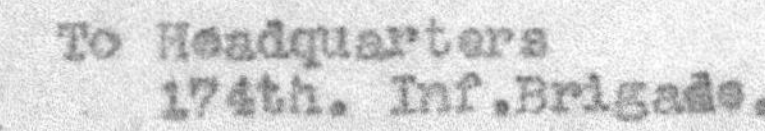

To Headquarters
174th. Inf.Brigade.

Ref.1/20,000 Report of attempted raid of night 5/6 November. 18.

1. PRELIMINARY.
(a) OBJECTIVE. Enemy M.G. at J. 3 c 70. 90. and to effect a crossing at this point.
(1(AN enemy M.G. had been identified at this spot by every Patrol issuing in this neighbourhood during the last 4 nights and had been a great source of annoyance to these patrols. It was desired therefore to attack this post and to ascertain how the enemy crossed the SCHELDT.

(11). IN order to effect this a raiding party was organised with two covering parties and a Raft party.

(b) (1). Theoriginal scheme did not involve a crossing of the SCHELDT by the raiding party, but after an interview withthe G.O.C. JURA yesterday afternoon it was decided to include a crossing and search of opposite bank where there was a small Brick stack and heaps of rubble.
(11). Immediately after the interview with the G.O.C. and the short necessary ~~interview~~ interval for getting out orders to the raiding Company as to crossing, steps weretaken to secure a raft.
(111). The R.E. Dump and ZINC works were searched by parties under Officers without result, and after communication with the R.E. at their rear Headquarters it was ascertained that there were no completed rafts at MAULDE. Pioneers wereset to work to construct one with large floats and Duckboards and a raft was completed but was found too heavy for practical use: the night was very dark, lights could not be used and it was Midnight when the raft idea was abandoned. only large floats could be found.

(c) A T.M. demonstration was arranged on the objective to cover the advance of the various parties.

2. In accordance with my O.O. No. 90. the covering parties went out at 2200 under cover of T.M's and reached their positions without opposition, Viz:- The HUT at J 3 c 75.50 and the POPLARS in J. 3 c 90.

3. Shortly before 0001 the raiding party set out and reached a point about 100 yds S.W. of the Objective at 0001, when a second T.M. demonstration accompanied by bursts of fire from the HUT and POPLARS was made.

4. At 0006 the raiding party advanced to the Objective, which was reached without opposition, but found it unoccupied by the enemy.

5. The following traces of recent enemy occupation were found :-
(a) A formal emplacement with signs of recent work.
(b) A track of rather confused footsteps leading to the emplacement.

6. The banks were searched for enemy means of crossing, but no boat or raft or material for a raft could be found.

7. No opposition was encountered from the further bank and no movement of enemy was seen or heard. A crossing could have been effected had any sort of raft been available.

8. The parties returned about 0050 without opposition.

9. Constitution of Parties.
(a) Raiding Party. 2/Lt. R.C.STECKLEY and 10 O.Rs.
(b) Hut Party. LIEUT. H.L.HUMPHREYS and a L.G.Section.
(c) Poplar Party. I Rifle Section.
(d) Raft Party. I Cpl. and 4 O.Rs.

(e) S.Bs. were kept in readiness on Canal bankabout J 3 c 30.20.

10. General Remarks.

(a) The main objects of the raid viz:-
To secure a prisoner and to effect a crossing were not successful.

(b) The attempt however had useful results viz:-

1. It reached a post which had been a constant source of annoyance for several days.
2. XXX It demonstrated recent enemy occupation of it.
3. It demonstrated possibility of effecting a crossing at this point. The ground of the route taken by the raiding party is stated to be waterlogged, but not flooded.
4. It seems probable that the T.M. demonstration may have caused enemy to abandon this post.
5. The enemy were very alert in the neighbourhood of the SAW MILL, both with M.G. and with T.M. and may have been anticipating an attempted crossing there.
6. The R.E. XXXXXXXXXX Sapper in charge of the R.E. Dump could not be found. I was not even aware that a R.E. Sapper was available here until so informed from the rear. The small floats and partly constructed rafts had been moved from their former places both at the dump and ZINC Works, and in the dark and without lights they could not be found.

P.O. 145 A
6/11/1918.

Lieut.Col.,
Cmdg.8th.London Regt.

War Diary

To Headquarters,
174th.Infantry Brigade

FURTHER REPORT TO BE ATTACHED TO RAID REPORT OF ~~5~~6/11/1918.

1. Evidences of recent occupation of S.W.bank of river were:-
(1) Emplacement at J 3 c 80 80 appeared beyond doubt in my mind to have been a proper one and earth on top and sides showed traces of recent handling.
(2) It was very dark and no individual footmarks could be distinguished. Path leading from River edge to track leading along road which runs along river bank could be seen. No cases/ cartridge could be found, but it was very dark.

2. The bank on this side of river is about 8 feet above water level and slopes at about angle of 45 degrees. In any case water level can easily be reached through opening in bank about 10 yards to left of emplacement. This opening is fully the width of the river and is full of water the level of which is the same as the river ~~th~~ itself and that seen on aerial photograph at about J 3 c 60 80. Opposite bank appears to be boarded to a height of 4 or 5 feet above water level.

3. In my opinion this would make a good place for a crossing because in addition to feasible banks
(a) Brickstack and rubble on opposite on bank more or less shield landing and afford protection when across.
(b) Approaches to this place are two and more or less under cover ,namely along bank itself using road or approaching river at right angles via a small ditch on higher ground between the flooded parts.

(Signed) R.C.STECKLEY.
Sec.Lt.

R. D. Derviche-Jones
Lieut. Col.,
Cmdg. 8th. LOndon Regt.

~~XXXX~~
P.O.147 A.
6/11/1918.

Appendix III

REF. Sheets 38 and 45 $\frac{1}{40000}$

DERA Dispositions

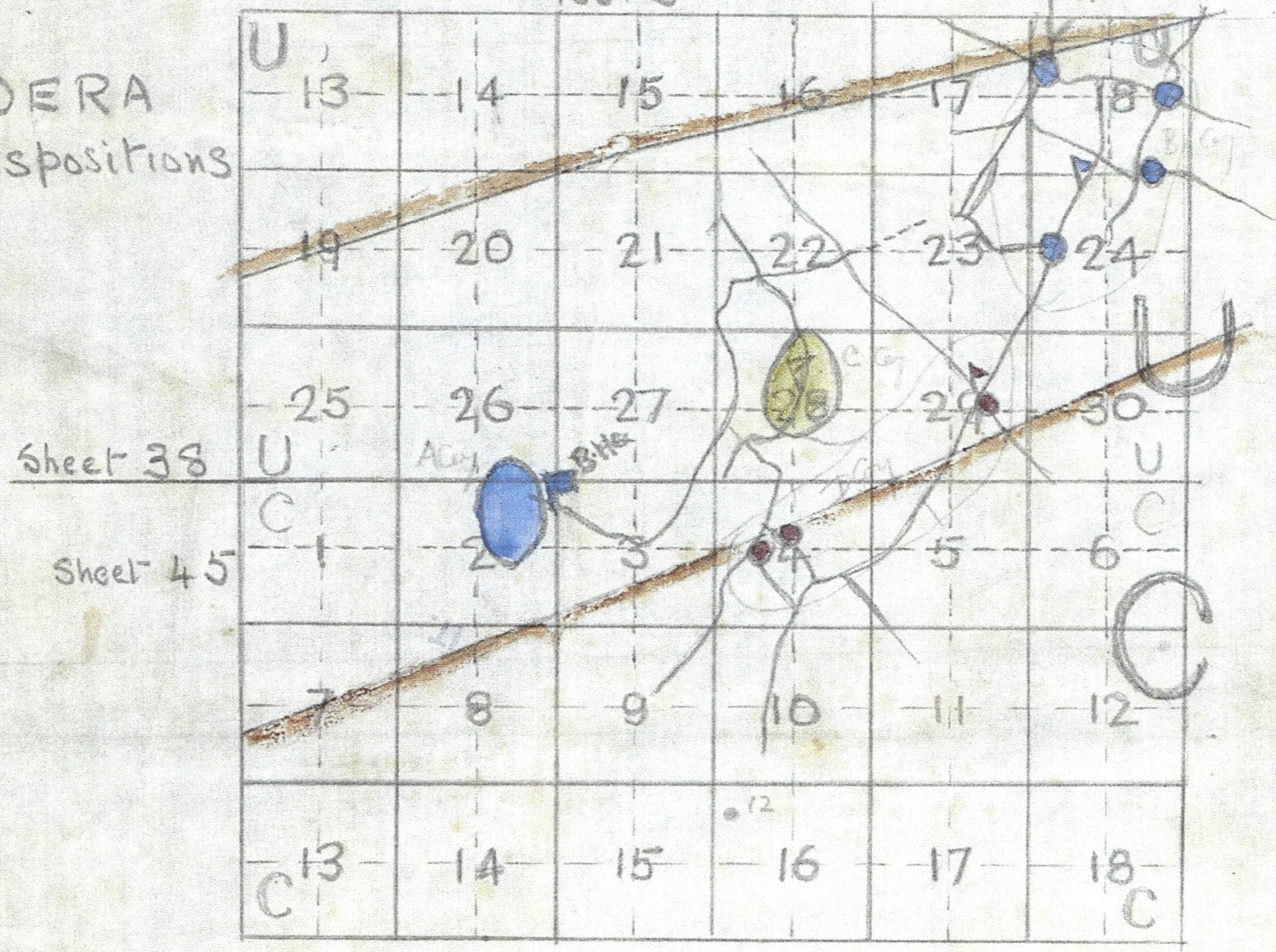

Sheet 38

Sheet 45

Appendix V War Diary

8th Battalion London Regiment. Copy No...2

ORDER No. 95.

18th November, 1918.

1. MOVE. Battalion will move to PERUWELZ Area tomorrow by march route through STAMBRUGES, GRANDGLISE, BLATON.

2. PARADE. Battalion will parade in BELOEIL STAMBRUGES Road. Order:- Headquarters, Band, "A", "B", "C", "D" Coys. Cookers with Companies. Mess Cart in rear of Battalion. Head of Column. 200 yards North of where FAVARCQ - ECACHERIES Road crosses BELOEIL - STAMBRUGES Road. Time. 1015.

3. TRANSPORT. Transport less Cookers and Mess Cart will move under orders of T.O., passing the Square, BELOEIL, at 0930. Route. North corner of FOREST DE BELOEIL South of first E in BELOEIL - Cross Roads ST. ANNE QUEVAUCAMPS, BASECLES Roads - BASECLES Station - LA BAITERIE - PERUWELZ. T.O. will arrange for reconnaissance of bridges at LA BAITERIE. Transport will not pass BASECLES until bridge has been reported on as fit for transport.

4. BLANKETS if drawn will be returned to the G.S. Wagons in the Square by 0815.

5. BILLETING PARTY consisting of 2/Lieut. REEVES-MOORE, representatives from Companies, Headquarters, Q.M. Stores and Transport and one runner, will meet at Battn.H.Q. at 0745 and will report to Staff Captain at Road junction West of P in PERUWELZ at 1000. Sig. Officer will arrange for ~~six~~ 7 bicycles to be available. The runner will meet the Battalion at Railway Crossing, South of second T in BLATON STATION, and will guide Battalion into PERUWELZ.

6. MESS STORES of Companies will be carried on Company Cookers.

7. CLEANLINESS CERTIFICATES to be handed to Adjutant on Parade.

Issued at 1800

Captain & Adjutant.

Copies to :-

1. File.
2. War Diary.
3. O.C. "A" Company.
4. O.C. "B" Company.
5. O.C. "C" Company.
6. O.C. "D" Company.
7. Headquarters.
8. C.O.
9. Second-in-Command.
10. T.O.
11. Q.M.
12. R.S.M.

To all Coys.
to be read out
on parade

H.Q. Coy. 70

(6)

WAR DIARY

58th (LONDON) DIVISION.

I wish to express to all officers, N.C.Os. and men serving under my Command my warm appreciation for the very valuable and gallant services rendered, and for the indomitable and cheerful spirit shown by them during the recent operations.

From the 8th August to 29th September the Division delivered 22 attacks, each carried out with the greatest gallantry and success.

From the commencement of the enemy's withdrawal in October, the Division continued to press back his rearguards with the same spirit and determination as was shewn on the battlefields of the Somme.

The co-operation of all Units of the Division and the untiring efforts of the various Staffs are points on which I wish to express my special admiration.

(Sd) F. RAMSAY.

Major General,
Commanding 58th Division.

17/11/18.

6th London Regt.
7th London Regt.
8th London Regt.
174th L.T.M.Bty.

BM/115

Forwarded.

The Brigadier ~~directs~~ desires that the above be communicated to all ranks.

J. McConnell

Captain,
Brigade Major,
174th. Infantry Brigade.

18th November, 1918.

To

Officers and men of the
8th Battalion London Regiment (Post Office Rifles)

I wish to congratulate the Battalion on the splendid spirit, courage and endurance shewn by all ranks, especially during the anxious days of the Spring and early Summer of this year, and the more stirring times of August up to the 11th November, a day which will be for ever famous in history, and to thank all ranks for the consistent loyalty extended to me both personally and as Commander of the Battalion.

In 1917, when the 1/8th Battalion was magnificently upholding its name as a fine fighting unit, notably at CAMBRAI, the 2/8th was carving a great reputation for itself at BULLECOURT and the YPRES Salient.

In 1918, after the amalgamation of the two Battalions the fighting qualities of the 8th have been well proved during the enemy attacks at the CROXAT CANAL, TERGNIER, VIRY NOREUIL, CHAUNY and VILLERS-BRETONNEUX, during the very strenuous fighting from MALLARD WOOD to EPEHY, and later in the pursuit of the enemy from LOOS to BAUFFE. The success which has always attended the efforts of this Battalion is due to the splendid co-operation between all ranks and to the indomitable spirit and devotion of each individual man.

I am indeed proud to have had command of such a splendid fighting force and trust that the comradeship engendered by the War may endure during the years to come.

R. S. Derviche-Jones

Lieut.-Colonel,
Commanding 8th Battalion London Regiment.
(Post Office Rifles)

In the Field,
November, 1918.

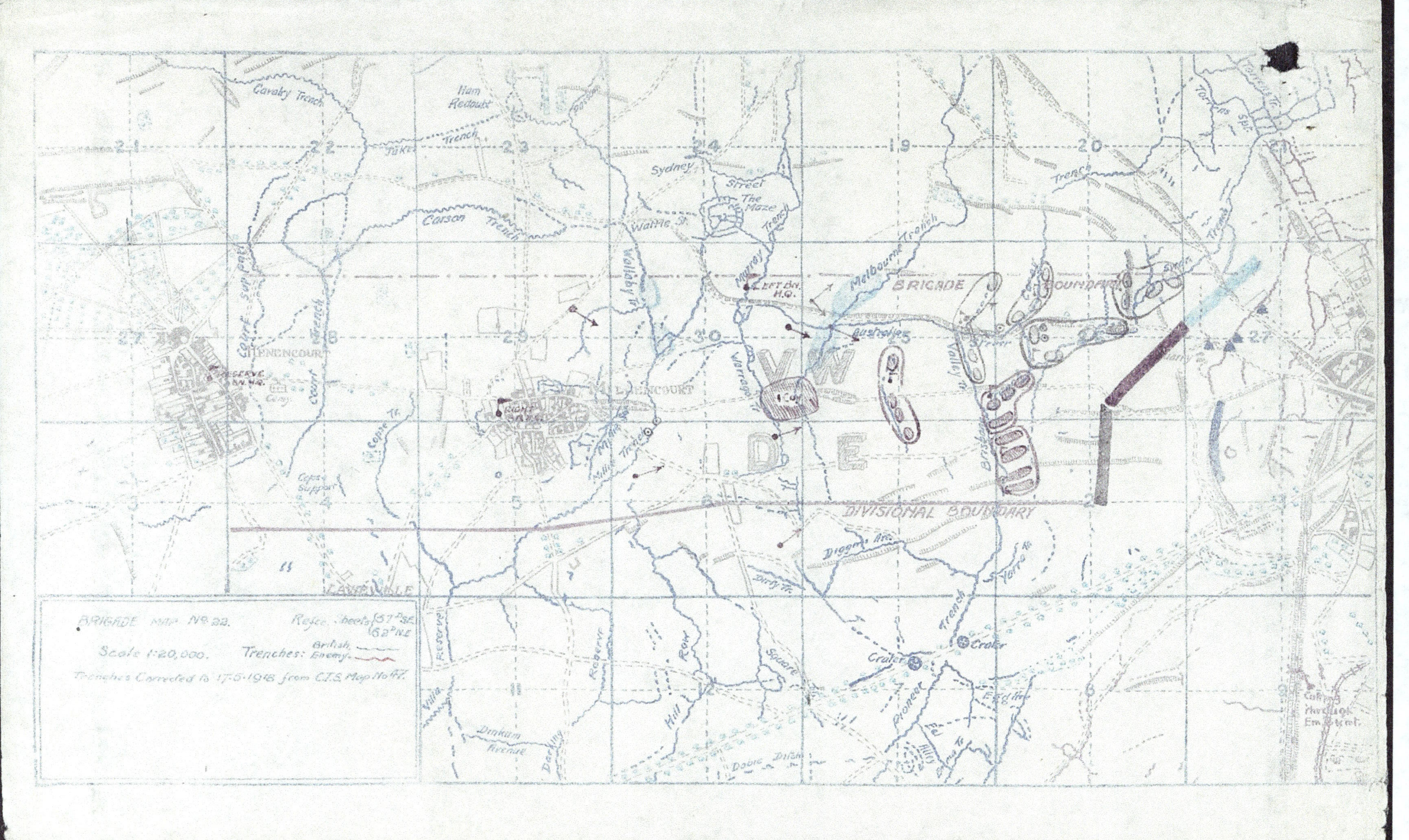
BRIGADE MAP No. 22.
Refce. Sheets 57 D SE / 62 D NE
Scale 1:20,000.
Trenches: British / Enemy
Trenches Corrected to 17-5-1918 from C.T.S. Map No 47.
Cavalry Trench
Ham Redoubt
Tokio Trench
Carson Trench
Sydney Street
The Maze
Wattle St.
Wallaby Tr.
Murray Trench
Melbourne Trench
LEFT BN. H.Q.
BRIGADE BOUNDARY
DIVISIONAL BOUNDARY
Australian
Valley Tr.
Brisbane
Warragul Tr.
Diggers Ave.
Dirty Tr.
Yarra Tr.
Crater
Pioneer
Trench
Square
Hill Row
Reserve
Dinkum Avenue
Dobie Ditch
Copse Tr.
Copse Support
Court Trench
Court Sup. Post
LAVIEVILLE
Villa
Torrens Tr.
Torrens Spt.
Trench
RESERVE BN. H.Q.

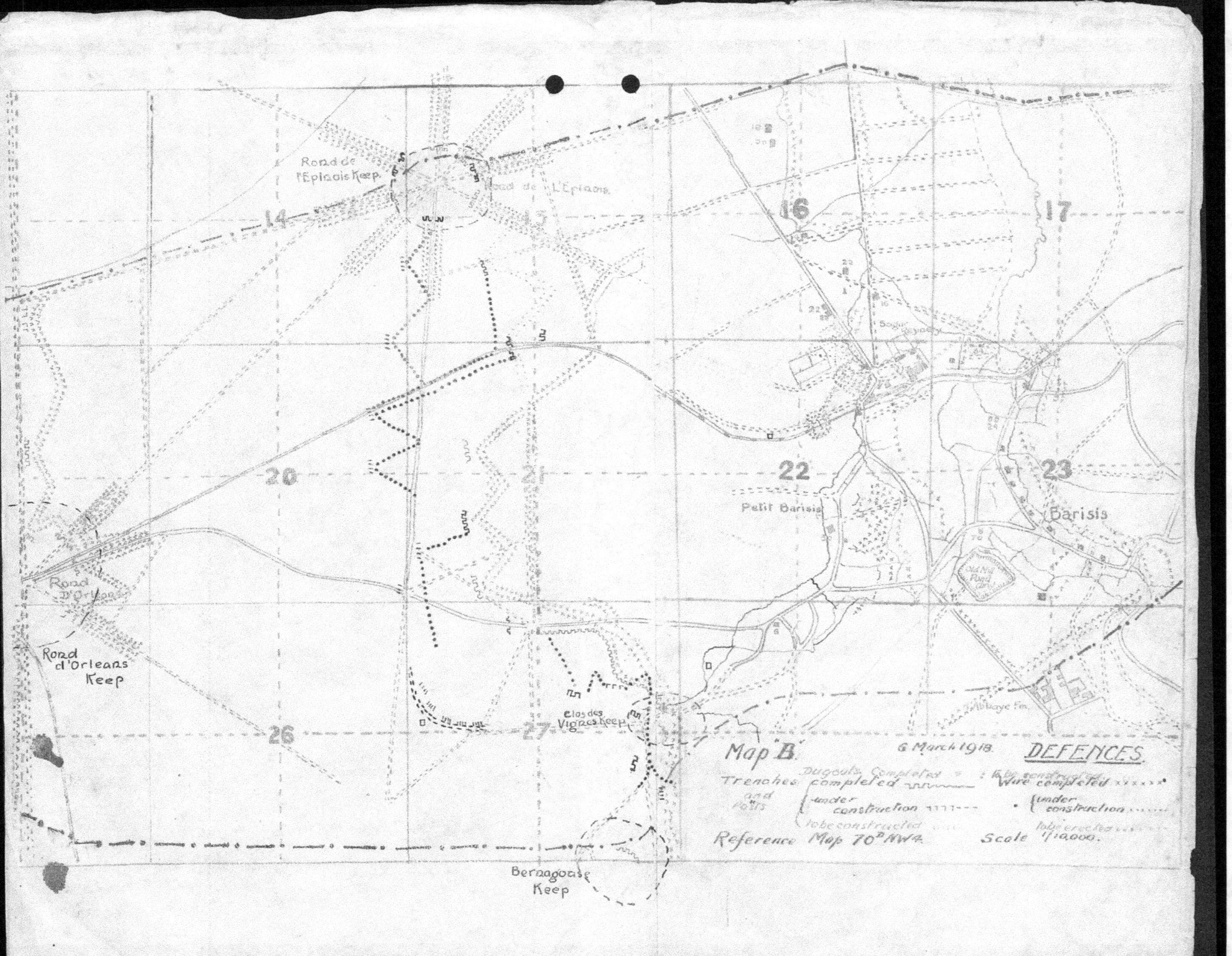

Rond de l'Epinois Keep
Rond de L'Epinois
14
15
16
17
20
21
22
23
26
27
Petit Barisis
Barisis
Rond D'Orleans
Rond d'Orleans Keep
Clos des Vignes Keep
Bernagousse Keep
Abbaye Fm.
Map "B"
6 March 1918.
DEFENCES.
Dugouts Completed
Trenches and Posts completed
under construction
to be constructed
Wire completed
under construction
to be erected
Reference Map 70D NW4.
Scale 1/10,000.

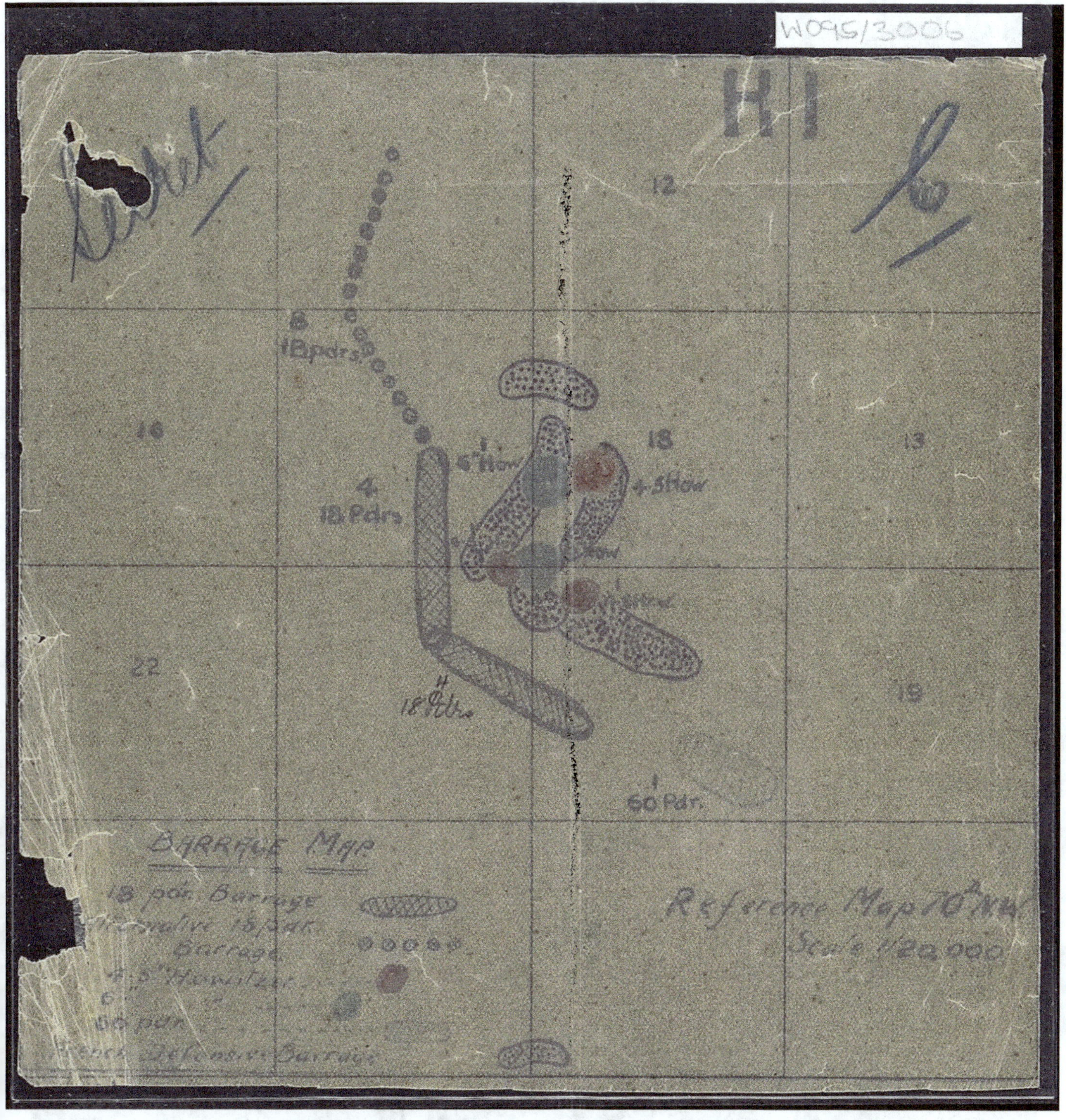
WO95/3006
H1
Secret
12
8
18 Pdrs.
16
4
18 Pdrs.
18
4.5 How
13
22
19
60 Pdr.
BARRAGE MAP
18 pdr. Barrage
Barrage.
4.5" Howitzer
60 pdr.
Defensive Barrage
Reference Map 70 N.W.
Scale 1/20,000

35. Æ. O. 370.
10.8.18 – 5.30.p.m
F=10¼"

Peziere
57ᶜ X. 25.c.05.50.

57ᶜ W. 30.d.40.05.

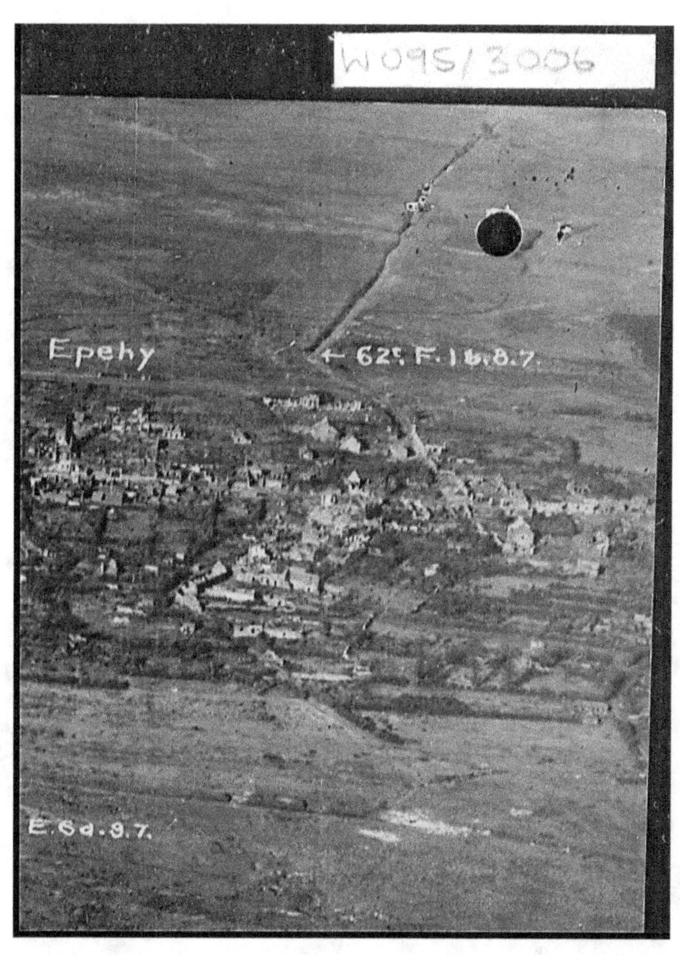
Epehy
← 62c. F.16.8.7.
E.6d.9.7.

7

Instructions regarding War Diaries and Intelligence Summaries are contained in F. S. Regs., Part II. and the Staff Manual respectively. Title pages will be prepared in manuscript.

Army Form C. 2118.

258

WAR DIARY

or

~~INTELLIGENCE SUMMARY~~.

(Erase heading not required.)

VR 25

Place	Date	Hour	Summary of Events and Information	Remarks and references to Appendices
			8th London Regiment (Post Office Rifles) — January 1919 —	

A5834 Wt. W4973/M687 750,000 8/16 D. D. & L. Ltd. Forms/C.2118/13.

Instructions regarding War Diaries and Intelligence Summaries are contained in F. S. Regs., Part II. and the Staff Manual respectively. Title pages will be prepared in manuscript.

WAR DIARY
or
INTELLIGENCE SUMMARY.

(Erase heading not required.)

Army Form C. 2118.

Place	Date	Hour	Summary of Events and Information	Remarks and references to Appendices
January	1919			
PERUWELZ	2nd		Lt Col. A.D. DERVICHE-JONES D.S.O: M.C. proceeded to MENTONE on leave.	
"	3rd		2nd Lt. C.R. CROSSLAND. M.C. proceeded to BOULOGNE on duty.	
"	4th		Battalion route march to BURY, returning via ROUCOURT.	
"	5th		Divisional Football cup – 8th Bn. beat 7th Battalion by 3 goals to nil.	
"	7th		Lt. H M FLOWER rejoined battalion from TOURNAI.	
"	8th		Capt. M W PETERS and 2nd Lt. H.C. FRASER proceeded to 290th Brigade R.F.A for a course.	
"	9th		Brigade Relay Racing – the short relay race won by the Battalion.	
"	10th		2nd Lt. C.R. CROSSLAND rejoined from BOULOGNE.	
"	11th		2nd Lt. H. ROSS proceeded to England for demobilisation. 2nd Lt. R REEVES-MOORE rejoined from hospital.	
"	"		Divisional football cup – 8th Battalion beaten by R.A.M.C, 5 goals to nil.	
"	12th		Lt. R.N. SHAPLEY proceeded to England for demobilisation.	
"	"		Lt J.H. HALLIFAX proceeded to England on leave.	
"	13th		2nd Lt. T FULTON proceeded to England for demobilisation.	
"	14th		Football – 8th Battalion beat 7th South Staffs by 1 goal to nil.	
"	"		Capt. M.W. PETERS and 2nd Lt H.C. FRASER rejoined from 290th Bde R.F.A	
"	"		Capt. M.F. BRICKDALE proceeded to Divisional H.Q. for duty.	
"	15th		2nd Lt F.W. BUCKLAND proceeded to England for demobilisation.	
"	17th		Lt W. B. MACBEAN proceeded to England on leave	
"	18th		Battalion route march to CHATEAU L'HERMITAGE, returning via LE TRIEUX DE RENGIES	
"	"		Inspection of billets by Divisional Commander.	
"	"		Divisional Tug of War, Semi Final. 8th Battalion beat 6th Battalion (100 stone teams), and 8th Battalion beat R.A.M.C (Catch weights).	
"	19th		Lt Col. A.D. DERVICHE-JONES, D.S.O. M.C. rejoined battalion from MENTONE	
"	"		Battalion attend Church Parade in the Cinema.	
"	21st		Capt. & Adjt. L.E.B JACOB proceeded to England on leave	
"	"		Sec. Lieut F.G. MACINNES went into hospital	

A5834 Wt. W4973/M687 750,000 8/16 D. D. & L. Ltd. Forms/C.2118/13.

Army Form C. 2118.

WAR DIARY
or
INTELLIGENCE SUMMARY.
(Erase heading not required.)

Instructions regarding War Diaries and Intelligence Summaries are contained in F. S. Regs., Part II. and the Staff Manual respectively. Title pages will be prepared in manuscript.

Place	Date	Hour	Summary of Events and Information	Remarks and references to Appendices
PERUWELZ	22nd		Captain J.M. BARRATT, M.C. & Sec Lieuts G.M. GARROW, J.F.W. KELLY and D.D.S. CREE proceeded to England for demobilisation.	[illegible]
"	23rd		Battalion won the divisional tug of war (catch weights), beating 58th M.G.B. in semi final and 10th London in the final	[illegible]
"	24th		Battalion concert.	[illegible]
"	26th		Church Parade in Cinema.	[illegible]
"	"		Rev. H.C. JAMES, C.F. proceeded to TROUVILLE on leave	[illegible]
"	28th		Lieut C.A. MONTGOMERY, Sec Lt H. PEACOCK, and Capt G.C. BARNES proceeded to England for demobilisation	[illegible]
"	29th		Lieut F.G. MILLS & Sec Lt G.P.R. TALLIN proceeded to England for demobilisation	[illegible]

[illegible signature]
Lieut Col.
Commanding 8th London Regt.

A5834 Wt. W4973/M687 750,000 8/16 D. D. & L. Ltd. Forms/C.2118/13.

4

WAR DIARY
or
~~INTELLIGENCE SUMMARY.~~
(*Erase heading not required.*)

Army Form C. 2118.

58

10 London ~~Regt~~

8 London Rgt

~~1/8~~ 26

Instructions regarding War Diaries and Intelligence Summaries are contained in F. S. Regs., Part II. and the Staff Manual respectively. Title pages will be prepared in manuscript.

Place	Date	Hour	Summary of Events and Information	Remarks and references to Appendices
PERNES-EN-ARTOIS	1919 FEB. 1st		Brigade Ceremonial parade cancelled on account of heavy fall of snow	
	2nd		Church Parade at 18th London Camp - Orders received to move into that Camp on 3rd Feb	
	3rd		Moved into camp just outside Pernes & shared quarters with 18th London	
	4th		Companies at disposal of Coy Commanders in order to arrange new quarters.	
	5th		Battalion baths at Raimbert - Various working parties at work on building a local camp & dismantling Ranges	
	6th		Whole Battalion employed on working parties - Major J. J. SHEPPARD M.C. left Battalion for demobilization	
			Working parties as on 6th	
			Working parties as on 6th	
			Joint Church of England & Nonconformist Church Parade in Camp Theatre - The Divisional & Brigade Commanders attended	
			Battalion Baths at Raimbert - Orders received to prepare draft of 100 NCO & men for 18th Battn Middlesex Regt - 33rd Division	

D. D. & L., London, E.C.
(A8004) Wt. W1771/M2731 750,000 5/17 Sch. 52 Forms/C2118/14

FEB 1919

Instructions regarding War Diaries and Intelligence Summaries are contained in F. S. Regs., Part II. and the Staff Manual respectively. Title pages will be prepared in manuscript.

WAR DIARY

~~or~~

~~INTELLIGENCE SUMMARY.~~

(Erase heading not required.)

Army Form C. 2118.

Place	Date	Hour	Summary of Events and Information	Remarks and references to Appendices
PERNES EN ARTOIS	1919 FEB 11th		Lt Col C.G. SALKELD GREEN DSO, M.C 7th Battn The London Regt assumed command vice Major C.J. BANTICK.	
			Draft for 18th Middlesex inspected by Lt Col Green	
	12th		Draft went for Route March in the morning	
	13th		Court of Inquiry President - Major C J Bantick, Members:- Capt G. Shillito & Capt H Ferguson sat to enquire into state of stores and equipment	
	14th		Companies at disposal of Company Commanders for training.	
	15th		Companies at disposal of Company Commanders for training. Football match in afternoon v 18th London - 18th won 5-1.	
	16th		A fire broke out in hut occupied by the Officers Servants at 0430 - Hut utterly destroyed -	
			Church Parade in Camp Theatre	
	17th		Companies employed on a working party on a local range demolishing firing points.	

Army Form C. 2118.

Instructions regarding War Diaries and Intelligence Summaries are contained in F. S. Regs., Part II. and the Staff Manual respectively. Title pages will be prepared in manuscript.

WAR DIARY
or
INTELLIGENCE SUMMARY.
(Erase heading not required.)

Place	Date	Hour	Summary of Events and Information	Remarks and references to Appendices
PERNES EN ARTOIS	FEB 1919			
	18th		Baths at Raimbert. Brigade Court of Inquiry sat to enquire into cause of fire on 16th inst.	
	19th		Companies at disposal of Company Commanders for training	
	20th		Same arrangements as 19th for training – New register under Representation of the People Act prepared	
	21st		Same arrangements for training as 19th – Work in progress repairing drains and roads in Camp	
	22nd		Same as 21st.	
	23rd		Church Parade in Camp Theatre.	
	24th		Draft for Middlesex Regt parading under Capt Welch M.C. for training	
	25th		Baths at Raimbert	
	26th		Draft consisting of Capt C.W. Welch M.C. 2nd Lt Ricks (R.G.L.I) + 83 O.Rs left for 18th Middlesex – Entraining Station Calonne Ricquart.	
	27		Battalion reorganised into one Coy.	
	28		Lorry placed at disposal of Battn for trip to Lille. – No men available for training.	

D. D. & L., London, E.C. (A8004) Wt. W1771/M2031 750,000 5/17 Sch. 52 Forms/C2118/14

5 8th London Regt March 1919

Instructions regarding War Diaries and Intelligence Summaries are contained in F. S. Regs., Part II. and the Staff Manual respectively. Title pages will be prepared in manuscript.

WAR DIARY
or
~~INTELLIGENCE~~ SUMMARY.

(*Erase heading not required.*)

Army F[illegible]

M 27

Place	Date	Hour	Summary of Events and Information	Remarks and references to Appendices
	MARCH			
PERUWELZ	1		Lt Col A.D. DERVICHE JONES left the Battalion for two months leave prior to rejoining his own Battalion. Major C.H. WILD assumes command. Brig Gen Maxwell left the Bde	[illegible]
LEUZE	8		Bde moved to LEUZE by march route.	[illegible]
	13		Capt PURKIS rejoined from leave. 2 ORs demobilised	[illegible]
	30		2nd Lt A. BUCK demobilised	[illegible]
	31		Major C.H. WILD proceeded on leave. Capt PURKIS assumes command.	[illegible]

8th BATTALION LONDON REGIMENT. No. ......

[signature] Capt
for Commanding [illegible] Battn.

A5834 Wt. W4973/M687 750,000 8/16 D. D. & L. Ltd. Forms/C.2118/13

174/58

8th BATTN. LONDON REGIMENT

ARMY BOOK NO. 152

LIEUT- COLONEL DERVICHE JONES

AUGUST 6 - 12 1918

SECRET 8th LONDON Rt Copy No.

OPERATION ORDER No.

1. (a) On a date & time which will be communicated later the 174th Infy Bde will attack the enemy's positions.
(b) The 6th Northants (18th Division) will be immediately on the left flank & the 10th LONDONS on the right flank.
(b) The operations by this Brigade are part of an attack on a large scale in which several Divisions will take part.

2/. The objectives of this Brigade are shown on the objective map attached.

4/ (a) The attack will be carried out by the 6th & 7th LONDONS & 1 Coy 8th LONDONS.
(b) The 8th LONDONS (less 1 Coy) will be in reserve.

5. ASSEMBLY
(a) The battalion less 1 Coy (B Coy) & two platoons of B Coy will assemble 25 yards behind the 3 left Companies of the 7th LONDONS

To O/c B. Coy

1/ Gas may be discharged on SAILLY-LAURETTE to night at 10.30 p.m. from Stokes Mortars

2/ Gas masks must be worn from then until 15 minutes after the completion of the ~~the completion~~ of the discharge, in case of ~~a~~ premature.

3/ O/c Stokes Mortars will call & see you

4/ Send Strength of your ~~[illegible]~~ Company by bearer.

5/. Your rations will be at 35 a 80 90 at 10 p.m

6/. ~~[illegible]~~ Owing to casualties your Coy will probably have to provide 2 platoons for carrying & 2 for mopping up.

7/. Be at Bn HQ to-morrow at noon

5 p.m. 6/8/18 O/c [illegible]

(b) ROUTES have been reconnoitred by Coy Cdrs

(c) Time will be notified later

(d) Formations:- in groups in file thus:-

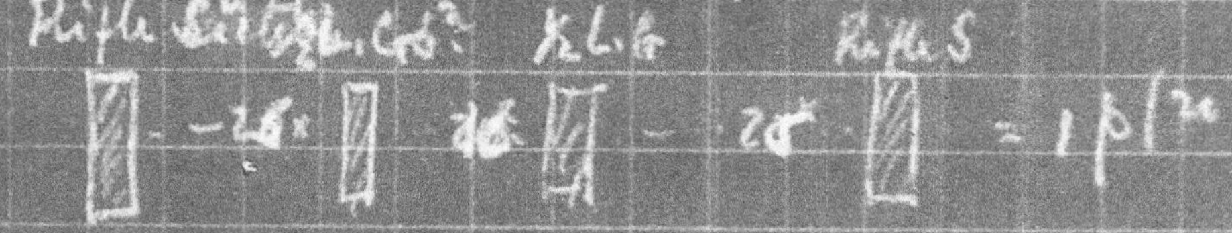

(e) 2/Lt. Knell will superintend the assembly & report assembly complete.

(f) Two platoons of C Coy will assemble 25x behind the right Coy of the 7th LONDONS at about

(g) B Coy will assemble 25x behind the right Coy of 6th LONDONS (Capt. JOHNSON) at about

moving in silence & getting into position in time.

(b) ~~Role~~

ACTION of 8th London.

★

I(a) B Coy will when assembled be under orders of O/C 6th LONDONS until their objective is captured & mopped up, when they come under orders of O/C 8th LONDONS

(b) This Coy will be formed up on

4 a ~~four~~ platoon front, ~~in~~ Each platoon in Sections in file - ~~[illegible]~~ If 2 L. Gs are carried by the L. G. Section this section will be split into two. Each platoon front

~~(c) The objective of this Coy is the area shaded on the~~ will be about 100 yards

(c) The objective of this Coy is ~~the~~ the area shaded blue on the attached map. This area is divided into 4 sections and a section is allotted to each platoon to mop up.

(d) Responsible N.C.O's must be

Touch must be maintained with
mpany of 6th on left detailed for
st edge of MALLARD Wood.

When mopping up in this area is
ompleted the Company will consolidate
tself in the area in depth, and
t patrols to its front. The West
dge of the Wood must be held

Company (less 2 platoons) will
hen assembled be under orders
f O.C. 7th LONDONS until it has
ompleted its special duty when
t comes under orders of O.C. 8th
ONDONS.

The special duty of these platoons
is to mop up the Copses in the
area shaded red.

The platoons will be formed up
on a two platoon front in each
thus:

R.S

LG LG

d) The area is divided into 2 sections one of which is allotted to each platoon.

e) As soon as the ~~senior~~ officer in charge of these platoons is satisfied that ~~these~~ this area is mopped up these two platoons will join A Co & D. Co in Brigade reserve ~~by~~ by the trees on the road at K 27 10.10.

III (f)
(a) ~~[illegible]~~ The remaining platoons of C. Coy are acting as carrying parties & will receive separate instructions. O/c Coy will detail an officer ~~to~~ as O/c working parties & will himself accompany the mopping up platoons.

III (a) The remainder of the battalion viz: A Coy & D Coy will be formed up each on a two platoon front each Coy in sections in file & will follow the left 3 Companies far as the trees on the road at K. 27 a. 10. 10, where they will act as Brigade reserve. The mopping up party of "A" Coy will join up here & be formed into a composite Coy with "A" Coy under Captn POULTON.

b/. On arrival at K. 27 a. 10. 10 these Coys will take such ground cover as is available in artillery formation: outposts will be placed to the front & on the left right flanks & careful watch on the front & both flanks will be maintained by officers.

c/. These Companies are not to be involved in initial fighting except in case of Emergency. Their role is for use in enemy counterattacks

Companies of the O/C Battalion is not there & will act on his own initiative, but reporting to O/C Battalion immediately any action is taken with regard to these Companies.

7. **ARTILLERY**

The attack will be covered by a creeping barrage, howitzers & heavy howitzers.

8. **TANKS** will assist in the attack.

The following signals will be used:—

(i) From ~~tanks to~~ Infantry to tanks.

Steel helmet raised on fixed bayonet denotes—

TANK ASSISTANCE REQUIRED

(ii) from tanks to infantry —

Administratio

7/8/18.

Formed at 1 p.m.

No. 1. C.O.

2. Adjt

3. O/c H

4. O/c B

5. O/c C

6. O/c D

7. 174 Bry

8. War Dr

a/ O/C D Coy will find two sections to act so to act as liaison with the 6th Northhants

i. at K. 26 a 80.70 on road

ii at K. 27 a 40.70 on road.

b/ The duties of these sections will be put in touch with the left flank battalion

i/ to obtain & give information.

ii/ to form a joint defensive flank

A & D. Coys. SECRET

10.m 7/8/18

54th Brigade is carrying out an attack this morning to recover CLOSE TR & STAFFORD Tr / the front line lost ~~this~~ yesterday morning.

The attack is being carried out in two waves:—

i/ 1st wave captures CUMMINS Tr.

ii/ 2nd wave leapfrogs to CLOSE & STAFFORD

As the 2nd wave moves up ~~you [illegible]~~ you will push out posts:—

i/ A Coy to occupy CLOSE Tr & gain touch with the left

ii/ D Coy to occupy CLOSE

174 Inf: Bde
from
O/C 8th LONDON

Report on Enemy attack of the 6th August 1918 near SAILLY-LE-SEC.

1/. From reconnaissance made of this Sector & from conversation with Major KEEP commanding 2nd BEDFORDS holding the line I came to the conclusion that to relieve this sector before daylight & in time to allow the BEDFORDS to side slip to the N the relief must not start later than 8.30 p.m.

2. Visibility was bad on the night of the 5/6th August

ed owing to a heavy mist & as I could not communicate with Brigade in time I took the responsibility of starting at 8.30 p.m., one hour before the scheduled time.

The arrangements for guides made by the BEDFORDS were exceptionally good & worked without a hitch. It was purely the awful condition of the trenches which delayed the relief.

At 4.15 a.m. on the 6th Aug. the Enemy started his barrage, a very heavy one of Shrapnel, light T. Ms. By this time my two ~~left~~ right companies had completed relief – ~~by depart~~ & the ~~Centre~~ BEDFORDS – had had a

off. My Left Centre Company had completed relief but their opposite numbers had not cleared off. Two platoons of my left Coy had completed relief & the remaining two platoons were in the act of relieving the outpost line.

5. The Enemy barrage caused considerable losses in my left Coy, reducing their strength from over 100 to 47.

6. Under cover of the barrage the Enemy attacked from the N.E. [illegible] across the front of the left brigade of the 18th Divn & also from the E on the front held by my left Coy & BEDFORD & by my left Centre Coy.

of prisoners by the enemy. Those in the outpost line who were unwounded came back. The attack on my front was gallantly repulsed by L.G. & rifle fire, by a bombing attack started by 2/Lt PATTISON on his own initiative which resulted in the capture of 8 prisoners & two M.G.s & by a sally by the BEDFORDS who brought in 18 prisoners & 3 M.G.s

8. At no time, despite the fact that the enemy had

to some depth in
was my first line
ed. The outpost line
en up in accordance
orders
platoons of the BEDFORDS
and Rudd slipped, on
to the north, being on to
osition though their left
was in the air.
ing to put on record the
work
ing of the BEDFORDS, who
particularly difficult
stances, behaved with
tional gallantry.

A. D. Burochi[illegible]
Lt Col.
8th London Regt

1. Lt. [illegible]NNELL an Australian officer
& Lt. CROSSLAND with a party of
80 stragglers of various units went
out about 8.15 a.m. with following
objects:–

a) to reconnoitre situation up
to & including whole west
edge of MALARD Wood

b) to clean up M.G. nests
still in copses in 26c & 31a

c) to collect & reorganise
troops ~~at~~ between our
front line & W edge of
MALARD Wood

2. This party is still out

2. A straggler (a Corporal) of the 7th was here short time ago & said he believed troops had gone round N. Edge of Wood.

3. Situation generally obscure but will be cleared up.

4. Have intercepted note from Colonel of 3 LONDONS to 173 Brigade - reads as follows —

"Situation obscure am lost
" touch with 2/2 & 2/4 Bns aaa
" MALARD Wood in our
" possession aaa Enemy hold
" Quarry. Have ordered attack
" on this point with
" Composite Company aaa
" Will report progress aaa

K 27 C 0 7.

N.B. This message is not signed or timed!

3. My Capt. THOMAS is wounded – casualties unknown.

4. 86 prisoners + 2 officers have passed here.

9.30 a.m. R. D. Sewell-Jones Lt. RGA. 8th LONDONS

parties of these men are digging in
a small hole line facing N.E about
K.26 c 8.6 to L.6.9
If [illegible] intelligence officer [illegible]
I have just found the former are
about 80 of my men
[illegible] under Lt. Johnson at K7 a.
I am now sending a runner
to tell Lt. Johnson to collect
these men & allow them to
join the others at K.26 c
If I should then have a
garrison of 124 men (there are
probably others I cannot find) with

[illegible] to the [illegible] in [illegible]
A & D Coys [illegible] off [illegible] the
[illegible] through [illegible]
[illegible]
The [illegible] was very [illegible]
[illegible] limited to 15 x; the
advance was so slow [illegible]
[illegible] found themselves [illegible]
of the 7th & advanced without
difficulty or casualties. The
[illegible]
with [illegible] taken [illegible]
prisoners (including [illegible]
commanders) in the [illegible]
[illegible] one of whom [illegible]
[illegible] commanded [illegible]

between the 8th [illegible] advance of
[illegible] [illegible] of the 8th Bn urgent
appeal for assistance & A Coy
advanced to a Quarry like hollow
N of MALLARD wood rendered
material assistance in clearing
this area of the enemy. Captain
Poulton was killed here, while
the enemy were putting up a
stiff fight. The Coy casualties
were heavy. The only [illegible]
remnants of [illegible] Coy are with
Captain Johnson.

W.D. [illegible]-Jones
[illegible]

1.30 pm

[illegible]

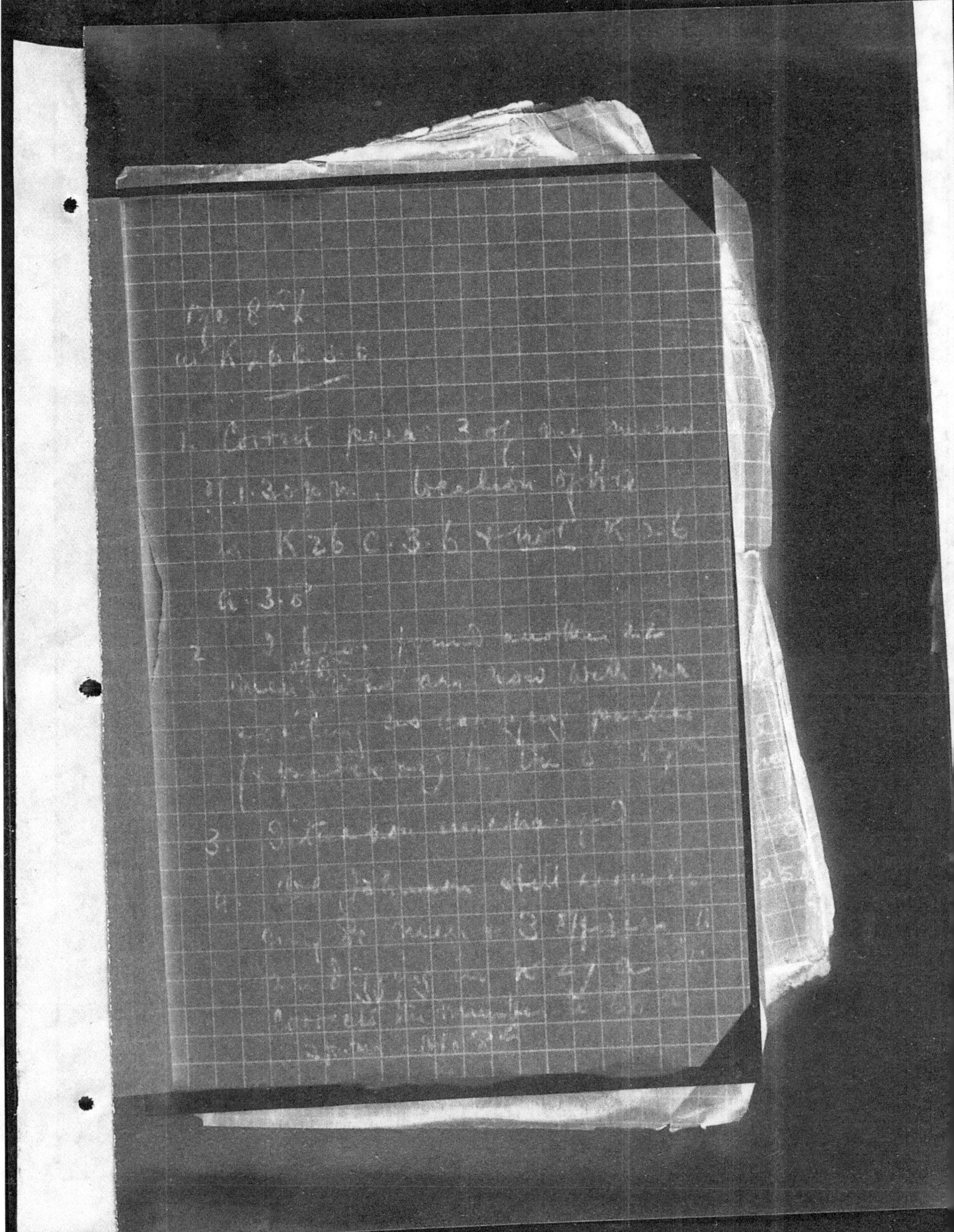

[illegible]

1. Correct para 3 of my memo

at 1.30 p.m. location of [illegible]

is K 26 C.3.6 & not K 5.6

A.3.6

2 I have found another [illegible]

[illegible]

[illegible]

[illegible]

3. [illegible]

4. [illegible]

[illegible] 3 [illegible]

[illegible]

[illegible]

[illegible]

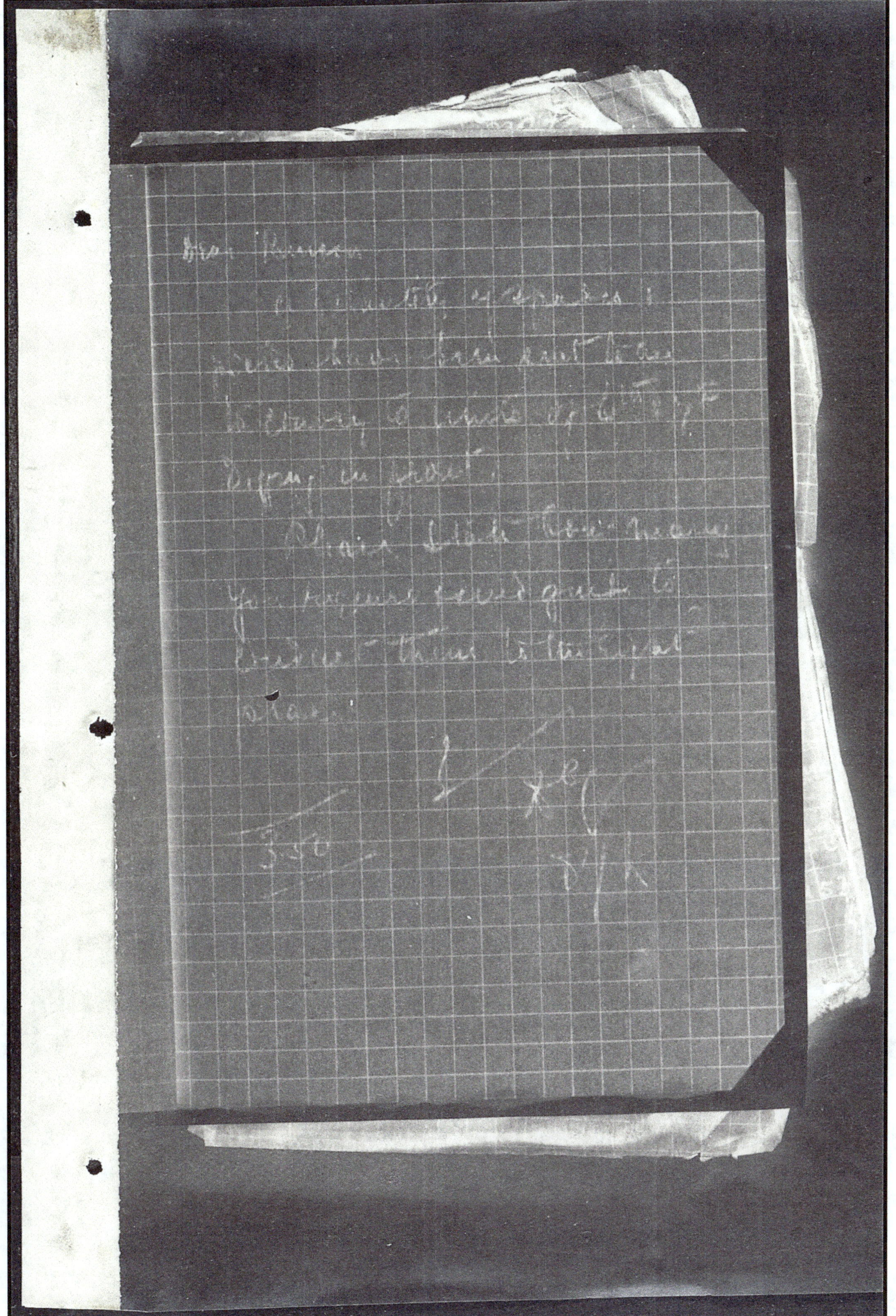

174 Infantry Bde
from
O.C. 8th London Regt

Preliminary OPERATION REPORT 7/8 [illegible]

1./ This Battalion was given the following special duties in these operations:-

(a) To mop up the [illegible] [illegible] MALARD Wood (B Coy [illegible])

(b) To mop up Copse in K.[illegible] (C Coy [illegible] [illegible] position [illegible])

(c) To form a reserve in K.26 [illegible] (A & D Coys [illegible] - C Coy being [illegible] to form reserve after mopping up copse.

2./ ASSEMBLY. At this point the following difficulties:-

(a) [illegible] battalion was holding the line & could not assemble in the position owing to the [illegible] [illegible] [illegible] of continuous position

(b) The state of the L.T. [illegible] [illegible] Extremely [illegible]

(c) The enemy [illegible] [illegible] [illegible] particularly [illegible] [illegible] [illegible] with H.E. [illegible] [illegible] [illegible]

[illegible] [illegible] [illegible] [illegible]

[illegible] reinforcements on. [illegible]

It was decided accordingly to instructions given that [illegible] of the [illegible] got in position by 2.30 a.m. The Coys of the 8th Bn in the line would go [illegible] from the front trench stretched out in the open into their formations.

B. Coys. to the jumping off positions and the 6th & 9th were already in position by zero.

3/. The ATTACK

a) The weather was very misty from zero until 9.0 a.m. Visibility limited to 20 yards.

b). The M.G. barrage started at zero with the artillery at zero plus 2.

c) Punctually at zero the brigade advanced over the top with the 2/13th. Both were just in time.

d) Coys of the 8th moved from the front line trench.

e) At zero minus 1 the enemy started a T.M. [illegible] on the front line.

f) Owing to the mist direction was very difficult to maintain and A

[illegible] [illegible] the [illegible]
Battalion only soon found themselves
[illegible] [illegible] [illegible] of [illegible]
of the barrage which was good. The
two Companies advanced to the
objective in K 26 c, which they
mopped up, capturing between 100
& 200 prisoners, 2 Battalion Commanders
& 2 ~~[illegible]~~ [illegible] them
[illegible] [illegible] to
Wood behind continued [illegible]
[illegible] [illegible] line of trees in
K 27 a which were [illegible] without
[illegible] [illegible] with but few
casualties. Soon after the [illegible]
R. found themselves in difficulties at
the Quarry Ravine at the N.W. edge
of MALARD wood & sent an urgent
[illegible] to Capt. POULTON A Coy
[illegible]
[illegible]
[illegible]
[illegible] [illegible] Captain
POULTON killed. Later [illegible]
[illegible]
[illegible] the [illegible]
JOHNSON

(2) D Coy [illegible]
[illegible] of [illegible]

1st Inf. Bde
From
O.C. [illegible]

1/ Total strength in all my Coys [illegible]

2/ K 36 a 8.6.

3/ [illegible] [illegible] [illegible] [illegible] reports [illegible] [illegible]

3/ Col. BENSON will [illegible] [illegible] before [illegible] [illegible] [illegible]

4/ Have we all messing & bathing through Bde.

5/ Cannot say [illegible] S.A.A. [illegible] required yet, but suggest a dump be made [illegible] should [illegible] opposite my H.Q. [illegible] [illegible] come up here [illegible] [illegible] [illegible] which [illegible] on the road [illegible]

R.A. Smith [illegible]

5.25 p.m.
8/8/18

the weather [illegible] [illegible] [illegible]
[illegible] [illegible] on the way, killing
about 30 Bosches & taking 42
prisoners which were handed
over to the [illegible] [illegible] on
continuing the advance. Capt.
[illegible] was wounded [illegible] the
first day [illegible] [illegible] most unfor-
[illegible] [illegible] [illegible] his absence
[illegible] [illegible] [illegible] [illegible] they
[illegible] [illegible] carried on under
command of Lt. BENSON

4. At 8.15 a.m. Lieut McK[illegible] with
a party of sappers, who had been
lent [illegible] [illegible] [illegible] assistance in
[illegible] [illegible] [illegible] [illegible]
[illegible] [illegible] Bosches [illegible] MALARD
[illegible] [illegible] [illegible] [illegible] [illegible]
[illegible] [illegible] [illegible] [illegible]
[illegible] [illegible] [illegible] M.G. [illegible]
[illegible] [illegible] [illegible] [illegible]
[illegible] [illegible] [illegible] assistance [illegible]
[illegible] [illegible] [illegible] [illegible]
[illegible] [illegible] [illegible] [illegible] [illegible]
[illegible] information

5. [illegible] [illegible] [illegible] [illegible]
[illegible] [illegible] [illegible] [illegible]

the battalion next. Companies of the
6th & 7th were able to reinforce with the
services of the men attached to them.

K. Units of the battalion near Bn. HQ
have been employed in digging [illegible]
[illegible] [illegible] R. A. C. [illegible]
by [illegible] position [illegible] holes in [illegible]
holes in the road accordingly.

[illegible] [illegible]
Lt. Col.
Commanding [illegible]

8 p.m.
8/8/15

3/. In the meantime [illegible] towards the south I stopped up [illegible] [illegible] on the way, striking about 30 Boches [illegible] 72 prisoners which were handed over to the 6th L [illegible]. In continuing the advance, Capt. Phillips was wounded [illegible] [illegible] [illegible] remain in position near their [illegible] where they [illegible] under command of Lt. BENSON.

4/. At 8.15 a.m. Capt. McKAY with a party of stragglers who had been lost in the mist [illegible] assistance [illegible] [illegible] W. MALARD [illegible] [illegible] [illegible] M.G. was [illegible] [illegible] assistance in [illegible] Italian [illegible] information.

5. By 11.0 [illegible]
3.6 [illegible] 3.0 p.m. [illegible]

showing, in particular etc. a bar in [illegible] with SHAPLEY

4/ It should be explained to A. Coy that those returned to them, A Coy OC [illegible] & I personally chose FARER & CLARKE – there is not the slightest reflection on FARER.

5/. Whether men were keener [illegible] [illegible] proud of them

Yrs [illegible]

D. [illegible]

12/8/17

174 Bde

OPERATION REPORT 9th Aug 1918

1. On the morning of the 9th the battalion was located as follows:—

a)

	officers	men	
H.Q	5	35	(including M.O. & staff)
A.	–	23	
B.	1	14	
C	–	5	
D	2	51	
	8	128	

at the Copse K.26 c 3.6

b/. 3 officers & about 60 men with the 7th battalion at the Ravine in K.27.c.

These were made into 3 parties for counter attack purposes

c). about 6 men with the 6th Battalion

c/. about 40 men of "C" Coy with Brigade for carrying parties

Making a total of 11 officers & 234 men

2/. Steps were taken for all men to clean Rifles, L. Gs & ammunition & to reorganise into Companies. The party with the 7th battalion could not be reorganised until they rejoined the battalion.

3/. a/ At 4.5 p.m I received a warning order (timed 1.45 p.m) from 174 Bde of the resumption of the attack & immediately sent a H.Q. officer to the 7th battalion to collect my party there & to inform Col. Johnson that I required these men.

b/. At 4.50 p.m I received detailed orders (not timed) from 175 Bde to resume the attack on the left flank & to get up to the barrage line by 5.30 p.m. The time the barrage would start. This line for my extreme left was 2500 yards away, as the crow flies, & nearly two miles by the nearest route.

c/. My party from the 7th arrived at 5.5 p.m. & those from Brigade Carrying party (40 men) as the battalion was marching off at 5.20 p.m. (these went straight on without rest after a long march up)

d/ I saw Col. CHART (Commanding the Rangers on my right) at 5 p.m. & arranged that as it was impossible to get to the barrage line in time, the two battalions should march by parallel routes together, so as to keep touch from the start

e/ The few minutes available were utterly inadequate to explain all details to my officers & I had to give rough guides as to route & objectives & send them off. The Companies were actually organised into platoons & sections which on the march & under shell & M.G. fire

3/ To assist the battalion I sent a HQ officer at the head & some time after the start when I saw that direction was being lost I sent another HQ officer forward to put matters right –

4/ The barrage started soon after my HQ had started at the rear of the battalion & we at once came under considerable shell & M.G. fire. I could see no sign of the 12th Division but I saw Enemy S.O.S. signals going up from that divisions front –

5/. My advanced HQ were established in a bank at K.21.c near Cox CHART. On the way there a shell knocked out nearly all my runners

175th Inf. Bde Order no 13?

SECRET

9/8/18

Para 1 The 58th Divn with 131 American regt: attached will attack today. The 131st American regt on the right. The 175th Infantry Brigade less 2/10 Battn but with one Battn 174th Bde, and 5th Royal Berks attached on the left.

12th Divn will attack on the left 175th Inf Bde. zero hour will be 5.30 pm

2(a) objective will be line K24 D15 K18 C00 K17 centre K11 C30 (railway bridge) K11 A14 (road junction)

(B) dividing line between 175th Inf. Bde and 12th Divn will be a line K15 C52 (road junction) K11 A14 K6 A31

The dividing line between 175 Inf Bde and 131st American regt: K27 B28 K22 central K17 central K12 D69

(C) the attack will be carried out by two battns

(c) The attack by 175 Inf Bde will be carried out by the 8th London regt on the left 12th London Regt on the right dividing line between the battns will be K21B54 K22A19, K16C95, K16B60 K17A05, K17A58.
each battn will attack two companys in front and two in support 5th. Royal Berks regt will be in support and in a position of readiness in the valley K25B
9th Battn will be in reserve and will concentrate as soon as possible in the valley K25B.

Machine guns one section will be attached to each of the 8th & 12th battns and will immediately place themselves under the orders of OC's of these battns. The remaining section will remain in support in the valley K25B

artillery arrangements
attack will be covered
by creeping barrage
advancing 100 yds in
four minutes
Start line of the barrage
line will open at zero
K15D05 K28A85. K35C65.
Barrage will lift from the
right zero plus eight
and from the left at zero
plus twenty, subsequent
lifts at the rate of 100 yds
in four minutes and
parallel with the general
line of first objective.
Protective barrage will
halt for one hour on line
300 yds N.E. of objective
forming up
Troops will form up for the
attack as close to the barrage
as possible
Tanks ten tanks of
tenth Tank battn will
cooperate five on the front
of the 131st American and
five on the front of 175th
Inf Bde.

MESSAGES AND SIGNALS. No. of Message

Code m. | Words. | Charge.

Origin and Service Instructions.

This message is on a/c of: Service.

Recd. at m.

Date

From

By

Sent At m. To By

(Signature of "Franking Officer.")

TO: 1/5th, 1/7th, 1/6th, 1/8th | 1/5th Bn. Gs. Staff Capt.

Sender's Number. G106. | Day of Month. 9 | In reply to Number. | AAA

The division will attack today aaa. Line will be reorganized as follows aaa. 143 Bde on right 144 Bde on left Boundary between Bdes [illegible] inclusive to 143 Bde. Brigade front will be held by 6th Bn on right & 7th Bn on left. Boundary between Battalions track at K.27 central aaa. 8th London Regt and Section "C" Coy MG Bn will be attached to 145 Bde and will assemble forthwith in Valley K26 C and K25 D 10th London Regt will be attached to 143 Bde Bn will act at once on receipt of these orders aaa. MGs will remain in positions

FROM 144 Bde.

1.45 pm

above may be forwarded as now corrected. (Z)

Send Constance at once to [illegible] [illegible] from 7th [illegible]

A. [illegible] Capt.

Censor. Signature of Addressor or person authorised to telegraph in his name.

* This line should be erased if not required.

CONSERVATION

→SP1←

007

www.ingramcontent.com/pod-product-compliance
Lightning Source LLC
Chambersburg PA
CBHW080831010526
44112CB00015B/2492
* 9 7 8 1 4 7 4 5 3 1 3 7 5 *